PEOPLE
OF THE
EARTH

PEOPLE OF THE EARTH

THE NEW PAGANS SPEAK OUT

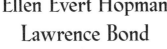

Ellen Evert Hopman
Lawrence Bond

Destiny Books
Rochester, Vermont

Destiny Books
One Park Street
Rochester, Vermont 05767

LIBRARY OF CONGRESS CATALOGING-IN-PUBLICATION DATA

Hopman, Ellen Evert.
    People of the earth : the new Pagans speak out / Ellen Evert Hopman and Lawrence Bond.
        p. cm.
    ISBN 0-89281-559-0
    1. Paganism—United States—Interviews. 2. Paganism—Canada—Religion—1960– I. Bond, Lawrence. II. Title.
    BL2525.H67   1995
    299—dc20   95-39794
                                                                 CIP

Printed and bound in the United States

10 9 8 7 6 5 4 3 2 1

Text design and layout by Virginia L. Scott

This book was set in Frutiger with Phaistos as the display typeface

On the cover (top to bottom): Susun Weed, Russell Williams, Cerridwen Fallingstar, and Phyllis Curott

Destiny Books is a division of Inner Traditions International

Distributed to the book trade in Canada by Publishers Group West (PGW), Toronto, Ontario

Distributed to the book trade in the United Kingdom by Deep Books, London

Distributed to the book trade in Australia by Millennium Books, Newtown, N. S. W.

Distributed to the book trade in New Zealand by Tandem Press, Auckland

Distributed to the book trade in South Africa by Alternative Books, Randburg

Contents

Foreword

W ho are the Pagans? The delightful book you are holding seeks to answer this question through interviews with modern Wiccans, Druids, and other followers of nature-centered spirituality. The answer lies between the lines and behind the spoken words. For many of you, it will validate, as it did for me, what you already know from years of study or practice: Pagans, as the title says, are *people*.

What kind of people is a question I tried to answer in social psychology, a discipline concerned with the behavior of groups. Although a lifetime of spiritual study left the answer in my heart, my brain needed to find the answer in terms that science would understand. I was surprised by the resistance I encountered in making metaphysical beliefs the topic of my doctoral dissertation. My advisor was concerned about my marketability with such a specialization. Other faculty warded off the idea with greater or lesser degrees of nervousness: Some politely claimed they didn't have the time to work with any more students. Others said they just weren't interested in the subject and didn't want to be associated with my project. One was openly hostile to the idea. In the end, it took me nearly two years to find four faculty members willing to supervise my study.

Even more surprising than the academic resistance I encountered was the response within the Pagan community. While more than five hundred people completed and returned my survey, I also uncovered a great deal of distrust and even hostility among a small minority who feared another witch-hunt. Some were afraid that I intended to discredit Paganism by developing an unflattering psychological profile. Others worried about personally becoming targets of persecution. A few complained that my standard questions were too biased by Aristotelian/Christian logic to capture any valuable information. Considering I can only report feedback from returned surveys, one can only wonder what was running through the heads of those people who relegated my questionnaire to the recycling bin. Given the hostility on both sides of the magnifying glass, the lack of research specifically targeting Pagan populations is unsurprising.

The earliest research on metaphysical beliefs dates back to the first half of the twentieth century, when psychology was still in its infancy. Several professors noted that better students believed in fewer superstitions, so they erroneously lumped together superstition, witchcraft, and magic, and prematurely concluded that all these beliefs were more prevalent among the unintelligent. This lead to the marginality hypothesis, which claims that believers are either members of small, socially disenfranchised groups that are too uneducated to see the foolishness of their beliefs or are so desperate to believe in something that they can't exercise proper judgment. Some of these "socially disadvantaged" groups included women, African Americans, the young, and the poor. Alas, this theory allowed bigotry to pass for science.

Most studies compounded this bias with a surprising level of ignorance. Questions about metaphysical beliefs were frequently insulting, inaccurate, or both. While the psychologists were asking "Do you believe in witches?" the witches were doubtless contemplating whether they believed in psychologists. Few witches ever got to express their doubts because most surveys went to freshman psychology students, a practice which makes about as much sense as surveying men about childbirth. To nobody's surprise, these studies offer little support for the marginality hypothesis.

Of the few well-conducted studies available, none focus on Pagans exclusively. Instead, they take a broader look at psychic fairs, Theosophy, or readers of the now-defunct occult magazine, *Gnostica*. From these studies emerges a picture of the generic occult practitioner as someone who tends to be older, white, female, better educated, and more affluent. This is a far cry from the stereotypically young, black, uneducated, and poor college freshmen the marginality hypothesis imagines.

Believers are actually far more often part of the mainstream than of the social fringes to which speculation often seeks to relegate them. In America today, believers in astrology outnumber the membership of any single religious denomination. Eight out of ten people believe in ESP. Every year, the metaphysical community spends $100 million in books and $27 billion in alternative medicine. The estimated number of Pagans worldwide increases every year, and *Megatrends 2000* predicts that alternative and New Age faiths like Paganism will become the "boom religions" of the twenty-first century.

In my study, I targeted the Pagan/magical community because I wanted the "real thing": people whose lives were actually shaped by their beliefs. The "typical" participant was a thirty-eight-year-old white female with three and one-half years of college. In childhood, half of my sample had been raised Protestant and another third had been raised Catholic. They kept their minds open to new beliefs and actively pursued new truths. Finally, they were far more likely than nonbelievers to have had a transformative metaphysical experience— a personal encounter with anything from angels to ghosts to UFOs—and to see control over their lives coming from within, rather than without.

The neo-Pagan movement that I encountered is a dynamic entity, whose origins are part modern invention and part adaptation of tradition. As such, many participants in Paganism forge a unique path, as is evident from the variety of opinions and practices described in this book. This quest for spiritual fulfillment can lead in many different directions, some strange and fantastic, some challenging and frightening. The path may call for a study of ancient traditions such as Druidism (see The New Druids). It may revive nearly forgotten concepts like the *Shekinah,* the Great Mother energy of the Kabbalah (see the interview with Elie in Paganism from Norway, Greece, Egypt, Israel, and Italy), and the sacred prostitute (see Sacred Prostitutes). For others answers may lie in modern sources, including the fantastic fiction of Robert Heinlein (see The Church of All Worlds). It may involve adapting old ways to new or unusual situations, as among military Pagans (see Military Pagans). Or it may find a union in politics (see The Politics of Persecution) or feminism (see the interviews with Starhawk, Margot Adler, and Z. Budapest in Writers). Whatever the path, its travelers are reinventing the traditions and rites of passage which are so widely absent in the West.

Who are the Pagans? Statistics are valuable but, like rocks in a tumbler, they grind away the subtle and beautiful differences that make everyone unique. Ellen Evert Hopman and Lawrence Bond seek to answer this question in a different way, through interviews with members of the Pagan community. They let the people of the earth speak for themselves—and speak they do, as diverse and fascinating individuals. The words tell a far more colorful tale than the numbers ever could.

Dr. Richard Kaczynski
Assistant Professor
Wayne State University

Preface

My own path toward Paganism was grounded in the experiences of childhood and started long before I realized I was on a spiritual journey. My father was a diplomat in the State Department and a Lieutenant Colonel in the U.S. Army. As a result our family traveled extensively, usually moving every two years and often to a country where none of us spoke the language. I was born in Salzburg, Austria, in the homeland of the Halstatt Celts, the place where the Celtic people first coalesced as a distinct cultural entity about 700 B.C.E. When my mother was pregnant with me and when I was a baby, there were digs going on in the area and Celtic artifacts and even bodies were being recovered from the local salt mines. My mother, an artist, was intensely interested in these archaeological finds. Some of my earliest memories are of her talking about the Celts.

My religious upbringing was eclectic. Both of my parents professed to be atheists, and my brother and I were cared for by a series of maids and governesses, most of whom exposed us to their religious traditions. In Spain I was taken to Latin masses in old cathedrals where the service began with music, candles, and the wonderful smell of burning frankincense. At the age of eight, I adopted the habit of having an altar in my bedroom, a habit that persists to this day. At that time the altar was dedicated to Mary, complete with flowers and other offerings. As a teenager, I began practicing Zen meditation to develop my inner being. By the time I was at Bard College, I was an initiate in Transcendental Meditation and Kundalini Yoga. Later, when I was at the California Institute of the Arts, I studied Tai Chi and Hatha Yoga, and read extensively in other traditions. Eventually, I settled down to study with a Sufi master whose teachings were supremely ascetic: no singing and no dancing.

I had a numinous experience while I was still with the Sufi master that transformed my spiritual imagination. My husband and I were driving down a stretch of highway that was bordered by forest on both sides. He was listening to a hockey game on the radio, and the announcer happened to mention that it was the day of the Winter Solstice. As soon as I heard what day it was, I felt a strange and compelling longing inside. I knew that there was something I was supposed to do, but I wasn't sure what. All I knew was that I had to get out of the car and into the woods.

I finally convinced my husband to pull over, and I walked straight into the forest. I kept walking until I came to a tiny stream that was partly frozen over. I knelt on the ground and cupped my hands in the frigid water. When I looked up, I could see the sun in the sky, and when I looked down, I could see the brown earth and leaves. Somehow I *knew* that I had found what I had been seeking. I was in the presence of the Fire, the Water, and the Earth. I anointed myself with the water and felt a sense of relief. I now realize that this was my first hint of the Pagan path that would unfold in later years.

At the end of eight years, I left the ashram, my marriage, and the teacher, feeling like I was "starving in the desert," and found myself drawn to the Native American path. My experience in the forest was echoed in their reverence for the sacred: animals, trees, plants, spirits, and human beings. I attended Native gatherings and local meetings with like-minded individuals for five years until some Native American friends told me that while it was a good thing for me to honor their ancestors, I should look to my own European ancestors. I immediately thought of the Celts, of whom I had heard so much from my mother, and of her French and German ancestors.

I became hooked when I first heard that there were practicing Druids and that one could study with them, learning about Celtic history and religion. I was already a great fan of traditional Celtic music and dance, and so it was an easy transition to the myths, the poetry, and finally the Gods and Goddesses.

I have been a Druid officially since 1985, and I am happy to say that I know that I have at last located my spiritual home. I have never once been disappointed in this path. Today my altar celebrates the Goddess in Her many guises—Brighid, Mary, the Venus of Willendorf, Isis, the Goddess Elen (the Green Woman and the Horned Goddess), Quan Yin, and others. There is a place for the God on my altar too, in His guise as the Horned One, the Green Man of the forest.

My own spiritual search led me to one of the most ancient paths and inspired me to seek out others who had discovered Paganism. Why would some members of the best educated, most materially comfortable generation of Americans look back to mystical traditions many millennia old? How are they finding fulfillment in one of the fastest-growing spiritual paths today? And what messages do they have for the future of our society? I began to interview fellow

Pagans, choosing some individuals who are prominent, well-respected leaders in their communities and others who are not as well known but who have equally fascinating stories to tell.

As I collaborated with Lawrence Bond to edit the interviews I had compiled, we were struck by the respectful tolerence of this amazingly diverse community. In spite of the many issues that hold potential for disagreement, the overwhelming majority of the Pagans we've met have embraced the tensions that inevitably arise as people create and redefine the boundaries of their chosen traditions. The emerging dialogue sheds light on the reality of being a Pagan in twentieth-century America. In this time of paradigm shifts, cultural upheavals, and ecological crisis, I believe that the Nature religions hold the key to a more peaceful future.

I am always amazed when someone tells me that they are a Pagan or a Druid or a Witch and that they cannot seem to find anyone in their area to worship with. During the last ten years, I have met with Pagans virtually everywhere I have traveled, from New England to California and from Ireland to Italy. It seems immensely sad that those who feel a calling to the Old Religion should find themselves in a state of isolation, and it is for those souls in particular that I offer this book. My hope is that this book will provide an avenue—through the people, organizations, and publications presented—for every person who has felt the call of the "spirit of the forest" to find a spiritual home.

May the Gods and Goddesses of all Pagan traditions be honored once again among the major religions of the world.

Blessings of Stone, Earth, Fire, Sun, Water, Sea, Wind, and Sky.

Ellen Evert Hopman

Acknowledgments

I wish to offer special thanks to Andras and Deirdre Arthen of the Earthspirit Community, Isaac Bonewits, and Oberon G'Zell for their assistance and encouragement in making the crucial first contacts for this book. I wish to acknowledge Mark Roblee for opening the gates to the Faery tradition.

Thanks are due to Ernie Urvater and to Paul Eagle for their technical assistance. Untold gratitude is due to Ted Mills, who has unfailingly encouraged me in all of my efforts. I also wish to thank Lee Wood and John Matthews for their sensitive and skillful editing.

In particular, I wish to thank all of the Pagans who opened their hearts and gave of their time. Everyone has been most gracious.

Blessings of Stone, Earth, Fire, Sun, Water, Sea, Wind, and Sky.

Willow (Ellen Evert Hopman)

I dedicate this book to my son Emrys and his generation. May they live and grow in a world that celebrates diversity rather than fears it.

Lawrence Bond

The New Druids and the Celtic Revival

The words Celtic and Druid seem eternally shrouded in a mythical mist that suggests ancient Britain, Pagan warriors, King Arthur's Avalon, and secret societies of robed initiates circling around Stonehenge at sunrise. Beyond these romanticized and largely inaccurate images lies the truth of a group of peoples who flourished throughout all of Eastern and Western Europe, as well as the British Isles, some eight centuries before Christ.

Some of the first written accounts of Druids came from Julius Caesar, who recognized their role as the administrators of spiritual instruction among the Celtic peoples. Entrusted to them were the history, mythology, physical and spiritual healing techniques, and oral and written language of the Celts. Over two thousand years later, with Europe and the rest of the planet divided up into separate countries and clearly delineated ethnic and religious groups, it would seem that the people who were once known as the Celts are looked upon largely as a footnote in the early histories of nations such as Britain, France, and Spain.

It is interesting that as the twentieth century draws to a close large groups of people are forming neo-Druidic collectives with the purpose of gaining knowledge about Celtic spirituality and practicing Druidic ritual and ceremony. The following four people interviewed were chosen for their diverse outlooks on this modern Celtic revival, and for the fact that they represent a distinctively American viewpoint on this ancient European form of spirituality.

ISAAC BONEWITS is an ArchDruid and founder of a modern neo-Druidic organization called Ar nDraíocht Féin, or ADF. He is the author of *Real Magic* and the forthcoming *Rites of Worship: A Druid Approach.* Bonewits is also a skilled musician and has two cassette tapes of Pagan-inspired music called *Avalon Is Rising* and *Be Pagan Once Again* (available through ADF and many Pagan catalogs). He was interviewed in May 1993 at The Brushwood Folklore Center near Sherman, New York.

When did you first realize that you were a Pagan?

I first realized that I was a Pagan sometime in my early teens. I realized that I wasn't a Catholic anymore at age thirteen when I left a high school seminary for kids, sort of like a prep school for future priests run by the Norbertines, an obscure order from Hungary.

On the last day that I was there they changed their minds and graciously decided to let me come back for tenth grade. They had been about to throw me out for having a bad attitude. I said that I didn't want to come back the next year, and they said, "That's too bad. Have you discovered that you don't have a vocation to be a priest?" And I said, "Oh, I have a vocation to be a priest all right, just not in your religion." And I turned around, got in the car, and my dad drove me home. At that point I had no idea what religion I was supposed to be a priest in, but I knew there was a religion somewhere where I was supposed to be a priest.

Shortly after that I made the acquaintance of a young woman from New Orleans, who was very much into Voodoo, that is to say, the Afro-American religion without the religious aspects, just the magical aspects. She showed me a few spells that she had been casting, and I saw the results of those spells. I was *very* impressed.

At that point I became voraciously interested in consuming all of the books on magic, parapsychology, and the occult that I could find at my local library. Not surprisingly, they included an awful lot of books on anthropology. The more I started reading about Pagan belief systems, the more they made sense to me.

As time went by, I went to college; I met a few Wiccans here and there; I saw a couple of the early copies of *Green Egg*; and it became obvious to me that I was a Pagan. Then I discovered Druidism, and I knew that was where I belonged.

I had a roommate during my last year in college named Robert Larson, who was a graduate of Carlton College in Northfield, Minnesota. That was the birthplace of the Reformed Druids of North America. He wasn't one of the founders, but he was one of the early members of the organization. He mentioned to me that he was a Druid and told me about the group and showed me their literature, such as it was at that point.

I said, "This is *great,* this feels just right!" So we organized a grove in Berkeley and started doing ceremonies, and I said, "*Yes*, this is where I belong." I've been stuck with being a Druid ever since.

So what is the essence of Druidism? What is the most sacred thing? What has kept you a Druid all of these years?

I can only say that I have a "vocation" to be a Druid, using the Catholic terminology, since I don't know any Celtic terminology to describe the same thing. Every time in my life that I have tried to stop being a Druid, that I have dropped out or semi-retired, gone on sabbatical, or anything like that, someone or something has come by and lifted me up by the scruff of the neck and tossed me back into it again.

To me the essence of Druidism is combining the best of head and heart and hand. Combining the intellect, the emotions, and the artistic creativity and craft that people have. It's using that to worship the Gods and to help ourselves to understand our lives better and understand what we are doing and where we are going.

So you founded a group called Ar nDraíocht Féin?

Yes, or it founded me, I'm never too sure about that. I've been going back through my records trying to figure out when did I actually start ADF. It's very difficult to put a clear-cut beginning line to it. The roots of it go back to the years I spent with the Reformed Druids of North America.

The RDNA did not consider itself Pagan. The RDNA, very much like the meso-Pagan or fraternal Druid organizations of England, believe that Druidism is a philosophy. A style of questioning and of metaphysical openness that is applicable to any belief system. On the other hand, I say that if you are gathering people out in the woods, you are singing hymns to the Earth Mother, and you are giving praises to the old Celtic Gods and Goddesses, you are practicing a Pagan religion.

Over the years I made a number of efforts to paganize the RDNA and to get the people of the RDNA to accept the fact that what they were doing was a neo-Pagan religion. I was met with varying degrees of success and resistance. Eventually, at one point there was a blowup in the small-group politics, and I just said, "This is it, I am not doing this anymore. I am tired of beating my head against a cement wall." I retired for a couple of years and focused on learning how to earn a living with computers.

Eventually I started getting back into doing ritual that for me was "Druid ritual." It was based originally on the RDNA stuff but increasingly on the studies I was doing of the Celtic materials. I have found early versions of the current ADF liturgy dating back as early as 1981. Yet to the best of my knowledge we didn't officially start ADF until around 1983 or 1984. That was when I was talking to friends about the research that had been mentioned to me by my Irish teacher concerning Indo-European studies. Things like the comparative mythology of Georges Dumezil and the discoveries that had been made of more or less intact Pagan traditions being practiced in the Baltic territories.

A number of friends of mine who were amateur or professional scholars said, "Gee, this is exciting. We ought to organize a group to look into this." The next thing I knew we had ADF.

Almost within the first year of putting ADF together as a network of about forty scholars, we had another hundred people joining us who wanted rituals, rites of passage, and music and art, who wanted a complete religion.

This was before we had finished researching what the old religions of Europe really were. To me it was very important that we plant our roots in firm ground. That we not indulge in the kind of romantic silliness that most Druid revivals of the past have indulged in. I thought we should find out what they were *actually* doing in Europe before the Christians came along, what parts of those religious beliefs do we really agree with today, and what parts do we think are no longer appropriate.

How is ADF different from other groups?

Most of the people in the rest of the Pagan community are very casual about their scholarship. They read something that sounds or feels good, and they go for it. This is probably the reason why so many women in the Goddess spirituality movement leapt on the Golden Age of Matriarchy idea, because it felt so nice. The fact that the evidence to support that was shaky to slim didn't seem to bother them much. They could always claim that it was the fault of those mean, nasty Patriarchal Evil Folks, or male anthropologists.

There's a line in [Lewis Carroll's] *The Hunting of the Snark* about how you close your one eye and then gaze fondly upon the subject with the gleam of true belief in your other eye and you will see the snark, which is otherwise an invisible entity.

The approach that an awful lot of people in the Pagan community have taken to scholarship has been to read until they find stuff they like and then stop reading. Or at least to stop reading anything that contradicts what they want to believe. ADF is to the best of my knowledge the only neo-Pagan tradition that is based on the idea of continual research and on changing and adapting our policies and procedures based on the results of that research.

One of the most revolutionary things we've done in ADF is to spread the idea that credentials should be verified. If somebody makes a claim, you should be able to verify whether or not that claim is valid.

Most other Pagan groups get a system together, and they stick with it. They may elaborate on it, but that's it; they don't really do any more digging.

You play the harp, don't you?

Yes and no. I was starting to learn to play the harp when my illness made it very difficult for me to move my hands fast enough. My harp lessons have gone on permanent sabbatical until I can get my illness under control. It's like severe arthritis that makes it difficult to play an instrument. Mostly I do songwriting and singing now.

So what is the role of the arts in Paganism?

The arts are one of the ways that you arouse strong emotions that are appropriate during religious or magical work. Emotions of awe, beauty, love, and appreciation. We integrate the use of the arts into our rituals as much as we possibly can.

Can you talk about what leads you to compose a particular piece?

Many times I'll either be out in nature taking a walk or meditating, and I'll see something that will strike me as being noticeable or worthy of attention. Worthy to be commemorated in some fashion. If at that same moment a stray fragment of melody happens to enter my head, bubble up from my subconscious, I start putting it together and making a song out of it.

A lot of the times I'll be reading about mythology and studying the stories of the different Deities, and I'll say to myself, "Gee, so and so is really a neat Deity; they really deserve to have a song." I also have a list in the back of my head of great old folk tunes. Mostly Irish and English folk ballads with some others from elsewhere that I'll think would really make a great song if I could just come up with lyrics for them. Once in a while they will click.

What's it like being a Pagan father, and how do you think you are different from other fathers?

Well, it's hard to say how much of our parenting style is based on Paganism and how much of it is just based on our personal beliefs and research into parenting skills.

For me the hardest part of raising [my son] as a Pagan has been explaining the world to him, since of course three-year-olds want you to explain everything to them. We try to explain it to him in ways that are simple enough for him to understand and accept, but not as simplistic as the mainstream Christian culture wants you to be. So I have to avoid black-and-white answers.

He'll say he wants to do something, like when he wants to levitate one of his toys. I'll say, "Well, on the earth-plane level of reality you are going to run into a problem with gravity." I'm being very careful not to tell him that too many things are impossible. Because I believe, just from my research into magical work for thirty years now, that it's being told that things are impossible that is probably the primary psychological block in releasing psychic phenomena. I'll say, "It's possible to levitate things, but you have to work at it very hard and it takes a long time to learn and you will probably be able to do it when you get older."

I'm trying not to tell him that things are impossible, but I am teaching him how to assess the odds on a situation. If you do such and such you *probably* will have this and that happen. It would be things where the average father would say, "No, you can't do that because you will always have such and such happen as a result."

I'd say the primary distinction between Pagan parenting and, say, Christian parenting, for example, is respect for the child. I think that may be the simple essence of what makes Pagan parenting different. Respect for the child. Not feeling that we have the absolute one, true, right, and only reality, that we have the God-given right to shove it down their throats. Which is the essence of Christian child rearing.

Can you shed some light on some of the problems that the Pagan community is facing?

I think the overwhelming majority of problems in the Pagan community are the normal problems of human interaction, especially small-group politics. Small-group dynamics do not change simply because your religion has changed, not unless you make a conscious effort to change them. The other main problem is simply growing pains. Our community has grown so rapidly that I believe our population is doubling every three or four years. This is astonishing growth for any kind of a religious movement. Most of that growth is hidden because we are so decentralized. In many ways neo-Paganism is a beautiful example of what Toffler would call a "third wave" religion, if he wasn't so hostile toward religion.

A simple example would be publications. Toffler talks about how there is a simultaneous concentration in the mainstream media. For example, in every big city in North America you now find only one or two big newspapers. It used to be that every city had five or six or seven or eight big newspapers. There are presently only a handful of the network television stations. All owned by the same people.

At the same time that's been happening, there has been the explosion in cable and satellite television and all the many stations that now exist. There's been an explosion of journals, small press publications, magazines, and bulletin boards. These are ways that people are communicating outside of the officially established mainstream media.

In Paganism what you see is an efflorescence, a growth of hundreds and hundreds of small, different groups who communicate and network with each other, who compete with each other because they are in the same ecological niche. If you look at it in those terms, then a lot of the personality problems and the politics that look so horrible to us from the inside look like very typical tempests in a teapot from the outside.

The Pagan community is simultaneously developing a national consensus on some basic principles and thrashing out through argument and debate and people voting with their feet how they feel about a whole host of other issues. I think this is very healthy.

So what is right about Paganism?

Most of the modern neo-Pagan movement is an outgrowth of Gerald Gardner's efforts to create what amounted to a Pagan house church movement. Small groups of people getting together to worship the Gods. Probably the biggest change we've seen in the Pagan community in the last ten years has been growing beyond that model, starting to develop large-group worship techniques. That's one of the things that ADF has been heavily focused on.

Our liturgical work so far has been mostly based on medium- to large-group liturgy, although we have a number of our folks now working on individual and family worship materials. Paganism is growing so rapidly that when you go to a festival you may have five hundred or a thousand people there, all wanting to do a ritual simultaneously. You can't use the same techniques for a thousand people that you use for half a dozen people meeting in your living room.

Because there is a natural human tendency, even among revolutionaries (perhaps even especially among revolutionaries), to want to fossilize and rigidify the "new view" as quickly as possible, there has been a lot of controversy in the Pagan community over the idea of Paganism becoming a mainstream religion. Many people in the Pagan community would really like it to remain where it was for the first thirty years, which is a collection of elite cliques who all prided themselves on how wonderful they were and who didn't want to interact with the riffraff, the mainstream population. That's where Paganism was for the first thirty years.

What has happened is, again, the decentralization and demassification. Many books, articles, television programs, and videotapes have been produced about Paganism now. It's relatively easy for anyone who wants to start their own Pagan group. These Pagan groups are not necessarily wired into any kind of organized structure. They are people winging it, based on a book by the Farrars or by Starhawk or by me. They don't necessarily consider themselves beholden to the authors of those books. They'll take what they want and mix it in an eclectic fashion and work and see what rings their chimes.

So where do you see Druidism in the future of America?

Oh boy . . . and the future of the world? And the future of the planet? [laughter]

And the solar system and the galaxy. Where does it fit in the Grand Scheme of Things? What is your personal vision for it?

What role do I see Druidism playing in the unfolding drama? Well, the ancient Druids, the paleo-Pagan Druids, both the Celtic Druids per se and their colleagues in the other Indo-European religions, were the repositories of cultural wisdom. They were the people who were responsible for making sure that the hard-earned knowledge and skill of each generation was passed on to the next. That's why they were so bloody conservative.

They led, at least the specific clergy part of the Druid caste, the rituals that united entire tribes, sometimes entire groups of tribes. It was their function to bring together people from widely separated places and unite them in the worship of the Gods.

I believe that modern-day Druids, at least the neo-Pagan Druids, have the ability to do exactly the same thing. We have the ability to bring people together from many different origins and help them to learn how to work together to contact the Gods. We need to unify ourselves so that we'll have a simultaneous movement of organization, as we have the already very active movement of disorganization.

The ancient Druids were really obsessed with order and fearful about chaos. I think the modern Druids have learned that order and chaos in a dynamic balance with each other are what produces the most healthy organism and the most healthy social structure.

Basically, I believe that in order for the planet to be saved Paganism has to become mainstream. Paganism has to be at least as much of a presence in the culture as the Unitarians or the Quakers—two groups which are influential all out of proportion to their actual numbers. My guess is that we have somewhere between a hundred and fifty and three hundred thousand Pagans in the modern-day neo-Pagan world community. I am deliberately being conservative here.

Are there ever people excluded from ADF?

We've had certain groups of people that we have not allowed into ADF because personally I don't think they belong in the neo-Pagan community at all. Neo-Nazis, people who think that Druidism is only for Celts and that if you aren't 100 percent Celtic on both sides of your family you have no business being a Druid. We've had some raving anti-Semites who have decided errone-ously that I'm Jewish because of the way my name sounds. They've been furious at the fact that somebody Jewish would try to be a Druid. I find that hysterical!

But it's very useful to flush these people out, because we don't want bigots in the organization. One of the things we've been stressing in ADF, and I think that the neo-Pagan community as a whole has been stressing, is that you can be proud of your ancestry without having to trash other people.

Americans are mongrels. America is a nation of people who cheerfully intermarry with people of other racial and ethnic backgrounds. A neo-Pagan religion for Americans and for the twenty-first century has to be open to people regardless of what their ancestry is. Racism is BS, and we don't need it in the next century.

Neo-Pagan Druidism is different from some other Pagan movements in that we're not sticking our head in the ground fantasizing about a romantic Golden Age. This ties into the scholarship again, because we don't whitewash things that our ancestors did that today we would consider extremely unpleasant or tacky. We're not reviving human sacrifice or the cult of the severed head and so on and so forth!

Green Man Grove has put out a series of very humorous announcements in their newsletter, where they made a bunch of those circle-with-a-slash-mark symbols and they had one that was a blood drop with a slash mark through it that said, "No human sacrifice." It also said, "In addition to the ADF ban on human sacrifice we have voluntarily decided to agree on no cannibalism at official events!" They drew a little severed arm holding a fork. Very quaint.

Possibly one of the major benefits of the neo-Pagan community is that so many of us have a sense of humor about ourselves and about reality. I think that's a good thing.

We have one foot in the past and one foot in the future. ADF is focused towards what the world is going to be like a hundred years from now as well as what's going on in the present. I think that if and when we finally get around to building starships, we're going to have Druid chaplains on those starships.

Druidism is a religious approach that says you can be a whole person. You don't have to suppress your intellect or your emotions in order to be a religious person. You can have your intellect, you can have your emotions, you can have your artistic creativity, you can have your physical needs, you can have all the different aspects of what makes a healthy, balanced human being. You don't have to suppress or hype up any one aspect of yourself in order to be considered spiritual.

How is Druidism different from Wicca? You mentioned before that 80 percent of people in the movement considered themselves to be Wiccans.

The differences between Wicca and other forms of neo-Paganism are actually fairly simple. It's important to emphasize from the beginning that these are not "good/bad" distinctions, because I'm not a dualist.

Wicca is small-group oriented. The average Wiccan coven is three to five people, despite the fantasy about there being thirteen. By the time there gets to be ten or eleven members in a coven it fissions. The actual cause of the fission is almost completely irrelevant. It's always small-group politics, somebody going to bed with somebody whom their partner didn't want them to go to bed with, or people come up with an excuse to blow up the coven. So it always stays three to five or six people because that is the maximum number of people who can effectively work the particular magical style that Wicca does.

Druidism by contrast is large-group oriented. We assume that there will be anywhere from a dozen to several hundred people at a ceremony. Our rituals are designed to have multiple contingency factors built in, and the clergy are trained in how to adjust the ritual based on the number of people present.

This is not something that is part of the Wiccan training because Wiccan training assumes that everybody is going to fit into a nine-foot circle. Wicca is primarily esoteric. Druidism is both esoteric and exoteric. That is to say that Wicca is based on intense small-group magic being done by a group of people who essentially become a family.

The Wiccan idea is that of a small group of people who know each other intimately on as many levels as possible, who can set up a very tightly focused group mind in order to do magical work. They are esoteric because of the heavy emphasis on secrecy, the heavy emphasis on not letting outsiders know the details of what they are doing. Druidism is primarily exoteric to the extent that we're focused on larger groups, on openness, and are inclusive.

Many Wiccans are not into the secrecy thing anymore. You have all of these eclectic people running around who are into public ceremony.

They are not into secrecy to the extent that they read books and write books, but coven business is still coven business. You don't talk about what's going on inside the coven with outsiders. Remember, I'm not talking dualism here, I'm talking about opposite ends of a spectrum of values, okay?

The Druids were the leaders of the tribes. They were the priests and priestesses of the Old Religions. Therefore, when they led a ritual their teaching and their religious and spiritual training were oriented to everybody in the tribe. There were esoteric things involved in the personal training of a Druid, and we have those things as well. We are developing those things in ADF.

Nobody knows anymore what the old Druid mysteries were. If they say they do, they are fibbing, to put it as gently as possible. But we are rediscovering what the esoteric mysteries are for a Druid in our time, in this particular planetary situation.

A Wiccan group is small, esoteric, and exclusive, that is to say that in order to get that small working group you have to pick and choose who you are going to let into your circle. So you exclude perhaps the vast majority of people who might want to join you. You only pick "the best," the ones you think will work best with your group. You are closed as far as outsiders coming in. That's a necessary result of that style of magical working.

A Druid grove is open. Anybody can show up, and as long as they behave themselves they can participate. There are few if any closed meetings that are for "grove members only." Usually those are business meetings, and they are boring. The emphasis is always on making the religion accessible to anyone who sincerely wants to participate.

How about the theological differences?

Theologically, Wiccan groups tend to be either monotheistic or duotheistic. Duotheism is the idea that all of the female Divinities who have ever been worshipped on this planet can be seen as aspects or faces of one female Divinity, the Goddess. All of the male Deities can be seen as aspects or faces of the God, or the Horned God. This is how metaphysical reality is divided within the system.

Many of the feminist Witches leave the Horned God out of it entirely. They either say he doesn't exist or that he is an aspect of the Goddess too. In any event, the Wiccan system is focused on blurring the differences between individual Deities in favor of emphasizing the Yin or the Yang. The monotheism comes in when the Goddess is seen as the only entity whose worship is important.

In non-Wiccan Pagan groups there is more of an emphasis on pluralism, on polytheism. The Goddesses and the Gods are seen as distinct individuals. They have their own needs, strengths, and weaknesses. None of them are omnipotent, omniscient, or omni anything else. The focus is on the unique individuality of each Deity and his or her relationship to you.

Do Druids believe in a Creator?

No. Because "a Creator" is one of those lovely, sneaky theological terms that has dozens of unverified assumptions buried inside of it. For example a lot of mainstream theologians have complained about people who worship Nature because they are "worshipping the creation rather than the Creator." The trouble is that the whole idea of "the Creation" is a monotheistic theological concept. It's not an eternal verity of human philosophy. The Universe just is. It's here. We're here. We have no idea where it came from and neither does anybody else.

On one level the primary function of neo-Pagan Druidism and of the neo-Pagan movement as a whole is to save the planet. To bring back that attitude of reverence towards Nature that our ancestors had, with the additional knowledge that we now have about biology and bioregions and how the environment actually functions. We can use that to halt the horrible destruction that the products of the mainstream religion have produced.

The current ecological crisis is almost entirely the result of Christianity—to a lesser extent Islam and Judaism, but primarily Christianity. The very idea that some Deity created the world and gave it over to human beings to do with as they choose. To trash it in any fashion they choose, and it doesn't matter because any day the millennium is going to happen and we'll all be washed away, so who cares?

That attitude, that contempt for Nature, seems to have been essential to Christianity almost from the beginning and is what has put us in the mess we're in now. The fact that a lot of the damage was done by scientist types who consciously don't follow Christian dogma hasn't changed it, because they are still subconsciously following Christian dogma. Despite the best efforts of people like Matthew Fox, for example, to echo Christianity or to make Christianity environmentally conscious, they're working against the whole inertia and the belief structure.

In neo-Paganism making the people environmentally conscious is working *with* the inertia of the metaphysical structure. Inertia works both ways. Something that is standing still stays still until you add extra energy. Something that is already moving will *keep* moving.

The neo-Pagan religions, and for that matter paleo- and meso-Pagan religions, already move in the directions of considering Nature sacred and considering it important to pay attention to your impact on it. Judaism, Christianity, Islam, scientism, and Marxism are all religions that are based on the idea that Nature is dead and human beings can do to it any bloody thing they want to.

In order to change those religions to make them environmentally conscious, you have to work against dozens and dozens of interrelated doctrines. To make Pagan religions more environmentally conscious, you can work *with* dozens of already existing assumptions that support that idea.

The reason I am phrasing all of this as carefully as I am is that our Pagan ancestors were *not* ecological purists. They changed the entire environmental state of Europe through what is called slash-and-burn agriculture. They completely transformed it from solid forest, from one end of the continent to the other, to pockets of forest and lots of farmland.

Pagans in the past have trashed their environment. They weren't aware that was what they were doing. They didn't know that cutting down all the trees on a hillside to build ships to go sail someplace was going to destroy the ability of that hillside to hold rain, and therefore change the ecology in that local area.

Ancient Pagans didn't know that; we do. We know that stuff now. We know that making major changes on a small scale in a small area will reverberate and have ripple effects on a larger area. I believe that if the ancient Pagans had realized that some of the things they were doing were trashing the environment, they wouldn't have done it. They would have been more careful. Because they believed that Nature was sacred. Even while they were changing it.

I believe that neo-Paganism is a synthesis of the best of both the mainstream and minority religions that have come before. I believe that neo-Paganism is the next inevitable evolutionary step in human religion. Monotheistic religions are polarizing now into extreme conservatives and extreme liberals. The extreme liberals are all dropping out and are either joining us or some other New Age group.

The extreme conservatives are fighting tooth and nail to preserve the political and economic and military power that they have held. They are going to lose, unless they manage to blow up the planet before we can save it.

Can you talk a bit about your experience of Pagan spirituality?

I would say that the single most powerful spiritual experience I've had in the last three years was watching my son be born. We had a home birth with a midwife. Arthur was born in our bed at home with a copy of the Bill of Rights framed at the head of the bed. Watching him be born, I saw the miracle of natural creation at its most powerful.

Personally, I think that anyone who has ever watched a child be born would find it impossible to worship a male creator. Which may be yet another reason Christianity has always tried to suppress midwives. They try to wrap birth around with taboos to keep the men away from seeing it.

Catching my child as he came out of his mother was incredibly profound. I looked into his eyes, and I saw a very old and very wise man. That experience gave me more belief in reincarnation than I had ever had. I'd always been kind of ambivalent about reincarnation. But that was *not* a blank slate there. That was very definitely a person. Arthur was a person from the day he was born. It was amazing. That to me was a powerful religious experience, and I would classify that as a Pagan religious experience. It was Nature, it was reality at its most basic and profound. It was deeply meaningful.

We've had some very powerful ceremonies here at the Nemeton we have built on this land [in western New York state at the Brushwood Folklore Center]. The Nemeton is a reconstruction based on our chief artificer's research into the archaeology of Celtic sacred sites.

A Nemeton is a sacred grove, or a sacred space in general, but it was always associated with groves of trees. Archaeologists and philologists have said that it means "sacred grove." In any event, we set one up here. We consecrated it last year with a full ceremony, and we had some incredibly powerful spiritual experiences. People were hearing voices. You could see ghostly figures running around the outside of the ring of people. The energy, power, and love that we got from the Gods and Goddesses on that occasion was just unmistakable and very hard to articulate!

Does ADF have a prescribed ritual form?

The trick is to have a standard liturgical outline that functions as a skeleton for your ritual. It is up to the Druids and the bards and the seers of the grove to put flesh on that outline. There are lots of different styles and ways the outline can be done. The primary advantage to having a standard liturgical outline is that you don't have to reinvent the wheel every time it's time to do a ritual, and people from various parts of your organization who are traveling through your territory can participate and know more or less what's going to happen.

For example, last year when it was time to consecrate the Nemeton, we had ADF Druids from half the continent and a dozen different groves here. In something like half an hour we were able to put together what the ritual was going to be. We pulled it off, and it was spectacular. You can't do that at your average Pagan gathering, where you have people coming from dozens and dozens of different traditions who all have different liturgical designs for how they do their rituals.

Aren't you afraid that you are on your way to becoming monolithic, orthodox . . . ?

No. I'm not afraid of that. Structure is not the same thing as tyranny. Part of the problem that the whole neo-Pagan community has is that since all of us are what the Unitarians call "come-outers," we've all come out of some other religious background. Many of us were burned very badly by our experiences with our childhood religion, and anything that even vaguely resembles it we tend to find makes us nervous.

But there are reasons why successful religions, whether Pagan or non-Pagan, have the standard liturgical patterns they do. From a magical point of view, patterns work. You don't want to tinker too much with a successful pattern. Especially if you happen to believe that the sun won't rise, the crops won't grow, and the herds will not reproduce if you mess up the ritual.

From a magical point of view it's very useful to have a standard design that you know works. From a social point of view it's really useful to have a standard pattern so that all the people who are participating know what they can and cannot do, where they are going to be able to contribute. That's what the Buddhists, Native Americans, or native Chinese would say.

Isn't it odd that the very best Christian buildings try to look like groves of trees—the Gothic ones?

Funny thing about that. But I am not talking about the aesthetics. I am talking about the simple practicality of when you build a building that is essentially something that is going to fall apart. You have to be constantly repairing it and working to keep it as it was before. With a grove what you have are living beings, the trees. A tree is planted either deliberately or accidentally by nature. It grows. It puts out its branches. It sends out its own seeds, which become seedlings. As the years go by, eventually the tree dies and rots and turns into humus, and all its children, the seedlings that came from it, are rooted in that humus. They grow and flourish and produce their own offspring.

We work with organic metaphors in ADF. I tried very hard at all times to see that when we came up with central metaphors for the organization they were organic. We assume that the liturgical outline is going to change over time anyway. Oddly enough there has been more bitter opposition from people for changing the liturgical outline than for there being an outline. The liturgical outline now has something like thirty-seven steps to it. A lot of people found that intimidating. This is because they have never sat down and done a liturgical analysis of an average Wiccan circle or an average Catholic mass or an average Buddhist rite, all of which can have anywhere from twenty-five to fifty steps in them.

A Native American ceremony, an authentic one, takes place over several days, and they are very precise about who is going to do what and in what order. They still have room for creativity within that structure, but they stick to the traditional structure, or it's not part of the tradition any more.

So having a standard liturgical design not only gives familiarity, which is comforting to many people, it makes it easy to participate if you come from another part of the organization. It is a magical system that we know happens to work, and it is part of what helps to define a tradition or a movement. ADF has, as part of its defining characteristic, this particular way of doing ceremony. The people who like it, like it, and the people who don't, go someplace else. We've had groups schism off from us, and for the most part we've been very happy with these schisms. That means that when somebody comes to us who wants to do something that isn't what we're doing, we now have places we can send them.

The point is that things don't have to be one or the other. A healthy biome has many different species in it competing in constantly changing relationship with each other. ADF has never been out to destroy all competing groups. That's the Christians' trip.

We believe that there is a role for organized large-group worship in the Pagan community, and what we envision, and are already starting to see, is that within a larger ADF grove there will be smaller groups. There will be covens. There will be healing circles. There will be bardic groups and artistic groups. There will be ecology action groups, as the people within a congregation form special-interest groups of their own.

Like Unitarian committees!

Exactly! There's an awful lot that we can learn from the Unitarians. In fact we have a fairly heavy overlap at this point between our membership and the Unitarians. A lot of them have joined ADF and Pagan groups in general. A lot of ADF people have joined the Unitarian church because there's a lot to learn from them.

TONY AND SABLE TAYLOR were originally members of ADF but split off from the group to form The Henge of Keltria, an international Druid organization dedicated to spiritual development through study and practice of the Druidic arts and Celtic magic. The Taylors offer both personal and correspondence courses, and are highly active publishers of Pagan-related material, including:

> *Keltria: A Journal of Druidism and Celtic Magic* is published quarterly and on time. This magazine also pays for articles, which is probably a first for a Pagan magazine.
> *Serpent Stone: A Journal of Druidic Wisdoms* is published infrequently and available on a per-issue basis. Back issues are available.
> *Book of Ritual* offers ritual basics and theology plus sample scripts.
> *The Henge: An Introduction to Keltrian Druidism* (booklet) describes beliefs and ethics, political and administrative structure, member rights and responsibilities.

While sharing many of the beliefs of Isaac Bonewits and ADF, the Taylors have some fundamental differences as well, which are explored in detail in this interview conducted by phone on February 12, 1994.

Sable, when did you first discover that you were a Pagan?

I have been a Pagan since I was a child, but I didn't discover that this was anything that anyone else in the world was until 1980. I found out then that there were other people who were as weird as I was.

As a child I was very interested in mythology. I made my own set of Runes; I had absolutely no idea what they were. I made them out of linoleum and painted them with red paint. I didn't know what to do with them or how to use them, but they felt good in my hands.

What religion were you raised in?

I was raised Methodist, but not very strictly. My parents didn't go to church very often. This was in Baltimore, Maryland.

Tony was probably the first real live Pagan that I encountered, but at that time I don't think he knew that there were other Pagans in the world. He felt like a loner, too. We actually discovered other Pagans in the early 1980s in the Pagan Special Interest Group of MENSA.

We would get together and talk about different kinds of Paganism and what different people were doing. Occasionally, we would have some light form of ritual or meditation.

How did you become a Druid?

That was a gradual metamorphosis. There was a mystique about it that called to me. There was something in my ancestral being that urged me to seek it out. It took me a while to realize what I was and that that was what had been calling to me all those years.

What I knew about Druids at that point was what I had picked up from *The Golden Bough* [by Sir James Frazier]. Reading about the Fire Festivals in Europe as a teenager started me on the path to Druidism.

When I met Tony, the two of us were drawn to this thing called Druidism, but we didn't exactly know how to define it. We started doing research, and we found out that there were occult bookstores, places where we could find information. The more we found out, the more we knew we were on the right track.

When did you both meet your first Druids?

That would have been Isaac Bonewits at the Pagan Spirit Gathering (PSG). I think it was in 1985. At that time Isaac was the only person who was putting his name out in public as being a Druid, at least in the American neo-Pagan community. He had the wealth of information from the old RDNA, and since there were no books on Druidism that I knew of, at least not on modern Druidism, he was the only contact point that we had. If there had been other contact points, we might have pursued them.

So we talked with Isaac, and we got involved with ADF.

How long were you involved with ADF?

I think it was about four years. It was kind of disappointing, because I had these great expectations that I was going to get all my questions answered, and that didn't happen. There simply wasn't enough information being disseminated by ADF for me to get the answers that I needed.

I wanted to know what Druidism was; I was still wrestling with it in my own head. I was relying on Isaac as my "high guru" to put the pieces of the puzzle together for me. I discovered that was a mistake; I can't put those kinds of expectations on another person.

Due to that and to some other disagreements such as administrative issues that Tony and I weren't comfortable with, and due to the promise of a certain amount of goods coming to us for the membership fee and not getting those, we left. We weren't seeing the publications that we had been promised, for example. We eventually just got frustrated.

We decided that we weren't going to wait for Isaac anymore, and we were going to do it ourselves. We then formed Keltria.

How is Keltria different from ADF?

Keltria works specifically within a Celtic framework. We don't have Greek Druids or Slavic Druids. We have Celtic Druids. We're more tribal than ADF. We recognize that within the Celtic culture the tribe and the clan were very important. We try to structure ourselves around that idea. We are not trying to be a fraternal organization. We like to work in smaller, closer groups that mirror the tribe—the feasting, the rituating, the camaraderie that exists within an extended family.

We are organized into groves that operate as extended families. The Druids within each clan are free to interact with Druids from any other clan. Just as the ancient Druids could move from tribe to tribe and be recognized and respected. We stay in contact with the other clans, even though we may have our own.

How is this different from ADF?

We don't specialize in large public ritual. We are certainly capable of doing them—we do them at PSG every year—but it's not our main focus. We have never done a ritual for the whole PSG, but we have done open, public rituals there on nights when people had a choice of four or five rituals they could attend.

We typically don't do things for the public at large. It's not that we are being secretive, it just doesn't feel like something to be scattered upon the wind. Our rituals are designed to speak to the soul, and they only speak to certain souls.

You are a composer of poetry and songs. Some of them are becoming widespread in the Pagan community. Can you list some of the ones that you have done?

There's one called "Fur And Feather." It goes like this:

Fur and feather, scale and skin
different without,
but the same within.
Many of body,
but one of soul
through all creatures
are the Gods made whole.

"Walk with Wisdom" is another one that has been picked up:

Walk with wisdom,
from this hallowed place.
Walk not in sorrow,
our roots shall ere embrace.
May strength be your brother,
and honor be your friend,
and luck be your lover,
until we meet again.

The other one that has kind of gotten around is "Mothers and Fathers of Old":

From far across this mortal plain
Mothers and Fathers of old
We pray that ye return again
Mothers and Fathers of old
To share with us the mysteries
And secrets long untold
Of the ancient ways we seek to reclaim
Mothers and Fathers of old.

You also helped to compose Book of Ritual *recently, didn't you?*

Yes. It's the first Keltrian *Book of Ritual*. In it we have rituals for the eight High Rites (Samhain, Imbolc, Beltane, Lughnasad, and the Solstices and Equinoxes) and also for the Mistletoe Rite. The Mistletoe Rite is held on the "sixth night of the moon"; that commemorates the gathering of the mistletoe, which was known as the All Heal. We use that ritual for healing and communion or "healing of the tribes."

You are a Pagan parent. Can you talk a bit about what that's like?

It presents its own challenges and rewards. I try to do something everyday with my younger children. The oldest is two, and the youngest is nine months, so the training that they are getting at this point isn't very spiritual.

When I had my first child, who is now nineteen, it was somewhat different because my philosophy at the time was that she should be allowed to be whatever she wants to be. Tony and I did not try to indoctrinate her into anything. As a result she doesn't know what spiritual path she wants to be on.

It's a matter of reaping what we've sown. If you don't give a child a religious background, they tend to grow up not having an idea of what they want to be. They then have to go out and seek it for themselves. She is wrestling with it right now. She is a spiritual person, but a lot of times younger people don't focus on spirituality; at least that has been my experience and observation. They are too busy living the empirical side of life. They almost have to settle down and possibly even have their own children before they start looking at the connection between past and future and thereby recognizing a spirituality through which they can express that vision.

Where do you think Paganism is headed right now?

I think it's growing. I think it is going to be the religion of the twenty-first century, but it has a lot of hurdles to get over such as battling the mainstream religions and being recognized. There are still people out there who think of Paganism as something satanic or a joke. They don't take it seriously.

We need to learn to organize. We need to get back in touch with the life continuum and realize that we are all connected to the past, to the future, and to each other. Western society tends to idealize individualism to such a degree that we have lost contact with community. We need to let go of some of that "rugged individualism" and feel our connectedness with others.

By doing that perhaps we will be able to get enough cooperation from each other that we can effectively build our temple. We will then become something that other people will be attracted to. They will look at us and say, "That person is a Pagan, maybe I should be a Pagan too."

Building temples takes money. There has been a lot of controversy about money in the Pagan community—whether to have paid clergy or not, whether to collect dues. What do you think about that? Can Paganism move forward with or without funds?

I think that just because of the way that our society is structured, we have to have money to move forward. The question is how are we going to get that money? Do we go out and hold bake sales? I don't know what we will be doing to get the money. But money talks in this culture, and if we want to be heard we have to have the money to talk with. We have to be willing to deal with money no matter how dirty some people may think it is.

You said that having the clergy would create the congregations. Do you envision a training program or a school?

Paganism is so diverse that you couldn't have just one Pagan theological college. One of the things that a lot of Pagans want to do is to stay away from that much structure because it leads to hierarchy.

But there are an awful lot of street corner preachers out there who have gotten themselves churches. They haven't been to the great Christian seminaries. So it can be done. It's a matter of having the right charisma and having the organizational skills to make it happen. But it does take a certain amount of money.

So, Tony, you have been waiting patiently. How did you arrive at Paganism?

I first discovered that I was a Pagan in the early to mid-seventies. I had been on a spiritual quest. I wandered through the Reorganized Church of Jesus Christ of the Latter-Day Saints. I wandered through the Baha'i faith. I had an introduction to Buddhism and Taoism, and I came to the conclusion that I was doing it all wrong.

What I really needed to do was to determine what *I* believed and then seek something that fit that rather than trying to find out if something out there fit me. I found that the relationship of myself to Deity fit within Paganism.

There is something about me that is fairly unique, even in the Pagan community. I am a true polytheist. I believe that the Gods and the Goddesses are very separate and discrete entities, not aspects or manifestations of a unifying God or a Goddess, as is usually stated in Wicca.

When did you meet your first Druid?

The first person I met who identified himself as a Druid that I took seriously as such was Isaac Bonewits. I had already been Druid-identified myself for ten years or better. I even had "Druid" on my dog tags when I was in the service from 1969 to 1979. At that time I was practicing a type of Celtic spirituality. I didn't have to get permission from the chaplain or anything like that. I just told them I was a Druid, and that's what they put on my dog tags.

What was it that led you to create your own Druid organization?

There were several fundamental issues. The first were some administrative and organizational difficulties that ADF was experiencing at the time that I had difficulty working with. Some of those actions were quite distasteful to me.

The other thing was the notion of a Pan-Indo-European form of Druidism. That just didn't ring true to my spirit. Lastly, I found that ADF was good at networking, but that it wasn't helping its people to establish a spiritual relationship with other spirits. There was not much of spirits joining and making a connection. It just wasn't in the ADF liturgical system.

So what is unique about the Keltrian liturgical system?

It is designed to focus around developing the individual person's relationship with the ancestors, the nature spirits, and the Gods and Goddesses of their tribe.

Another difference is that Keltria is very egalitarian in terms of its officers.

Both males and females are equally recognized and accepted and desired for any position, which is quite different from other Druidic groups, many of which seem to be quite patriarchal.

What is the focus of the journal?

The present structure of *Keltria* is to take a theme or special focus for each issue. We then have three areas within the magazine called the Bardic Path, the Druid Path, and the Seers Path. Those paths relate to the three worlds of land, sea, and sky, of mind, body, and spirit, and of past, present, future.

Do you find that Druids around the world are on a similar wavelength?

There are very fundamental differences. Some Druids throughout the world are not even neo-Pagans. They are reaching back to a former Celtic experience that they want to reclaim or recover. I've run into a full gamut of a few smaller groups [of English Druids] that do appear to have some sort of racist agenda that is also a nationalistic agenda. They are seeking to reestablish Celtic nationalism.

But the vast majority of them seem to be neo-Pagan or meso-Pagan. The latter are groups of people with a fundamentally Christian worldview, yet who have a Pagan overlay of ritual or practices laid on top of it. The neo-Pagans have a truly Pagan worldview, but they do not have a tradition that carries back into ancient times.

How do you think Druidism can affect American culture?

Druidism has a couple of major aspects which if developed in the mainstream could make a substantial difference. The first one is, of course, the reverence for nature. The idea that the earth is something that needs to be taken care of, loved and cherished, and so on. The second thing is the relationship that Druidism provides with the ancestors. Fundamental respect, love, and nurturing of the ancestors is something that our culture has really lost. This includes grandparents and parents. All elders are to be respected. The third notion is the one of tribalism. In the Keltrian Druid perspective there is a set of Gods and Goddesses amongst the group of people who worship together. The honoring of the tribal Deities becomes a mechanism for the extended family.

We recently had some people from our grove, our tribe, who were in a significant auto accident. There was no problem in having a car loaned to them until theirs could get repaired because they are part of our family. In American society we talk about the breakdown of the family, yet that breakdown can be redirected into a whole new context. I think that's something that Keltrian Druidism can provide.

Sounds like good solid Republican family values.

That's right! I think we do have good solid family values. They just look a little different. I think the nuclear family is just too small to be stable. It needs more support along the sides, and I think that Druidism affords a way to get that.

ALEXEI KONDRATIEV is a Celtic scholar and linguist. He has in the past served as president of the Celtic League American Branch, a New York–based organization that works to unify the Celtic "fringe"—countries and geographic areas that still speak Celtic languages and operate in a Celtic cultural context in order to protect them from cultural and political demise. He is the author of a forthcoming book on Celtic spirituality, titled *The Apple Branch*. The interview was conducted at the Etheracon conference in Poughkeepsie, New York, in January 1993.

First of all, are you a Pagan?

That's hard to answer actually, but it's a yes. I've never thought of myself as a Pagan in a sectarian sense. In fact, it's hard for me to think of my religious convictions in any kind of sectarian sense. Several religious paths are congenial to me, and they each affect my life in different ways; each responds to different concerns that I have.

I think that I was sensitized to a Pagan type of spirituality from very early childhood. I was born in 1949. The first things that really excited me and focused my interest as a small child were natural phenomena. I was not the sort of little boy who would be concerned with cars and machines, airplanes, motorcycles, or things of that nature.

I was interested in birds. That was the first thing that really caught my attention. I had a passion for ornithology which has continued to this day. I also had an interest in wildflowers and insects and things like that. From very early on it was a very systematic sort of inquiry.

I read a great deal of scientific and technical books on the subject, which kept my intellectual curiosity alive, and at the same time I loved being out in the countryside experiencing the whole range of habitat. I would go to a marsh or a meadow and watch the teeming variety of organisms that were about, not knowing what they were or how they interacted, just being in awe of the fact that they were there. I think these were some of my earliest spiritual experiences.

I was actually born in New York, but my parents were first-generation immigrants from Europe. My father was Russian, and my mother was French; she came from a French aristocratic family. We went back to my mother's family when I was about a year old; then we shuttled back and forth across the Atlantic. I'm still doing it. I didn't speak English until I went to school.

My upbringing was here in the States and in eastern France. I have a very strong attachment to that area of France. I am oriented to a very rural way of looking at things from spending a lot of my childhood and adolescence in the Saône valley.

As I grew older I had a number of experiences that I now, after studying anthropology, recognize as shamanic awakenings. I had the period of almost psychotic dismemberment, watching the world fall apart around me and then be very painfully reorganized. I saw the world in a new light as I also discovered new powers in myself. I also sensed new responsibilities, and I began to feel a layer beneath everyday existence, something that was not everyday consciousness.

I had loved myth and fairy tales from a very early age, and I began to discover an actual "hands-on" relationship to these things. This led me to a personal relationship with Divine figures. Not necessarily Divine figures out of literature but figures that I experienced firsthand in the environment around me, which I tried to communicate with.

I did not think of myself as a Pagan at that time. I also had a Christian awakening experience shortly after that. This did not contradict the shamanic experience at all. It was just an awakening of spirituality in another area. I really didn't have much contact with people who were formally Pagan.

I did have contact with the occult community; I was interested in ceremonial magic and the way it related to shamanic thought processes and activities. But I really only became involved with the Pagan community in the last dozen years. I was reluctant to get involved with neo-Paganism because my experience with such things is a very private and personal one. There is something about sharing those experiences with a large number of people. It's not so much that it cheapens them, it's that there is only so much that comes across when it's filtered for a large public. At Pagan gatherings you get an impression of a very trashy sort of spirituality. We're playing this, it's a game, it's fun to come out in nature and behave in a very uninhibited way and do things that we don't really believe in.

I actually discovered Paganism from science fiction fandom. I read and write science fiction and fantasy. I discovered that a lot of fans were starting to become neo-Pagans. I realized that many of them were really atheists who were bored with the traditional atheism because it was simply not fun.

So it took me a while to really become interested in neo-Paganism as a movement and as a community. Most of the people I met in it I liked. They were the type of people I had associated with in the sixties, in my hippie period. These were people who were interested in following their own spiritual path, their own inner calling, as opposed to just following the dictates of society. In that sense they were kindred souls for me; I was not interested in following the dictates of society either. I wasn't sure that these people were going about it in the most elegant and productive way, but there was an attraction and a kinship there. Then I gradually met some people whom I really admired.

The first person that I met who was of that caliber was Judy Harrow. There was a very small panel held in somebody's room at a science fiction convention that was about neo-Paganism. I heard Judy talk about Wicca or Paganism, not as something that you kept secret from the world, as you hid yourself away to do a lot of self-congratulatory things, but she actually talked about it as a responsibility, a calling. She also showed respect for the paths of others.

I've often been turned off by Paganism that is rabidly anti-Christian. I consider myself to be Christian, too; I don't have any kind of bone to pick with Christianity as a spiritual path. Christian institutions are another thing. I was glad to hear Judy talk about how she was nauseated by someone desecrating Christian symbols. This was a Witch who was at least able to go beyond that sort of narrow sectarianism. Then I met other people who were involved with her and found out that she was actually a "heretic Gardnerian."

Judy and I don't see eye to eye on an enormous number of things, but it was the fact that she respected other people's traditions and she was intelligently committed to all sorts of things. It was not just an escapist thing for her. She was interested in the social and political problems that affect everybody, and I think that when neo-Pagans are aware of those problems, they are far ahead of everybody else.

Once you got that glimpse of the passion and the integrity that a few Pagans had, what was it that you found valuable enough in Paganism that would keep you involved?

It was around 1982, when I had been involved for a few years with the Celtic League—not a Pagan group, by any means. It's an organization that has as its agenda the unification of the Celtic peoples as they exist today, their political and their cultural liberation. That is a very long-term project that involves educating a lot of people about who the Celts really are and what is really going on in the Celtic world today.

I was interested in the Celts primarily as an anthropologist; that was what I had studied. I now write and teach Celtic mythology, the Irish language, other Celtic languages, and history classes relating to the Celtic world at the Irish Arts Center in New York. I always try to remind Irish people that they are not the only Celts, that they are part of a larger continuum.

At one point, after I had exposed some people in the Celtic League to the writings of Starhawk and some others, it was suggested that people of a like mind in the Celtic league put together a circle. The idea interested me.

At that time there was this marvelous store in the East Village in New York City called the Rivendell Bookshop. It was run by a wonderful Scottish lady named Eileen Campbell Gordon from Inverness. She was an extraordinary person; everyone who met her was very much marked by her. The bookshop was dedicated to Celtic studies, fantasy, and the occult. Eileen was very knowledgeable about Celtic reality. She had a very strong intuitive sense about it. She was very intolerant of phonies. She reluctantly became involved with the Celtic circle, but as she saw that the people in the group were sincere she went into it more deeply. Eventually she became the focus of the group. She and I co-led the group using material from years of study of the Celtic civilization. Eileen was able to contribute some family traditions as well.

Eileen was our touchstone of authenticity. You could always absolutely trust her as to whether something was a real tradition or not. She knew when something "felt" wrong, and we wouldn't do it. This lasted for about five years. I think that this was my best group experience working with a Pagan tradition and with ritual.

The group unfortunately fell apart in 1988 due to personal frictions of the kind that often happen inside a circle, and the next year Eileen died. After that it was very difficult for the group to coalesce again.

Not having a group after that, I felt rather destitute, so I began to get more involved with other Pagans. None of them were really from a Celtic tradition—they had other agendas, cultural backgrounds, and concerns—but at least they had a certain vision in common. I stayed in touch with the more creative and interesting of them.

I now work in an eclectic Wiccan group into which I add a certain amount of Celtic input. Sometimes I resurrect some rituals from the old group and try to adapt them to the new one. Of course, the people in the group are not as interested in Celtic culture as the other ones were. You can't feed them as much of the material and expect them to digest it.

My working partner is into Hinduism, and he contributes that point of view. The group seems to be one where you follow your own path and develop it sincerely. It's not necessarily the group that I would most like to be involved with, but it's where I am right now.

What is the most significant aspect of Paganism for you?

I think it's the atunement to the natural world. I think that this is the sole real value that Paganism brings to modern spirituality, which the other religions simply don't. That makes it all the more important. It's very important for people to develop that atunement to nature. It is not just an intellectual understanding about what nature is good for, that we live in a physical environment, and all of our nourishment comes from it. That we would not be able to survive outside of it. It's a gut feeling that this is so that we need to develop.

You live in New York City. How do you retain that mystical connection? How do you stay in relationship with nature living in that environment?

New York City is not what people imagine it to be. I live in Flushing, Queens, which is a fairly green suburb. I have a garden, I can plant things, there is green all around me. It's not like I look at a brick wall outside of my window, though some of my friends do. I'd have a very hard time living that way.

I've never lived in a completely urban environment in my life. Even in other parts of the city you always have the sky; you don't have to go very far to find water. The native configuration of the land is still there, even though we've put buildings on it.

The northern tip of Manhattan has a very beautiful park, which is currently being terribly misused and is under a great deal of stress. It's the last natural forest on the island of Manhattan. It's also a very powerful place. At some point about a hundred years ago some trees were planted on top of the hill there, but it's been wild for quite some time. There is a beech tree there that sends out this enormous vortex of power across the entire hill. I notice that other people have found that beech tree independently, and it is obviously the focus of rituals. So there are magical places that are within a subway ride of anyone living in Manhattan.

How does being a Pagan affect other aspects of your life? For example, your work life or your personal life? Has Paganism made your life different from what other people's lives might be?

That's a very good question, and it's a hard one to answer because there are so many levels to that. I could say that it affects my life in that I've been unable to make certain choices that other people might make. For example, I've become much more aware than the average person about things that lead to polluting the environment, shortcuts that people take which are actually very destructive. I think that when you are a Pagan, and you are not the sort of Pagan who is playing SCA [Society for Creative Anachronism, a medieval dress-up group] games, but you are someone who is really attuned to the real world, you can't do some of those things anymore. You are too aware. You walk through a forest and you see that people have left their beer cans and their dirty bottles, and you are offended by that. You are constantly trying to act on that awareness.

I think that on a more personal level you are aware of your own physical existence and the way that it interacts with the environment in an intimate way. You feel the changes that are happening in the Earth. Pagan ritual is based on the changes of the seasons, and you see those changes as something that people are meant to follow. Not something that people are meant to supercede or ignore by turning winter into summer and vice versa. You learn to accept and appreciate what Nature gives you.

I recently read in the *New York Times* that there is a Russian project that is underway to put reflectors into space so the Arctic regions can be illuminated at night in winter. You can have day instead of night. I see that as a wonderful example that could only have come from a communist country, where environmental literature was not permitted for a very long time. It's the sort of megalomania that was born in the late nineteenth century.

There are "techno-Pagans" out there who might disagree with you.

There are different meanings to the term techno-Pagan. I don't necessarily advocate a Pagan lifestyle in which you try to live at a medieval technological level. I think computers are wonderful things. I have a computer, and I wouldn't know what to do without it, because it facilitates a great deal of my creative work. I don't think that inventing the electric light or printing was a terrible thing either. It's how you relate those discoveries and how you implement them to the central philosophy that you have.

You could be a techno-Pagan who liked to wear funny clothes and who pretended to be a medieval Welsh person or whatever on a Sabbat (holy day) and then went out and raped the environment for money. I don't think that there are that many around. Then you could be a techno-Pagan who, on the contrary, realized how much easier it would be to run an efficient community using some of the nonpolluting technologies which are being developed now. Which could only have been developed through going through a period of industrial revolution with industry that was very harmful to the environment.

If we change our attitude, then we can actually use the insights we have gained to clean up and develop a far more efficient way of dealing with those same problems.

There are a number of Celtic reconstructionist groups out there. What makes your approach any different?

I am concerned with and interested in the *modern* communities. What I want this to do eventually is to serve the modern Celtic-speaking communities. This doesn't mean that people in America or Australia can't be part of it. I think that the diaspora has an enormous role to play in Celtic consciousness because the Celtic communities are so downtrodden and have been psyched into thinking of themselves as inferior. They have been made to feel that they should give up their culture.

It's often the people who have lost their culture and who have struggled to regain it who are those who return some kind of respect to it. In the end what I want to do is return that kind of respect to the Celtic communities themselves. I would like to see them take control of their destiny again at a deep level. Not necessarily by becoming Pagan but by empowering the deeper aspects of their heritage. They have an enormous amount to teach to the Western world. They can play the same sort of role in Europe that some Native American movements are trying to do here, in North America.

What about your vision for America and for the world in general? As a person with Pagan leanings, because you say that you are a Christian also, where would you like to see the world go in the future?

I think that there is a very great hope for America in the type of Paganism that has taken root here. If you look at the neo-Pagan movements in Europe today, precisely because they have roots in their local communities, they often develop very strong nationalist and even fascist agendas. They've been doing this since the nineteenth century. We had a rather horrible example that led to World War II.

Today there are some rather left-wing, ecology-minded Pagan movements in Europe, but there are far more of the nationalist ones who say, "Let's go back to the faith of our ancestors, which was the best faith in the world, better than the faith of those stinking neighbors of ours!"

In America there is this illusion of internationalism, which is not actually there. America is a big blob in which you never really meet any strong cultural barriers. But it has allowed people to look beyond all that and to find a way to relate to the land directly and to develop ritual ways of celebrating that. It helps, of course, that there is a great deal of unspoiled wilderness.

Americans have this rather progressive, tolerant, egalitarian approach to Paganism, which is starting to be exported, in some ways unfortunately. I like the ancient Paganism, the old Pagan traditions that are still there in the countryside and which I grew up with in France. The old peasant rituals, the old way of relating to the land simply because you have to live on it. Seasonal blessings of the crops, going to a certain place and leaving an offering. You went to a certain place, and there was a presence there. You didn't quite know who it was or even why you left the offering, but you did it just for safety's sake or because your ancestors had always done it.

There was a pond not very far from where we lived, where people threw stones into the water as an offering. We never really talked about why this was done, it just was. Sometimes there were little altars that people would make in the woods where offerings were left. There would be a small stone table, and you would leave a flower or some small gift.

Traditions like that are common throughout rural Europe. Nowadays, of course, they are disappearing. I was back in France after an absence of eleven years this summer, and I was shocked at all the things which had disappeared. Rites of passage, for instance. Before, when people turned eighteen, there was a rite of passage that they went through. In the nineteenth century, young men would be conscripted into the army. The ritual itself is obviously much older. It had elements of chivalry, the "knight's vigil," elements of rebirth, going into the womb and being reborn. You had to sleep in the baker's oven—it was a huge oven—you were hermetically sealed in so that you could not see the light.

Born again!

Yes. There were other things that obviously went back to a much earlier substratum than any idea about going into the army. There was a kind of procession where they had an image of the Virgin Mary that they had printed privately each year and which they would give out to people at each household that they went to. She was called Our Lady of September.

September is the time of the harvest.

Yes, I suppose that she is the Lady of the Harvest.

She is the harvest Goddess.

Yes, and the Harvest Home is the patron feast of the village.

So they would get out this image, and they would blow a big horn. There was another one into which people would throw coins and another one into which people would pour spirits, so that by the time they got to the end of the village they would be quite tipsy and not moving in a straight line any more.

That was one custom that had continued all the time I was in France, and I just learned that it isn't being done any more. The reason was simply that the people had been forced off the land. It's becoming very hard for traditional farmers who relate intimately to the land, in the way that peasants always have, to survive economically.

These traditions that I grew up with and which survived for thousands of years are very fragile. The changes are very evanescent. For example, it might be in the way that the land and the fields are laid out or in the way that people relate to each other in the agricultural work. A certain sense of respect for the land is disappearing.

I remember when I was a child they were building the first highways. I was told how some of the huge oak trees that had been standing for centuries had to be cut down to make room for the road. The old people would take their hats off as the trees were being cut down.

Horrible things happened in the 1970s when the bureaucrats in Paris decided that there had to be a rational way of "normalizing" land use throughout France.

Did the people try to go back to the old way after that?

In some places they did. I'm not sure to what extent. But there was a lot of consciousness raising about this later on, how the old way actually was better and worked better.

How has your life been most affected by being a Pagan?

It all goes back to what we were saying about being sensitized to the environment and one's day-to-day interaction with it. On another level it's fun to meet very different types of people. It's also empowering for me because I happen to be a gay person. When you come out as a gay person, you get to meet some very creative types who are opposed to the usual stereotypes and cliches of society. You belong to a community, and it gives you strength and it gives you self respect.

The Pagan community is sort of the same thing. You have these intuitions about how the environment is very important, you react in a very personal and visceral way to Nature. The rest of society tends to deride that; they see it as a very extreme position and they don't take you very seriously. Suddenly you meet people who are not just environmental activists in the theoretical sense, but who have that same deep feeling that you have about the Earth.

What is it like to be gay in the Pagan community?

It's better than it used to be. I remember a time when the form of neo-Paganism that one was most likely to meet, on the East Coast anyway, was Gardnerian inspired. This was before Starhawk and the blossoming of leftist environmentalism. You had these so-called "English traditional" groups who were very homophobic. They said, "This is a fertility religion, and it has to do with sex and the only type of sex that is fertile is between a man and a woman, in such a way that a child can be produced. Therefore, all other types of sexual activity are wrong, or if not wrong they certainly have no place in ritual." There was a certain discrimination against gay people.

There were a lot of gay people who were involved with those groups who had to fake heterosexuality in rituals. I hated that. I hated the whole idea of living a spirituality that denied who I was. Why not simply belong to any of the other homophobic religions?

It was only in the eighties that we started having openly gay activities at the Pagan festivals, where people didn't have to apologize for it any more. Largely through the influence of Starhawk it became a pluralistic multiform celebration of humanity with all of its impulses.

Nothing that happens in nature is strange to nature. It's there, and you have to deal with it and learn about it. Paganism became so much more tolerant and inclusive. In the Gardnerian perception if two men or two women try to work together, they will be cursed by the Goddess. They are the Pagan equivalent of damned.

Can you give some specific examples of some times when it was awful to be gay and a Pagan?

I recall something at Panthaea a number of years ago. That is the festival that takes place in the Hudson Valley around Columbus Day every year. There was a certain rather well-known neo-Pagan singer who is the leader of one of the "older" traditions, who was pontificating about whether it was appropriate for gay people to be in a ritual, to what extent gay people could participate legitimately. I had not been expecting that sort of thing; it was such a "blast from the past." He said the usual things like, "Their sexual energy doesn't work in the same way, so they will disrupt the entire circle. *Real* magic is heterosexual magic. When gay people are in the circle, they have to warn you that they are gay so that you know that their energy will go the other way." Of course, I've been in a circle with people of all kinds of orientations. Energy doesn't move in the rigidly polarized manner that a lot of magical theoreticians like to believe that it does.

I've seen less and less of this. Usually when it comes up, people do challenge it. There are certain members of the gay Pagan community who are much quicker to anger than I am. Even when such matters arise in a diplomatic way, they will jump up and make a scene.

Was there a time when it was absolutely marvelous to be gay in the Pagan community?

There are now gay Pagan groups that actively explore the gay Pagan experience. They study how to use that experience of the body and the way that the body raises energy to connect with and draw energy from the environment. There's the Lavender Pagan Network; there is a group called the Middle Pole in New York, a varied group of people who have a lot of different ideas about things. They are very creative, very much into being gay and making that into something positive, not a burden that you have to bear in society because you are different. It is a plus, something that you can use.

You are a historian. Do you have any further insights into the history of the Pagan movement that you would like to share?

When I first became interested in Paganism, there was this prevailing view that, as Selena Fox once put it, "Wicca is simply the old Celtic religion." A lot of people say that. It's sort of a Pagan dogma. The idea is that the Witch was an ancient priestess. I don't believe in Wiccan mythology. It's only because Americans have no sense of history that they swallow these really strained models of the Middle Ages that are served up to them in these Wiccan books about "The Burning Times." Of course things didn't happen that way.

Have you seen the video called The Burning Times?

Yes. It has these marvelous glitches like calling the city of Trier French; there are all these signs in German, and they keep calling it a French city. It said some good things, but it was trying to keep to the party line, and by trying to be historically plausible at the same time it was contradicting itself.

The myth of The Burning Times as it is currently enunciated in the Pagan community says that some time in the Middle Ages the church created the Inquisition as a way of destroying its huge Pagan rival. The entire countryside was Pagan in a very self-conscious, self-empowered way, with clergy and all of that. That it was a parallel religion that somehow endangered Christianity, and these people were the original Witches. The Inquisition sought out these Witches and obliterated them for political reasons. *Nine million* people died as a result.

The truth is, of course, when the Witchcraft laws were repealed in the 1950s in England, Gerald Gardner "revealed" the tradition was still alive, and he brought it back to the modern world.

If you really study what happened in the Middle Ages and the Renaissance, the church did create the Inquisition as a means of silencing its political rivals, but these were not Pagans. They were mostly other Christians, those who felt that they could live without the church's authority. Also some Jews and Muslims. Gypsies didn't really appear in Europe until the Middle Ages were over. The Albigensians were the main challenge. They were particularly heterodox and had gained the allegiance of a large number of people. Tons of people died, but they were Christians or Manicheans. It had nothing to do with Paganism or anything resembling Wicca.

The Witch trials were really a Renaissance phenomenon. As the Inquisition was trying to ferret out all the enemies of the church, they had the secular authorities as collaborators. After all, it was the state that executed people, not the church. They followed the church's recommendations. Europeans were carrying this folk myth that you can see in many different societies. It says that there are these people who have the means to harm you supernaturally. They are present in the community, and you don't know who they are because this harm takes place invisibly. So you have to ferret them out with specially trained people. Once you find them, all of your problems will be solved because they are the source of all of your difficulties.

As feudalism was falling apart at the end of the Middle Ages, this type of anxiety was very widespread. People tended to accuse each other of being dangerous. They developed a whole ideology of who these people were. They were people who had sold their souls to the Devil. They had been given power to harm others supernaturally as a result, and such people had to be found out and dealt with. This was actually a very minor part of the Inquisition's activities. Most of the people who were actually found out, tried, and burned were Christian heretics. They were the ones that the church was most afraid of.

So far as the Witch trials were concerned, those who have studied the actual trials in Europe concluded that they killed about twenty thousand people. This is what you can actually come up with from the records, but it could be as high as a hundred thousand. That's a very high estimate and not very likely.

Where did the nine million people figure come from?

Apparently, there was a woman writing around the turn of the century who threw out the figure of nine million. Nobody knows where she got it. Very possibly Gardner used the figure in his writings, and that is how it became popularized. People who just read Wiccan books and who never check any other sources have repeated this figure over and over.

So I don't like this myth of The Burning Times. It's inaccurate, and I like real history. It creates a holocaust mentality that is really invalid. It's like saying that the Jews got massacred in World War II, and everybody feels sorry for them, so let's claim that we got massacred in an even *worse* way.

Let's remember that the Witches who were killed were not Pagans! They were people who went to church and who were unpopular for some reason in their community so someone came up and accused them of Witchcraft. It was a horrible thing, but it didn't have quite the massive impact that Wiccan literature claims.

Speaking as a woman, when I look at woman's history, I tend to disagree that it didn't have a massive impact. If you were forced to watch a number of women in your community get killed, even if it was just a few, it would have a profound effect on the psyche of all the women in the community. And also on the men.

It does, yes. Though in Germany almost as many men were killed as women.

How many gays would have to be burned publicly at the stake before gays would begin to feel terrorized?

They did burn gays. I'm not saying that this whole episode is insignificant. What I am saying is that it has no relevance to Paganism. It's not part of a confrontation between Christianity and Paganism. It's a horrible thing that happened in the history of Europe. It's roots were not religious at all; it was social and economic. Anybody in power who was trying to stay in power would have done the same thing. It's the ideology of power, which can take a lot of different forms.

I can't imagine that Pagans would be immune to that kind of political power themselves. I know some people in the Pagan community who would be very glad to make heads roll to ensure that *their* view of things was the one to get implemented.

In the Pagan community there is this very romantic feeling about things Celtic, about Druids and the Golden Age . . .

When I first got involved in the early eighties there was this belief that Wicca was the "Old Celtic Religion." This was accepted unconditionally by everyone. There were those who were saying the opposite, but they were a minority. There is the romantic appeal of the fact that the Celts are the "other" in European history. The civilization that did not conform. People tend to project all sorts of nasty things onto them. Like they were violent and dirty and couldn't follow the rules of civilized society. They were bloodthirsty headhunters and murderers, or they were wonderful, moody romantics who were intensely creative and in touch with nature. You can project everything onto them that your society is not but that you would like it to be.

The Celts tend to function like American Indians, and they have been used in the same way. Their traditions have been stolen and used to playact. I think it's vital to recognize, just as in the case of the Native American tradition, that these are a real culture, a real people, with their own destiny, history, and identity, whose traditions belong to them. If you learn enough about them that you can become one of them, then you have the right to become an exponent of those traditions. But you don't have a right to say that you are an exponent unless you make that effort. You can assimilate things from any culture into your life, but you cannot claim to be an exponent of that tradition.

This is what much of *The Apple Branch* is all about. People are very interested in following a Celtic way, and they have to realize that this is a path that belongs to a particular people who are still existing in the world today. They are not people from the Middle Ages or the Iron Age. They live today and are the living descendants of those who produced the beautiful artifacts and stories. If you don't respect that and are just interested in consuming their culture for your amusement while those people die away—which is happening also to the Native Americans—you are guilty of a great injustice.

Today people are giving "shamanic" workshops, which they claim are traditionally Native American, and they give people the sense that they are recapturing this thing that they have destroyed. Meanwhile, they let real Native American communities die away in poverty and alcoholism. The same thing is happening in the Celtic communities. They are extremely impoverished; they have a very slim economic basis for survival. They are dissolving into the mainstream culture through emigration and assimilation.

If people really love this culture, they have to revitalize it, learn about it, apply pressure. Find out about the economic and political strategies that are driving these people out. They are the same ones that are affecting the Native American communities.

The Wiccan Tradition

Perhaps the most misunderstood term in all of the Pagan community is the word "Witch." To the general public the word is still tied to Halloween and old hags with warted noses; mass-produced and badly written books and movies; and the twinkling nose of Elizabeth Montgomery on the sixties sitcom *Bewitched*. Those with any predisposition for world history might associate the word "witch" with persecution, as in the Salem Witch trials, one of the dark moments of this country's history, or with the gruesome activities of the Inquisition of medieval Europe. Still, none of those images is at all accurate in describing the realities of the modern existence of Witchcraft, Wicca, or those who embrace the term "witch."

Witches are an intricate part of the Pagan world and are as diverse as the misconceptions about them. This chapter will introduce you to four people—two women and two men—who are Witches. Hearing their stories, you will get a sense of history and tradition, as well as a much clearer view into those who claim both the heritage and the title of Witch.

YVONNE AND GAVIN FROST are founders of the Church and School of Wicca in New Bern, North Carolina. They are the authors of *The Witch's Bible*, *The Magic*

Power of Witchcraft, Who Speaks for the Witch?, The Prophet's Bible, Astral Travel, and *Tantric Yoga, the Only American Yoga.* They are well-known practitioners and teachers of their Craft. They were interviewed at Wellspring '93, a Pagan festival, at the Brushwood Folklore Center near Sherman, New York.

When did you first discover that you were a Witch?

Yvonne: I discovered that I wanted to aspire to the Craft in 1968 when Gavin and I became close. I had been shopping around for a religion after I walked out of the Baptist church. I was raised as a Baptist in Southern California with a strong background in western Kentucky fundamentalist hard-shell Baptist training. Just one step short of "foot washers." This was a very tough, hard, *grim*, background. A family context with no love or warmth at all.

So finally I voted with my feet and started shopping for a religion I could feel comfortable with. I did what a lot of people were doing in those days, the early to mid-sixties. I investigated Buddhism, and that was fine but not for me. I went to several other things and looked into them. I was investigating spiritualism, a kind of Christian nomenclature for psychic activity, when Gavin and I met. They do a lot of seances and dark sittings and psychic readings and what today is called channeling. It was lovely, but it still wasn't quite enough.

He described to me what he had learned from the Craft, and something just clicked. It may have been a past-life memory, but anyway I asked him if I could ever aspire to the grand title Witch. One thing led to another, and we were given guidance, and teachers appeared as they tend to do when the student is ready, and then there was an initiation. I have said with more pride than any other statement in my life, "I am a Witch." I practice the Craft. That is my religious activity and belief. No statement could make me prouder.

Gavin, when did you first discover that you were a Witch?

Well, I was brought up in an Episcopal, Church of England type of religion, in England. The church was not very much impressed upon us; we didn't *have* to go or anything like that. So I got interested in megalithic monuments, being a mathematician, and particularly when I went to college, because one of my professors was Glyn Daniel, who wrote the book on megalithic monuments.

Later on I got involved in some missile programs for DeHaviland aircraft, where I worked on Salisbury plain. Since all the work we did was at night, I had days to look at the monuments. I also got interested in the "Druidiots," as they call them in England. The people who dance around Stonehenge at Midsummer's Day. Through them I met a guy called Graham Howe, who wrote *The Mind of the Druid*. I went to his lectures. I still have the lecture notes.

From that I got interested in the Wiccan movement, and I got initiated in Cornwall after going through several different tests in 1952. That was a long time ago! That was when the Fraudulent Mediums Act was repealed, and there was a very high interest level in this sort of thing.

So was that Gardnerian Wicca?

Oh, God, no. Gardnerian is just one offbeat brand. This was, if you like, a British aristocratic tradition. That's the best way to describe it.

Was this an old tradition that had been handed down?

Who knows? Of course not. It was invented, I believe in Oxford and Cambridge. I've been talking with Aidan Kelly about this, and some of the things look as though they came from around 1860, which is old as Witch traditions go. But we really can't tell. It might have been just a bunch of students who got together in Oxford or Cambridge and put the tradition together.

Then I got involved in making a living, came to the United States, and lived in Canada and Southern California, where I continued to work in aerospace.

You have been a Witch for many years, as long as I have been on the planet! What in particular has kept you going? The religions that you were born into obviously didn't have much to hold you. What is the essence of Witchcraft that has kept you interested for this many years?

Gavin: I think that it's because it's an experimental religion and because it's changing all the time. The tradition that I was initiated into would be far too chauvinistic to go over today.

Yvonne: This world is full of people who are in pain. And it's full of people who want to dominate other people. The Craft offers a better way to live than that. Through the Craft I have found answers and comfort for a lot of pain in my life. I have found answers to questions I couldn't even ask because I didn't know how to ask them. A lot of my life is about reverence and gratitude.

This planet is a school, untidy as it is, it's a schoolroom. And the assignments we are given are like term papers. We have to write term papers in order to move to our next level. They may be firm assignments, but they are not a punishment. They are *the* means of development. Death is graduation, if you want to pursue the metaphor. And that is just so infinitely comforting to me that I want to share it if I can with people whom I see in pain. It keeps me going. Yes, there are tears, yes, there are times when I don't want to face the next assignment because it looks so daunting. But with the help of my guide I know I will complete my assignment in time.

Each of us has a spirit guide. Each of us who is into puberty and beyond, that is. We are given our guides at puberty when we begin to make the break from the umbilical relationship with our parents. We work with that guide until succeeding assignments bring a change of guide. We are each given a guide who is like ourselves; that's the law of attraction.

My guide is someone like me who has the same kind of interests and the same kind of background and tastes in things. Otherwise, we couldn't work together. This is probably the third or fourth one that I have had in this incarnation.

How do you know when they change?

Yvonne: Well, your life goes through about forty-eight hours of pure random chaos during the transition time. You think to yourself that this *must* be the changeover from one guide to another! That's different somehow from the feeling you get when you are having a big heavy challenge, a big assignment to deal with.

Gavin: You can think about progressive reincarnation as that we are here to learn and that we are here to expand our consciousness, and to expand everybody's consciousness, and that the whole universe is expanding. That the spiritual side of the universe is expanding along with the material side of it . . . everything falls into a logical pattern. At least it does for me.

We get in trouble with the rest of the Pagan community who can't grasp the idea of reincarnation as a progressive thing. I get into further trouble by saying that it looks to me as though women are higher on the progressive reincarnation ladder than men. It's pretty obvious that women can have more experiences, childbirth, for example, and then more nurturing and more selfless experiences.

What about a woman who has never had a child?

Gavin: Well, they can have those experiences. If they don't, it's their choice. Maybe they have only just come into being a woman. In their next reincarnation they will be forced into having a child. They will have to come back to have a child because it's a learning experience for a woman. Or maybe she had it last time! Or she had twelve last time. Who knows? The only way to get a clue about it is to go into some kind of hypnotic regression. Then I turn around and say that maybe that crossover time from male to female is where we get our gay people from. Because maybe they are spirits who should have come back in a different physical body. That *really* gets me in trouble.

You said that if you progress, you increase the size of the Deity. What did you mean by that?

Gavin: If you imagine the Deity as the interconnection through the web of the wyrd [fate and the ability to control it], between all of the spirits in the universe, the more larger spirits there are in the universe, the larger the web, the larger the interconnection. So the larger the Deity. That is what I meant when I said that the Deity is expanding at the same time that the material universe is expanding. The two are expanding in parallel. If the universe starts to collapse in a few billion years hence, then you have deincarnation.

That's like the Hindu idea of the breath of Vishnu. Where creation is his outbreath as he dreams, and then he inhales . . .

Gavin: Correct. Brahma is dreaming of us during the outbreath, but if we don't think of Brahma dreaming of us, then Brahma won't exist, therefore *we* won't exist.

So you have been Witches for about forty years, how has the fact of being a Witch affected your life? You both worked in the aerospace industry, so how was it to be a Witch in that context?

Gavin: The funny thing is that Witches in those days were very much in the closet, but I wasn't. It helped me a great deal to be a Witch because a lot of upper executive–level people in those kinds of industries are very open minded, believe it or not. People along "mahogany row," as we used to call it, tend to be intelligent and pretty open minded.

The place where it does people harm in their job is when they are in the closet, and they don't admit to it. In some lower-level jobs women especially can get a lot of pressure put on them by the bosses. Nowadays it's a federally recognized religion, and they shouldn't stand for it.

When I became director of international sales, it was a great help. Especially when working in countries like India, where I could be much more open with people about religious matters. I worked in Thailand and China and India and Pakistan. I didn't have the Christian thing hanging over me.

Have you ever been harassed for being a Pagan?

Yvonne: We've had a bullet through the window in Salem, Missouri. Some people closed the bar one night and got out in their pickup truck feeling spunky, and everybody knew who we were, where we lived. They drove by and shot a hole through our kitchen window that faced the road. The bullet landed in the brand new kitchen cabinet of an old schoolhouse we were remodelling.

I was *annoyed!* We called the sheriff, who compared it to one that had been found in the flattened tire of a big earth-moving machine up the road, and I think someone experienced some consequences for their actions.

We got a lot of community support for that one. We were raising peas to support the school. Everybody knew that we were hard workers, though there were the usual stupid stories that always seem to follow Witches around. This was 1971 or '72.

You mentioned the Church and School of Wicca. Can you talk about how that was born?

Gavin: The church was born in Missouri. We saw more and more of this business of students, college-age people, trying to get power. Anton LaVey [a Satanist, not a Pagan, and the author of *The Satanic Bible*] was pretty big and we couldn't have Wicca associated with that kind of activity.

Yvonne: They were doing really dumb stuff. They thought they were going to do some juju or some "magic" out in the woods.

Gavin: So we decided to start advertising and run a course and form a church. We would not hide behind anything; we would be public Witches. We would be a Church of Wicca. We became the first federally recognized Church of Wicca in the United States.

Yvonne: We founded the school in 1968 or '69. We had our first student in 1968, by mail. We fought until 1972 for federal recognition as a religious activity. In '72 we got our Letter of Determination from the IRS. That is the official document that says, "Yes, you are a Church." We were living in Missouri, but that is a federal document. It transcends state lines. It's a religious association.

We immediately put ourselves under a vow of poverty. We own nothing. If I were to leave the Church of Wicca and the life I am now living, I would have to wind up sitting on the curb naked. I own nothing. The church owns what we use, and we are the custodians of the church's holdings.

Is there a staff that runs the church?

Gavin: There is a staff that runs the school. We have three people who do logistics for the school. There is a board of trustees in the church, of course, that has regular meetings, and that's it.

Of course, there was a high level of interest in the church from the beginning, and even the smallest ad in those days brought a lot of response. After we had been running the school for about six months I gave up my job in aerospace.

Yvonne: We sawed off the limb we were sitting on and went independent. What has supported us ever since is the church. All the work we do is connected to the church or the Craft in some way.

Gavin: From having gold credit cards and international air travel cards and a car funded by the company, we went to subsistence farming and eventually in a couple of years we went onto food stamps.

Yvonne: If you want to learn humility, that's the way to do it. Sever all connections with a regular cash flow. There are those who claim that sainthood is accelerated by sleeping in ditches and eating out of garbage cans, but I don't think that's true. I don't think that kind of life would say much for the Craft as something to espouse. So we try to exhibit that we live in some modest kind of comfort. We have adjusted our expectations from what they used to be.

We used to have big steak dinners for visiting aerospace people. But it's a matter of ranking priorities. You think about what is important in your life and where you invest your strength and your activity, and some things fall by the wayside. Some things lose their importance, and other things gain importance.

There is a controversy raging in the Pagan community about whether clergy should be paid.

Gavin: I believe that *no* Pagan church at any time should keep any financial records. I believe that *very* strongly. The God Moloch is with us all the time in this society. Materialism is rampant. We are a religion which does not believe in materialism. Either we have faith that the Goddess will provide, or we don't. If the Goddess will provide, She *will* provide. If we don't have that faith, then we shouldn't be in this religion. Once we are in this religion and the Goddess does provide why should we fall down to the laws which don't apply to us? The IRS and people like that do not guide us. We are not materialistic.

Yvonne: There is a separation of church and state, ostensibly in this nation. So the IRS has no need and no right to poke into our activities, because we are separated from the state as a religion.

Gavin: I also believe that the legitimate clergy should be supported by their church. In the Amish system twenty-five families support the pastor and his wife. Why couldn't the same thing happen in the Pagan community? The answer is Pagans are cheapskates! I've seen them come begging at the door and refuse to pay $5 for a lecture and then smuggle in bottles of Chivas Regal. I've seen them refuse to pay a dollar to support candles and wine at a ritual, and they have just driven up in a brand new BMW. I think that's the experience we all have had. I don't know why, but it all probably comes back to the stupidity of old man Gardner.

Yvonne: Right. Gerald Gardner was living on a comfortable civil servant pension when he wrote that people should not be paid for teaching magic or the Craft. It was easy for him to say because he had his pension all buttoned up! That contrasts painfully with what we are experiencing. We gave up a substantial and impressive paycheck because we didn't have room in our lives to live the Craft and earn a paycheck. So we had to choose between the two and ended up devoting our productive energies to something that we believed in. We have to have cash flow of some kind. As reverent as we may be, the post office will not send our mail for free, and the filling station won't fill our tank for free.

How is your church different from other Pagan groups?

Gavin: We reach out to an entirely different audience than most other Pagan teachers. We are reaching out to the vast mass of people. Our course is an entry-level course, but it requires discipline. It requires the reading of twelve books.

Although we sign up something like two hundred people a month, we only initiate one or two a year. We have a high dropout rate because of the discipline requirements.

What qualifies someone for initiation?

Gavin: They have to complete the course. They have to do thirty-three hours of community service. They have to have a full physical, they have to *ask* to be initiated, and they have to have dedicated themselves to the Craft at a public meeting at least six months ahead of time. They make their own tools, their own mead, they have to do a lot of things that other groups tend not to ask. There are a few groups that require this kind of dedication, but very few.

It disappoints us greatly that so many people are getting in so easily. American-style initiations are entirely different from the European style. An American first-degree initiate gets to be one if they show up for a couple of meetings. It seems to be getting that way.

Our initiation is about the equivalent of a third-degree American, the way we see it at the moment. It's a whole question, one which I am not clear on in my own mind, about the difference between discipline and free style. Yvonne and I are trained dancers in ballroom dancing. So if we go to a free-style dance, we don't enjoy it. This business of just standing there and shaking and throwing your body around is something we don't really enjoy. We think that Wiccans should be disciplined.

What about people who feel that they hear a profound inner calling and they have read Scott Cunningham's book for the solitary practitioner, and they went off in the woods and had an experience with a tree, and they decided that they were a Witch?

Gavin: They are *not* Witches. They are somewhere along a shamanistic path perhaps.

Yvonne: If they have had real instruction, that means something about living a life of decency and reaching upward to higher levels in a religious sense, with reverence and gratitude, and they are living a life of decency that they have thought about. If they have seriously considered what the hell their life means, then maybe they are on the path. But this casual thing of, I have to get a robe and the sleeves have to touch the floor when I hold my arms out straight, and now I am lighting a candle and now I close my eyes to meditate, and now, gasp!, I'm a Witch—that ain't shit.

I have to ask you this. You know that it's coming. You have talked a lot about living a decent life and a life of morality and spiritual advancement, but you guys were almost made pariahs in a certain sense because of something that you wrote in a book, The Witch's Bible, **which some people in the Craft took great exception to because it involved the idea of ritual defloration of adolescents. I would like you to elucidate further on this topic.**

Gavin: In every single society, if you go back and look at any of the old American Indian shamanistic works or books on the roots of civilization, you will find that the maiden was deflowered by the shaman as a rite of passage and initiation to bring her into womanhood. I think that we have lost lots of rites of passage and I think a lot of the trouble we have with our young people is that they don't know where they fit into society. If we brought back more of the rites of passage, we would be better off.

You just said that the young lady would be ritually deflowered. Why didn't you say the young man?

Gavin: He was. The book talks about cutting the foreskin. We are not talking about circumcision; we don't believe in that. There is another skin that goes between the tip of the penis and the foreskin and down the front of the penis, which is cut in many societies, especially in the Australian aborigine society, where they do a lot more than just cut that piece of skin.

So do you still advocate the ritual defloration of adolescents?

Gavin: In today's society we cannot do that. We are saying that today we have a real problem in America and in many of the Western societies where a husband can't bathe his baby girl. He would be afraid that some aunt or some relative would come in and say that he molested her.

Yvonne: It's the crime of the decade. It's very trendy right now to talk about child molestation, incest, all those hideous, horrible things. People are saying they can't live their adult life because they had a traumatic experience as a child. They can't even remember it, but they had a traumatic experience. Some adult did them a "bad" against their will. We've had to say that we are updating the teaching that we present as the best we know for the Craft and yet saying that we are not going to advocate it. Our original intent was to describe an anthropological phenomenon that was universal among preliterate societies.

Gavin: We are the only group of Witches who actually teach and practice the ancient six principles of Witchcraft. The flight to the orgy on a broom, which is astral travel. We teach that. Flying ointments came much, much later.

The second one was the business of renouncing their religion and announcing that they would accept the religion of Witchcraft.

Yvonne: Number three was the "pact with the Devil" where they signed over their soul. Blah, blah, blah, gasp, gasp, gasp.

Gavin: With us you have to make a pact that you are going to be a Witch.

Yvonne: If you want initiation bad enough, and of course it's always optional because the candidate has the choice until the last minute.

Gavin: Another principle is working magic. We mean *working* magic on the physical plane as opposed to religion, which is reaching upward to spiritual levels. Magic on *this* plane of existence. We have been discussing this with Ian Corrigan. Why in Druidic liturgy do you work magic at the end of a ritual, and why do we do it at the beginning? That is a continuing discussion. We teach what Yvonne calls "paycheck world magic."

Yvonne: There has been so much sloppy semantics, and that is one major cause of the conflict in people's minds about what they are doing and what we are doing.

Gavin: We gather for meetings at night, and we try to do our meetings at the right time. Within a couple of days of the full moon and when the moon is actually passing directly overhead. That doesn't mean that we will meet on a

Friday night because Thursday is impractical because somebody has to go bowling. We do it on the right night or not at all.

Yvonne: That sets us apart from those who want to scorn us because they can't be bothered to do it right themselves. They need to study what is right and discipline themselves to do it right.

Gavin: We teach sexual promiscuity. Nature is sexually promiscuous, and I think the human species is one of the sexually promiscuous ones.

Well, maybe the male of the human species . . . I'm not promiscuous!

Yvonne: Actually, we teach freedom of decision. We don't teach promiscuity. We don't teach anything that would be called "naughty." We encourage people not to feel guilty, to separate moral and ethical issues from practical ones.

What if it hurts the person that you are with?

Gavin: Then they have a lot of learning to do.

Yvonne: We teach people to "harm none."

What about in a marriage where there is a contract?

Yvonne: What have they agreed to in the contract? If they have agreed to complete monogamy, then that's fine. They should observe complete monogamy. If they have not agreed to it, they have options.

What are some problems with Paganism today?

Gavin: One of the problems I have with the present Pagan festival movement as opposed to the general Pagan public is that it has become very elitist. It's not reaching out to the people. The thing we do all the time is we reach out to the "common man" and the "common woman."

Earthspirit has started reaching out to the New Age community through their journals, and they are already getting hell for it.

Gavin: Yes, of course! But New Age journals are already too late. They are not with the people. They do not represent the mass of people. The people who read New Age journals are upper-income people. We reach them through the *National Enquirer.* Ten million circulation. All those people out there!

What does your ad say?

Gavin: It says, "Wiccacraft, harness its powers."

When you put an ad in the National Enquirer, what are the kinds of things that people write to you about?

Gavin: A lot of them are looking for a love spell or a money spell, you know: "When do I get paid and when do I get laid?" But we get a lot of very serious people. We really do.

Are they educated people?

Gavin: No. Some of them can't even write two sentences together. But spiritually some of them are *amazing*. Evolved people who just don't know where to look.

We do get all sorts, and of course we have a public telephone number. People call us on the phone, and the girls in the office have lots of fun answering them.

MIKE MARRA (THEITIC) is the high priest of the Coven of Minerva. He was interviewed by phone on May 7, 1994, and was kind enough to give an overview of the "Witch Scene" in New England, which has often been ignored by other authors.

Are you a Pagan?

Yes, I am. I am also a Witch. I have been since the mid-seventies. I was studying Craft in the early seventies, but I wasn't initiated until 1976.

What was it about Witchcraft that caused you to be interested in it, and what about it kept you interested?

I found that the things I enjoyed such as nature and the out-of-doors were things that most Witches also enjoyed. They had their parties and festivals outdoors, and I wanted to be a part of that. It was tough at my age because I wasn't allowed to attend a lot of things; I was only thirteen. Because of that it lent a bit of mystery to it, and there was a curiosity behind it. That drove me a little further. I found out later that some of the mysteries in the traditions, some of the lore and legends really attracted me. I felt at home when I started to read those things, much more than I did in dealing with the church and saints and the organized religion.

When I was hunting for the Craft in my early teens, there was nothing available back then. It was the late sixties, and you could find a mass-media paperback by Sybil Leek, but that was it. There were no tapes, no videos, there were very few books on Witchcraft, and there were no periodicals. There was almost no way of finding somebody who was doing this, and at the time I actually didn't know that it was Witchcraft that I was looking for. I just knew it as a feeling and a search for something. It took years before I found out what it was actually called. All I knew about were some of the things that had occurred in my family. I come from an Italian heritage, and my grandmother had some home remedies for ailments, and she would do things to keep away the evil eye. She would check to see if someone had some negative influence put on them by another person, and she knew what to do to take care of that. That's about all I had to work with.

There were only a few people who were public at that time in New England. One was Laurie Cabot in Salem. When I went up to visit her, she was running the Witch Shop. Another person was Ted Mills in western Massachusetts. He is a jolly guy with a great sense of humor. At the time he ran Parker Coven, and when I went up to visit him, he had a lot of people around who were very happy people. I remember them playing music and singing. I didn't get very involved with them, but I knew them socially. That was in the mid-seventies.

The people around Ted Mills seemed to be very sincere. One of them who I remember was Jeanine Strong, who was a very pleasant woman with a very nice attitude. One of her students actually came to me when Jeanine moved, and she is now my coven maiden. Jeanine is now one of the heads of Parker Coven.

Elizabeth Pepper was also a public figure. She is the author of *The Witches' Almanac*. She moved to Newport, Rhode Island, and I met her there in the mid-seventies. We found that we had a lot of things in common; she grew up in similar places to where I grew up in Rhode Island, and we became good friends. Elizabeth Pepper is a very quiet and secretive woman. She is a Scorpio, which probably contributes to that reserved quality. She has been a student of the occult since her early childhood. She is also the author of *Magical and Mystical Sites* and *Witches All*.

Is there anyone else in New England who is important?

Recently Joyce Seigrist has come into Rhode Island. She founded Rosegate in the late eighties. It is a relatively new tradition that deals more with metaphysical principles than it does with old Craft teachings. What has made Rosegate popular is that they were able to receive a tax-exempt status in Rhode Island as a church of the Craft. That had not been done in Rhode Island before. Rhode Island is a very tough state to get tax-exempt status in. That brought her publicity, which put her in several national magazines. She got interviews with people from all around the country and outside the country as well. I believe that she was interviewed by some people from Japan and from Australia. She was quite busy for a while doing talk shows and interviews. Her group is extremely public; they do public Sabbats. They publish a newsletter called *Rosegate Journal*, and information can be had about their group through that.

Andras Corban Arthen of the Earthspirit Community is one of the people who was traveling around in the mid-seventies and meeting with different groups. He is a very charismatic spirit.

Being a traditionalist, I know most of the Rhode Island traditionalists very well. Most of them don't want to be mentioned. As a matter of fact, I might hear from a few people who will ask me, "How could you *possibly* have done an interview?" But that is something I'll have to live with.

Do you have a mundane job, and how has being a Pagan influenced that?

I am a production manager in a mid-sized company. Being a Pagan has made me understand people a lot better. There are aspects of people that make them get along or not get along. I have found ways of getting along with all of them by feeling more of what the people are feeling. I understand people's natural growth processes. That has come from the practice of my religion.

Have you ever run into any prejudice at work or in other places?

I did run into prejudice when I was in high school. I was fired from a job for being a Witch. I didn't tell people I was a Witch, but someone found out. What I have done with my current job is that I didn't tell anybody what I was until they learned to know me and what I was like to work with. Once I had made a lot of friends and people understood that I was competent, then I began to let a little out here and there. Now people have come to accept me because they are not afraid of me. They had a chance to understand who I was before they understood what I was doing.

Can you talk a bit about your tradition?

I am a high priest of the Coven of Minerva which is a branch of the New England Covens of Traditionalist Witches (NECTW), which is a name given by Gwen Thompson in the early seventies. She was a hereditary Witch. Her family tradition had stayed in the family until the mid-sixties, and then she brought it out to the public. It was a folk Witch tradition. A lot of its teachings appear to be Welsh, but she insisted on being called Celtic traditionalist, and she did not like being termed Welsh. She was responsible for several other movements in the United States.

The NECTW are the diehard traditionalists that remain right in line with Gwen's family teachings. There are several covens of that tradition in Rhode Island. Each family tradition tends to be unique unto itself. They stayed secret until the late fifties and early sixties, and most of them are still underground. The few that came out tended to come out because the family lineage was ending and rather than letting it die out, they became public.

The teachings are pre-Gardnerian. We all work robed, with robes and hoods. We still acknowledge the triad of the Goddess (Maid, Mother, and Crone), with the Goddess as the Mother of all creation and the God as the God of hunting, death, and rebirth. The Moon Goddess is represented in the high priestess, and the Horned God is represented in the high priest.

We don't believe in a devil, and we do follow the Wiccan rede ["An it harm none do what thou willt"]. We use the long version of the rede, the old version with twenty-six verses. We practice harmony with the environment and with nature. We respect the beauty of the earth and the life of all creatures.

I think that one of the things that separates the family traditions from the post-Gardnerian Wiccans is that most family traditions have an emphasis on magic as opposed to an emphasis on religion. We teach a little bit about spiritualism, and we emphasize heritage and lineage and the forces and the powers of nature. We recognize that those powers of nature have names and that they have become Gods and Goddesses, but a great deal of the emphasis is on how to do the magic to make the world a better place and ourselves better individuals. We still respect the laws of karma, and we have legends that have never appeared in print because they are kept within the family.

How do you see your path in relation to the earth?

Currently, I feel that I need to defend the Earth. Our original purpose was to work in harmony with Her and understand Her ways—to feel the winds, to be able to call the winds, and feel the pulse of the Earth and to sway with the tides so that we would be more in tune and more in harmony with the Earth. After all, we are supported by the Earth and She doesn't really need us. We need Her. Right now I feel like a warrior on Her side.

Where would you like to see the Craft go in the future, and where do you think it is headed now?

I see the Craft going two different ways. I see the public Craft, which is in some ways capitalizing on the Craft in the New Age way, and I see some of the underground Craft that is rejecting that approach and is burying itself further down, digging its heels deeper into the earth. I think they are both extremes.

I think there is a place for public Craft, and there is a place for private work. I think that publicly it would be nice to make people aware of our principles and our beliefs, to gain some legal respect for us so that we can do rites of passage and deal with our living and our dead in a way that's respectful to us and within the legal and social constraints within which we live.

Privately, I think that we need to maintain our secret rituals, our mystery legends, and our lore. I don't believe in public initiations, I don't believe in revealing some of our symbolism, which is so rich in magic. But I also don't believe we should hold on to our principles and beliefs and keep them from the public. I think that only instills fear, and that's not good for us either. There needs to be a balance between the two.

ALLYN WOLFE is the grand summoner for the New Wiccan Church International and state magus for the New Wiccan Church of California. He also serves as editor of the magazine *Red Garters International*, and is the author of "Good News, Bad News: West Country Wicca," which appeared in *Red Garters International*. He was interviewed by phone on February 10, 1994.

First of all, are you a Pagan?

Yes, I am. In the sixth or seventh grade one of my classmates, the daughter of a local minister, announced that only the people who went to her dad's church were going to go to heaven. This struck me as a rather ridiculous notion, so I insisted that she prove it to me. Using the Bible, she proved to my satisfaction that her position was the only tenable one and that everybody else was wrong, at which point I abandoned Judeo-Christianity. I figured I just wasn't interested in a religion that worked like that.

What brand of Christianity were you raised in?

Equal parts Protestant and Catholic from both sides of the family. Of the two churches, I liked the Catholic better, because before Vatican II it was just more entertaining.

So what is the most vital and important aspect of Paganism for you? What is it that keeps you interested in it?

The Gods. I like being in a live religion. It's not a case of a revelation from the past where somebody else saw the Gods and that was real nice, and we've been living on hearsay ever since. The Lady is a very real presence to me.

My actual conversion to Wicca was a bit odd. I had always attended churches, synagogues, snake handlings, and anything else I could attend because I always found them interesting. I also went to a few flying-saucer-cult meetings. There was always the sense that there was something behind each of these paths, that it wasn't all just made up. Well, except the flying saucers.

A friend and I had been working on our own bootstrap Wicca while we were both in college. Another friend had actually gone out and got himself initiated. I watched him for about a month, and he hadn't grown mold so I figured it didn't look *too* dangerous. So I decided I'd get initiated too, because you just can't get baptized, ordained, or dipped too many times.

So he took me out to the suburbs, and I met a nice, pleasant middle-aged housewife who told me the ancient-stone-age-to-the-present history of the Craft that her teacher had told her, which I knew was crap. I kept a straight face and went along with everything.

The night of the initiation there were three of us undergoing the process, and I was scheduled to be the last of the three. They left me in a back bedroom to meditate on the coming transformation, and I was still trying to work out in my own mind what I was going to do. Was I going to pretend that I got the "zap" and stand in with the ranks, or was I going to let them know that nothing happened and let them go blue in the face trying to do magic on me, or was I going to really run with it and make a big display of "I've got the power" or whatever, and see what kind of an impression I could make with that? Or would I just hang around until I got a handle on what was going on and then drop out?

It never occurred to me that this middle-aged housewife might know something that I didn't—*in a big way*. They trotted me around the circle and did various things, and then it came time to pass the power and suddenly the queen seemed to recede at a high rate of speed without appearing to get any smaller, the rest of the room went out of focus, and there was a sensation across my skin like static electricity.

I was so utterly surprised that anything like that could happen that my brain locked. In the procedure you were supposed to withdraw when you had enough, but I was just too astounded to be able to do anything. She figured out finally that I had enough, and she withdrew. I wound up just sitting in the corner, burnt out for the rest of the meeting because I wasn't prepared for the reality. That's when I converted. I was just kidding, but the Lady took me at my word.

What do you think was going on?

My initiator was a real channel for the Goddess: an alternative I had not considered. I had read all the then-available books. I knew the history. I was the one who was supposed to know where reality lay. This lady had the widely accepted ancient stone age Wiccan survival story, which I knew to be wrong. It just turned out that the power lay in something other than what I was expecting.

Was she your teacher after that?

Yes, her name is Lady Lydea. I trained with her for several years, and as a matter of fact we are still in contact. That was April 30, 1973, and just last week I was helping her buy a new car.

Was what she taught you traditional English Craft?

Yes, there's some history behind that. Sometime in the early 1960s someone brought English traditional Craft to California's Central Valley. From there it split into several groups, with differing sorts of orientations, the usual sort of development. One batch of them decided that they wanted to expand the focus, and so they started devising additional rites, creating new degrees, and rewriting the core material. They called themselves the Majestic Order. At that point it changed from what most people would consider fairly standard Gardnerian-style Craft into something considerably different. That was the group that I originally joined.

The order eventually became rent with internal political problems, and several of the members decided that they wanted to get back to the original way of doing things in the group that the Majestic Order had sprung out of. So we contacted the other side of the family, which hadn't been going through changes. That group is now called the Order of the Silver Crescent. They regard themselves as the guardians of the "old tradition" per se. We then took what we considered the best of both groups and also carefully checked the texts against the published Gardnerian and Alexandrian material and produced a synthesis called Kingstone Wicca.

How do the Central Valley traditions compare to Alexandrian and Gardnerian Wicca?

The main differences are that we are robed instead of sky clad at our rites, males can start covens on their own and initiate on their own, there is no same-gender initiation, and we use consistent cord colors: white for first degree, red for second, and blue for third. For the most part we look like British Gardnerians, otherwise.

At first we thought the tradition was a hybrid between a Magisterial group and a Gardnerian one. Since then we have come to realize that we are a survivor of the era when Magisterial Craft was *becoming* what is now known as Gardnerian-type Wicca. Our books preserve many documents in versions prior to those discussed in *Crafting the Art of Magic* [by Aidan Kelly].

The Magisterial covens historically were the ones the church records describe. The Magister or Magus, dressed in fantastic horned disguise, was the God incarnate, the center of worship. Then you had the Queen of the Sabbat (a.k.a. the Queen of Elfhame), who presided over the ceremonies, and her assistant the high priest, who'd eventually inherit the God position. When the fellow with the horns stopped showing up, the queen continued in command, and that is how you get the matriarchal focus in most of the traditional Witchcraft groups that now exist.

Was Alex Sanders a "student" of Gerald Gardner?

There has been some embarrassingly ill-mannered debate on that. I would refer you to page 166 of *The Rebirth of Witchcraft* by Doreen Valiente, where she states that Alex Sanders [prominent English Witch] went to the Isle of Man and apparently got *Book of Shadows* from Gerald Gardner. That indicates that Gerald thought he [Sanders] was a real Witch. On the other hand, Patricia Crowther is quite adamant that Sanders was not initiated. So apparently you have one Gardnerian authority agreeing that he is and the other saying that he is not.

So what is the New Wiccan Church?

It is a confederation of English traditional elders (third degrees) who have essentially formed a church to handle the common needs of the Craft for them so that they don't have to constantly duplicate effort. For example, the church serves as a placement organization. The New Wiccan Church advertises *everywhere*, and when applicants fill out the placement forms, we do the general prescreening and then send them on to the NWC elder who most closely matches their requirements. If we can't find one for them in the church, then we try to place them outside of the church.

How does this differ from, say, the Covenant of the Goddess?

The main difference is that COG is a general Witch organization, and that could include anything from Strega (Italian Craft) to Hexen (Germanic Craft) as well as English traditional and New Age Witches. The New Wiccan Church deals only with English Traditional Witch organizations that have traceable lineages and initiations that are similar. The NWC is a special-interest group.

We're all in this together because we all look like "Wicca" to each other, whereas "Witches" could be a much wider variation. For example, we don't have an Egyptian Witchcraft tradition in the NWC.

My job as grand summoner is to crawl up everybody's family tree and figure out who is related to us and therefore eligible for NWC membership, and who is not. As a consequence I am constantly digging into other people's dirty laundry, and a lot of them don't like it.

What do you mean by dirty laundry? What kinds of nasty, smelly things do you find that get people upset?

Generally speaking, most of the Witch traditions in the United States are either derived directly from Gardnerianism or done in imitation of it. In some cases it's done in counter-imitation of it. There are a lot of people claiming "ancient family traditions" which are in fact clearly derivative of Gardner's work [see the article "Good News, Bad News: West Country Wicca"]. As research has improved, there has been a lot of "back-pedaling." We in Kingstone saved ourselves a lot of embarrassment because, early on, we decided that we must be somehow derivative of Gardnerianism, so we just accepted it and moved on. It later turned out that we are likely from a co-lateral branch off of the same people that Gardner was working with. Humility saved us a lot of embarrassment.

There are some people who say that Gardner made up the whole thing himself, and there are others who believe that his work was "Divine inspiration" from the Goddess, or the teachings of a genuinely ancient Witchcraft tradition. To your knowledge, who were the people that he was working with? Were they working with a truly ancient tradition, or were they just making it up in the fine old neo-Pagan tradition?

Well, that's a hard one to figure. For sure, Gardner did *not* invent Wicca because he in fact was working on something else when he met the New Forest Coven. He had been doing some sort of ceremonial work and had himself compiled a manual called *The Book of the Art Magickal*. In this book he says the magus does this, the magus does that. After he meets a Witch, presumably the woman called Dafo, he starts writing in bits for her to do. He says that the ceremonial magician should do this and that and then he adds, And if you have a Witch, the Witch should do thus and so . . .

So he starts writing parts in for his girlfriend or magical partner, whatever she was. She was clearly a Witch before he was. So you begin to see the sudden development of Witchy parts in *The Book of the Art Magickal* and then everything stops.

The next appearance of almost the same material is after he leaves the New Forest Coven and now he is doing his own thing. The first question is, Why did he change back from what he was doing in the New Forest Coven? There is a rumor in the Craft community in England that the old coven told him he could start his own coven but that he was not to use any of *their* material.

Cecil Williamson was running the museum on the Isle of Man (which Gardner later purchased), and he was having Witchcraft association meetings to which Gardner would show up. Gardner's methods differed considerably from those of the other people attending this meeting. He could not have invented the Craft because he joined an organization of people who were already practicing and in fact differed from him in practice.

Can you talk a bit more about the New Wiccan Church?

Presently the church has branches in the Midwest, Great Britain, and in the three West Coast states of the U.S. We are unique among Wiccan organizations in that we now have an organization that meets our needs and for the most part the *squabbling* has stopped. Up until the New Wiccan Church almost all Craft disputes were handled by the principals arguing with each other, snubbing each other, insulting each other, and telling their descendants not to deal with the other people. There was no formal mechanism for solving any of these problems. In our church we agreed that all the elders were to submit to judgment by the other elders for their behavior. We finally had a mechanism by which if a problem arose, people qualified to judge it and to deal with it were in place.

What kinds of problems would be likely to come up?

All kinds. For instance, because the covens are traditional, they tend to be conservative, and there is the issue of secrecy. At my initiation I took an oath that the material I received from the tradition could only be transmitted to certain people provided that they had undergone essentially the same procedure.

People like to innovate, and unfortunately rather than rewrite the Sabbats, which dreadfully need it, most people want to rewrite the initiations. The result is that the initiations keep changing form, and people are unsure if they can honestly exchange information with other branches of their same tradition because things have changed so much.

You've obviously seen a lot of water go under the bridge. If you could speak to the Pagan community as a whole from the point of view of what you have learned, what do you think you would like to say to them?

If you are only working by yourself, it doesn't matter to anyone else what you do or think. But if you are going to deal with others you are going to have to have, out front, an explicit process so that everybody knows where everybody stands. That way there will be no complaints about "We expected you to do this, and you did something else."

The New Wiccan Church functions very much on the idea that things have to be spelled out and defined, so that we don't have the problem of expectations not being met. If it's not written down, you can't expect it. If it's not explicit, it's not agreed upon. If it's not agreed upon, you can't complain that it isn't done your way.

Once you have an agreement, you can explore the possibilities and come to new positions, but you can't just assume that everybody out there holds the same position you do—for instance, on animal rights. You will have to talk with people to see if you can get agreement, or maybe there won't be agreement, and you have to let that one slide.

The Heartland Spiritual Alliance was established in 1987 as a legally recognized not-for-profit organization to assume the responsibilities of the Heartland Spirit Festival (formerly called the Heartland Pagan Festival). The HSA is an eclectic, ecumenical, religious, and educational organization composed of eco-spiritualists. This Pagan gathering is a four-day event held over Memorial Day weekend; it brings together well-known keynote speakers and musicians to coordinate an exchange of ideas and knowledge in workshop spaces.

The HSA has expanded its interests to include the Pagan Parenting Group and a publishing venture with the Kansas City Covenant of Unitarian Universalist Pagans (CUUPS) group, which produces a bimonthly newsletter. In addition, they are a contributing sponsor to a Pagan radio program on KPFI and are in the process of raising money to purchase land for a camp for Pagans and like-minded groups.

RHIANNON is a Witch of the Scottish traditional Craft. She is a trained psychiatric nurse, and president of the Heartland Spirit Alliance. She was interviewed on January 12, 1994.

What has kept you involved in Paganism? What is the essence of it that has held your interest?

I think I came to it through ecology. In school I was very active with that. I am of the Vietnam era; I was doing much protesting as the war was winding down in 1972. We were also putting a lot into the push to clean up the world. I realized at that time that we are all stewards of the earth.

Can you talk about the Heartland Pagan Festival?

The Heartland Pagan Festival is now called the Heartland Spirit Festival because we have so many kinds of people who come, and we didn't want to limit it to just one faith. I have always been involved with the interfaith idea. That comes from us believing that everybody should believe what they want.

The Heartland Spiritual Alliance is an organization that was incorporated to continue what was started by the Heartland Pagan Festival, the first one of which was nine years ago and had about two hundred people. It took place Memorial Day weekend. The next year they had some internal strife, as Pagan festivals sometimes do. That year I attended and taught some classes. The third year I was vice president and since then I have been president. This year we had over five hundred people at the festival.

During the process of pulling all that together we had trouble finding a place to have it. We got tossed out of a Sunflower Camp, a Campfire Girls' camp, because they said our philosophies didn't match. What happened was that a neighbor of the camp who was trespassing at a time when we were supposed to have it exclusively saw a young man in a loin cloth. They could have seen much more; I was really pleased that they hadn't run into anybody running around skyclad!

We then went to a Boy Scout camp, and they declined to let us come back there supposedly because it was the last weekend before their season and they wanted to give their people time off. But when I got them to really talk plainly with me, they said they were upset about the fact that in our brochure we had stated that if people were going to be trysting in the woods they should stop by the first aid cabin and pick up condoms.

My response was, "So you are telling us the Boy Scouts of America are against safe sex?" And they said, "We are against sex at *all*. We are talking about children here." I told them that out of five hundred and fifty people, there were only about thirty children. That five hundred and twenty were consenting adults, and we were promoting the safe sex idea. Of course that didn't go over.

Also during this time there was a Men's Festival and a Midwest Women's Festival, who were also having some hassles. They happened to be gay and lesbian. The lesbians were having a tough time with the rangers at a state camp who, even though they said they would not come through, were riding through the camp on horses and ogling the women and making them really uncomfortable.

The men were actually raided. They were tossed out of a park. I think the police found three joints and one underage child. They took the child away from the father and put it in a foster home until the mother could drive up and get the child. I think that's a travesty. Later all the charges were dropped.

After this I started thinking that we should try to pull together a place that would be safe for people to come together and be with nature and be allowed to be who they were. I started to work with the Heartland Festival Alliance on a campaign to look for property, which we did for about two years. The property we finally purchased was the first one we ever went on. It is one hundred and sixty-eight acres, about forty-five miles northeast of Kansas City. We have named the land Gaea. There are nine cabins on the land and a dining hall, a pavilion, a two-story main hall, an office, and a caretaker cabin. Everybody volunteers to work there. Not only are they volunteers, but they are also financial supporters. We had over five hundred gallons of paint donated last year to spruce up the buildings.

There is a twelve-acre lake. We have developed a Venus Mound which is a wonderful place. Some people came and put a statue on it. Things appear there, people leave offerings. We also have Herne's Hollow, which is dedicated to men's mysteries. There are horns hanging in a tree and pictures of Herne.

How do you pay the taxes?

We don't have any. We are tax free because we are a nonprofit education center. The way we get money for the land payments is by renting it out. The goal is to eventually be self-supporting.

How did you get the money for all of this?

I had $6,000 that I had inherited from an aunt, and I raised the rest of it, which in the Pagan community is kind of incredible. It took several years to do it. We asked people for donations, and we started having a silent auction at the Heartland Spirit Festival. This was another reason why we changed from a Pagan festival to a spirit festival. We had raffles, that sort of thing.

I'm fortunate to have grown up with some of the big name Pagans, and I got some really good support from them. Janet Farrar and I are friends, and she helped. There were enough people who knew me well enough to know that if we didn't get the land, they would get their money back.

Have you had any problems with being on the land?

We work very closely with the police department. This is *not* Pagan-owned land. The majority of the people involved are Pagans, but it is an interfaith retreat center, and we are very specific about that. Yes, there are Witches on the property from time to time, but no, it's not a Witch camp.

Locals do come by and wonder what is going on. We've had kids crash down the gate. But I'm not so sure that is because of religious orientation as much as that it's country-type people in a place that was abandoned for a long time and now their access to it has been cut off. We did press charges on the gate. Once they realized that we were a religious organization, we became less interesting to the community. Next fall we want to have a spirit day for the teens so they can come out on a Saturday and swim and fish and have a pep rally. That way they will see that we are just normal people, and they will leave us alone.

You said you have done interfaith work?

I've been on the Kansas Interfaith Council for nine years now. It is an organization that was set up by CRES, which is the Center for Religious Experience and Study. We have eighteen different faiths in Kansas City. I have been very well received as a Pagan. I just participated in the World Peace Celebration on New Year's Eve. I did a litany and a prayer.

What do you do for a mundane living? And how does being a Pagan interface with that? Is there any connection, or does it influence your work?

I'm a psychiatric nurse. In my work with patients I have found that the empathy level is recognized. I think I have a more accepting attitude. I'm less judgmental about what people are into.

Can you describe some magical things that have happened to you personally or in group settings?

The magic that I am most pleased about is that I have a child that is a surrogate child. His biological mother and I are friends. We met and within a year of that time she was pregnant. I believe that she was sent to me. We had lots of people help raise energy for that conception. He's four years old now, and she is very good friends with us.

Do you have a vision for the future of Paganism and for the future of America and the world?

Oh gosh, this is where you say, "I want us all to live in peace and unity," the normal Miss America speech. Basically, I would just like to be able to be who I am and do what I do and have people be okay with that. There is a lot of religious oppression in the world. I would like my son to grow up in a world where he can celebrate Beltane and Summer Solstice and Lammas and Samhain and not have to hide that. He may grow up to be a Republican Christian for all I know. Kids have a way of being surprising—maybe it skips a generation! But he should have the freedom to be who he is.

I feel that the more people know about us the less there will be to be afraid of, so I think that by doing things like Gaea and by working with interfaith councils we can make things better.

RICHARD AND TAMARRA JAMES are the founders of the Wiccan Church of Canada, as well as two occult shops in Ottawa (593½ Bank Street) and Toronto (109 Vaughn Road), Ontario. The Wiccan Church of Canada is committed to the academic study of the historic Pagan ways of worship. They basically offer an open-to-the-public Wiccan Sunday school, with worship services every week, and they are developing a priesthood of a public church. They were interviewed March 3, 1994, by phone.

Richard, are you a Pagan and when did you first discover that you were Pagan?

Yes. For me "discover" is a weird word. I guess it was 1977. I was driving down the street one day with my lady love in the car on Santa Monica Boulevard in Los Angeles. She said, "There's a place we have to stop!" I pulled over, and we went into this place called The Sorcerers Shop. There was this strange and odd person who was running the place who greeted us by saying, "Do what thou wilt shall be the whole of the law." That's an Aliester Crowley type code sentence. He was a little disappointed when we didn't come back with the correct response, but we got along reasonably well. He invited us to circle the next week, and we went. We discovered there that not everybody was into Aliester Crowley; they were mostly a group of Wiccans. I found that what they were doing agreed with me, and I started to learn.

What religion were you raised in?

I was mostly raised Unitarian.

What was it about Witchcraft that attracted you to it?

Multiplicity of Deities. The Unitarian people have a tendency to pray "to whom it may concern." They are not sure about the quality, number, gender, or anything else of God. They happen to be wishy-washy when it comes to the religious expression of anything. I found that it was nice to have the freedom to address Deity in the way that I wanted according to the needs of the moment. That one could firmly address Freya and the next week just as firmly address Chango.

Can you talk about your church a bit?

After our extended visit to Los Angeles, during which I was introduced to the Craft, we moved to New York City. We had an introduction to the Earth Star Temple and the Blue Star Tradition. They had this little shop called Zipporah and the Wizard, and there was another shop called the Magickal Childe run by some other people. We took a look at the way that Earth Star and the Blue Star Temple were being run, both being connected to shops, and we thought that was a pretty good idea. We also thought that we could do a better job of it, but being Canadians if we were to try to do it in the U.S., we'd probably wind up getting thrown out of the country. So we moved to Toronto, and we opened up our first little shop. The people who came to the services that we had in the back room of the shop decided to form an organization which became the Wiccan Church of Canada.

Can you describe your tradition?

We decided that a greater degree of public access was a good idea. We don't screen people before inviting them to circle. It's a church; people can just walk in the door. We are committed to a greater degree of academic study than the usual. A little bit of worship leads to a certain knowledge of the Gods. After that, hopefully, one really wants to acquire more knowledge of the Gods. What we do is to basically offer publicly available Wiccan Sunday school.

So our tradition is a little bit academic in terms of studying historic Pagan ways of worship. We do public worship services every week just like your average Presbyterian church, and we need a group of people who are competent to lead these worship services. Our tradition has grown up around the need to have people who can do that teaching in a very public forum.

The core of our Wiccan tradition is about developing a priesthood of a public church, which is kind of antithetical to the old private coven approach.

How many people are involved in your church?

There are three congregations and a small handful of associate covens, which are training grounds for people. There are also some associate covens which are composed of groups of inmates. They don't have much say in the way that the church is run, but it gives them a point of connection. We have about one hundred official members, and there are about three hundred people who regularly attend and take part in services.

Because of our history of teaching people we realize that not everybody is going to get along well with Celtic Deities or the Greek Deities and so on, so we change the focus from week to week. One week we will do a Norse circle based on our study of the old Norse ways, and the next week it will be a Sumerian rite based on old Sumerian worship. We'll work with just about any tradition after a reasonable amount of study to make sure that we aren't screwing it up.

You could be considered an elder in the Pagan community because you are one of the heads of a larger church. Do you see any problems that the Pagan community is facing?

There are some political problems. For example, our church applied to be a religious charity in Canada, and the government said no, just because they didn't feel like doing it. This means that we have to go through a long process of educating the government and the public so that eventually we can acquire for Wiccans and Pagans the kinds of rights that other people take for granted.

I read somewhere that your church was the only officially recognized Pagan one in Canada and that you had rights to go into jails and hospitals and so on. How did that happen?

That started because a person who was loosely associated with the church ended up being thrown in jail because he committed a crime. He announced that he was Pagan and that he wanted a Pagan minister to come and visit him, so we had to do that. That was our first introduction to the institutional setting. It was a little bit difficult to do. When the chaplain of the institution didn't want to cooperate, it was a matter of getting hold of the chaplain's boss, who was a little more educated. The boss called the chaplain and told him that the law said he had to let us in.

It was a matter of us behaving in a reasonable fashion. If we had gone in and behaved in a manner that the institution didn't like, they would have had a case for not letting us back in. We played by the rules, and now Tamarra is the chairperson of the multifaith branch of the local interfaith council. Our approach has always been to pursue things through the proper channels.

What effect do you think your path could have on Canadian culture and on world culture?

If you were to live in Canada and listen to the Canadian Broadcasting Corporation, you would rapidly discover that we are part of an ongoing cultural tendency towards multiculturalism. Canadians don't believe in the value of the American melting pot. Canadians are very hot on maintaining ethnic communities. We are a part of that, and there is a certain degree to which Wiccans and Pagans can speak about things like polytheistic religion in a way that is a little more comprehensible to your average WASP Canadian.

Does your path deal with the earth in any way?

Our path, in common with other Pagan paths, addresses the Earth Mother as principal Goddess. What we try to do is encourage people to encounter environmental issues in a way which is informed by their Paganism rather than encounter Paganism in a way which is informed by their commitments to environmental issues. We think that a commitment to the Gods is more basic than environmental issues and all other issues.

Do you practice magic?

Yes. I think that overt spell work, which is what I think you are asking me about, is a minuscule part of what we do. In the process of circle and worship and learning there is magic of the "Ah Ha!"—the sudden realization of "something."

The magic that we work towards is that self-fulfillment of coming to a realization of our own relationship with the Gods. For us that's a whole lot more important than doing a spell to get Johnny a job.

So, Tamarra, are you a Pagan?

Yes, I am a Pagan. I started to move to it when I was about fourteen. I actually became Pagan when I was sixteen, in 1967. I was rebelling at the time. I lived in Victoria, and my mother was a fairly important person there, and I was having an identity crisis. My mother was the first female president of the Chamber of Commerce and the first female alderman. She ran a charm and modeling school, she was in *Who's Who,* and she was pretty high profile. Everyone that I was introduced to said, "Oh, you are Helen's daughter." So I had a postpubescent identity crisis, and I decided to go hippie. I was right in the heart of the hippie movement.

I also had a number of bad tastes with Christianity at that point. I had gone to the Anglican church with the rest of my friends, and the time came when I started my period. My family dealt with that really well. They took my sister and myself out for a fancy dinner. My grandmother gave me my name and that sort of thing.

What do you mean by your grandmother gave you your name?

There is a name that you don't share with anybody. My grandparents were farmers, and they had some old-world ideas. There is a name that you get when you are born, but it is told to you when you are older. That was just a family thing. I liked the way that they dealt with things better than going to church and being told it was the Curse of Eve.

In the course of the hippie thing I was reading every witchcrap book that I could find. I was feeling fairly powerless, and I wanted to be powerful, so I was reading spell books and that kind of garbage. I was hanging around with a group of older people, carrying these books, and dressing all in black and being very Witchy and stuff. It embarrassed my mother very much, which was what I had set out to do!

But gradually I got turned on to better books. On my sixteenth birthday I was invited to a circle, and what I discovered was that it was something entirely different from what I had been reading about. It was something new, yet it felt like coming home.

How was it different from what you were reading about?

I had been reading about spells, and what I came to was a communal sense of things, an idea of Goddess that before was only half formed in me. Most of the spell books didn't talk about Goddess. They were fairly ceremonial.

I had spent my formative years on a farm, so I had a respect for nature. My grandparents were farmers, and there was this idea of respecting the land because your whole livelihood comes from it. Gram used to get us up to watch thunderstorms. She was an herbalist; she had a lovely herb garden, and I started learning herbs from her when I was little. Years later when the press had misquoted me about something, my grandmother said, "What is all this Witch-craft stuff anyway?" So I told her where I was coming from, and she said, "When you put it that way, I guess I am one." But it wasn't the words she normally would have used. She was a country person.

The principles that you learn in the country are at home in Wicca, like getting your hands in the earth and recognizing the seasons. My grandmother had what I call a "Goddess bowl." So did my mother. I have them both now because Mum gave me hers when I bought a house. It's a bowl that has a Lady statue in it, and every season we would put different things in the bowl. That was a special treat for us. In the spring we would put flowers in the bowl and in the summer the first fruit. In the fall, colored leaves and in the winter, holly. I grew up with country things like that.

What for you is the most important part of Paganism? What is the essence of it for you?

Being mindful. It's recognizing your connection with everything else and the sacredness of everything. It's being the best that you can be in whatever you choose to do. Your whole life, as far as I am concerned, is an offering back. Nothing is disconnected from anything else.

It's the realization that the air that we breathe has been here from the beginning. That the water we drink is a part of the primordial water, it's been blood, it's been rain, it's been waterfalls and snow and juice and sap. It just keeps going around.

It's knowing that your body has been plants and animals and that somehow there isn't a real distinction, we are all part of this Mother Earth.

You are a cofounder of the Wiccan Church of Canada. Can you talk about how you gave birth to that?

When we came to Toronto we opened the store, and we decided to have a little coven and an open circle. We hoped to meet people through the open circle and create a coven out of that. What happened was that somebody threw a brick through our window the night of our first circle. The story hit the newspaper, and the next day there were Pagans coming from *everywhere*. We suddenly had a whole community of people.

A few months later this guy walked in, and he had a bunch of papers in his hand. He said, "I got these when I was going to start a Pagan church, but you guys are closer to that than I'll ever be," and he dumped the incorporation papers in our lap.

So we asked the people who were coming to our circle if that was what they wanted to do, and they said yes. So we did it. It was that serendipitous.

How does the church handle finances?

We have a donation jar. The shop keeps the jar, and people put change in when they make a purchase. We have a little sign on it that says all proceeds are for the WCC. Occasionally, we will do a fundraiser like selling plants in the spring. We start the herbs from seed, and people can buy them for a few dollars. We will accept donations anytime, anywhere!

Can you give an anecdote about something magical that you have done or that has happened?

A very dear friend of mine is in the hospital just now. He fell down and hit his head and bled into the brain. We told people about it, and the entire community of people who knew him began working together. They were burning blue candles to Iaso, a healing Goddess whom we are quite fond of out here. She's a daughter of Asclepias. Everybody was burning lights for him and doing meditations for him. There was a little shrine on his bedside in the hospital. The doctor came in on day two and said that he was experiencing a pretty miraculous recovery. They hadn't expected him to recover as quickly as he had or as well as he had. That's just one example, and things like that happen here all the time.

Most of our magic is healing and community support. I have personal experience on a spiritual level with the Gods and the Goddesses, and many of the people that I know do. That is absolutely magical. But also magical for me is the fact that I can put a seed in the ground and plants come up. I'm pretty simple about a lot of things and pretty scholarly about other ones. I think that we can't afford to lose the wonder. Everything in the world is magical.

The
Faery Faith

Mention the word "Faery," and you will find the Victorian image of gossamer-winged sprites etched into the minds of most people. Children's book illustrators starting with the great Arthur Rackham have contributed to and elaborated on these fanciful images for the past hundred years. But long before that, people in every culture and in every region of the world had their tales of "the little people," "the good people." The Irish have their sidh, the Scottish their wee folk, the German their dwarves, and Scandinavian countries their Tomtems. Indeed, many believe that these were races that accepted and lived by the ways of magic as easily as we now accept the "realities" of computers and air travel.

The first two interviews are with modern practitioners of the Faery Faith, a tradition that is as ancient as some of the oldest trees on earth. In both interviews the name of Victor Anderson is mentioned with a great deal of reverence, as he is one of the few direct descendants of this ancient faith. He is the keeper of the flame, and it is with great pleasure that we present a very rare and in-depth interview with Mr. Anderson as the third part of this chapter. But first . . .

ANNA KORN is a priestess, botanist, and long-time friend of the late Gwydion Penderwen, the much loved and well known Pagan poet and bard. At the time of the interview Ms. Korn had recently served as national recorder (secretary) for the organization COG (The Covenant of the Goddess). She was interviewed by phone on March 3, 1994.

If you are both a Pagan and a Witch, what does it mean to be a Pagan, and what does it mean to be a Witch?

I see Paganism as the overarching classification of a number of religions and practices, of which Witchcraft is probably the most numerically predominant. To be a Witch, in my opinion, means tapping into an ancient energy of wild nature. And also peaceful nature energy.

I relate a lot to plants, both as healers and as teachers and communicators. Though lately I have been working to recover what the Witches might have been doing with animal familiars. So I can't say that I solely work with plant energy.

I am an initiate of a number of different traditions in the Craft. I started out as a grove priestess in the English Dianic system with Morgan McFarland and Mark Roberts. That was in the mid-seventies. At that time Witches and Pagans were so rare that when you met someone whom you could relate to, you would immediately take up with them. Later, I met Oberon and Morning Glory G'Zell and did work that was probably more shamanic/eclectic. Now I'm more active in a British traditional Wiccan context.

What religion were you raised in?

My parents were kind of unusual in that they had been in a Vedanta temple for quite some time. My father was interested in Buddhism and particularly in Zen. We didn't have any specific religious training when we were little; if we wanted to go to somebody else's Sunday school, our parents would let us.

It was pretty clear that they didn't think too highly of Christianity, and my mother was sort of an angry ex-Catholic. Nearly everyone in our family was a scientist. My father, even though he was a Vedantist, had a lot of different religious directions that were mostly eastern.

So what was it about Paganism that attracted you?

I think it was something that was always intrinsic, something that had always been attractive from the time I was small. I would make charms when I was little, and I learned about plants and about folklore. Those were the type of books that I chose when I was a kid. I remember reading *The Golden Bough* [by Sir James Frazier] when I was quite small and thinking that it was a really magical book. I did "kitchen Witchery" when I was little. Also sympathetic magic, learning the language of the flowers, and Indian uses for plants in our area. Things like that.

You said you have been working with animal familiars and with plants. Can you give some examples of that?

I've been gardening quite a bit in this house that I moved into about three years ago. I have quite a few herbs and flowers here, even though the yard is quite small. I've always been close to animals of all sorts, and when I was a kid I had many different kinds of pets. We had snakes, we had a monkey, we had horses. I've always felt very close to cats.

Gwydion was incredibly close to cats and had an approach that I really haven't seen duplicated very much. I have been trying to explore that with our cats, and I'm now planning a workshop around this topic, about working with familiars and about animals and divination. Gwydion had this way of palling around with animals that was very interesting to see. He would talk to cats one on one. We lived in a cabin in the woods with our two cats, and we would have four-way conversations. I suppose that people who know cats well can generally understand what they are saying.

He also had a very teasing relationship with them. He used to play the "kitty pipes" with his cat Pandora, who was really a very smart-alecky cat. He would put Pandora under his arm and put the tail in his mouth and squeeze. The cat would go WRRRRRRROWR! Pandora didn't really like it, but she went along with it.

Gwydion has been referred to as a Pagan saint by several people. Can you comment on that?

Gwydion was an incomparable poet. He had tremendous psychic gifts. Sometimes he could be extremely stubborn and obtuse. I think that it's important to realize that he had very human qualities.

What do you think was his greatest contribution?

His music and his poetry. Gwydion also had psychic power, and he was a master of the art of fascination and of sending power with a glance. He had eyes that were very very blue; sometimes they could be like the blue of the sea or the blue of a sunny sky or ice blue. He could really zap people with his eyes.

He was extremely focused on internal practice, which he didn't talk about very much. He did a lot of work in trance. People at parties thought he was a sort of a wet blanket because he would retire early, but he was spending a large portion of the night in trance. He would remain almost motionless, looking very much like a dead king on a bier with his beard pointing almost straight up.

I think that we Pagans often focus more on the celebratory parts of Paganism and maybe not enough on the work involved in developing some of the psychic gifts that are a part of our heritage. I can't say that was true of Gwydion. He was extremely disciplined in his psychic work. I think that he had the knowledge that he was going to die young. You could see that by the way in which he lived his life. He definitely identified with the archetype of the sacred king who was born to be sacrificed. That comes out again and again in his music.

I was with him for seven years. I was living in a different place when he died, but we were still very close. He came down to see me the night before he died. He died in a car accident. The car went off the road and rolled in a ditch. He was thrown out, and the car rolled on top of him and crushed him. There is some belief, and this has been obtained from psychic contact with him, that what caused the car to go off the road was that he swerved to avoid a deer.

He had ties with deer as sacred animals and had done something that the Irish would never do with an animal that they identified with as sacred. He had shot a deer that he found in his garden, which is the usual rule in the country: "If it's in the garden, it's dinner." This was not the wisest thing in terms of sacred history for him to do. He did prepare the skull by painting it shortly before he died. He was also very close to foxes, and they were probably even closer to him in terms of being his sacred animals.

He was part of the Faery tradition. Can you talk a little about what it's like to work in the Faery tradition as compared to the Gardnerian tradition, for example?

There is a great body of lore in both traditions. I've done quite a bit of trying to gather Faery tradition stuff together because I don't think it has been collected as completely as the Gardnerian materials have been. The lore has been scattered because the way that Victor Anderson taught was that he rarely gave all he knew to any one initiate.

He basically taught each initiate what they needed to hear or learn. A more timid person might be given something that would increase their confidence. A more arrogant person might be taught something that was perhaps a humbling lesson. Consequently, we get teachers who have individual material that is not at all the same as any other teacher. It's really quite scattered and disparate.

I don't think that any one person can pull the teachings together. I think that it's very important for the various practitioners to work together on this. I think that the tide is turning, and that's beginning to happen now.

If you were to characterize the Faery tradition, how would you describe it?

I think it's many headed. Less of the material has been written down in the Faery tradition. Victor Anderson and Gwydion Penderwen were the main sources in the United States. In later years Gabriel Caradoc ap Cador was a source.

Gwydion had been going to visit Victor since the time he was about thirteen years old. As Gwydion grew and developed his own interests, he contributed most of the Welsh and Celtic material within the tradition. He and I worked together on the tree alphabet and the images that were raised in *The White Goddess* [by Robert Graves] as they filtered into poetry.

Victor has always been very close with African practitioners of Voodoo and other practitioners. He also has the experience of past-life remembrance that goes back to Polynesia and especially to Hawaii. So he brought in the African and Polynesian stuff while Gwydion drew much more heavily on the Celtic.

Gardnerian Wicca has certain tenets like the Wiccan Rede and not charging money for the Craft, and the Lord and the Lady and Drawing Down the Moon, etc. How is the Faery faith different?

They both have a belief in the Drychton [Anglo Saxon word meaning "lord" or "ruler"], a power that is both male and female and which is the power behind the God and the Goddess. In the Faery tradition the Drychton is actually visualized as having more female characteristics, although if you ask Victor, he will say it's the Mother-Father God.

In the Faery tradition there is a belief that as the light from the stars bounced off the curved mirror of space in the directions to the left and to the right, it produced the other Deities, the Gods on one side and the Goddesses on the other. The Faery tradition has specific Deities. It has both outer-court and secret names for them. There are specific visualizations for the guardians of the quarters as well as for the above and below. There are specific Deities that are worked with, and there are specific power-raising techniques and power-circulating techniques that are taught which seem to be pretty unique to it. At least they don't seem to exist in any other branches of the Craft that I am familiar with.

Like in many of the initiatory traditions there is a dependence on the passing of power from person to person, from teacher to student. It's an ecstatic tradition rather than seeing itself as a fertility tradition.

And what is the object of that ecstasy?

Union with the Gods, identification with the Gods, becoming like the Gods.

You have worked in Gardnerian Wicca as well. Can you talk about that?

I come from the California Gardnerian tradition. I can't say that we see ourselves as terribly schismatic in the sense of wanting to break away from any other group, but we do have a particular way of seeing things that is perhaps in part engendered by being in California. We are in a real hotbed of Pagan development and evolution. It's an area with many progressive political ideals, so many of the things that the Gardnerian practice has been criticized for in the past have really been examined here.

Many of us have met and discussed at length over the course of about a year and a half what our practice and beliefs are really like in the context of the

Gardnerian tradition. As a result of those discussions we have come up with a declaration. The main distinction that we make and that cascades down to other smaller decisions is that we treat the sexes as equal. We don't see that there is a matriarchy within the tradition. We don't see it as a priestess-predominant tradition. We're trying to see it in a post-feminist way. We are trying to have equality between the sexes within the circle.

When Gardnerian Wicca came to this country, it was a priestess-predominant religion. The women and the men within the circle would not even get the same teaching material. We think that it is important to accentuate the wholeness of all humans, whatever their gender.

We feel that gender equality is key and that has certain corollaries such as inclusivity for gay members of the Craft. We feel that the almost exclusive emphasis on heterosexuality within the Gardnerian context for the last thirty years has probably mistakenly brought about an emphasis on a fertility religion as opposed to an ecstatic religion in the popular mind.

What have you done with COG?

Back in 1976 or 1977 I met Alison Harlow. That was when COG was first getting together, and it sounded wonderful to me. At that time I wasn't a member of a coven that was a member of COG, but I began getting the newsletter and tuning in to what COG was doing. Initially and for many years it was just a California thing. Witches would get together once a year and have a meeting. I moved to California in 1979, which was after the total eclipse that occurred in February right over a replica of Stonehenge.

All sorts of California Pagans came up to Oregon for the eclipse. It was just wonderful meeting all those people. My life in Oregon was kind of winding down at that time, and shortly after the eclipse I moved in with Gwydion, so I feel that was a kind of astronomical key turning in a lock. It was an opening of a new door in my life.

Many of the people in this area have been COG members for a very long time and have a very open, inclusive attitude about the Craft and the variation that it affords for many different people's spiritual paths.

I became locally active, I held quite a few officer positions on the local level. Then I became national recorder. Last year the organization raised quite a lot of money and sent a delegation to the Parliament of the Worlds Religions in Chicago.

You are a botanist. Can you give some examples of ways that you have worked with plants in a magical context?

I try to integrate them into my life. It's not something that I just do in circle. Besides tuning into the plants as food and incense and medicine, I listen to the trees. I go out and hug the trees. I listen to the plants to see what they have to tell me about the weather, the climate, the environment, how the earth is faring in a particular area. There's much you can learn through being quiet and listening.

Do you have a favorite herb or a favorite plant?

I like alder trees very much. Alder trees out here on the West Coast are quite different from the ones on the East Coast. On the East Coast they are a small, very dark-barked shrub that grows by the waterside. Here they are water lovers too, but they are silver and they are much bigger. The bark is silvery gray, and they talk about flowing and how fiery energy can come out of watery energy. They tell about endurance as the waters ripple away at their roots.

FRANCESCA DUBIE is a shamanic healer, Faery priestess, poet, and psychic. She is the author of a self-published chapbook *Her Winged Silence: A Shaman's Notebook*. She is also founder of The 3rd Road school. The 3rd Road is a living branch of Celtic shamanism, popularly called the Faery tradition. It is a school for Pagan religion and an institute of healing for people from a wide diversity of religious walks of life.

The institute, like the temple of an ancient city, is the nucleus of a community where students come together to worship, study, heal, work, and play. The 3rd Road offers ministerial services including baby blessings, alternative-style weddings and handfastings, spiritual cleansings, and exorcisms.

Ms. Dubie was interviewed by phone on March 9, 1994.

Are you a Witch or a Pagan?

I am both.

When did you discover that you were a Witch and a Pagan?

That's never an easy question for me to answer. I fell into it. As you know, I am a Faery shaman. The word "shaman" is just another word for Witch, Witchcraft being Northern European shamanism. I really got kidnapped into it; I think that most shamans like me did. It was nothing I chose.

When I was young I lived in Vermont, and I was terrified because I had to walk through the woods at night to get home. It was dark and it was unlit. I was terrified because I was afraid the fey folk were going to steal me. They do live in Vermont. They are very much a part of the wilderness there, and I had such a fear of them. Yet I was also fascinated by them. I thought they'd put me to work in their gold mines; that was my youthful fear.

What finally happened with the fey folk was that I bit by bit moved more and more towards their magic and didn't fully realize yet how fey my own blood was. I do not mean that metaphorically. I don't really speak in metaphor.

About eight years ago I was working professionally as a psychic, and I was pretty used to psychic phenomena. If somebody's dead father showed up in the middle of a reading, that was not new to me. One night I fell through the veil; in other words, the fey folk kidnapped me. The next day I woke up and I went for a walk, and the trees were talking to me and the sidewalk was talking to me and the buildings were singing and spirits were talking to me all day long. It was no longer something that was contained in the readings. I was living on the other side of the veil.

I didn't have any trouble with it. I was having the time of my life! It was the first time I felt like I was at home. I went to a therapist, and I asked her if I was having a psychotic break. I told her what was going on, and she said no. She knew that I was already used to psychic phenomena. So you know that what was going on for me was something spectacular if I was already used to that sort of thing. She told me that it wasn't a psychotic break but that my consciousness had been expanded further. She told me not to use it as a drug, that I should use it to serve people etc. etc., and I'd be okay. I have followed her advice, and I've been living on the other side of the veil ever since.

That sounds like a very wise and unusual therapist. Was she a Pagan?

No, she wasn't. She was a Freudian, believe it or not.

What I realized was that I was too foolish, as I think most shamans are, to make the choice for myself. I had to be kidnapped. Now I know that I probably wouldn't be alive if I hadn't gotten on the other side of the veil. But I was too foolish. I didn't know what was best for me, and the Gods had to kidnap me.

What religion were you raised in?

I was raised by a Witch as a Catholic. We neo-Pagans always talk about Paganism as something new because it's new to the media. But at least in blue-collar neighborhoods Paganism is not that unusual. Until at least a couple of generations ago it was very typical for Pagan practices to be happening in Christian families. It may not have been under those names.

In Ireland they say that if you scratch the surface of a good Irish Catholic, you will find a Pagan.

Absolutely. I was raised by a woman whose Italian family of origin called her the family Witch. She read cards and was enormously psychic. She would not teach me a thing about it. I don't know why. I think part of it was that she was trying to be a good Catholic.

So why didn't you end up as a nice Catholic girl?

The fey folk kidnapped me!

When I was fourteen, I was involved with the Junior Ecumenical Council. That was 1964. I've always been a seeker, I have always been looking towards the spiritual. It's not because I'm so good or anything. Some people like hammers and nails, some people like spirituality. Some people like music, some people love to dance. I'm comfortable in the spiritual realms.

A friend of mine was just reminding me that at age fourteen I complained about Catholicism because they wouldn't let me be a priest. Catholicism didn't address me because I am a Pagan! I am a Pagan at heart.

What was the first training that you got other than the fey themselves?

My main teacher was Victor Anderson. I had a fortune teller once tell me, and she didn't know anything about Paganism, "Your job in this lifetime is to teach the Faery magic to the human race." My jaw just dropped. This was after I met Victor.

I have past-life memories of doing this over and over again with human beings. Of bringing my fey blood into human arenas and teaching the magic.

I met Victor two weeks after the Faery kidnapping. I went to him, and he said, "You have found the Faery secrets on your own. What you did was very dangerous; you are lucky you didn't blow your brains out." And it's true, the Faery tradition in the old form is a very dangerous kind of magic.

He said that was why shamans used to have covens. The old shamans used to go on a hill and confront the Gods themselves, and they finally learned that it was safer to do it in covens. He offered to take me under his tutelage. Two weeks later he gave me a formal Faery initiation.

People say that he rambles. I do not think that is the truth. I think they are not listening to what is a very sensitive, delicate mind that moves in spirals, that moves in patterns that have a lot more to do with physics than mental constructs.

He's passionate, he's ornery. This is a man that is physically blind and yet has married and raised a family. He's celebrating his fiftieth anniversary this year. He owns his own home. So the orneriness is almost raised to the power of Divinity. This passion and this almost sacred anger that he has helps him accomplish things, I think.

When I spoke with Victor he said that the Faery faith was a completely separate lineage from what most people consider to be Witchcraft, from Gardnerian-inspired Wicca. Most people have no concept of what it is. Can you talk about that a bit?

A lot of Gardnerian magic is based on dualism. Faery is based on truer physics. For instance, I tell my students to look at an electron and a nucleus. What you have there is mostly emptiness; life is not this balance between matter and emptiness. If you look past the lighted atmosphere of earth, you will see darkness. There is not a balance of dark and light. What we have is a reality that is mostly darkness and mostly emptiness, and that's the Mother. We start there.

Out from that Mother emerges the God, whom She is totally in love with. So we have a feminine-based reality, but that does not mean that the feminine is better. An aspect of that feminine is the masculine, and She loves him. It is not a love that is given or withheld or any kind of a power trip; it is just true love. The question of better doesn't even enter into it.

It's a very dark tradition. Most of the Wicca that we see is not that dark. The Faery folk were a very dark race, dark racially, dark in the sense that they were close to the earth; they were close to the mysteries of the spaces between the stars. The people who came after them started talking about that darkness as evil and scary and all of the racist implications and the hatred of the earth that came with that. And the hatred of women as beings who were close to the earth.

The Faery were dark in the most holy sense of darkness. A very unthreatening darkness. The darkness of a mother tucking her child in under the covers at night and whispering, "Gee, I love you." That nice safe feeling you get when you snuggle under the covers at night. That darkness.

Historically, the fey folk came out of Africa. They were an aboriginal group that traveled throughout the world and took their magic everywhere. Every culture has a story of ancestors or people that came who were small, dark, and bearing magic. You hear it in the tales of the Menehune in Hawaii. You hear it in the Celtic lands as the story of the small, dark, fey folk. Do understand that when I talk about Faery, I am shifting somewhat between myth and history as two different sorts of beings. Who was it that said you should always swallow two contradictions before breakfast?

In Irish tradition they talk about the sidh. They were big people; they were huge, in fact. They were called the mighty sidh. They were not small; they were bigger than everybody else . . .

There are three streams that I pull from. There is the one of the small people we just talked about. There are the spirit fey. And there are the large ones you mentioned. I have no trouble with those contradictions. The large people can almost be talked about as Gods from beyond, from another realm.

Yes. That is how I relate to them . . .

Absolutely. I relate to them quite peacefully in all three ways. One of the reasons that it's so difficult to talk about the Faery tradition is that you can't talk about it in summaries. It takes seven years to learn the tradition. It would be like telling somebody how to be an M.D. in a paragraph. It's a highly evolved system, and it doesn't work to do charts and diagrams. I am sure that someone, somewhere will give you charts and diagrams of Faery, and you know what? The fey folk will giggle at it.

That is not how you capture Faery. You capture it through rigorous training and through poetry. There is a myth that Dagda [a Celtic God] drew a veil between the realm of humankind and the realm of Faery so that their destinies would no longer be intertwined.

It's really clear that the veil has been lifting. I've thought a lot about this. I think this is part of why Starhawk's book *The Spiral Dance* had such an enormous impact. I think the veil is lifting because the two races need each other again. I think that humans really need the poetry.

What I mean by poetry is not words on a page that nobody can understand without twenty years of college, but words that evoke courage to help people in their struggles—for example, the political activism that has sprung up with Starhawk in the Faery tradition, or embodied poetry which is smiling. Poetry that is just mischievous acts in life, that bring us alive.

You have a school called The 3rd Road. Can you talk about that?

When I started it, people told me that opening a school of Witchcraft was ridiculous. That was about eight years ago, and they couldn't conceive of it. I think that part of it is that it's very hard for people to put the sacred together with money. What I love about Paganism is that it has immanent Deity, which means we have to bring it into money too, right? I think part of it also is that it's hard for people to accept things that are new.

What kinds of things do you do in your school?

I think what's unusual about the way that I teach is that I believe all this stuff is real. The Gods are not a metaphor for me; they are spirits with spirit bodies who exist. The psychic mysteries are real; they are a fact.

I teach the science and the religion of magic and of the old religion. One of the bases of Faery tradition is that in order to run what is a very wild and dangerous magic, there is a certain purity that is needed. Not purity in the sense of a holier-than-thou, Victorian model of purity. But purity in the sense of purified of all that keeps us from being fully human and fully muscular and fully visceral.

Unless you are that way, you cannot run the Faery magics. Can you imagine some uptight Victorian dancing in a faery ring? They'd go mad. So there is a very heavy emphasis on personal transformation in the classes. It's also not just a class in how to run the energy, how to be a cauldron for the magic. The goal of magic is self-realization, and through that self-realization to be of service to the community.

One of my beliefs, one of my experiences, is that we are taught that we have to sacrifice ourselves in order to be "good." That if we are going to help others, it's through self-sacrifice. While there is some virtue to that statement, it's a dangerous half-truth. The fey folk revel in the self and in passion. I teach my students that if you pursue what gives you the greatest pleasure in life, that is the thing that will be of most service to the community.

"Follow your bliss," said Joseph Campbell . . .

However, one of the other things I teach at the school is that an ecstatic path, following your bliss, is very different from a sloppy or undisciplined path. In this culture we are pretty much told to dichotomize into these false polarities between ecstasy, integrity, discipline, and pleasure.

Part of what the Faery tradition is about is wholeness. This is also a big Kahuna principle. That you bring together mysticism, practicality, passion, service, intellect, intuition, visceralness, and even aestheticism. That takes years of discipline and supervision to achieve.

You mentioned the Kahuna. Did you study Kahuna magic and healing in Hawaii?

No. That came through Victor. A lot of the Faery magic is in Hawaii. The Menehune brought it there. So much of the Celtic tradition, for example, has been lost, and less of it has been lost with the Hawaiian.

You do psychic counseling—what is that?

Let's call it shamanic counseling. A lot of people who are working in psychologically based treatment modes, psychologists, therapists of various sorts, have started to bring in shamanic tools over the years to implement what is basically a psychological treatment mode. They are finding that they are able to be far more effective that way. But that's not what I am doing. As a shamanic counselor what I am doing is wearing a lot of different hats. I am working as a psychic.

One of the things that I don't see happening in counseling and that I don't see happening in a lot of systems of Witchcraft is what I am doing—moving people's energy. It's one thing to recognize a problem, that you have a fear or a morbid belief system, but talking it out in therapy isn't enough sometimes. So I do rituals with people to actually help them to move the energy.

I am also working as a mystic in those situations. Part of what is a shamanically based treatment mode is that I am "John the Baptist." I come in from the desert every couple of days to counsel people. And people need those visions.

Much of what I hear from clients is, "This is the first time in my life I've had permission to paint, change my job, be myself." I think that one of the strongest messages a mystic has is, "Yes, trust that. Trust that. Trust that." *Have* your head in the stars. Part of what you do also, because you are in an earth-based religion, because you are a priestess or a shamanic practitioner, is to help them ground into reality so that they don't fly away.

This is America, and it's a very cruel culture that really does not support its people. If people get too enthusiastic about following their ecstasy, this is a dangerous place to do that, isn't it?

That has not been my experience. I've done this counseling for a long time, and I'll see my clients five years later. I didn't put a bandaid on them. I'm seeing vibrant women and men. They are so out in the world that they scare me. It's so beautiful.

You were initiated by Olivia Robertson of the Fellowship of Isis. Did you go to Ireland to do that?

Yes, I did. I had a vision of Olivia. I was told that I had to meet this woman, and when I met her she was *exactly* as she had been in my vision. I had a weekend in Clonegal, and I needed to grab this woman's attention fast because I wasn't going to be in Ireland for long. I spent a weekend with her, and from then on I didn't leave her side until I left Ireland. She initiated me practically right then and there. There was no preparation. This is what always happens in my life; I get kidnapped into things.

I really wanted her blessing because I felt that this was a woman who I would become. Not in the sense of running a huge organization, but in the sense that she lives with her head in the clouds and her feet on the ground. She and Victor Anderson are two of the only people I have met that even other Pagans consider eccentric. Since I've always been in that category, she was very precious for me to meet.

You also taught in England for a six-month period. How does the English Pagan scene compare to the American Pagan scene?

It's much Witchier. Over here a lot of what is seen in the media is based in academic perspectives and feminist perspectives, as opposed to a real cultural base. An anthropologist once said that "When the anthropologists arrive, the Gods leave."

The Witchcraft that you find in England is much closer to what you would find in Appalachia and in blue-collar neighborhoods in the States and in black neighborhoods. It's much closer to the real thing. It's not Wicca.

What do you mean by "the real thing"?

It's much closer to traditional practices. It's not Gardnerian based. Even the Gardnerian-based stuff is *nothing* like the Gardnerian magic over here. I'm not a Gardnerian, but I lived in a Gardnerian household over there. They were more Witchy. Everything wasn't a metaphor for something else; it was just Witchcraft. The way Witchcraft has been understood in the States is in psychological terms rather than in terms of mysticism or actual physics, actual magic. As if it wasn't real.

Symbols and archetypes?

Exactly. The word "archetype" comes from the Greek word for God. Archetypes are fine if you realize that they are real, that the Gods exist. The Gardnerians over there were much more in tune with that.

Did they revere Gerald Gardner as the keeper of a genuine ancient tradition?

I was living with an initiate of Gerald Gardner. To tell you the truth, I think that Gardner had more authentic magic than people give him credit for. For most people the fey folk have not put the salve on their eyes, and they wouldn't know real magic if they saw it. In other words, if he borrowed something from the Key of Solomon [an ancient Hebrew magical text], they think that invalidates everything else that he did. Whereas traditional Witches have always borrowed anything from anywhere. Whatever works.

I visited with fam trads [family tradition Witches] in England. There is no question in my mind that Gardner got some traditional stuff.

Have you met any genuine fam trad people in America? All of the people I have met here who claim to be fam trad are actually doing Gardnerian Wicca.

Cora Anderson, Victor's wife, comes from a fam trad. I'll tell you, I won't do the fam trad stuff I learned. I always revert to neo-Paganism when I am in a group situation. You do fam trad with your family; it's a family system. You are vowed into the family, and you don't spill it around.

I was talking with one fam trad person I know about the fact that in the Faery tradition there are elemental correspondences for the directions, and that has always rung wrong with me. It was not in keeping with everything else that I had gotten from the tradition because it was too conceptual: "Go to the east for air . . ." If I want a glass of water, I go to my kitchen, which is in the north part of my house. Water is not in the west in my house. So this is a question that I discussed with about seven different fam trads. Maybe there's a lake in the north, then what? It was too much like cutting existence up into a block of cheese that was in squares.

That's not even physics. Physics is much more chaotic than that. I rub my nose and atoms move on the opposite side of the world. It's this wonderful, supposedly chaotic dance.

Are there any issues floating around in the Pagan community that you see as problems or things that need to be discussed?

The hot one right now is the professional priesthood thing. I would like to see a professional Pagan priesthood, as opposed to academics calling themselves priests. Knowing the history of ballet does not make you a ballet dancer. People seem to think that an academic study of Paganism makes you a shaman. There are systems in which you train as rigorously and as deeply and as thoroughly as a ballet dancer trains. You learn a skill, you learn an art, and yet it's funny that Pagans don't respect their own magic enough.

Do you have a vision of where you would like to see Paganism go in the future?

As much as I'm for a professional priesthood, one of the wonders of Earth-based religions is that we are hearth centered. That we can do the basic kinds of things that a Christian minister would do in the community, pastoral counseling, teaching, performing ceremony, weddings, etc. I think that what's wonderful about Paganism is that we do have the coven, or the family model.

A coven is a nonbiological family. Spiritual practices, religious practices, and personal experiences get a chance to happen in small groups. I guess that's what I would like to see continue.

Is there anything else you have been thinking about?

My favorite soapbox right now is the class issue. Disenfranchised groups are often empowered by Pagan religions. If you look at the Italian myth of Aradia, she was sent down to the Italian peasants to help them rebel. Over and over again there are stories of the fey folk helping the oppressed. The Native Americans have used their magic to try to empower themselves. But what often happens, and it really infuriates me, is that the ideas get appropriated. I think it's also a lack of respect for poor white culture. It's classism. By disrespecting it and turning it into some sort of intellectual upper-class paradigm, then we disempower poor whites. That's one of my pet peeves right now.

We're talking about a professional priesthood, and nobody is looking at the biggest professional Pagan priests around, the fortune tellers. There are still people practicing very traditional magic called fortune tellers. But they are too hokey, too weird, too macabre, too mystical. Good grief! These people are in the community practically hearing the confessions that people are afraid to bring to the Catholic priests. They are dealing with social dilemmas that the social workers aren't getting. Half the time they are referring women into battered women's shelters. They are telling young pregnant girls what they can do about it. They are counseling people in ways that priests and psychologists may never get a chance to because some people will not go to a priest or a psychologist.

But we are not looking towards that model. I think it's in part because we are afraid of our Paganism, because we don't trust our magic. That's too hokey. It's not Episco-Pagan enough. And it really bothers me. Of course, a lot of my anger comes from being a working-class woman, but since I believe the personal is political, that's fine.

Is there anything else?

There is one other thing I want to say. The fact that Paganism is based in small family units gives people a chance to talk with one another instead of being talked *at*, like in a church or some lecture authority on TV. Because of that, Paganism gives us a chance to develop our own myth, our own sense of being uniquely sacred.

I hope that when people read your book, they don't just read it. I hope that they sit down and talk with each other about it, because that's where the magic will come from. Not from reading it and then considering themselves an authority on your book. Because magic tells us that we are all our own authority.

VICTOR ANDERSON, the most important exponent of the Feri/Faery Faith in America, is also the person responsible for bringing it to this country. Victor has been a teacher and friend to some of the most influential personalities in the Craft today, including Starhawk.

Victor's wife of fifty years, Cora Anderson, has authored the definitive text on the Faery Faith called *Fifty Years in the Feri Tradition*, which is available by mail. Getting Victor on tape proved to be an almost impossible task. The first hour-long session did not record, and only half of the second session was salvageable, as the tape inexplicably turned to gibberish whenever he touched on the deeper mysteries of the Goddess. Before the third interview was conducted some heavy Hebrew and African (Dahomean) prayers were said and written on a sheet of paper that was placed on the tape recorder. That time it worked.

This interview was pieced together from conversations by phone between May 9 and May 13, 1994.

So are you a Pagan, and how long have you been one?

I would answer that very simply. I have been a Pagan all through this life and all the lives before that I am able to have any memory of.

Where did you get your training?

From the Gods and from those who were of the same way and path as myself. I have always been of the mystic. I studied Kabbalah extensively in Spain in previous lives. In this life I teach Kabbalah.

Do you have your past-life memories intact?

I remember a lot about my past lives. I remember the Japanese, the Siberian, the Hawaiian; I began doing this when I was very young. When I was born as who I am now, I did not lose my identity. I remember what it was like to be born. I remember where I was previous to my birth.

I have been all over this good old world. I saw the Russian Revolution, I saw World War I; it was a really interesting little trip I had there. I can also remember our Civil War; I remember the sound of the guns—I was just a tiny little boy. They mistook me for a Negro because I was Hawaiian. Later I was in the medical corps.

I remember back to when I came from another star system to the earth, but that does not make me like a New Ager who says, "Behold, I am from Mars!" or some such rot. I am a human being, a child of our Mother Earth, but the universe is the universe and we should not think of our earth as something separate. It's just like if you come from one of the South Sea islands. You might come from Samoa, Tonga, or Tahiti; you are still Polynesian. It's the same way when you are a human being. A soul is a soul. If you can remember back to another time when you had a life on another world, so what? They are just planets.

Did most people who are alive today come from other worlds originally?

I don't think so. It's difficult to explain. I would say that there are old souls and there are new souls. Souls are not something that were created just once and left hanging around to be born thousands of times. That's ridiculous nonsense. There are souls that are very young and souls that are quite old. I am sure that there are people who can remember that they came from another planet, but that is not something that makes a person better than anybody else unless they came through as an advanced person, as someone who is really seeking knowledge.

I belonged to a small blue-skinned people who were about four feet, eight inches tall. Some of those people lived here on earth too. The very nature of the human form as it is now being understood by the study of DNA shows that what we are is an expression of the elements of which we are made. It is not completely ridiculous to think of the human form or even the form of a cat as being from another galaxy or a planet that is distant from here.

If the elements follow their own nature, they will link up in various ways. That is the way we look at so-called "alien" life. We are often ridiculed when we speak of aliens with human shapes. Yet those are precisely the kinds of beings who would be most interested in us, because they are more akin to us.

I do not believe in using the UFO theory to explain everything that happens.

What about all of these UFO abductions that people are claiming are going on right now. Do you think that is really happening?

I think some of it is. Abdul Al Azarid, the mad Arab who wrote part of *The Necronomicon* warned us to "beware of the cruel celestial spirits." One of my ancestors was Ali Ben Rashid, who helped invent algebra. The word "algebra" comes from *algebran*, which means "the numbers." The word "chemistry" comes from our word for the dragon—*alchimer*.

Victor, you and I have had some discussions about sexual practices in the Craft. Could you please restate your position?

"The quickest way to create evil spirits in the human body is to give the pleasures of the Gods to a herd of swine." That means that sexuality itself is not what is wrong; the erotic is not what is wrong. "Sin" is to hurt. In the Hawaiian language they say, "No hurt, no sin." If you have the right kind of sexual conduct and activity, it's not the passion or the erotic or the intensity that is the problem. It's the vile practices such as sadomasochism, refusing to respect the commitments of others, and throwing sex around like a child playing in its own excrement. That's what we despise.

We also say that Aidan Kelly's book is an insult to the Italian people. He uses vile language and uses the four-letter "f" word all over the place. He quotes me and twists it into something filthy. I said, "The union with God is ultimately sexual." I meant that in the highest and most beautiful sense. I don't mean celibate or pseudo-pure. I mean natural, very natural. He took that and used that as justification to put forth the so-called Ten Commandments of the Goddess in his book. There is no such thing as the Ten Commandments of the Goddess. There is no such thing as a Dianic Book of Shadows. He gives spurious and false ideas about how the Italian Witchcraft got started, about how the Strega [Italian traditional witches] got started. He claims that these people were the beginners of the Craft. That is not true. The Craft has been here since before Roman times. It existed all over the world as the religion of the common people and the hidden way that was pre-Christian. It was the worship of the Gods.

I am intimately connected with Italian Witchcraft—*Vicia, La Vechia Religione*—as well as the Craft in Mexico and the Hawaiian Islands. I deeply resent the kind of filth that Aidan Kelly has put forth, and he lied about me also. I did not have childhood diabetes; I never had it. My blindness which I suffer from now was never complete. It lasted for a period of about three months, and it was due to an accident when I was two years old. No disease or neglect caused it.

I was trained in the recovery of sight by Mexican *brujas* [Witches] and Yaqui Indians in Mexico. I was not born in Gemini, New Mexico; there is no such place. I was born in Clayton, New Mexico, in Green County. I could look across the Rio Grande and see Mexico. I grew up with Mexican people and with *indios* [Indians]. My tradition is authentic. If anybody else wants to practice something, no matter how weird or offbeat, let them do it. If they want to shit, let them use their own latrine, but leave my house alone.

How can one identify the "genuine" Faery tradition?

We worship "God" as a feminine being. When we say "Goddess," we don't mean something aside. We mean the Deity. It is the same as Ishtar, as Astaroth, as Belili. The Ancient One, the Oldest of all Deities, the Mother of All the Gods. The Holy Ghost Herself. We speak of Her as the Holy Virgin. Not because She doesn't have sex, but because She is complete within Herself. She is both male and female, the same as Cibele.

Another difference is that we came out of Africa, more than twenty thousand years ago. We have scattered all over this world. The Menehune of the South Seas, the Leprechaun of Ireland, were all named for our people. These are small humans, not just nature spirits. They are "the Little People." We came out of Africa as a pygmy population. We became large when we mixed with other races a long time ago in Ireland and Scotland and Spain. Before that we were very small. I am racially related to the Little People. Kelly says that I made that up because I got it out of a book. I say to him, "Did Martin Luther King get his negritude out of a white man's library?"

I am connected with Santeria and Voudon, and I am proud of it. That happened because the Faery tradition came out of Africa. It is African. It is just as African as if my skin were black. There is more in it that is not of the white man's way than there is of it.

We are old, we are not just in the Celtic areas. We are in Siberia and Japan and all over the South Pacific. The Native Americans of the mainland know about us. We have a code of honor that is just as powerful and demanding as Japanese Bushido. Many of our religious concepts are identical with the religious teachings of Shinto.

One reason I was taught about these things is because I am part Native American and part Polynesian, and I *know* what I am talking about. The white-skinned peoples, before the coming of the Christians, had the same beliefs. The Druids, for example, were the flower of the Faery tradition. In places like Finland and Norway they had the same beliefs. It was called *Vitka*, which is the origin of the word "witch."

Does anything of the Druids still exist, and if so where would one find it?

In Wales and in certain parts of Ireland but especially in Wales. There is a Storm-Faced God in Wales who is an ancient remnant. If one went to Carnarvon in Wales and showed that one was interested in their music or their language or even in their ways, if one showed a loving interest in the people and if one showed respect for the Goddess Cerridwen, then they would look you up. You can't look *them* up because if you try to find them, you never will. But they are there.

They speak of the Holy Wells and they speak of the Three Form Goddess: Anna, Nimue, and Mari. Hw [pronounced "hoo"] and Esus are the Divine Twins who are Her consort. Esus is a word in a Gallic tongue which was spoken in northern France and parts of Britain at the time the Romans got there.

Esus is actually derived from the African Esu [pronounced "eshu"], which is very old, actually older than the human race. Esu was sometimes mistaken as the Devil by Christians who tried to convert the slaves who were brought into Brazil. In our tradition we have an image of Esu in red, like a human person with horns and an erect phallus, who holds a trident in his right hand. The Christians mistook him for their Devil because they took our Horned God for their Devil.

Hw can be either one of the Divine Twins. It means "The One Who the Mother Sought in Her Desire." It is considered to be one of the aspects of the Divine Consort. Darvel would be the God of the waters, or of the underworld, but it would be the same God.

There is a word "Hw," which also represents the female, the Goddess Herself. "Hw Holi," just like the dove says. That is in the Welsh tradition. Even our word "Cerridwen" which means "white treasure" is Welsh. We use Welsh, Irish, Hebrew, and many different languages in the Faery faith.

In the theology of my religion, of my Craft, God is a feminine being, but She is both male and female. She is called the Holy Virgin because She is complete within Herself. But She is not without sex. Through Her Divine lust She desired two bright spirits whom She brought out of the darkness and carried within Her until they were worthy to be Gods and brought them forth as the Divine Twins which are Her dual consort. They are exactly alike and one can play one part and one can play another, or they can both blend together like two flames of a candle. They are the God.

Is one dark and the other light? Are they the powers of Dark and Light?

They can be. But they are *exactly* alike. It is said in Islam that Allah lit seven candles before the throne. That comes from the older, pre-Islamic idea that the two flames were lit before the Deity.

I am not completely sure myself whether Mohammed was as much against women as the people who put up what he said and called it *Al Quran*. What about the woman who stood with him at twilight and spoke to him at length and he would not allow any of his followers to hear what they were saying? She was a prophetess. He also was said to have ridden upon Buraq, which was the white mare. The same old Goddess of inspiration, the same muse. Like Epona of the Celts.

Islam means living in peace. They are not really living by "Islam," I don't think. When I meet someone who is pure Arabic, I will touch my heart and say, "*Salaam alaikum*"—"Peace be with you always." I do not feel I am saying anything contradictory to what I believe if I say "*Allahu Akbahr*," but I know that other people wouldn't understand.

In Islam they have the three parts of the soul just like we do. One is called Nof, the other is Ruh, and then Al Sir, the Secret One, the Bright One, which is also referred to in the Quran as "The Star of Allah" that watches over us at all times, asleep or awake. It is the spirit of the soul, the soul star.

Robert the Bruce of Scotland always got the Little People out of the way when he fought the British. He told his soldiers, "Be sure and evacuate the women, children, and the Little People." They had a treaty with the small people. They knew they weren't big enough to fight with the weapons they had in those days. They would get behind a tree like the tropical pygmies and shoot you with a poisoned dart, but generally they got out of the way. They were feared by all different races because of their magic.

The Scandinavians treated them beautifully. They never abused the Little People. They would trade with them—iron for cured meat and fish. The Little People were expert hunters and fishermen, and they needed iron to make weapons with. They called them *Vitka* (female) or *Vitki* (male).

People often confuse the nature spirits with the Little People because the Little People were so skillful in speaking to the nature spirits. The nature spirits were the Gods of the Little People. They spoke to the Gods of the forest and of the rivers, and their Supreme One is the same ancient Goddess. The word "Vitka" became "Wicca" and "Witch," so a Witch used to be a race as well as a person who practiced the Craft.

Is that why they used to say that "the Sight" got handed down? Because it was genetic?

True. "Snow White and the Seven Dwarfs" was started as a legend of a coven led by a female priestess. There were originally eight dwarfs, which would be the nine with their holy queen. She was a woman of Wales who was blond, very fair rather than dark. Later they cut it down to seven dwarfs. As a matter of fact, the dwarfs were her eight husbands, literally, and they were of the Faery people.

We say that if all three souls are straight within you, you can speak to the Goddess directly, as lovingly and as normally as you speak with each other. The Gods need us and we need them, and there is a Divine Mother Goddess who is complete in Herself.

Do you have anything to say about the people who are practicing Druidism today in America or in England?

I have no ill will toward them. They are doing the best they can to follow the old ways. They are fulfilling a need, and I would certainly not say a thing against them. I may not agree with them, but I will not say a thing against them because they are doing as well as they can, and they *are* doing some good things.

The British Druids have been keeping the respect for Stonehenge and Glastonbury alive. In the United States there are some genuine ancient Druids in the southern states. I am very reluctant to say much about them, but they do exist in the Appalachian mountains, in Alabama and Tennessee and Kentucky. They brought it with them from Scotland and other places.

There is a lot of misunderstanding about Druidism and about Witchcraft. The word "Witchcraft" means "the Craft of the wise" and even in one sense "women's wisdom." A lot of people in the Pagan community are just throwing things around, and they hurt people by doing that because they make us look like irresponsible people.

Do you feel that this is a universal religion that is found everywhere?

Yes, indeed.

And is this something that people can discover on their own if they develop a relationship with the land?

Yes, indeed. I have the degree of Grand Master in my tradition. But is has to be understood that I earned that degree in the same way that a Japanese martial artist earns his or her degree. I worked for it. We are not an elitist religion that says we are the only ones who have the truth. Our religion is of the soil and of the common people, the working people. It is a religion of freedom. We have people who are specialists just like you would have specialists in the field of medicine or physics or anything else. We love and respect our masters and priests in the same way that the Shinto people of Japan respect their Sensei and for the same reasons.

You seem to have ties to many different cultures. One time when we were talking you mentioned the Strega in Italy and a certain cave outside of Palermo, Sicily.

Yes. In this cave is this bowl, and at the bottom of the bowl is carved a queen bee, like a cross between a bee and a lady. There are five drones circling around her. Then there is a jar that people use to put their offerings in. [Honey is offered to the Goddess as Queen Bee in the bowl.] There is a statue in the cave—as we would say in Hawaii, a Tiki. It's a statue of a Goddess as Melissa. She is called Our Lady of the Labyrinth. I am not permitted to give details, but there is a picture there of a man reclining at the feet of a priestess who is holding an object in her left hand and there is a bee over her head. I am telling you that so that those who know will understand that I know what I am talking about.

The tradition of bringing offerings to a cave or to the Goddess, is that a part of the Faery tradition?

Yes it is. Of course, we don't have caves here.

I have news for you, I just spent the whole morning in a cave here in Massachusetts, and I made offerings to the Goddess, so we do have caves! I took Mark Roblee, who is one of your priests. We were chanting and singing.

Isn't he wonderful? I've taught him a lot, and he has learned a lot on his own, and he has learned from Francesca Dubie. I have also given him the head-washing rite of the Vodoun. The word is *Maître tête*, which means "master of the head." I am not completely sure of my spelling, though I do speak Creole.

What does that mean when you are a "master of the head"?

The head refers to your personal God, your third and high Spirit. The soul is made of three parts. In Hawaiian we speak of the part of the soul that occupies the part of the astral body that is shaped like ourselves as *Unihipili*, which means "the breathing, emotional, sticky one."

The other part of the soul is *Ke Uhane Malama,* which is the auric body, or the "body of light." The third part is *Ke Aumakua.* That is your personal God, your parental spirit, the highest part of you.

Is that what we would call your "higher self"?

In a sense it is. But people stumble over the word "self." The word "self" is not so easily translated back from the real Hawaiian meaning. The word is *Uhane Kahi Kolu,* which means "the soul-which-is-three-in-one."

That sounds very Celtic.

It is. In fact the black bird symbolizes that same Higher Being. [Crows and ravens are sacred to the Goddess Morrigan, Cerridwen, and others in the Celtic tradition. In the northern traditions of Scandinavia female sorceresses often use the crow as a spirit animal to help them "fly." Male sorcerers commonly use the raven as an aid to Astral Travel.] There are three grades of spirit or selfhood, but they are like the orbits of the atom; they are not empty. There are three definite entities that comprise our soul, and each is whole and conscious of being us. But they can live separately if they are split apart.

Is that something that you want to do or not, split them apart?

Of course not. In Hawaiian we call it *Ka mahele* or "the fission." It happens when a person dies a very cruel death or when a person gets schizophrenia or a split personality. So the Unihipili is the one that takes care of your physical body, keeps your memories, creates your passions, your fears, and your desires. That doesn't mean that the other two don't do that. That's another thing that the *Haoli* [white people] make a mistake about. They have to label everything and put it in jars. Those of us that are Kahuna, we don't do that. We see all life as one. You don't have to say that this one does that and the other one doesn't. We are a trinity. The minute you say that, then they speak of Father, Son, and Holy Ghost. But if you say, "You are a trinity," they get mad. When I say things like that, people think I am hitting Christianity in a mean-hearted way, and I am not. I am simply pointing out where they don't think right. In reality, the Christians worship the same Trinity that we do, only in sort of a twisted way. The Holy Ghost is the oldest of the Gods. She's the Mother of All.

She is Sophia, Holy Wisdom.

That's right. And what more beautiful word than "Holy Ghost"? She who haunts the Universe and sings Her lullaby between the stars in the darkness of the night. As one Catholic priest friend of mine put it, "The warm-breasted dove that circles the earth and fills the waters with love."

You can read all about this in Cora's book *Fifty Years in the Feri Tradition*. I met her in her astral body years before we met in this plane. We were married in three days, and we have been together for fifty years. No fights, no quarrels, we work together. That's something, you know? We just celebrated our fiftieth anniversary, and we are as much in love as ever.

There is a Hawaiian family that has adopted us as their love parents; they just threw a big celebration for us for our fiftieth wedding anniversary. There were over fifty people there, even from Hawaii.

So you don't feel a need for a group marriage or many wives all over the place?

I'll tell you why I've had to be very conscious about that. You have to remember that I am not pure white. I am part Polynesian. In Hawaii and in Tahiti we did have polygamy. But it was based on what we call *Aloha*, love and respect, tenderness. We didn't dichotomize between sex and love. We didn't even know we had bodies until the missionaries came and told us that we did! The body is you. As long as you are alive, it is you. It is the lower part which we call "the body of two waters," *Kino Wailua* [lower body, root chakra]. That is the Unihipili and the Ke Uhane Malama together.

Some people will tell you that the spirit body looks exactly like the physical body, but it does not. It is approximately human in form, but it can change its shape. When you look upon it with etheric vision, you will see it as a sort of blue gray, extending about two centimeters off of the flesh. It can glow pink in certain people.

I've seen that in people who were very developed.

If you jog or exercise or breathe deeply, it can glow a brilliant pink, but when you are quiet it will go back to the blue gray. The aura, of course, has different colors in it. The true auric body extends about nine inches off of the body. It is kind of flat. The *Ke Aumakua* [divine self, upper body] dwells at the top and it's very hard to see, but when you do see it, it appears as a ball of blue light. It is about nine inches or less in diameter.

Does everybody have it?

Oh yes, indeed. It can grow if it takes on extra astral matter, extra "manna" or "life force." It is both male and female. In some cases they will refer to it as "your Heavenly Father," but it is also "Father-Mother." This is the original God that was spoken of in the very ancient Jewish Craft. "Thou shalt have no other Gods before me" means don't let yourself be used by Gods that are not yours; if you have all three souls straight within you, don't do it.

If you know these things, you are a Kahuna. That means you are a specialist. I am Kahuna Ana Ana, which means I have some powers which are pretty strange! I believe that the Kahuna tradition is a martial art just as truly as the Ninja are in Japan. It is a martial way. It is not pacifist in any sense. If they can't have the same regard for their honor as the Bushido, then they should not play with it.

These things are very difficult for most people to understand. One time I was speaking to a lady who was taking notes. I was speaking about the Hawaiian Fire Goddess Pele, the one who is associated with volcanoes. I referred to her as "our Fire Goddess." The lady wrote down in her notes, "The Fire Goddess of the Faery tradition lives in a crater in the Hawaiian Islands." That's what people do with these things!

Can you talk some more about your Spanish and other traditions that you have brought into the Faery tradition?

As I have said before, I have Spanish roots. That gives me a tie to the near eastern black people. Their roots are actually in Iran as well as in the Arabic traditions of Spain. Because of that we also refer to God as Allah. We don't see any reason to think of Allah as strictly the male chauvinist idea of Deity as it is in Christianity and Islam as it has been practiced for so long. The word has an *ah* on the end of it, after all, which means "The Supreme One." "Al-lah."

Didn't Allah have a female aspect originally called Allat?

The supreme Deity was first worshipped as a feminine being, just as we do. Allat was one of the names of the Deity manifesting powerfully in the Mother.

That was also the Father-Mother form. The other word, "Allah," was used to bring in the male potency of God. The color of the ray that came through with that was green. That is why in Islam the flag is green.

According to Islam the color of the highest heaven is green . . .

Yes, and I am speaking of the mystic tradition of Islam. In my tradition of the Craft we regard the word "Allah" as most holy, never to be defamed, never to be disrespected. If the people in Islam do all these terrible things like abusing women and cutting off people's heads, that is their sin. But we will not disrespect the name of God. Allah is holy. That's our attitude.

The Craft also has roots in Araby. Words like Esbat [minor festival] and Sabbat [high or major festival] are Arabic in origin. Many of the priestesses in England during the terrible persecutions were shielded and taught by Arabic men and women. Everybody in Araby is not orthodox Islamic, you know. There is an underground there just like there is here.

What do they worship?

They worship God, but they have a different idea about it. What the people of the Craft are against there is destructive kinds of worship. They had one God put on them just like it was done in Europe. The religion of the Arabic countries was gradually formed into this monotheistic idea because some people were disgusted with losing their power by having a natural, polytheistic religion. There were also people in Araby who were abusing the polytheistic religion.

Old Araby was quite feminist. We don't have to think of Allah and Allat as two different Gods, although they will say that in Islam.

The Kaaba was originally a shrine to the Father-Mother, Allah-Allat.

Yes. Those of us who are part Arab can hear the words as they really are. Others use a word, and they know what it is supposed to mean, but they don't *hear* it correctly. They hear it the way they would hear the word "green" or "red." Those of us who are part Arab can hear the words in a different way. That is why we can speak about it with some enlightenment.

As an elder, are there any problems that you see cropping up in the Craft that need to be addressed?

Yes. The first is the problem in dealing with human relationships. That needs to be straightened out. They are also too prone to deal with our theology and magic as a system of beliefs. They are making the same mistake as the Christians, fighting over a cauldron which was almost emptied during the Burning Times.

They are having parties and all kinds of ridiculous nonsense instead of paying attention to the real magic. They should be recovering how we are made as human beings, how our relationships work, how we relate to the Gods and the Goddesses and how they relate to us.

The Gods are not just concepts. There was an article in *Green Egg* about Pan, and they treated him as an abstract symbol or an archetype of a principle in nature and not as a person. In Greek the word *pan* means "all." He would be the Horned God, the same old God of hunting and dancing as in Ireland. One of the Greek names for the Goddess is Ibanagia or All Holy One.

I would like to say to the younger people who are coming up in the Craft that the Gods are real. We belong to the same life chain, the same ecology as the Gods. They do not have physical bodies as we do, but they are our Divine parents. We are their children, and we are all living the same life, the life of the universe. We should remember that God is Self and Self is God. God is a person like myself. Always keep your own identity, always have dignity and respect for one another, especially for commitments and bonds.

Remember that whenever you make love or have sex you are repeating the same process by which God Herself gave birth to the universe. It has to be treated with respect because all things which are worthwhile are dangerous. All magic which works is essentially black. Treat it with reverence or let it alone. Don't play with your sexuality as a baby plays in its own excrement. Try to be decent. Have honor. Honor yourselves and your loved ones. If you don't respect yourself, how do you expect anyone else to respect you?

Learn to perceive before you believe. Perceive first and then study scientifically to learn what you must believe. You don't have to accept everything you believe. If you believe that there are vile spirits, you don't have to go out and worship them.

Also don't be ashamed of the word "belief." It's not a bad word. We all have theories because we are not all-knowing. Even blind faith will have a purpose. If your loved one is in the hospital dying and the doctor says "he or she might not live another hour" and you believe with all of your soul that the person will, it *will* help, whether you have a reason for it or not. There are things that are older than what we call reason. They were there before our brains ever evolved.

Also try to remember that we are animals. We are not some special thing made into the image of a male God. We are animals, and many times we are far worse than our four-footed sisters and brothers. Try to remember that "the black heart of innocence," as is so often spoken of in our Craft, is purely sexual in meaning. It means "How beautiful is the black lascivious purity in the heart of children and wild animals." And "Except ye become as children ye cannot enter the kingdom of the Gods."

The quickest way to create evil spirits in human bodies is to give the pleasures of the Gods to a herd of swine. Don't be swine. Walk on two legs and say, "I am and God is," whether you mean the Deity or all of the Gods within and throughout and round and about without doubt.

Is there anything else you want to say?

Yes. They have the idea that everyone who gets initiated is made into a bona fide Witch right there, all ready to go. That is not true. An initiation is literally a marriage to the Goddess and the Gods. To rejoin the life chain from which we evolved both spiritually and biologically is an engagement to Our Lady and Her consort that just sets us on the path.

The Goddess says to her priest, "I love you with the same love a mortal woman loves you with but raised to the power of Divinity." And to the woman she says, "I love you with the same love that a man or woman loves you but raised to the power of Divinity."

The ultimate nature of the union with God *is* sexual, so don't abuse your sexuality, or you will go through life after life undoing what you have done to others and to yourself. Take part in the creation and evolution of your ecology, or the Mother Earth might conceive of you one day as a cancer that needs to be gotten rid of. As a priest of the Goddess and the Gods, I have warned you of this.

Remember that your teachers are to be respected in the same way that the Japanese respect their Sensei in the martial arts. I am a Grand Master because I earned that in the same way that a practitioner of the martial arts earns that.

It is not true that a person has to have a highly trained priest or priestess to form a coven and worship the Gods. Anyone can do it. To say that you couldn't would be like saying that you have no right to play music unless you have a professional teacher. But don't claim Grand Mastership unless you have earned it. People are always hollering about how Witchcraft is not a hierarchy and so on, but it is also not just a "dog eat dog" thing where everyone has a right to their own opinion in the most pseudo-democratic way possible. That's no way to do anything; that's anarchy, it isn't the Craft. It's just a bunch of people using their psychic powers as an excuse to get out and have a rip-roaring, so-called good time, when all they are doing is destroying themselves and other people and their relationships.

I say wake up and respect your Sensei and your teachers, whatever you call them in whatever language. Let's have honor. Honor for yourself and for others. My Craft has a code of honor that is as strict as Japanese Bushido, and in many ways it is quite identical to Shinto.

Is there anything you would like to say to Americans about American culture?

One of the cruelest things they have done to themselves is having an insulting idea about God. They picture God as a monster. We in the Craft speak of a "false God." People are doing terrible things in His name, making the people believe that he is the king. But God is God. These televangelists and these people who are against abortion are against the dignity of sexuality, against a woman's freedom. These same people are hollering about killing off everybody, the Jews and the Negroes, and having the white race reign supreme in the name of Yahweh. They are under the influence of a vile spirit. Cora explains in the book *Fifty Years in the Feri Tradition* who that spirit is. The Mormons have a peculiar way of believing the same thing. It is a little different from our belief, but it comes from the same source.

The Little People called him Bung. There are actually two of them. They are not the Divine Twins. Bung the Good is also a Prince of Darkness, and he is against Bung the Filthy One, and they fight constantly. Each hates the other. That is really what people should have understood instead of inventing the Christian's Devil, which is mostly spurious and false.

Even the word "Satan" is not evil. Even the word "Bung" itself is not evil. It simply means someone who strikes something. Sir Arthur Conan Doyle mentions this in his book *The King of Elfland's Daughter*. He went to New Zealand and noticed a striking similarity between the Maori people and the Little People that I am related to. He tells about that in his book *A Journey of a Spiritualist*.

What I want to tell America is to get rid of racism. Stop abusing the Negroes because when you are, you are abusing your own ancestors. We *all* came from Africa. Those who walked out of Africa were bleached white by the northern climates, by the cold, because they no longer needed melanin in the skin.

Then we came back in the name of the false God and enslaved the black man. We committed vile sins in our Mother's own house and fouled the cradle of our birth. Now we had better start paying for it by treating these people right. Because they *are* our ancestors. Don't despise Vodoun because it's one of the forms of the oldest of all religions. Don't hate Santeria because we have animal sacrifice. We don't have human sacrifice; that is a lie told by the white man. And stop thinking that you are better than everybody else, the Mexicans and everybody else. Texas was stolen from Mexico, and Mother Mexico is not for sale. I am not a racist, but I know a gringo when I see one and I don't like them.

Paganism from Norway, Greece, Egypt, Israel, and Italy

Paganism as practiced in the United States is most closely associated with the traditions of the northern regions of Europe and Britain. This includes many Witches, Druids, and other Pagans that draw from mainly "Celtic" origins. But just as in this country there was a staggering diversity of religious beliefs among America's native peoples before the coming of white European settlers, there was and continues to be a rich tapestry of non-Celtic traditions that can still be considered Pagan being introduced in America from around the world.

In this chapter we are introduced to two followers of the Egyptian Goddess Isis, a Greek traditionalist, a Jewish Pagan, a Norse rune mistress (spaewife), and an Italian Strega.

SOLFINNA (SUN FINDER) is a Norse traditional priestess and teacher of rune magic and lore of the spakone, or spaewife. She brings a distinctively non-Celtic branch of European Paganism to America. She was interviewed at Ecumenicon in Washington, D.C., in July 1993.

Were you raised as a Pagan?

In a way, yes. One of my grandmothers was Norse traditional. She had to hide it though, because it was not done to be non-Christian in a Christian world. But she managed to teach me plenty before she died. My mother was essentially a "blue domer," as in the blue dome of the sky. That was like a liberal Unitarian type with overtones of Christian Science in the sense of "let the body heal itself out in nature."

I am a Norse traditional spakone [pronounced spaukoona], a spaewife; that's the English word that is the closest correspondent to it. Wife in the sense of older woman rather than married woman.

Crone?

Not necessarily crone, but mature woman. One who does divination, one who can do some of the older folk things, folk wisdoms, lores. I don't have too much in the way of herbalism, some runes.

Is there anything that you can tell us about what your grandmother taught you when you were very young?

My grandmother would go up in a room, and she'd tell me about the way of the water, how water moved, how you just sank into various things, how you became them. It was like an art lesson. She was also a very fine artist. She'd say we were going to have an Art lesson. The rest of my family didn't know it was capital A, not lowercase a. So in teaching me how to paint the sea, she would teach me to *see* the sea. Or when looking at a flower, she'd teach me how to see it, to observe it. And she'd be passing along as much as she could about old ways.

In my studies since she died I've learned how much she had forgotten. Fortunately, there are enough ethnographers, enough researchers who from medieval times in Scandinavia have documented a lot of these things.

What we are talking about then is family tradition. When did you first discover postmodern American neo-Paganism?

When I first discovered that was after I got out of college, out of grad school. I think it was when I first started working at my university job, and there was a bookstore downtown which was called the Sixth Sense. They had these wonderful candles, and all these books on all this stuff, and so I bought one or two and I talked to people there, and it was so obvious that what I was doing was different from whatever they were doing.

Then they put me in touch with a local Gardnerian coven, and we sniffed each other over. You know how dogs sniff each other over to say howdy. So we sniffed each other over to say howdy, and they said, "Please come over to play with us." I was so strong in my tradition, and terribly curious: I'd never practiced with anybody in a circle. I was so excited, but they were getting it out of a book. It was cookbook stuff. I didn't feel any power in their circle. It turns out they were far more interested in sucking my brains then I was in theirs.

So they went from wearing their black robes to wearing white robes the way I do. They were fascinated. It was like somebody picking up an aborigine who was a full practicing shaman of his people.

Did your grandmother teach you about the white robes?

Yeah, pretty much. She wore what she had. You didn't have necessarily white, but it was light, something you could you really move in. As in the Sami [Lappish] way, with the Norse way there is a great deal that you are guided to by your spirits for your own sense of what is magically right. For example, a Tarot deck does not feel right in my hands. I have never even attempted divination with the Tarot.

So this stuff from my grandmother, much of it was lost, filtered out from her mother and back because it had to be so hidden. Husbands didn't know about it. I'm the most open one probably in easily six or seven generations.

And this is women's magic?

Yes, it's called *Kvennagaldr*. That mean's specifically women's magic. Or women's *galdr*. Galdr being a magic form in which one uses a song or some sort of spoken element. That is only one segment of what I do. For example, I could be called in for birthing magic when a woman is having a birthing, to keep away evil or malign influences.

Have you done this?

Yes, not with childbirth, but with protecting and leading up to the birth. In the Norse healing circles that we do at Etheracon and Ecumenicon, we've done fertility magic for those who want to conceive but haven't for some reason. We set up a ring. We have a circle of fifty-plus trained people, and we put our minds right down to where the basics are—in other words, "Humma Humma!" In other words, insert part A into slot B. Put it right down there where the erotic is.

We have that next to last because we have that sort of for dessert. We have the harder healing ahead of time, but everyone can hardly wait for the fertility magic. It's a wonderful thing. We send it around and send the energy into the couple, both to the man and the woman, that they may conceive a healthy child.

Have any babies resulted from this?

Oh, yes. The Sheeleys' baby. It was born prematurely. They thought it was going to have all sorts of breathing problems, but it was fine. Last year at Etheracon, there were two or three babies in the circle whose parents we'd done the magic on the year before.

Is this something you got through research or from your grandmother?

It comes from a lot of sources. The basics I got from my grandmother, but you tune up, you never stop learning, and in many cases as you develop and learn, it blurs where everything comes from. A lot of the basic philosophy and basic goals, ways of looking at things, ways of seeing and of becoming I learned as a child. For example, on a foggy day you become the fog so that if you wish to clear the fog away from a place to which you are going, you wish away the fog. Since you are part of the fog, you know how to push it away.

You are a teacher of Norse Paganism. How is that different from Wicca or the Druid path?

We are influenced by elements in the Sami tradition, which is the Lappish shamanic way, particularly in the northern areas of Norway and Sweden. There's a great big overlap, pun intended, in the traditions . . . particularly in the folk-healing things.

How is your group different?

We are unique in that we don't necessarily have "high priest" and "high priestess." We have guides rather than priest and priestess. It's much more of a folkish way of doing it, rather than an organized way. The nature of the group is that people are welcome to experiment. People are welcome to bring in new things. For example, one of our people is a quarter Comanche. So he can do his stuff in the circle as well. The Norse types shamelessly borrowed and stole from anybody. And we shamelessly teach and get stolen from in return. I am trying to teach some of the Norse words. It's difficult for some people. It's work. But they are learning with the rune staff.

The rune staff is a length of wood which is rectangular or square in cross-section. It's not round or dowel type. Upon it is inscribed or written a wand spell. The business end or the end which is not in your hand generally has a depiction of a horse's head on it. On the end towards you, you would have your name written in runes, in bind runes, which are runes written on top of each other so the pattern looks sort of like a snowflake. It's a secret kind of writing so that you and the Powers That Be would know what was meant, but somebody else would not be able to pick out your working magical names.

With the rune staff, you are able to learn what the runes are and the powers associated with them so they can be used for visualization. Unlike a lot of the "neo" groups, we do not do ridiculous things like forming our bodies into runes shapes and meditating on them.

There are a lot of "Norse" groups out there these days who are unfortunately not based on the traditional things. They are based on nineteenth-century and later "wannabeism" . . . the German, Pan-Germanic movement. They think they are Norse groups, but they are German wannabes.

Can you give some examples of some Germanic practices they might be doing in the name of Norse Paganism?

For example . . . using the runes. Runes were never German in origin. Runes originated in southern Denmark, Fresia area, probably for trade. Magic came much later to the use of the runes.

And they weren't Irish either...

[Laughter] . . . they weren't Irish either. But there is probably a connection between the Celts and the Norse in that the Celtic ogham has families of letters.

How are runes used in your tradition?

Most of the rune use in our tradition was not magical. And another shocker to these New Age groups is the greatest sophistication in rune magic came in Christian usage, not in Pagan times. A lot of the Pagan stuff is more shamanic. There are certain rune things that are magical, but it's not the magical runes! That is a much more romantic later period.

We're very eclectic. I try to teach as much as possible of the traditions that I know. And we do a lot of comparative stuff. We just head over to the university library, and if somebody comes up with a nice dry academic reference, that's really good, everybody goes, "Oh, goody!" And they get bored stiff by some of the books. There are many books out there by publishers who do not do their homework. They do not do their research. A lot of the stuff they claim, they have no base for.

We're trying to go back to how it was done by the people back then. Adapting some of it for living in the twentieth century. We do have [deodorant]. We do have flush toilets. There are certain benefits. We have hospitals that work. You don't have to go to a shaman hoping that he or she can go on a spirit voyage to the Land of the Dead so he can be told how to cure a patient.

Presumably everyone in your group was raised as a twentieth-century American, with American TV and the American educational system. How does the ancient Norse worldview fit into that?

It fits in very well because there are so many things people are hungry for that the American culture does not give them. For example, our quarter Comanche is hungry for what his ancestry was, what was lost by being in a modern, mundane American family. A lot of people want a non-Christian, nonmainline, nonorganized type of spirituality. We are fortunate in that in this culture one can be something really eclectic like a Unitarian, and get tax deductions from the state. You can tell a Republican blue-haired little old lady that you are a Unitarian, and she won't necessarily think that you are a kook.

We as Pagans are actively hunting for the spirituality that our forefathers fought for. We call ourselves Americans, but we all came from somewhere. One of our people has French-Canadian and Cherokee ancestry. She's looking for the Cherokee part, but she is also looking for the early French and Celtic traditions of her ancestors.

You have been writing and teaching about these things for a long time. What is your personal goal with all of this? Why are you putting out this information?

For one reason because there is so much misinformation. So many of the "Norse" groups are based on things written by Guido Von List, who was from the 1700s. He was a racist-supremacist who "discovered" the runes and this particular path. It was just something that he cooked up, but he got a bunch of his buddies to believe him and he got some patrons behind him. Some really powerful people used his writings to further their agendas—Adolf Hitler for example.

Was Hitler looking at the writings of Guido Von List?

Yes, his propaganda was directly based on those writings. The Thule Gesellschaft was Heinrich Himmler's creation especially. The Waffen-S.S. used the runes. There was a lot of this in the beliefs of the military elite of World War I as well, particularly in the Prussian military mysteries.

Too many of my parents' friends were in the resistance against the Germans. I get really scratchy when I see this stuff being passed off as "Germanic." They talk about the Vikings, but they have no idea what was really done. A great deal of the literature has only been published in Scandinavian tongues. This makes it inaccessible to the English-speaking people. There is a great hunger for this stuff.

What would you like to see happen to Norse Paganism in America?

I would like to see *far* more research done. I would like to see people who claim to be Norse Pagans actually learn the language. Then they could read the material that's out there. They could go overseas and look at the Viking ships and the rune stones. The *real* rune stones—not the Kensington stone. The Kensington stone is located in Minnesota. There are a number of people who believe that it was left by a Norse expedition to America in the 1300s. I am *absolutely* sure that this is a stone that was carved in the 1700s or later. Some of the runes are from Dalarana province or Alvedal. Rune use in those areas of Sweden has been documented to the beginning of World War II. The numbering system used on the stone is in the Latin way, not the tally way of the earlier times. They have the practice carvings from the guy who carved it. They know the whole story. All the more power to them—it makes a great tourist attraction.

If somebody could prove the date to me with laser scanning or something like that, I'd say Great! But you see I am scientifically trained. When you have been academically and scientifically trained, you want to see the proof.

THOTH is a gay Witch of an Alexandrian-derived tradition that worships the Greek pantheon. He also works as a ceremonial magician in a Pagan Kabbalistic system, and is a former editor of *Tides* magazine (no longer in publication). He was interviewed at Starwood, at the Brushwood Folklore Center near Sherman, New York, in July 1993.

Are you a Pagan?

I am a pantheist. When you delve into mythology, you begin to see the personification of various aspects of The One. Hence, you get the Mother Goddess of the Grain, Storm Gods, Sky Gods, Water Gods, Water Spirits, Air Spirits, all the different aspects. Take the Egyptian mythologies, for example, and the God for which I am named, Thoth. He is specifically a God of magic and the God of writing. He creates language.

For the Egyptians the art of writing was essential to their culture, so they personified language with an individual God and the sounds of the throat. That to me is the strong point of pantheism, that when you need to work on a particular element of the universe or your own universe, or what have you, you can find Gods that represent a specific point and you can work with that God, that symbol, or however you choose to view the Gods. A monotheistic or monistic God like Yahweh in the Judeo-Christian tradition is too vast, too illimitable. It has its appeal, but it's so remote.

Wasn't Jesus supposed to be this human intermediary for people to relate to so that God wouldn't be so inaccessible?

Yes. That is what the church has done *to* him. If you really delve into the epigraphy, what we have of his teachings, they are by no means that. It is what later interpreters have done to his work and what the church had designed the teachings of Jesus to be. I don't want a mediator between me and God. I am the mediator between me and God. I don't need to accept someone else's sacrifice. I am capable of making that sacrifice myself.

Most Pagans feel that way. They want to be the direct link to the Divine, however they perceive the Divine. This is one reason why there is a controversy between paid clergy versus laymen. Ultimately, it seems that a good portion of the various Pagan and neo-Pagan movements have always believed that everyone is a priest and everyone is a priestess. That you don't need an intermediary between yourself and the Divine. Paid clergy in our type of community would be setting up and following the old Romano-Christian imperial model. I think it's a terrible idea. I don't think that our community can successfully follow the old models of a pastor who has a parish who is supported by tithing. It is just not going to work.

What about the people who devote their entire lives to planning festivals and creating festivals?

They should be paid as administrators, not as clergy. I don't see any problem if people want to join a big umbrella organization. Their dues and membership fees should be paid as administrative costs. A distinction should be made between someone who is being paid as an administrator and someone who is being paid as a spiritual leader, because there's a big difference.

You are a Greek Pagan. What does that mean?

The original Gardnerian/Alexandrian material was very fragmentary. You found yourself invoking Cernunnos and Aradia in the original *Book of Shadows*. You were invoking an Italian/Etruscan Goddess and a Gallic/Celtic God. They are connected, but it's vague.

Years ago the coven with which I work wanted something more complete. We decided that we didn't have particularly strong ties to Celtic society. This was in the early seventies when we knew less about the Celtic people than we do now; we were limited to Lewis Spence and a few other people for our sources.

Our group has very strong Greco-Roman roots. Even our American society has those roots. Our architecture is Greek influenced; our politics are Roman. When we looked into the Greco-Roman tradition, we found that it fit perfectly. The mythic cycles of the Greek religion fit the traditional Wiccan wheel of the year—the harvest Lord and the Maiden and the Goddess and so forth. And so we chose to work with the Persephone myth.

Throughout our Sabbat cycle and all of the thirteen moons, we have a ritual cycle that tells the story of Persephone. It's timed according to the Celtic harvest cycle as opposed to the Greek because the Greek growing periods were different than what we have in New England.

When we perform the mythic cycle in our rather ceremonial Alexandrian-derived way, it is very much like Greek passion plays. Like the Eleusinian mysteries or like reading Sophocles or Euripides. The main officers, a priest and priestess, and two other officers are the principles, and the rest of the coven functions as the chorus. We chant or intone our parts; we don't just speak them. When the energy comes, you have the workings going on between the various officers and the chorus. It works like a good production of a Greek play. It's all done with the characters interacting and chanting the lines and the chorus weaving in and around.

We have several very well-educated people in our group, Ph.D.s, people who work in classical studies and ancient religions and who read the languages. So we can really draw on what we know as the scholarship continues to unfold about Greco-Roman religion. The aspects of the Gods as we worship them are very Hellenistic. We draw upon the Bronze Age and up for the elements of ritual, but the images that we use, visualizations and so forth, are from the Hellenistic period. That was the height of the mystery cults.

If there is a parallel to what we do as Wiccans, as Greek Witches, it would be the Eleusinian mysteries, the way that whole festival was choreographed with the passion plays. When you first went to the Eleusinian festival, you took the kukeon, which was a barley-water drink flavored with mint. It was probably a hallucinogen of some sort, because the barley that grows in that region is highly susceptible to ergot. The alkaloids in ergot, which are highly hallucinogenic and safe, are also water soluble. The poisonous ones are heat activated, hence the problems when you bake it in bread, which results in ergotism. So what they were using was probably a controlled hallucinogenic experience.

You were trained for a year and a half prior to the event in the symbolism. Then you would make the fourteen-mile walk from Athens to Eleusis. On various points along the way you were challenged, you were entertained, and there were several points where you took sips of this drink, the kukeon. We know about this because it is told to us in the Homeric hymns.

Once you got to Eleusis the compound of the temple had stations very much like the medieval passion plays. You were taken around, and you would see various elements of the myth of Persephone's journey. What went on in the mythic cycle at Eleusis is very much what we are in to. What is the Wiccan wheel of the year about? It's the death of the Harvest Lord, and the Maiden coming back bringing spring and leading up to a bountiful harvest and then having to return to the Underworld in winter time. That is in essence the Persephone myth.

For us the Harvest Lord is the sun. He's an aspect of Apollo. We invoke him as Helios, Hyperion, and Apollo, the trinity of the Sun God. Throughout the cycle of the year he starts out as Helios and then becomes Hyperion and then Apollo. At the end of the year he has to make the decision to become the consort of the Goddess, at which point he is sacrificed as the Harvest Lord. Then he takes his seat on the throne at Samhain as the Lord of the Dead next to Persephone, who is once again installed as Queen of the Underworld.

There is no feminine aspect for the Sun?

Not in our system. That is where the Alexandrian derivation comes in. The Goddess is the moon.

My understanding about the sun being male and the moon being female and the female being associated with the dark and the passive and the male with the bright and the active comes from Kabbalah. I know that is based on a very general reading of Kabbalah, not necessarily a deep reading of Kabbalah, but you say that you are also a Kabbalist. Can you talk about that a little?

What we have done with the Kabbalah is very similar to why we decided to work with Greco-Roman religion. It's because we have very strong ties with it in a spiritual sense. None of us are Jewish. We don't have a single person from a Jewish lineage in our group, and it's not part of our cultural background. But the glyph itself is universal, the Tree of Life. The whole beauty of the theory is that it encompasses everything in the Universe. You can find correspondences for everything and fit it on the Tree of Life. That is why the glyph is so important and why it has been used for centuries, and perhaps millennia.

We threw out the Hebrew and replaced it with Greco-Roman and Egyptian symbolism. By doing so you take Malkuth, the lowest sphere on the tree, the Earth Center, and you put Persephone there. Right away at the bottom of the Tree at the Earth level we have Persephone on the Tree of Life. That is where Wicca ties in to our ceremonial magic; it's how the two systems are linked.

Each sphere has a Greek God except for one, which has a Roman God because the Greek version of that God was much less developed. That is why

I keep saying that we are very Hellenistic, because the Greco-Roman symbolism really came into its own during the Hellenistic period from the time of Alexander's conquest in 330 B.C. to about A.D. 300, and the Hellenistic influence continued all the way up through the fall of Rome in A.D. 410.

So we have been able to create a Pagan Qabalistic system that ties right in with our Wicca. Our Wicca is our religion. It is devotional, it is emotive, it's what we do to tie us into the cycles of the planet and the moon and the sun and our environment. Our magic is our science.

You can wield magic on the Tree. Pantheism has personifications of Gods that you can work with specifically, and the Tree of Life provides you with a pattern to work with those personifications. It puts a limited number of Deities into a system with checks and balances.

If you are working with the sphere of Hod, the sphere of the intellect, the sphere of ideas, and you put a Greek name to it like Hermes, the messenger, and directly opposite him you place Aphrodite, who is the sphere of Netzach, the sphere of love and beauty, you have the two poles. You therefore have the intellect with Hermes and emotion with Aphrodite.

If you need to work on one or the other, you can work with both and create the hermaphrodite, which is the middle pillar and is the Baphomet symbol of the OTO [Ordo Templi Orientis, a tradition of ceremonial magick]. We don't actually use that image, but Baphomet is the androgyne, the balancing point between the two pillars.

In the Celtic tradition the harp does that. You have the belly of the harp, which is female, and the neck of the harp or the fore pillar, which is male and fits into the female part, and then you have the bridge between the two on top.

That's what I like about the Tree. It is all, it is sexless. It is the ultimate of androgyne to work on the Tree Of Life. You are constantly balancing. If you are working with one sphere, you are working with the stereotypical feminine, the passive, the receptive, the dark. But to move up the tree, you have to become active and fertilizing, not passive.

You may be able to do that as a feminine force, a feminine Goddess. Take Athena, for example. She is no cowering, receptive, passive figure. She is bravery, courage, wisdom, which are also attributes of Mars in the Roman period. In the Greek period when the Athenians went to war they invoked Athena for bravery and courage.

You don't have to fall into the stereotype of feminine being passive and masculine being active. We don't work that way. But we do invoke the Goddess as the moon and the God as the sun. Everything that we do is an attempt to reach the middle pillar between them. We believe very strongly that we all have the masculine and we all have the feminine. It's a matter of how and when we manifest it.

I personally believe that it's completely possible to draw the moon down on a man. Drawing the moon down actually comes from the ancient Greek. It is a technique of theurgy, a type of magic where you invoke a God down into an object for the purpose of worship. There are several accounts in ancient Greek literature about "drawing down the moon." That's probably where Gardner got it from, unless he got it from Crowley, because Gardner didn't read Greek, but Crowley did. In the original Gardnerian/Alexandrian Wicca, Drawing Down the Moon was the most important part of the circle. It is what you did when you cast your circle. The circle was not complete until the forces of the Moon Goddess were drawn down onto the priestess as a vehicle to manifest those forces on the physical plane. That was the core of original Wicca. The subsequent festival celebrations were secondary.

In traditional Gardnerian/Alexandrian Wicca you probably won't find many people who would do that on men because they deal very strongly with a sexually-based polarity system, the Alexandrians a bit less so. And that's fine. If it works for you and everyone agrees with it, that's great.

But nowadays gender is not so concretely defined. People do not want to limit their identity to their sexual orientation. I believe that we have evolved to the point where it's quite possible for certain men who have an affinity for the Goddess to manifest the moon.

Can you talk a bit about being gay or bisexual in the Pagan movement?

You will find a lot of gay people, a lot of bi-identified, and transgendered people in the Pagan community. That goes back to the attraction of pantheism. The neo-Pagan religion offers a flexibility and a freedom for acceptance and empowerment that institutionalized religions that castigate such sexual identifications don't offer.

A lot of gay people turn to Paganism because they are comfortable working with a God/Goddess polarity form of Wicca. There are a lot of gay and bisexual people who are not comfortable with that, so they seek out traditions that are less polarity oriented.

I am an avidly gay-identified Witch, very vocal and public about it, and I work with the God and the Goddess. We keep polarity in our circles for the most part. I don't view my Gods as limited by their genitalia or by who they sleep with.

When I'm invoking the Goddess, I don't think in terms of a sexual attraction to Her, though even as a gay person that energy might be there at times. My worldview is that the moment you divide the One who is at the top of the Tree of Life, the Kether, the un-manifest, it has to become two. In order to talk about the One, you first have to have two.

What is the most basic division in the world? The division between male and female. I don't have a problem with that. Some gay people do have a problem with it, but that's okay. They don't have to work this system. It's not the only system.

Have you experienced gay bashing in the Pagan community?

Yes. There have been instances where invitations to join open circles have been revoked once it was realized that I was a gay-identified individual. Most of these were with people who worked in more rigid-polarity traditions. That's really the only thing I have come across, people who don't think that gay men are capable of manifesting the God.

If anything, I believe that we are even better at manifesting the God because we *also* understand the Goddess. And many times we understand Her better than straight men do because there are elements of femininity that we encounter that most straight men never do.

Is there anything else you would like to add?

As far as being a Greek Pagan, I think it's very important for people to understand that Greek mythology as it was taught to most of us in school was Greek mythology from a very British or Germanic perspective. Edith Hamilton, for example, even though she was a woman was trained in that patriarchal system.

I have met a lot of resistance from Pagans in the community to the idea of being a Greek Wiccan. One time I was castigated by this Celtic Witch, and when I asked her to name her own pantheon, she named Cymric Gods, Welsh Gods— she couldn't name a single Celtic pantheon that she worshipped. I believe very firmly that if you are going to work in a system with any kind of continuity, you have to stick to a pantheon to a certain extent. You have to go into some depth. You can't invoke Kali one day and Durga the next and then bop over to the Morrigan.

The coven I work with has never missed a Sabbat in twenty one years. You won't find many groups that can say that. I guess what I am getting at is that there is real continuity to our system, and I hate being castigated for being a Greek Pagan when people don't understand what the Greeks were all about. The mythology is not the religion.

I look at the Greek Gods and Goddesses and what I see is a very dysfunctional family, and I don't want to relate to that. I had enough of that in my own life, thank you very much!

Those are myths. Myths serve a function that can be completely separate from religion. They are very often a cultural narrative. We are postmodern now, postenlightenment, postfeminism, post this and post that. We don't perceive the same way that the ancient world did. We will never know exactly *how* they perceived, but their religion was integral to their culture so what better way to have cultural narrative than to personify it using religious figures? We have myths today that are not religious. The myth of the Wild West, for example, gunfights in the street. That never happened.

Yes it did, for forty years.

But it has been mythologized, and it has absolutely nothing to do with religion. So cultural narratives can form that are not religious. Perhaps the only way that the Greeks could express these cultural narratives was in terms of personifications of their Gods. But the Greek religion was very distinctly different.

There are kernels of religious truth in the myths, but in order to find them you have to know the culture and the language of the Greeks. You have to know the people as much as they can be known, and it is a beautiful, complex system.

They even have the Tree of Life. It's the Caduceus. The snakes coil seven times across the staff, which symbolizes the seven chakras, the seven points on the Tree of Life. The wings are the initiate. The symbol depicts the travels of the serpent down and up the Tree Of Life. And this is just one symbol of their very complex system.

If you don't feel an affinity to what you think are more "appropriate" forms of Wicca, then take a look at other things. Really delve into them. There are systems out there that are complete. But you are not going to pull a Llewellyn book off the shelf, any book, published by Yale or whatever, and get a complete system.

For white Americans of European descent the Greek system is probably even closer than the Celtic tradition. The Celtic tradition is so fragmented that you really have to reconstruct things, whereas with the Greeks there is less to reconstruct because we know a lot more about them. They had a written tradition unlike the Celts, and we live in what is basically a Greco-Roman culture. From architecture to law to medicine those roots are there. If we are looking for ancestral roots, we can find strength in these Deities. We can reclaim them. We don't have to think of Zeus as a nasty patriarch who is controlling everybody's lives, because he wasn't. He was the enthroned God of Chesed on the Tree of Life. For anyone who is familiar with that sphere, it's the square, it's the realm of concepts. It's the form. We can reclaim that, in all it's beauty.

THEODORE MILLS (LORD THEO) is a high priest hierophant of Isis, Wiccan elder, and medicine man. He is also the founder of the Parker Coven and is the author of "Quest for a Witche's Jewel," published in *The Witches' Almanac* Aries '92–Pisces '93. He was interviewed near Northampton, Massachusetts, in the fall of 1993.

How long have you been a Pagan?

Probably all of my life but actively since 1967, outwardly anyway. I've been practicing the Craft from the time I was very young. I have a background in it, being that I'm a descendant of three of the "Witches" that were hung in Salem, Massachusetts. I don't think that that's *why* I'm a Pagan; it's just a benefit, you might say. It gives me a little courage to know someone else was there, too.

I've been a Pagan all my life. The word "Pagan" covers so much territory. I think that calling yourself a Witch, a Wizard, or anything that you might call yourself is not as important as what you do, as the way you utilize the power that you supposedly have. I'm a healer; I think that I heal people spiritually. I get letters from people all over saying that I've affected their lives for the better. I suppose there's a few that may say otherwise, but they haven't surfaced yet.

At eighteen or maybe nineteen I started really seeking for my spiritual identity, and then it came about as a manifestation of the Mother. I was visiting my people down South, and I was in my room. I looked up and I saw this bright light on the wall, and I thought at first that it was a spotlight from outside, an automobile light. Then it dawned on me. How could that be since there's a park opposite the window, and there are no lights from cars that could flash onto the wall?

I kept looking at it, and pretty soon things were moving around like in mist in the bright light and you could see shadows and things. Then all of a sudden this woman's face appears. She has long hair and it's black, at least it looked black in the vision, and she has emerald green eyes. Her black hair was moving as if there was a wind, but you didn't feel any wind. She just looked at me. Her skin was like pearl, very translucent and beautiful. She had red lips—not red in the sense of lipstick, just a beautiful natural red. I was pinching myself because I thought I was sleeping, and I was trying to wake myself up. She said, "Care for my children." That's all she said, and she was gone. I got out of bed fast, put the lights on, and I thought I must be losing it. I didn't say anything to my folks, and I thought it must have been something I ate.

Then I was in the library in New Orleans looking through the books on mythology and things like that because I was interested in those things, and I turned the page and there stood Isis. I said, "That's who I saw on the wall!" The caption said, "I am Isis, I am all that is and ever shall be." I thought, "What do I have to do with an Egyptian Goddess? I'm not an Egyptian. Why would she come to me?" Then I thought, "Well, if you are the one that came and you want me to take care of your children, you have got to show them to me, you've got to bring them to me, show me who your children are because I don't know them."

I went home, and the first thing I got was a message to leave everything and go back to Massachusetts, so I did. This was in '67. I started to find out that I wasn't the only Witch in the world. I started seeing newspaper articles about Sybil Leek and the New Forest Coven.

Anyway, it just developed over the years. I was going out into the city, and I was talking about Isis in churches and synagogues. Not in the manner of a teacher, but in the manner of a person who knew and was telling very personal experiences to the people. And they were very interested, because I had very definite connections with the Mother. I would hear her speak to me. She would chastise me when I would do things wrong. If I was using the Craft for personal things, she would say, "Listen!"

For people who will be reading this who are totally unfamiliar with Paganism, could you talk a bit about Isis? Who is Isis?

I think Isis is many things to many people. Hundreds of names if not thousands of names. As She Herself says, "I am all that is, has been, or will be." Therefore, She is from the beginning of time. She's always been. You have all these different interpretations of who She is, but to each individual She shows Herself in the way that She wants them to see Her and what's relative to their existence and their life.

You may see Her in a totally different way than I do, but She's still the same; the Mother is just dealing with us in the same way that our own mothers would deal with a variety of children in the house. Each one has to be handled in a different way. So for people who worship the Virgin Mary, for example, that's only another manifestation of Her.

So she's another manifestation of Isis?

That's right, She had a virgin birth, too. Isis is a virgin Goddess. She said, "The fruit that I have brought forth is the sun." The Great Mother the Virgin Mary, She brought forth another great light to the world. But is that light any different than Osiris? No.

You mean Horus?

Horus was Her son, but Osiris was Her spouse and Her brother. She restored him to health. In the Christian religion they say, "And the angel spoke unto Mary and she conceived under the Holy Spirit," right? The same thing happened when Isis conceived Horus. She brought back Osiris from the dead, but he was a spirit and his spirit entered into Isis and She became pregnant with Horus.

Where does the God fit in? Do you see him as co-equal with Isis?

I don't see anybody as co-equal with Isis.

So for you Isis is the Creator?

The Creatrix. And the reason for that is, and the Catholics themselves say it, She is the Mother of God. Well, if She's the Mother, She ought to come first. That makes common sense. The church likes to explain that as a mystery. They can't explain it so they say, "You must accept that on faith," and that's it. So it doesn't make the God less significant for what he does, but it does put the Goddess in a good position for being the One.

What is the most important aspect of Paganism for you? What is the thing that has kept you involved all your life?

The peace and tranquility I have in my life. That I'm able to bear things that are not easy to bear, as you see me sitting with my nose hose on. I have emphysema. I used to travel all over the world, all over the country, and I can't do that anymore. For some people that could be very devastating, but I say to the Goddess, "This work I have to do in a restricted sense, I must be doing it to learn something. Perhaps I'll be here for someone I might not have been here for if I'd been roaming around the world."

If I had not suffered, what could I help people to do? I had to experience loss. You've got to do that or you won't be able to weep with the people that are weeping. You have got to give them the love they need, the comfort they need.

You founded a coven called Parker Coven, which has since passed on to new leadership under a new name. Can you talk a little bit about what led you to found it and how Parker Coven might have been unique compared to what other people are doing?

Parker Coven was founded in the late sixties. Parker Coven now has three branches; it's gotten big.

Where did the name Parker Coven come from?

I picked that name out because three of my ancestors were hung in Salem. They were Mary Parker and Mary Anne Alice Parker and Rebecca Churchill. One of Rebecca Churchill's daughters married a Mills.

None of the women that were hung in Salem were actually Witches.

Well, who knows? What is Witchcraft anyway but a belief? You'd be a Witch, even if you weren't one, if you knew anything different than your neighbor. If you were cross-eyed, if you had a wart on your nose, anything, you could be called a Witch.

What was Parker Coven all about? Was it Egyptian primarily?

Yes. Primarily they worshipped Isis, the Great Mother. We have all of this knowledge pertaining to the symbols of Egypt that has been handed down from history. We also work with what we get by revelation, and revelation is more important than what you see in the books, always copying what you think is the "right" way of doing something. There are books and books and books, and some people say, "I'm this and I'm that," and they're accepting what somebody else said is the right way of doing things.

Was this your revelation or was it a group process of revelation?

It was my own revelation, but I think they themselves have had revelations since then. My revelation created the coven, and my method of doing ritual was eclectic. It came from many traditions, and the Goddess decided what she liked and what she didn't like and when it began to flow, you began to get results from the rituals, and then you knew that you were on the right path.

I'm what they call a medicine brother, to an Apache medicine man, and even the Hopis and the reservation up in Arizona recognized that I worked with the Thunder Beings. It's obvious from my life that I work with the Thunder Beings. Sun Bear also worked with the Thunder Beings, and Sun Bear told me that he recognized me.

When you say you work with the Thunder Beings, are you able to create thunderstorms, or what do you mean by that?

That's my big thing, thunderstorms. But I don't create them just for the sake of creating them and say, "Look what I can do."

Why do you create them?

When there's a need. When there's a need for purification to create negative ions in the air, for healing.

Did you learn this from Native Americans, or who did you learn this from?

Some of it I learned from Native Americans. I have a photograph in one of my books of me raising a storm and the storm that came.

When I was in the hospital in '81 I was dying. They didn't expect me to live. I didn't want anything done to me, I wanted just to die and I was ready to go. I ended up in intensive care, and there was a tremendous electrical storm. It was really weird. I went back and forth between this world and the place of departed spirits, the place of shadows, and they kept sending me back. They wouldn't let me through. All of the sudden I looked, and there were three men, three people in monk's robes standing by the side of my bed. I couldn't see any faces, but they had lifted my arm up and they were doing something under my arm. I didn't feel them doing anything; I just knew that they were. Then I went back up to the place of departed spirits, and this time I saw the light, and I started going toward it. I didn't wait for anybody to tell me I could. I started toward it, and as I got toward the light . . .

When you say "toward the light," you're talking about the bright light that people typically see in near-death experiences?

Yes. It was very bright. The darkness was all around the light, but I wasn't conscious of the darkness. I was concentrating on the light. I got up there, and a woman stepped out into the light. I can still see her. She had long hair. I couldn't see her face because the light was behind her, all I got was the form of a woman. I reached out for her, and she took my hand and she kissed it, and I went zipping back into my body and then I woke up. I was totally alert, and I knew what was going on, but I couldn't speak because I had a respirator down my throat.

My doctor came, and he said, "When I get you out of that I want to know how you people do those things." I didn't know what he was talking about, but when I went downstairs people were looking at me like I was some kind of strange creature, and so I wondered what had been going on. I got up and I went into the bathroom and I looked in the mirror because I felt like I was a "walk-in." You know what a walk-in is, don't you? I thought maybe some other spirit had walked into my body. When a person dies, sometimes their spirit leaves and another spirit moves in. People often say that when they got back from the hospital they were nothing like they were when they went in; their whole life had changed.

That night I looked at myself and under my arm I had a perfect crescent, like a half moon, under one of my arms. I showed it to my friend Jim, and I said, "What is this, anyway?" He said, "I don't know." I said, "It's a crescent, where did it come from?" The doctors didn't know, the nurses didn't know, and I said, "Never mind, I know."

Twelve years later a nurse who was working with the oxygen company that services my respirator told me [she was there that night], and she described exactly what I'd seen that time at the hospital. There were three people, three monks wearing cloaks who had come into my hospital room. She said she hadn't seen their faces, and I said, "Wasn't there a terrible electrical storm that night?" And she said, "Oh, it was terrible. It struck the hospital and all the lights went out. When I went over to the emergency room there were three men wearing cloaks, and I couldn't help but wonder where the security guard was. I didn't have the time to think about it, and then the lights came back on. Then lightning hit again, and we had to run around and do everything by hand until they got the lights going. I didn't see them come, and I didn't see them go. And I didn't hear them speak." I didn't either, but I was thrilled to think that somebody else had seen them besides me.

Rev. Cara-Marguerite-Drusilla, L.P.H., The House of Life, KMT, is a cofounder of the Lyceum of Venus of Healing and priestess hierophant in the Fellowship of Isis. She is also a member of the Assembly of Religious Leaders of the World at the Parliament of World Religions, which met in Chicago in 1993. The interview was conducted on January 8, 1994.

How long have you been a Pagan?

Since birth. I grew up a Pagan. My father was a priest of Isis. My mother was an eclectic healer, so I grew up with the Pagan Deities, especially the Egyptian ones.

Where did your father get his training?

From his parents. He grew up a Pagan, too.

What country was this?

The United States. My father was an Egyptian priest by design. He was American, and he was in the military. My family is an old southern family. We came to the United States in 1640 to escape religious persecution just like everybody else did. They were Pagans when they came here. They were from England and the Netherlands originally.

How has being a Pagan affected you as a person living in American culture?

I belong to a group now called What's Next. It came out of the Parliament of the World's Religions. This group is composed of Catholics, Protestants, Jews, Moslems, Sikhs, and me and a couple of people from my group. We are working on pluralism and the fact that we need to accept differences, we need to live together and work together in peace and harmony, or we are all going to die.

What was the Parliament of World Religions?

The Parliament met for the second time in 1993. It met for the first time in 1893. The basic idea behind the Parliament was pluralism. It met in Chicago at the Palmer House. The whole ten days of the Parliament was an opportunity for people of different religions to come together to learn from one another and to argue with one another if they needed to and to find places of common ground. I think that we did some remarkable things there.

How were Pagans received there?

To my knowledge we were received as equally as anyone else. I was very cheered by these people who were looking for ways to work together. Sitting in a room with two hundred and fifty of what were considered the leaders of the world's religions, it was apparent that all of them were concerned about the same thing—survival.

No one had a problem with diversity. They recognized that the fact that we have many religions makes us very strong. It's when you have just one that people get into trouble.

I have heard that the first Parliament, which was a hundred years ago, was the "coming-out party" for the Eastern religions. Some people have said that this one was the coming-out party for Pagans.

I believe it was. Absolutely. The thing that was remarkable and the thing that I was very proud of was that on whatever level Pagans were working at this Parliament—from people who were doing nothing except attending to people who were giving lectures or major presentations or whatever they were doing—everything that the Pagan community did was impeccable.

After leaving it I was in touch with a number of people who were at the Parliament, not all of them Pagans, and every one of them had the same kind of reaction. That something magnificent had happened, and that what they needed to do was to stand back and think about it before they could decide what to do next. It was a remarkable ten days. A remarkable time for people to come together.

Can you talk about the Fellowship of Isis?

The Lyceum of Venus of Healing is a member group of the Fellowship of Isis. FOI began thirty years ago. It was started by Lawrence Durdin-Robertson, who was a vicar in England and who discovered the Goddess. He, his wife, and his sister began what was essentially a small study group where friends would come and talk. They had a very strong Druid background. Their friends were quite eclectic, and they grew up with many of the thinkers and more interesting people of Europe. Robert Graves, for example, was their cousin. Olivia Robertson, Lawrence's sister, grew up sitting on Yeats's lap.

I don't think they ever imagined that there would be a Fellowship of Isis in thirty years' time. The remarkable thing that happened was that they discovered the Goddess *truly*. Today FOI is in seventy-six countries, and it has a membership of close to thirteen thousand people.

FOI is an eclectic umbrella group that recognizes the Goddess in all her many forms. To be a member of FOI merely says that one believes in Deity and that one believes in *the* Goddess or *a* Goddess and that one is willing to work towards a life-affirming way—to live lightly on the earth. Not to be an exploiter but to be a caretaker in a real sense. Under FOI there are Iseums, Hearths of the Goddess, and Lyceums, which are schools. Everything is autonomous. FOI is the validating group.

As the head of the Lyceum of Venus of Healing I teach, I counsel, I can marry people. We are a *nome* [in ancient Egypt an area dedicated to a certain number of Deities and run by a priest and priestess]. We are Egyptian; we follow the balanced pantheon of Egypt and the law of Maat. Our nome is dedicated to Venus Victorious, Venus as Love because we believe that love is the most powerful force in the world. With love one can do anything. There is so much hate in the world that people forget the power of love. [When you are] armed with love, there isn't very much that anyone can do to hurt you.

We honor both Gods and Goddesses, Isis, Amun-Ra, Sekhmet, Tefnut, Shu, Maat, Kephera, Toth, Anubis, Set, Horus, Osiris, Hathor, Nut, Geb—we honor the balanced pantheon. We also honor the Aten, with His many radiating arms coming down from a great center of light. We believe the Aten is a symbol: all people, all life are walking the parallel lines of the Aten. We are walking parallel lines together, all creation, all living beings. That is a very powerful image.

We don't look for enemies. I have more friends in the strangest places. At the Parliament one of the nicest people I met was Cardinal Joseph Bernadin of the archdiocese of Chicago. He was one of the "superstars" at the Parliament. He came to me. He wanted to meet me, and we talked for quite some time. One of the things that I found extraordinary was that in the opening plenary when the dignitaries were all sitting on the stage, and nearly everyone said something by way of welcome or hello to the assembled groups, Cardinal Bernadin stood up and talked about Catholicism as his "tradition." To my mind that is a *great* step forward for a Roman Catholic cardinal, as a prince of the church, to put it.

That's a very Pagan way to put it, isn't it?

Yes, certainly. I had just had twenty minutes with him prior to going on stage, and I thought this was marvelous. This kind of thing happened throughout the Parliament.

ELIE is an Israeli Pagan, who was raised in a kibbutz. She is the author of the songbook and musical tape on Jewish Earth spirituality called *Earth Is My Temple* and of many informative articles, including "Shir Bereshit" (Song of the Beginning), "On Hebrew Paganism," and "The Hebrew Earth Festivals." She has also published in Israel "Ahavat Aretz" (Love of the Land) and "Derech Ivrim, Derech Falcha" (Ways of the Hebrews, Ways of the Land). She was kind enough to grant an interview in 1993 at Starwood.

Are you a Pagan?

If a Pagan is somebody who prays to Gods or Goddesses, no. If a Pagan is also somebody who is interested in Earth spirituality and Earth mysticism, then yes. It depends on how you define it.

Can you talk about how you were raised, the religion that you were raised in?

Actually, I was raised with a form of Earth mysticism. I was in a kibbutz, and the kibbutz is a strong embodiment of what is in essence Earth mysticism. It was all about going back to the land and redeeming the land, and by doing that *we* would be redeemed. We would heal the land from a couple of thousand years of neglect, and *we* would be healed by that. Our wounds as a Diaspora people and so on and so forth. The perception was that working the earth and being close to the earth was healing.

Do you think that this is part of the Jewish tradition?

It is part of the Zionist outlook, which, contrary to a whole bunch of bad press it's been getting in past years, is all about going into the desert and making it bloom. That is supposed to be a way to help people be more complete.

Can you talk about tree magic and tree worship in the ancient Jewish tradition?

Just about everywhere in the Middle East there were sacred groves, and the trees were holy to the people. This is not a neo-Pagan reconstruction. This is a known, historic fact. In the days when the religion of Yahweh was competing with the religion of the Earth there was a whole bunch of back and forth about how important the high places are. The priests from Jerusalem wanted the temple and the temple priesthood to be important; these would be the ancestors of Orthodox Judaism, and they tried to wrestle the locations of worship away from the locations out in the countryside. These places in the country were usually a tree. It was known as an Ashera. The word *Ashera* means three things in Hebrew. It means a personified Goddess, a column of wood or an artifact structured like a column to resemble a tree trunk, or it means a tree used for ceremonial/secret/Pagan purposes. If you look it up in any modern Hebrew dictionary, those are the three meanings. It's also the name of a Canaanian Goddess.

So the Goddess was synonymous with tree?

Yes, She was. She obviously has evolved beyond that, and She existed all over the Middle East. She had different roles in other Semitic pantheons where She was more connected to more stratified, hierarchical temple-type Paganism. She was a mother of Gods or a ruler of Goddesses, but as a figure the Tree Goddess Ashera was pretty common in various forms in the Semitic north and northwest.

So what happened when the worshippers of Ashera met the worshippers of Yahweh?

They clashed! Since the only accounts we have of it are in the Bible, by which I mean what you would call the Old Testament, according to what the texts say, the Yahwist priests evidently won. One of the things that did happen was that over time they gained the monopoly of worship. It became the monopoly of the Jerusalem temple. Before that all sorts of holy days had been celebrated in the countryside. People would pick themselves up and go to the local high place. There would be priests there with a little altar and the Ashera, an actual tree or the semblance of one, and they poured wine on the table and they chanted and walked around it. It's all in the Bible, you can look it up.

In Sheol there was such a thing. Some of the holidays that were later incorporated into the Jewish tradition were originally Earth-religion holy days tied to a Nature calendar. Any rabbi will confirm that for you. Most of the ancient Jewish holy days were Earth holy days.

People had scattered farms and villages, and they would meet at the local high place or holy place. One of the things the Yahwists did was to build a temple—this was only one of the reasons for building it, but they wanted to concentrate worship in the temple. Which meant bringing it under the control of the priesthood who were in the temple. They went around the country and they broke the altars and they cut the Asheras. They did exactly what the Christian church did a long time later to the European Pagans.

Were the Ashera people more matriarchal or more female-oriented?

I am not going to make myself very popular by saying this, but, although we need the mytho-poetry—because I really think that as Pagans and as contemporary people we need the mytho-poetry of "Once upon a time there were free women who were fighting and there were kings and queens and whatnot"— it's a beautiful poetic fiction. It serves a poetic as well as a spiritual purpose, and I don't sneer at it for that reason. As Joseph Campbell said, "Poetry today does a lot of the jobs that mystic religion used to do once upon a time." Or even what bards used to do, who were both poets and people of Spirit. So I am not going to knock the beautiful legends. But they were legends.

Women did not rule. They had different roles over time in the Middle East. There were more female Goddesses. And there were times in which the role of the women Goddesses was not limited to the kitchen and the gynecological department, which is what developed later on with the Greeks. What were the Goddesses good for under the Greeks? For having babies, overseeing birth, and a few other things that are in the "female" sphere. You have to go quite a bit back to ancient Acadia to find Annat the warrior Goddess, who is a Goddess of Love and War. She is not Venus with the pretty little veils and flouncing about. She is a scarred Goddess, who represents love as in love-drive, lust. She is a maiden Goddess not a virgin, and not a married Goddess. She has a certain Amazon feel to her. Over time even she got relegated to baking cookies and having babies and overseeing those jobs.

So the Goddesses have had an evolution, too. I don't see it as "The males showed up and banged the women on the head." If women had been that strong they wouldn't have been banged on the head that easily. And I don't believe there was a matriarchy. This is strictly subjective because there is no proof either way. But that women's Goddesses had wider ranges of responsibility, so to speak, in ancient times, and that these roles got reduced is something that can easily be proven. But I don't believe that the societies were matriarchal. Some of them were freer than the Western societies are, but that doesn't make them gender equal. I believe the only gender-equal ideal that has existed is the modern one. I am glad that there is that! If they can catch their inspiration from the poetry of ancient times, that's wonderful. If that is going to give it the juice that is needed.

You said that when you were raised in the kibbutz, they taught you an Earth-centered Judaism?

It was an Earth-centered spirituality. They might not have called it Judaism because they identified Judaism with what one would think of here as Orthodox Judaism. They would say, "We are not religious people."

Are there people in America today or in Europe or in Israel who are practicing this kind of Earth spirituality? How would they do that?

I can't say if there are any here. I know of a couple hundred people who did in Israel.

Can you describe some of the observances? Did you follow the Earth festivals of the year the way that Pagans do in this country?

What all of Israel has done that is secular is to retain the cycle of nature that is at the root of virtually all Jewish holidays with the exception of maybe one or two and simply strip them of the overlay of rabbinical "God you are so great and we are so miserably small" and so on and just go back to an Earth feast. Kibbutzniks are farmers.

It makes sense to be planting trees in January, which is the planting season, and there is a holiday on the Jewish calendar, always has been, called the New Year of the Trees. It comes in January, and it is celebrated by planting trees. All the school children get a tree, and they go out and plant. This is done to make the country green, but it is a very ancient Jewish/Hebrew holiday. It used to be the New Year. The New Year was shifted to the October New Year that is known today.

Another one would be Passover. This could not have been the Exodus holiday, because Moses went to Pharaoh and said, "My people have this big holiday they want to celebrate." How could they celebrate something that had not happened yet? What they were celebrating was a lambing festival. The birth of the lambs. To this day they celebrate the birth of the lambs at the kibbutzim. They have a big party, dance around the fire, which is the way things are done in Israel.

There is a harvest festival in the fall, and that later became the New Year. It is called Succoth. It was probably a Pagan festival. There are rabbinical sources that tell you that people would go up to the high places, pour wine on the altar—the Ashera—the priest would say a blessing, and people would probably carry a Goddess in procession—that is not clear—and they would sweep the ground, probably in front of the advancing statue, with fronds.

What I have seen Earth-spirit-oriented people do in Israel is to build a booth and spend six nights in it. The booth has to be half open—that is Orthodox—so you can see the stars, because our ancestors were under the stars when they did this. They will carry a small tree in procession, which you could consider an Ashera if you like; some people will sweep the ground in front of the tree. A little bit out of spite, because the rabbis of the first and second century said, "We don't do *that* anymore," they would do what the "ignoramuses," the *Am Ha Aretz*, the people of the land did. This word is the exact equivalent of "heathen" in English. It means the folk who dwell in the countryside who are not following the court and the high church religion, or the high temple religion, but who are still tied to the Earth ways. These are the ignoramuses who still sweep in front of the Ashera and who still go up to the high places even though we destroyed them a long time ago. You find this in the Talmud, the rabbinical literature.

The habits of the folk obviously lasted quite a while. At the time of the Babylonian captivity the Jews were deported. You can't maintain an Earth connection if you are deported from your own land. That is probably what did more damage to what was left of Earth religion together with the purified Orthodoxy, Yahwism, that was distilled during the Babylonian captivity.

What is left today of the Succoth?

In Israel everybody celebrates it the Pagan way. But they don't sweep unless they are a deliberate Earth-religion group. They build the booths; they spend six or seven days under the stars. They will have special traditional foods that vary by community; some have milk foods, some have potato foods. September and October are quite mild there, so they camp out and have a good time. It's a family holiday.

Chanukah happens around the time of the Winter Solstice. Is it related to what is going on in the sky?

I'm not enough of a scholar of the Jewish tradition to tell you, but there *must* have once been a connection like that. Chanukah now is supposedly the holiday that was celebrated when the Yahwist temple was desecrated and the Maccabee brothers chased the bad guys out of the country and reconsecrated the temple. And lo and behold there was a miracle, and for seven days and seven nights the oil lamps burned.

Betzalel is a person who is quoted in the Bible a whole bunch. He was the chief of the craftsmen who was in charge of making the beautiful vessels for the big temple in Jerusalem. The instructions of how to make these various implements were quite detailed—size, proportions, and ritual necessities. One of the rituals was that you had to make a menorah [candelabrum with seven candles used in Jewish Chanukah ritual] with buds on its branches like a budding almond.

Nobody knows what the old menorah really looked like, the big one in the temple. The only depiction we have of it is on the arch of Titus in Rome. When the Romans stole all the vessels in the year 70, they then glorified their victory on this sculpture and you can see them carrying away a menorah.

Nobody knows how precise that rendition is. The interesting thing is that it was forbidden to make a precise depiction of the menorah. In Judaism the Divine may not be represented in pictures. If you look at it, it's a tree.

Does the Roman sculpture show a menorah with buds?

No, the Roman one is the type of classic menorah that you see on other sculptures. It shows things that look like joints of the metal, but they are really stylized buds. Some Kabbalists will say that there is a connection between the menorah, which is built to look like a budding tree, and the Tree of Life. And the Burning Bush.

What is this about a burning bush?

This is my interpretation. It is partly mytho-poetry and partly not. In the Bible, when Moses goes to meet God he sees a burning bush. The startling thing about the bush was that it wasn't burning. It was burning, but it wasn't being consumed. Now I have seen such things in the Sinai. There are a number of bushes with so much resin on them that they self-ignite in the heat, and you can see them burning for the longest time. Unlike regular wood they take a while to burn because the resin burns off first. If Moses had never been in that particular part of the Sinai before, he might have been very shocked by this phenomenon. The Sinai is very different depending on which area you are in. He may never have been in that specific area, the mountain area, which would have been quite different from where his wife's flock was running around.

The Bible says that the voice of God called to him from in between the burning branches. So you can see a clear identification between the Godhead and the burning bush; they are not separate. God isn't hiding in the bushes! So I think it's the concept of the Shekinah. The Shekinah is the Presence. It is the one that sat on top of the Arc of the Covenant like a cloud. Basically letting you know that God was having "office hours." If you want to come talk to Him, you can do so now. The Shekinah announces the presence of God. In the bush She is the one that calls to Moses. This is our interpretation, and some mystics will say the same thing. She is both God and the messenger of God. There has been a lot of debate among Orthodox Kabbalists on how separate the Shekinah really is from the Godhead. Is She another face of Him? Or It? Is She separate? Some Talmudic texts and some Kabbalistic texts have the Shekinah having arguments with God.

Orthodox Jews who are into serious Orthodox Kabbalah will tell you that you cannot really tell them apart. Which means in modern terms that you can just as well say the God is female as that God is male.

On the Sabbath when you light the candles on Friday nights is that the Shekinah?

Some mystics have said that the Queen Shabbat is the Shekinah. And that when you welcome Her, you welcome the Shekinah into your house.

Isn't it the mother or the wife or the woman of the house who brings the Shekinah?

The woman is in charge of doing the Shabbat blessing. She is the high priestess. She lights the candle, and she does the blessing. This has always been like that as far as we know. This is an obvious leftover from the days when women had some sort of priestess role.

There is some very interesting work being done now by the so-called reconstructionist/feminist rabbis in the East Coast of the U.S. They are going back and they are looking at the ancient biblical texts, particularly the one that talks about the Exodus, to see what was taken out of it. There is a small passage, for example, where Aaron, the brother of Moishe—Moses—revolts against Moses. He says, "Who do you think you are? Are you the only one who speaks for God?" If you notice in the text it says that Miriam and Aaron went. When the Hebrews left Egypt, Miriam led the women in a dance of triumph. There is a chant of Miriam, the Song of the Sea. There is about a line and a half of it left in the Bible [see Exodus 15:20]. The text has been mauled. If you read it in Hebrew, you can tell it's been chopped. Scholars will tell you that the priestly scribes chopped a piece off of the song. Probably Miriam had a major ritual role. The feminist revisionist rabbis of today speak of Miriam the prophetess, Miriam the seer, Miriam She Who Spoke to God together with Aaron and Moses. You can't argue against it. There is no proof either way.

There is a place in the Talmud where they were discussing, orally rehashing, what they knew had been in their ancestors' traditions. These were people who were learned in the ways of the Hebrew tradition. It was a bit like people arguing a point of law and somebody writing it down. At one point you have several very wise rabbis in about the second century discussing what was *really* in the Holy of Holies in the innermost chamber of the temple. Well, one of the things that came up in this discussion was that the great rabbi so-and-so, who heard it from another great rabbi so-and-so, said there was the Arc [of the Covenant], there were the famous two cherubim, two angels touching wings over it, but inside of it were a man and a woman with wings, joined at the hip. I like to believe that this is the Divine Dyad. The Shekinah and the Godhead, two and yet one at the same time. This is written in the Talmud; it is not mytho-poetry. The interpretation might be, but nobody has a better one than mine.

So there was a lot of debate over whether there actually was a representation of the Shekinah in the temple. We will never know, because of course it got destroyed. By the time the Romans showed up, there was nothing in the Holy of Holies because the Babylonians had destroyed it.

In the Talmud they were arguing about what joined at the hip meant. Were they making love? Was this some kind of holy matrimony? Was it joined at the hip to signify a tree? A trunk with two big branches? This is what I like to think of. But they didn't arrive at a solution.

So you see that Orthodox Judaism has a strong feminine element. You don't need to go very far from Judaism to be an Earth-spirit person. Whereas if you are a Christian, you need to move much further out from the teachings in order to also be an Earth-spirituality person. Or so my Christian friends tell me anyway!

Does it seem to you that Jews of today are looking at that aspect?

Many of the Jews I have met here could be Anglo-Saxons from a very strict north England church. They have no body connection. They have lost their connection to their senses; they have lost their Earth connection, in other words.

The Zionist movement was aware of this, because one of the things it was saying was that the Jews, because of too much study and being cooped up in towns and being an "artificial" people because of the persecution and their inability to carry out the jobs that "normal" people had, had gotten themselves into an anomalous situation. They lacked the stability of Earth. I have seen these Jews at festivals. I was told, and I don't know if this is true, that a large number of Jewish people in America today are Pagans. I believe that what they are looking for is roots. Because all Pagans seem to be looking for roots in this country.

What about bringing the Jews of this country back to the Earth-connected aspect of their own religion? Wouldn't that feel better?

To my astonishment the local Orthodox people are not even aware that this mystic streak of Judaism exists. This would allow them to straddle and be both a Pagan and a Jew. I am talking about the American Jews. They are not aware enough that in their own people's tradition, the tradition of the Hebrews, there is so much Earth spirituality and Earth connection. And connection to the feminine aspect of the Godhead. I have nothing against them going to Wicca, but then they complain that they don't feel at home. It is very North European.

So what are you doing to reach out to the public with this?

I recorded the songs because a lot of the work I do involves self-healing and shamanic stuff. I had some songs, some of which were Israeli, some of which I had written, that in my view have the texture and feel of Earth spirituality in a Hebrew context. These are the songs of my people, the traditions of my people and our own history. Or it reconnects with it in some way.

I sang the songs at festivals where people were drumming and chanting, because these are mostly drumming and chanting tapes. If you work with them properly, in the sense that you use them the way they were intended to be used and that you have the training, you can move into altered states of consciousness.

LAURIE BRUNO is a Strega, which is an Italian traditional Witch. She comes from the ancient Sicilian traditions and is part of Our Lord and Lady of the Trinacrian Rose. She was interviewed by phone on March 27, 1994.

Are you a Pagan or a Witch?

I am a Witch. In the Italian tradition where I come from we are called "Strega" for female and "Stregone" for male. We are also called "Imago" for male and "Imaga" for female.

What kinds of Pagan practices did you have at home?

Honoring the Mother and the Father, honoring the seasons, respect for all humanity, respect for the animal kingdom, respect for the plants, respect for all of nature. The biggest word in the Craft today should be respect. Sometimes it gets lost.

What we had was a religion of humanity, the Craft of the Wise. When somebody says they come from a Witch family, I look at them and their immoral behavior and I say, "I doubt it." The ones who practice the *Religione Vecchia*, the "Old Religion," practice the religion of all the Gods which were created. It is a religion of decency.

You said that as a child you celebrated the seasons. How did you do that?

When the season of springtime came, we gave our offerings. We would take a red egg and put it where the sun rose, at the area of our home where the sun first came up. We would do that at the Spring Equinox. It was planting life, to cause growth. Remember that the Mediterranean was a different climate than here. Mayday was called Beltana, it was the time of the growing season, the time of fertility. Men would go with their wives or with the love of their life and be "close" to each other. It was the season of fruitfulness, that's what you would respect it as. We would go ahead and bring forth the good things to help the earth to bring the life force in. Understand? The children would go out and plant the seeds. Flower seeds, anything. We would say, "Grow. Enrich."

When we came to this country, we came to a place with the climate of the Celtic nations, right? So this was why we celebrated in the Celtic way. August would be Lughnasad for Celts. In Italy they would be honoring the Goddess Ceres at the time of the cereal in July. The image of the Mother would be carried; wheat and corn would be tied together, and it would be offered. It was also a time of fertility rites.

Children did not engage in sexual union. The Craft is not a gang bang in the Black Forest. When you see some of these movies they do in Hollywood . . . forget about it, that's not the way we honor. The way we honor is with respect to ourselves and to our people. Caring. Nurturing the earth. Giving honor to the Mother who grows things and to the Father. We would go into the fields with the fire and carry it around the fields and praise the Lord of growing things. We would say, "Grow! Grow! with the life force."

What about winter?

Befana is the old Witch, the old Strega *nonna* who would come around and bring gifts for the children. It was a festival of light returning. She is an old Witch. In legend it was said that she would come to help the children celebrate and bring gifts.

Do you think that she was originally a Goddess or the Goddess?

I feel yes. And most of us know, yes. I would call her Hecate, the grandmother Goddess, the Crone Mother. She is the ancient Crone Mother. She is a grandmother spirit. We call on her as Hecate Triformis, the Goddess of Three. This is who she is.

Some of the practices of our people are secret, and they are kept that way. You could say that they are jealously guarded because we see a lot of the Celtic ways being screwed around with anyway that people want to turn them. We teach our people the old ancient ways of the religion of Eleusis, the Eleusinian mysteries.

They say that no one ever revealed the Eleusinian mysteries. Are you saying that the Strega have them intact?

My family has them intact, and my coven are taught them, down to the drink and the sacred meal. I am not going to give you that because that is a secret of my family that has been guarded with their lives. We know that it still has to be guarded. It would be a nice thing for the outside world to know, but they would abuse it and, excuse me for the expression, bastardize it. I will not have that happen.

I was the first in my family to come out in public. My ancestor was Giordano Bruno. He was a philosopher, and when he was about sixteen years old he became a Dominican monk. He was burned as a heretic in the year 1600. When this happened, the rest of us knew to stay underground. He was burned because he spoke out against many injustices, and because he felt that there was a multiplicity of universes. He spoke about that and wrote about that. He felt that the sun was stationary, and that it was the earth that went around. At that time this was heretical learning.

Was he a follower of Galileo?

No, Galileo was a follower of Bruno. Bruno lived quite a few years before Galileo. Bruno was in the court of Elizabeth I of England. He was patronized by her and by Sir Philip Sydney, one of her courtiers. He founded a sect called The Giordanisti.

When I mention the Strega or La Vecchia Religione, people usually gasp. They seem to think that the Strega are very powerful, and they are also frightened of the Strega. Why is everybody frightened?

The Strega get business done. Even the Mafia respects the Strega. The Mafia use the *corno*, the symbol for the God with their hands. They copied the Strega a little bit. That hand position is also the crescent moon.

Some people think it means Satan.

It's not! Satan has *nothing* to do with it!

What about the Mal Occhio?

The evil eye? Have you ever seen somebody envying people? That is Il Mal Occhio. The evil eye is envy. They say "the evil eye can kill."

If you had to characterize Strega, how would you compare it to English traditional Wicca? What is its essential uniqueness?

Respetto per tutto. Respect for all. *Honore.* Honor the Gods. Honor of yourself. The definition of Witch for me is this: "W" is for the warrioress. The

"I" is for initiation. The "T" is for the truth. The "C" is for courageous, and the "H" is for heritage. There are those people who call themselves Witches and in their case the "W" stands for Warlock, Weasel. They initiate treachery, cruelty, and hatred. That's *not* the Craft a Strega belongs to. The Strega is the warrior/warrioress who champions the injustice, who will help anyone. Okay? Anyone who does evil is not of the Strega, my people. We are doing the good things, and we take away the evil things. Understand?

"Witch" is the Anglo-Saxon word. That's fine, we are in America now, we will go along with the name they give us, but Strega we are proud to be, Strega for all eternity we are. We've paid in blood, and we have cared for the people that came to us and we *never* abandoned anyone.

What do you do for a living?

I am a psychic. I have also worked with the police. I charge for my readings, $25 a reading. I don't charge a hundred, I don't want to gouge people. I want the little people to come to me. Sometimes I read for free if a person is on welfare. I will not take a penny from them because I care. I do the readings out of my house, and I also go to their houses. What I don't like is the prostitution of our Craft. I've seen numerous people do this. I don't have to mention their names because they know who they are. They know who the hands of the Gods are on. "You shall not prostitute your Craft."

What about the teachers today? I am thinking of a couple I know who have two kids, and they are working full-time as teachers and counselors to the Pagan community. They need to get paid, don't they?

What are they teaching?

Witchcraft.

I teach Witchcraft too, once a week. You know how many hours a day I counsel people for free?

Believe me, I am on the phone at six in the morning with people, "Oh Laurie, my son is in jail. What am I going to do?" "What jail is he in? Where is he?" Out of the bed I go, no makeup, no nothing. I take a shower, I run out the door. My son is wondering where I am going. I have to go pick up this boy because he's in jail, and his mother is beside herself. So how much would a Pagan counselor charge for that service? Thank you, no thank you.

Have I ever had good luck? I'll tell you what happened. After my husband passed away, I was down to my last nickel in the North End. I had nothing. I didn't have a car. I had nothing. He came in a dream to this Strega and said, "You play five, eight, five, one." Then the Strega woke up and said, "Louie, can you get the guy to put $5 on that number?" My Louie said, "What is this, you *give* people numbers, you don't play them." This was back in 1983. I went ahead and I played the number. Five, eight, five, one came out that day, and this

Strega won some money. So you see? Strega got paid back by the Gods in another way. How many Pagan high priests could say that in one day's work? So the Gods smiled on this Strega because she went out and did something. I gave back to the Gods.

Strega went over to the Buick dealership in Medford and said, "That's the car I want, the black car with the burgundy interior." On the inside of the car is the vehicle identification number. It's the Strega's husband's birthday. So Strega that night looks up in the sky and says, "Thank you. These were the things you owed me because of how mean you were in life." I have seven stitches in my head, but in death he looked after me.

There was an old lady in the neighborhood who had a lot of problems. She had a stinking refrigerator that never worked right. That day someone delivered her a refrigerator filled with food, anonymously. That's how the Strega work. No pat on the back, no newspaper, no TV. Just trust in everything.

In what religion are you raising your children?

They want to be Catholic? I let them be Catholic. If they can tolerate that I am a Witch, I can certainly tolerate their Christianity. My son is back and forth with it, but I don't force my Craft on them. Why should I? That's horrible. Hey, how do I know they aren't supposed to be Christians in this life? I leave it to the Gods.

They have seen me honoring the full moons, and they respect me. My son will peek in every once in a while. My daughter does her honoring of the Gods, but I've told her, "Sometimes you have to stay underground because the people in your neighborhood may not have open minds."

My daughter took a dead goldfish a couple of years ago. She was crying because it died. She said, "Oh, Goddess Mother, help me." She called the Magna Mater, she started to call them all. Then she cupped her hand and filled it with water and put the fish in her hand. She said, "Please, if you exist, help me."

She blew on the fish, and it started to move around in her hand. Then she got scared, and she put it back in the water. She called me right away, "Ma! Ma! The fish is alive!" I said, "Of course the fish is alive, why shouldn't it be alive? The Goddess knows, the Goddess chose. She made you wish and there it goes!" I said, "Yvonne, the good energy you put forth from yourself, the caring that you took, maybe it made a miracle."

My daughter's children are brought up Christian, and that's okay. I can tolerate people of every religion being with me. My boyfriend is a Catholic. I have a statue of Saint Anthony in the house, and I have a statue of the Blessed Mother. Isn't the Blessed Mother part of the Goddess? She is. She is another emanation of it.

It is all the same: Mari/Mary. When you see the little Italian ladies praying to the Goddess, to Mary, a lot of them are praying to the ancient Mother. We have been covering up continually so that we could survive. Remember that 80 percent of Italy's Witches, the Strega, survived. In Europe 80 percent of the Witches were burned. Why? I'll tell you why, because the Strega knew how to hide. They knew how to play the game. *Ave Maria, Ave Diana. Bella dia di Diana. Madre di stella, madre di tutto universo, mia madre.*

How many Strega are there in America?

They are underground. The Strega have been around for hundreds of years all over the United States of America. Some are in Canada as well.

Are they good Catholics, going to church and lighting their candles?

Mari-Diana. We play the game. This is how we hid and survived. We know what they did at Eleusis to us. The religion of the Great Mother started in the Fertile Crescent and worked up north. Our church is called Our Lord and Lady of the Trinacrian Rose. The rose is the sacred flower of Sicily. Trinacria is the ancient name for Sicily. If you look at the island of Sicily it has three capes on it, like a triangle. And if you look very carefully, it will remind you of the Triple Goddess.

The rose can never be crushed. It will always spring up again. It has thorns, but in the center it has a heart. Strega have thorns, but we do have a heart. Our family is very very old. I've seen so much. My mother says, "Please don't go out and teach because they could hurt you." My mother has the old fear because they saw the Burning Times. One of my ancestresses was a healer in the time of the Black Death. She was hung upside down in the marketplace because people went to her and were healed. She would open up the lesions, use a suction device, put some salve on it, and then seal the wound, the pustules. Then the people would recover. This was in the 1300s, in Messina, Sicily. They killed her. The religious ones hung her upside down because she consorted with the Arabs, and because she was a Strega. A healing Strega was even worse because they went against the will of the God. Believe me, if Jesus Christ were alive today he would sit with the Strega and the Celtic Witches far more than he would with the church of Rome.

You often see Italians in Italian neighborhoods wearing a nice gold cross with a nice gold horn next to it . . .

They should never be hung on the same chain. They say, "I am Christian and Craft together." The horn is the carryover from the Old Religion. Don't you love it! Women and men wear the horns and the little fist with the thumb and the little finger coming between the index finger and the middle finger. That's *mano in fica*. Those are the three we wear.

Is there anything else you would like to say about the future of the Craft?

I feel that we as priestesses and priests of the Craft and of the God and Goddess should always be there in the forefront and make ourselves in a comely manner to all people. In other words, don't behave in public showing that we have no respect for ourselves.

Public drunkenness, rude behavior, things of this nature, if we do them, we are just throwing mud on ourselves. Worst of all we are throwing mud on our God and Goddess. I don't mean to be a puritanical imp, but what I am saying is that if you wish to drink, then drink in your house. Don't go and act like a complete donkey in the middle of the public.

A woman who is a representative of the Goddess should never be immoral anywhere in public. She should never be immoral *anywhere*. She is a representative of the Goddess Mother, and that's her duty. Otherwise, it's just throwing mud on our people, and we don't need that.

What about group marriage? What do you think about that?

No. I'm sorry. Group marriage does not go. I don't throw my love away. I have been with my man now for eighteen years. I'm a little chubby lady—I'm not built like Marilyn Monroe, believe me. I'm a chubby grandmother, but, believe me, he loves me the way I am. And he adores me in our private moments.

I'm Italian. I'm no prude. But I will tell you this: I want people to respect us and be decent. What is group marriage for? Is it a kind of gang bang in the Black Forest? Sorry. That's not our Craft. That's Witchcrap! I'm sorry if I offended you with that, but I had to say it. Group marriage is just giving license to people to do what they want. Do you know what comes from that? AIDS and all of the sicknesses. The Goddess said, "Our body is our temple." It's Her temple, so why don't we respect it? The Craft that I know teaches responsibility and moral attitudes also. I will keep our ways always in my heart. I don't condemn you if you don't. But in the future what are you going to represent to everybody that looks at you?

A lot of people would say that Paganism is a religion that celebrates sex and that gives people permission to explore because "All acts of love and pleasure are my rituals sayeth the Goddess . . ."

Baloney. That's piganism. "All acts of love" means to love the children, to love humanity, to love all creation. It doesn't mean "Give me a gang bang in the Black Forest."

The saying is "Love and pleasure . . ."

I get pleasure out of taking care of children and loving them and also loving the man I am with. I understand what pleasure is. I'm not a prude, but I feel moral obligation and moral fiber. In order to be respected and cared about by everyone out there we have to show them an example. Please, if you want to go out and have free love, you don't have to join the Craft. My coven believes that, and they range from eighteen years old to fifty-five. Believe me, we don't go dancing around with each other. Give me a break! We have our husbands, and we have the men we are seeing one on one. And believe me *our magic does work!*

Let me tell you something, I am fifty-four years old, and I never went through the change of life. I have an active sex life with the man I am with. What I worry about is how the rest of this world will take us when we sit there and talk with them over a table. Do you want them to look at us and say, "They have gang bangs in the Black Forest, and they want us to take them seriously?"

Imagine a fundamentalist looking at me or you and knowing that we did that and them talking to us? We *have* to talk to these people. We *have* to have the decency. What you want to do is your business, but don't pull it into the public spotlight. In the long run the people that have these polygamous things going on end up in front of a psychiatrist's couch. Or they end up with me for a reading, and I try to straighten them out.

Polyamorous? No. Polyfoolish. "All acts of love?" I could tell you about acts of love. Taking care of everybody that walks through this door in a decent way. Loving my children, my family, the man I am with. Every day it's a new time with him, and I have been with him for eighteen years.

Goddess–centered Paganism

F eminism can be defined in an infinite number of ways, just as being a Pagan can mean vastly different things to any number of people. Then what or who are Pagan Feminists? Certainly, it can be said they are people who strive to help women re-empower their lives. In the case of the following two women interviewed, both prefer being called Witches to Pagans, feeling the word sets them apart in both tradition and more specifically as women. They both could be considered female separatists in their view that women need a tradition that is completely removed from any of the past's male-dominated religions. In their need to establish a strong voice for women they both have started new traditions, which draw upon ancient wisdoms while bringing them firmly into the twenty-first century.

ORIETHYIA is a lesbian, Dianic, Amazon, feminist poet. She is the founder of the woman-centered Artemisian Tradition. A talented individual, indeed, Oriethyia brings her fresh and vital insights to such diverse fields as Tarot reading and computer programming, which she does for a state budget office. She was interviewed by phone on February 23, 1994.

First of all, are you a Pagan?

I don't call myself a Pagan, I call myself a Witch. The difference is *pagan* means "of the earth"; "Witch" leaves it pretty clear that you are also talking about power because the word is so loaded. If in my work environment or my personal environment I talk about being a "Goddess worshipper" or a "Pagan," those things are true. But they are not the be-all and end-all of the truth. If I don't call myself a "Witch," I'm begging the question.

That is not a statement that I assume everyone can or should make. I use the word "witch" for the same reason I use the word "dyke." For the same reason that I remember being so overwhelmed by the Black Power movement in the sixties when African-Americans said we should not use the word "negro" any more and that the correct word was "Black."

For me it's about reclaiming the word. Every time you use it, you have to be prepared to slip into education mode, and that's not always the most pleasant thing. I've had my share of less than satisfying experiences in responding to someone regarding my calling myself a Witch.

When did you first discover that you were a Witch?

In grade school I read everything I could about the myth cycles of the Greeks and the Romans, to the point where I took rather a ribbing for it. I was especially fascinated by the Goddess stories. I was raised as a Roman Catholic, so I also read all of the stories I could find about the women saints. I think I was looking for the folks that looked like me, a sisterhood of sorts that was not exactly present in my life. There was a mythic urge and a Heraic urge [in the sense of Hera, Greek Goddess, queen of Olympus and hera as opposed to hero] in me.

Then came a lot of years doing overt radical feminist work and radical lesbian feminist work. I was a member of one of the early gynecological self-help groups. That was back in the days when self-help meant gynecological self-help.

I remember a bunch of us sitting around together one day talking about the self-help movement and about reclaiming herbal wisdom. At one point I looked up at the group of women I was working with and said, "You know, if this was Europe back in the sixteen hundreds, we'd be toast." The sense was that what we were about was the equivalent of fighting the enclosure movement in Europe.

For me much of the radical feminist work was very much akin to the enclosure movement. In this case not about enclosing the land but about enclosing women's minds and bodies and the insistence that those barriers come down.

So what does that have to do with Dianic Wicca?

I am one of those women who, the more radical I became, the more I got off the beaten path in terms of women's politics. It became clear to me that politics alone was not any kind of a full answer as long as we were operating in structures in which the head honcho, spiritually, is the top dog. I am talking about "God, the Father" and then the pope. Any rigid hierarchical structure, especially ones that say, "You women can polish the bishop's shoes, you can teach our children, you can bring the next generation into the world. That is the most important work in the world. By the way, don't expect to be taken seriously in anything except the prescribed roles, and don't expect to be allowed into any of the halls of power. Do not even discuss what power looks like." It became very clear that it was going to be crucial to step off of that path. I needed to ask myself what the world would look like if God were a woman. What would it look like if Divinity had a female face? That path leads to the realization that one does not have to invent this. It has been done before, in the past.

I discovered some writings by Z. Budapest and others. I said to myself, "Aha! This is the stuff I was looking for!" Subsequently, Starhawk started writing, and there was more of the material I had been looking for.

What was wonderful for me was that what those women were writing was the spiritual sister to the political work that I was doing. The spiritual part that I had been feeling was missing from the political work was there. There was no compromise necessary. They were of a piece.

For me finding a religion in which the Goddess was present and supreme was crucial and absolutely a homecoming. So for years I called myself a Dianic Witch. My understanding was that Dianic Witches put the Goddess at the center of the universe and that they saw Her as the constant. If and when there was a male consort, he was the variable. He was the nonconstant. He was the changing. She was also the changing one; so let's not get too rigid in our roles or our symbolism.

The only other Dianic Witches I had known were women. I had assumed it was a "women-only" order until I walked into a Wiccan bookstore about five years after that, and there was this very nice man behind the counter. We started chatting, and I asked him if he had any books on Dianic Witchcraft. He said, "Oh! I am Dianic too!"

So I lived with that for a while and then a few years later decided, Screw it, rather than fight over who got here first, just declare a new tradition and call it Artemisian. I now call myself an Artemisian Witch, after Artemis, the Greek aspect of the Roman Diana.

Artemisian Wicca basically says that while most of the religious world is putting a male face on religious power and Divinity, we are, as a spiritual affirmative action program, recognizing the female face of Divinity. Also, she doesn't have to have a consort unless she damn well feels like it. Don't talk to me about balancing out male and female energy because by declaring a women-only, Goddess-only tradition, we are doing our best to balance out the male-only predominance in the culture.

In your tradition are you basing any of what you do on ancient teachings or writings?

We are not based on any ancient sources. I would say that we use them colloquially in the sense that everything is a potential source, as long as it is honored and respected and not just ripped off from somebody whose stuff looks more interesting than yours. I say that specifically because there is a tremendous amount of rip-off going on of indigenous people's traditions around the planet. Including Native American and African traditions.

Artemisian magic is about saying, "Let's forget for a moment about external, cultural overlays and start from *here*. Start from my femaleness. What do I understand about the world from my femaleness? What do I understand about reality?"

What makes the tradition unique is that it starts from the place of saying, "Wait, everything else being stripped away, where is the center of femaleness in this?" It's not simply a "biology is destiny" trip.

When you say "the center of femaleness," can you explain what that means? What "feminine" means in this context?

Feminine has been so skewed to mean whatever the power structure at the given moment wanted it to mean. The center of femaleness is the thing that mandates me to have the discussion about what one learns in the gut and the heart and in the mind and in the spirit. When you have been given the opportunity to respond to potential or actual victimization and choose not to be victimized. That does not mean that you choose not to be assaulted at some time in your life. It means that you choose to not have it turn you into a victim. You recognize what it means to be overwhelmed at times. You have the potential to learn to be strong and powerful in yourself.

Aren't these qualities that men are trying to develop, too?

Yes, and bless every single one of them who is trying to do it. There are things that come up in men-only circles that cannot happen if women are there. There are things that will come up both energetically as well as verbally and physically in a women-only circle that cannot happen if there are men present.

I can't tell you the number of circles I have been in where I have been totally frustrated because it was a big group of women who had never been in a women-only circle before. The first time this happened I was ready to leave the gathering because of the comments I was hearing. It was totally heterosexual and totally Noah's Ark. The Noah's Ark conspiracy is where we all have to go through life two by two. I'm not saying that there's anything wrong with heterosexuality, but if it's the only thing in my face constantly, it gets a little old.

So this was getting really tedious with that sort of thing going on for the whole weekend. I almost left. Then there came this part where the men were to go off together, and the women were to go off together.

So a good friend of mine said, "Stay at least for the women's circle." At the end of the women's circle women were breaking down and crying. They were saying that now they understood what "those feminists" were talking about. After about the fifth woman said that, it hit me, how only a handful of us had ever been in a women-only space. They didn't understand what I was saying because they had never experienced it. Of course, it sounded like Venusian to them.

Artemisian Witchcraft has many of the same beliefs as the Dianic, with the exception that it is understood that if you are an Artemisian Witch, you are at least enough of a female separatist that only women are Artemisian Witches.

Can you talk about what it's like to work magic with a group of women as opposed to working with a mixed-gender group?

My sense of working with women is that when women get together to do magic, the first thing we do is take our skin off. I don't know if it's because we women grew up together trading secrets and confiding in one another. Of course, not all women have that experience, and not all women work magic that way. But there is something about a women-only circle that for me is stepping in and taking my skin off. We get really real with each other, and very fast. I have heard men talk about men-only circles and how infrequently they have felt that they really cooked and worked. They hear women friends talk about women-only circles, and they are always so astounded about the way that women get right to the emotional core faster and arrive at consensus faster.

How does the Artemisian tradition relate to the earth?

As sister. I am so tired of the mother, mother, mother thing. These days I am insistent on seeing the Goddess and the Earth more as sister. Mom is the one who is supposed to take care of everything. If we keep waiting for Mom to take care of it—Mom isn't getting the alliance and help that she needs.

What do the priestesses of the Artemisian tradition do to help their sister?

Whatever they feel called upon to do. Some women are the compost queens of their neighborhoods, teaching people composting and doing it themselves. For some it's being very actively involved in environmental groups. For some it's saying to friends, "Yeah, that's a really gorgeous crystal. Can we think about the fact that there are people who are strip-mining Central and South American countries to get these gems because we are turning them into a commodity? Ripping that stuff out of the planet may not be the best thing for the earth. When you are done with your crystals, might you think about putting them back in the ground?"

We do anything and everything that seems appropriate. From overt political action to regularly taking time in circle to specifically focus energy of love, nurturance, and healing back to the earth.

You are a poet. Talk about the role of poetry in Pagan worship, Witchcraft, or ritual.

For me poetry and ritual are synonymous. Poetry is the language that ritual is written in. This is what's true for me. In the way poetry is about reading between the lines to understand something, ritual is about stepping outside of the day-to-day language and the day-to-day symbol systems. It's about speaking in metaphor. Someone once said, "It's all real, it's all metaphor, there is always more." I love that. For me that's where poetry and ritual share space. It's all real. Take it for exactly what it says. It's all metaphor. Take it for the mystery.

Poetry for me is the language that magic lives in, that it works through. It is more closely than prose the language of magic.

Do you use poetry in spell casting?

Yes and no. Yes, in the sense that for me some of the most fun stuff is making up a spell on the spot that's a rhyming verse, especially since I never write poetry that rhymes. There is something in the rhythm of it and the playfulness of it. Even a silly-sounding rhyme. If you can be lighthearted about what you are working on, it lends magic to the magic.

Sometimes I use poetry specifically in ritual work, and sometimes when I open my mouth to speak, whatever is coming through in the ritual comes out as poetry, even if it was not necessarily my intent.

Can you remember an instance when you did a spell that worked, and can you talk about it?

A good friend of mine had been doing some therapeutic work on releasing old family patterns, getting past them and understanding her role in them. She was feeling rather frustrated. She wondered why, if she was so smart, was she still stuck in the same place?

So I said, "Let's do some work around that." She, two others, and myself decided to get together. Carol was the person who was the focus of the ritual, and we told her to just show up. We said we'd pick her up and go out to Lois's place to do a ritual. We didn't tell her what we were going to do or what she was going to do.

Lois and Dale and I decided to cast the circle and name the quadrants of the universe in the way that humans divide up reality. We decided to invoke the Goddess energies that we thought were most appropriate and do the chanting and dancing that would help us shift gears.

The idea came to "banish" Carol to an arc of the circle with Dale, who would be her companion. Lois and I would then kick the fire into high gear, and I would slip on my black hooded robe which Carol had never seen me use. By now it would be dark, and when she turned around she would only see a tiny portion of my face that was visible and the black robe blending into the black night. I would be holding my battle ax, my labyris, in front of me. Only my face and the metal of the ax would catch the fire, and that's who she would confront.

Carol didn't know any of this, of course, and I wasn't 100 percent sure what I was going to be doing as the crone, once she turned back around and came toward me. I only knew that I was going to be manifesting a very loving but older and stern figure.

Once I began to manifest that crone figure, Dale, who was her "childish" companion, was going to step away, and Lois was going to step in as her adult ally and interact with me, so that Carol would not be standing alone in the face of this sternness. That would give Carol a chance to face that sternness as both a child and as an adult.

I could only do this with Carol because we knew each other long enough that I had a really good sense that nothing was going to come jumping out of her psyche that she couldn't handle.

At some point in the ceremony we did everything that we intended. I sent Carol and Dale off to the side before I slipped into my crone gig. They were both holding teddy bears. I called them back, and they turned around toward me. As soon as they spotted me, the two of them burst into giggles, which I had not expected. So I just pointed and turned them back again to where they had come from. This happened three times. They just kept giggling, and I wasn't sure how to make it happen so that the gears would shift, so that Carol would be confronted by this image rather than giggling at it.

The third time when they came back, suddenly *boom*, she was in it. At some point in the ceremony, about fifteen minutes into her confrontation with the older, sterner image, all of a sudden I felt myself being about fifteen feet tall looking down at a very small Carol. The sensation was there for several seconds, and then it was gone.

Some part of my brain registered this, but I didn't get caught up in it because I didn't want to lose what we were doing. On the drive home Carol said to me, "I have to tell you something. Right about the time when we were doing this thing in the circle I was two feet high and you were enormously tall."

I pulled the car over to the side of the road, and I just looked at her, and I said, "Say that again?" She did, and it was at exactly the same moment that I had that feeling.

The ritual had worked in the sense that she had become child again, and I had become the overarching, overriding, overbearing older adult figure with more power to her less power. Over the course of the ceremony that evened out. By the end of the ritual she was absolutely holding her own with me and with Lois and with Dale.

It was the first time ever in ceremony that I had felt that drastic a shift. I thought to myself, "Aha! It's not only metaphor."

For another perspective on Pagan feminism we have **SUSUN WEED,** who is a Green Witch and founder of the Wisewoman School of Herbal Healing. She is the author of *Wise Woman Herbal for the Childbearing Year, Healing Wise,* and *The Wise Woman Way for the Menopausal Years.* She has also released a video, *Weeds to the Wise,* and an audio tape, *Menopause.*

Are you a Pagan?

I'm a Witch. If being a Witch makes me a Pagan, then I'm a Pagan. A Witch is a person whose life is understood as their art and whose spirituality is their life. So that life, art, and spirituality are all one thing to the Witch. Furthermore, I am a Green Witch, which means that my art is the wise use of all of the greenery around.

When did you first discover that you were a Witch?

You know, other people discovered that I was a Witch before I did! People started calling me a Witch when I was eighteen or nineteen years old, and I thought they were putting me down. It took me at least another decade before I came to really understand that in fact not only was I a Witch, I was also a bitch, a dyke, and a slut, and those four words are the words of women of power. That's why they are used to put women down. So I have claimed *all* of those words for myself.

There has been a systematic destruction of all things that remind women that they have power. The difficulty with this is that women *have* power, even if they are not reminded of it. It bubbles up and it rises up and it is unquenchable.

The ultimate weapon that has been used to try to dissuade women from being powerful was to take the sources of woman power and describe them as evil, describe them as things that you would be embarrassed to be—such as the bitch, the witch, the dyke, and the slut or the whore.

There are some women who call themselves sacred prostitutes.

Yes. In the bible we read about the Whores of Babylon. Those were the priestesses of the temple. As I understand it, from my readings about those ancient times, this was very clearly defined and understood. The gift of the Goddess included sexuality. The temples offered sexuality. Women would go there before they were married to spend time as sacred prostitutes and sacred whores in order to be the Goddess. They were seen as the Goddess in those situations.

What was your religious upbringing?

My father is Jewish. My mother is Catholic. They lived in Dallas, Texas, where you can't be either of those things. So they sent me to Baptist Sunday school, where I asked a lot of awkward questions. Basically I was a religious eclectic from the very beginning. My mother was struck by a sudden fear when I turned eleven. She hauled me off to catechism and communion so that I would be a good Catholic girl. I really got turned on to the incense, the singing, the Latin, the colors, the costumes, and the stained glass. They would bring the incense down the aisle, and at age eleven I would just faint with ecstasy. I was all set to go through Catholic sainthood when they ripped it all out from under my feet. They started doing the mass in English. I totally lost interest.

I went the way of many people of my generation, which was to explore atheism. That was kind of not satisfying; there wasn't much ritual in atheism. Then there was Zen. I really liked that, and I would say that Zen was my first introduction to the Tao. The Tao is one of those beautiful expressions of the Wise Woman tradition. It's almost like this last voice from the Wise Woman tradition that we had as it began to disappear and the patriarchal voice got louder and louder.

What is it about Paganism that you find valuable and that has kept you interested for the last twenty years?

I was building my own house by hand, and as I was digging the foundation, digging with hand tools these thirteen-inch diameter and four-foot deep pits, I realized that Goddess respected me. There was an actual communion between me as an individual and whatever God/dess was. That is what continues to inform, enrich, and enjuicen my life. I don't have to go to a priest. I don't have to have anybody intercede with anything for me. As I said before, my life, my spirituality, and my art are all one with every breath!

What you are saying sounds very similar to the way a Quaker might believe, the "still, small voice that comes from within." How is being a Pagan different from, say, being a Quaker?

I like to dress up in bright colors, paint my face. I like to take off my clothes and dance naked in the woods. I like to sing and dance with other women. So far as I know Quakers generally don't do those things. I have spent time with Quakers, and I feel extremely comfortable with them, and they feel comfortable with me, so long as I keep my clothes on.

I had heard that at one point in your career you were not allowing any men on your property. The way it was explained to me was that somehow by having men on the property it would damage the healing energy of the land. Therefore, only women were allowed on the land. Where are you with that now?

I spent seven years as a lesbian separatist. For me it was literally a period of being deconditioned. All of my conditioning as a woman had been to defer to other people, specifically to men. I found that I really hit a wall in being able to change that. The conditioning was constantly being triggered. For me, it was necessary to totally take myself out of that in order to find that still, quiet, *female* voice within me.

I found so much pleasure and so much richness in being exclusively in the company of women. I find that for other women even a short period of time, three or four days, exclusively in the company of women really "wakes up" their bitch, their witch, their dyke, and their whore in a way that they are not afraid of.

The men who come know that they are coming to a place that is sacred to women. If they are willing to come there to honor women, to honor the Goddess as evidenced in every woman, then they are welcome to come. They can attend the classes that are held for men and women.

Has any man ever given you a hard time about this?

Ever? Sure. But rarely. One of my first apprentices was a woman of very large stature. She was *not* fond of wearing clothing. I think one of my friends invited her out to have dinner with the caveat that she wear clothing. She asked her if she owned any!

Clove is very close with the animals on the place. One evening at sundown we heard from underneath the house the unmistakeable uproar of a duck being attacked by a raccoon. Clove immediately went into this tiny crawl space under the house. She was trying to scare off the raccoon. So she's under there and at this point some uninvited visitors drive up in the driveway, several men and a couple women. Clove is under the house screaming at the raccoon, "Get the fuck away from here! I hate you!" Needless to say, the uninvited visitors left very, very quickly—and they wrote me a very nasty letter!

Good thing they didn't see her as well! You are handfasted to a male now aren't you?

Yes, I have a consort. I am not married in the eyes of God or man or the Goddess. I have a commitment to be monogamous with my consort for thirteen years and thirteen weeks. Believe me, I tried everything I could to get out of it. This consort was given to me by a woman lover as a birthday present. For the first year of our relationship, it was really wonderful because I never saw Michael, whom we called Michelle, unless Jane arranged it. So I never knew if when I had a date with Jane, Michelle would be there. I didn't have to worry: should I call or not call.

Then Jane decided that she never wanted to see Michael/Michelle again, and that was pretty much the end of it. The three of us had been in a yoga class together, and after class a couple months later, Michael/Michelle walked up to me and said, "I love you, you know." I turned around and gave him this glare. I said, "Don't be silly; I'm a lesbian," and I stalked out of the class. He continued to pursue me. One of my ultimatums was that I would not have anything to do with him unless he called me the Goddess. The very next day I got a letter from him addressed "Dear Goddess."

One of the things that I have found is that if the Goddess/God or the Great Spirit, or whatever you want to call it, has some idea about what you are supposed to do with your life, you have two choices: you can do it, or you can not do it. If you don't do it, you get to go on a long detour that takes you exactly back to that spot. I am too old for detours! So I will spare you the details, but I will guarantee you that I squirmed and I tried whatever I could, asking astrologers, doing Tarot readings, past-life regressions, everything to give me some sign that I could get out of this. Every sign was that I was supposed to do this. So I am now a lesbian with a consort!

I still to this day don't know how it happened. But one thing that I have seen that has been quite amazing is that the apprentices who come to live with me, many of them for the first time find that they can be wholly, truly, and completely themselves around a man. Because of the nature of this particular man.

You are the founder of the Wise Woman tradition of herbalism. Can you talk about that?

I'll give you the Reader's Digest version. Basically, I see that there are three ways to approach healing. Actually, ways to approach life, because people have gotten into the Wise Woman tradition and understood the difference between that and the heroic and the scientific. Then they apply it to teaching, to psychology, to government, to anything.

The scientific tradition, which is not restricted to scientists and in fact a great many scientists have nothing to do with, defines reality as that which is measurable and replicable. So if you tell me that you have used an herb for this person and you got X results and then I do it, I have to use exactly as much as you did, do it exactly when and how you did it. I have to be able to replicate your results. If I can it's true, and if I can't it's false. That's the scientific tradition.

This is a linear thought mode; A precedes B precedes C. There is cause and effect, and you can always find the cause. It is Newtonian science from the clockwork universe; it runs by laws, and we can find those laws.

If we get into real science, if we get into quantum physics, into chaos theory, we are no longer in the scientific tradition. Once we get into variables, that is not the scientific tradition. We have to understand that the scientific tradition doesn't necessarily mean science. It means what we think of as "scientific." Double-blind testing and fixity. We are looking for fixity.

There is no definition of health in this tradition. Health is the absence of disease. As one doctor said to me, "How do you expect me to know anything about health? I just spent eight years studying disease and death!" Death is the Big Word that is not mentioned, because death is the failure. It must be prevented at all costs.

The heroic tradition says follow the rules, and if you don't follow the rules, you bad, dirty, filthy sinner, you've got to get clean if you want to come back in here! So the heroic tradition focuses on purification, cleansing, getting rid of toxins, and being "in balance."

The problem with balance is that balance equals stuck—because you are not inside the circle of the heroic tradition, and you are not outside of it. You are trying to be in two places at once, and so you are in neither. Life is not fixed. Life is not balanced.

In the Wise Woman tradition we stop pushing away what we don't want, and we stop clinging to what we think we want. We are in the place of "I don't know." Which also happens to be open to the universe.

The scientific tradition is a line, the heroic tradition is a circle, the Wise Woman tradition is a spiral. There is no inside or outside to a spiral. There is no place where a spiral starts or ends. So we have that wonderful "I don't know." What we do have is real wholeness.

Real wholeness involves this *and* this. The scientific and the heroic traditions have either/or. The Wise Woman tradition has both. For example, I will put my arm behind my back. I will forget that I did that and tell you that I now have a terrible pain in my shoulder. I have done just about everything I could think of to relieve the pain. I have had a massage, acupuncture, herbs, homeopathy, I've gotten therapy, I've cleaned up my diet, I've had colonics, and my shoulder still hurts—could you possibly help me? What could you suggest that I could possibly do to help my shoulder?

The obvious answer is that I've got to get my arm out from behind my back. Because that's what's hurting my shoulder. Right? I mean, I could do surgery, I could do any technique in the world and my shoulder would still hurt because my arm is still behind my back. That's the part of myself that I am in denial about.

"What do you mean I am in denial! I don't see anything. I'm not in denial about anything at all! I can see every single part of myself. The only problem is my shoulder hurts!"

Well, my shoulder hurting is already the solution. The problem is that my arm is behind my back. So in the Wise Woman tradition, rather than relieve the problem, which is actually the solution, we ask instead what needs to be nourished here. What needs to be nourished is the part that is in denial. So here's my right hand; this is the wonderful Susun. She's such a good person. She's a loving mother, she's a great friend, she would never let you down. She is exactly what society says she should be. My left hand is the bitch, the dyke, and the whore. Watch out!

Sacred Prostitutes

In her excellent fantasy series *The Earthsea Trilogy*, author Ursula K. LeGuin tells us "Words contain Power." The young magician in her books learns that to know something's "true" name is to know its power. This is something Pagans have known for aeons, but names can also cause many misconceptions, pain, and suffering. Take the name "prostitute." One immediately sees an image that is often seedy and unsavory. When we add the term "sacred," we are faced with an apparent conflict. To many ancient societies, however, sex was considered sacred, and whole systems of reaching spiritual, emotional, and physical ecstasy were developed.

The two women interviewed have re-embraced the words, concept, and practices of the "sacred prostitute." They believe by removing the (often Christian) conception of the human body as something to hide away, not discuss, and feel guilt over, and replacing it with the more ancient conception that the human body is a temple to use and celebrate, we can obtain higher forms of spiritual awakening and ecstasy.

Whether or not we agree with the viewpoints of either of these two women after hearing their stories, in a time and culture in which the human body (particularly the female body) has become something to exploit, market, and violate, it is refreshing to hear these women celebrate the sacred aspect of their bodies and sexuality.

D'VORA is a psychiatric nurse and lay midwife. She is also known as Queen of Thelema, the Empress, the High Priestess of Weirdness, the Propstitute, Sex Magician, Cat Woman, and as a sacred prostitute. She is the author of "Reflections from the Orgynizor," an article in the publication *Mezlim* in its "Sacred Prostitute Issue." She was interviewed in 1993 at Starwood, near Sherman, New York.

What is your background?

I am a registered nurse in New York state. My background has been in the women's movement. I have worked with the La Leche League with breast feeding, and I have been a lay midwife, delivering babies at home. I became a nurse *after* all of that which I think is very important. What I want to bring into my healing work is everything I learned "out there." I want to do the things that you don't learn about in nursing institutions or hospitals. I'm bringing in holistic and alternative approaches.

My degree is a master's in Community Health Nursing. I went to a small Catholic college, and I did my master's on using ritual as a healing tool. I did a qualitative study. I interviewed a family that designed and enacted a menarche ritual for their daughter. They used a Wiccan high priestess for that purpose to teach them how to do it. She happened to be *my* high priestess, so she linked us together, and I interviewed the family about what had happened. I used "Wiccan," I used "priestess," I used all the words.

At the time I was working on an eating disorder unit, and I was interested in anorexia, women not wanting to become women, holding their bodies back from looking womanly and not having periods and so on.

I learned something called therapeutic touch, polarity, and all kinds of healing techniques over the years, and I incorporated that into my practice. I currently teach nursing students energy-field healing, and I bring all of my magical work into the healing space, or what I call sacred space.

How long have you been a Pagan?

1981 was my first Rite of Spring. I had been a hippie, I was interested in ecology and all that natural stuff, and I never thought that there were people out there who were actively doing Witchcraft. I had read about it—I thought it was very romantic. So I arrived at this festival to sell stained glass, and I saw people dancing in a field, naked around a fire, with horns on their heads. There were these wonderful little pan figures, these men with tails and horns, and I just knew I was home.

What is your particular practice?

I call my personal practice being a sacred prostitute. To me that means running a sexual current. It's a very powerful current. We all are sexual, even babies are sexual. I was a midwife and nursing and having very small children, and as they grew I realized what I was doing to my own body—that I hated my own body. I realized that this was happening because of the culture. When I joined the women's movement, I learned to be free about my body. We were looking inside each other's vaginas with speculums and exploring what we really were all about. All this made me realize that this is a *very* powerful current.

At one point in my life I had become bulemic. I was destroying myself because I hated my body. To me that had a lot to do with sexuality. As I became a healer, I realized that, in the hospital particularly, many people are severely hurt by not knowing their boundaries. They open themselves to a very magical act by being sexual and don't know how to control or modify or modulate those energies, and they lose it and they become very sick. That means that we have incest and all kinds of sexual abuse going on with families. I see the end result of this in the psychiatric hospital. There's the woman who is starving herself, there's a woman who is cutting herself . . . .

The healing process for *me* was to unleash my sexuality and say, "I am free. No holds barred. I am free to use my body the way I want to." That means free to not use it as well. That is a common misunderstanding. When people hear the words sacred prostitute, they tend to leave out the sacred part.

There are a lot of people, men and women, who are working this current. I personally know of at least fifty who are actively doing this. When people talk to me, they get really turned on and they ask if they can learn more about it.

I'd say most of magic is sex. When you are doing the Great Rite in Wicca, for instance. But it's usually symbolic. The real thing doesn't happen very often. The Great Rite in most covens is the symbolic act of taking an athame [dagger or sword], which represents the penis, and putting it into a cup or a chalice that represents the womb, the feminine receiving power. This represents Tantra, the union of opposites, alchemy, everything that Jung was talking about. Usually afterwards people go home and make love if they have a partner to "ground the energy" with.

Sex is the one arena where most people can experience the ecstasy of the union of opposites. In orgasm you have some sense of what the true ecstasy of Yoga is all about. It doesn't necessarily take sex to get there. You can do it through breathing, through Yoga asanas, through meditation. There are many ways to get there, but the sexual one is most common. Most people can have sex and have a really good time and feel high. That's why it can be used so effectively. Because it is so powerful, it gets misused, and that is what I wanted to learn about for myself. I don't want to teach or practice or promote a philosophy with my clients. If people are coming to me who are wounded and I am wounded too, that's no good either.

Jung is a spiritual leader for me. I consider him to be a gnostic with a gospel, a spiritual word. He says you cannot help anyone unless you go through it yourself first, unless you have been there. One has to take the plunge and go into the dark side of whatever experience is frightening. For me that was sex.

That's a loaded statement, because that is like saying that a person can't be a therapist unless he or she has experienced rape, incest, divorce, child abuse . . .

I hear what you are saying. But people have to be willing to deal with their own dark side, whatever it is, in a meaningful way. There are too many psychiatrists out there who don't see a psychiatrist themselves, who aren't paying attention to their own growth and development. That means going into very painful places.

Obviously, you don't have to have had a divorce to help someone, but if you have dealt with pain and grief and loss effectively and used the techniques that you are asking your clients to use on yourself, it's more authentic.

You use the words "sacred prostitute." When most people hear the word "prostitute," they think of giving money for sex.

I think that would be perfectly valid. I originally was inspired by a Jungian writer named Qualls-Corbett. Inner City Press put out a series of Jungian treatises, and I was using Marion Woodman quite a bit in my work. I saw *The Sacred Prostitute* listed in the back of one of the books, and I decided to check it out. What she describes is her conception of ancient times when women were honored as wives and mothers and there was a type of mundane prostitute that men would go to for quick sex. There was another type who was a priestess, a sacred prostitute. The sacred prostitutes were in the temples. A priestess would have sexual union with someone with the idea of reaching some kind of enlightenment. This captured my imagination, the thought that sexual union could be a path to the Divine. The book also suggests that what we are doing is developing an inner anima and animus which need to be married.

I've since learned much about alchemy, because that is what alchemy is all about. It involves maturing and knowing your inner feminine, the anima, and your inner masculine, the animus, and wedding them. That is hard work.

I had realized that my little girl inside was a frightened little girl. Because of my work in the feminist movement, I had matured my animus; my masculine energy was out front. I was abrasive, and I could just chop anything down with words, but my soft self wasn't there. The sacred prostitute work seemed like an approach to finding that soft self. The inner marriage is the *most* important thing. What it takes to get there is the path you are on, and I chose an overtly sexual one. I decided to truly be *in* my body.

I was a Wiccan first, an initiated Gardnerian Witch. I chose to deal with what I euphemistically call "demons," the energies and dragons that come up in dreams, and meet and greet them.

Before I became a Pagan I hated my body and my breasts. If I was going to truly love my body, I needed to truly make love to other people. To truly *love* them, whatever and however their body was. Black or white, large or small, fat or thin. Things that I had cultural biases toward I wanted to overcome. I set out on a path to make love to it until I could find beauty in it. I wanted to find beauty in my sexuality, in all forms of it—to feel free. And I have!

This doesn't mean that it's always safe or that it's always pleasant. Many times it's ecstatic. I've also spent many months being celibate. The sacred prostitute path doesn't necessarily mean jumping on every available cock.

But why use the word "prostitute"? That usually means a woman who takes money for sex.

My belief is that there's absolutely nothing wrong with taking money for sex. Wives do it all the time. Everyone thinks marriage is so sacred, but if you think about it, it's actually an economic relationship that you have created.

That's one part of it. Hopefully, people get married because they feel a spiritual or a friendship affinity. They don't get together for purely economic reasons . . .

In my experience the spiritual part is what people would *like* it to be, but it's not. The economic demands of marriage as an institution override what could be a spiritual course.

I'd rather keep the two separate. I live with people in an economic arrangement out of love—my children, others in my life—but my spiritual/sexual partner will be something separate, I think. I'm not saying that an economic marriage isn't valid or doesn't have its place. But to me it's not necessarily a spiritual relationship.

Can you go into some of the specifics of what you practice?

My method is informal. I don't have a formal group like a coven. I happen to belong to a coven, and I find that takes care of the organized activity. What I do is very spontaneous, very eclectic. I've been working with large-group ritual, and this summer I am creating a ritual about the alchemical union of opposites. The imagery is very ecstatic. I don't have men dancing with flaming cocks or wands on fire—it's not overtly orgiastic, but that is in there as an underlying current.

The space that I am in now is one where sexuality is a blessed thing. The group that I work with is very sexually open. There might be people making love in a room while others are sitting and talking or looking. The freedom of it is very appealing. There is certainly a dark side to it, in that for many people this would be very frightening. But to be able to go into a safe space where sexuality is open is really very freeing. I don't think *everyone* is ready for that. Obviously, this is a path that you have to be prepared for.

The one experience that stands out for most people is an article that I wrote for *Mezlim* about an orgy that I held. I like group sex, I like anonymous sex, *I like sex.* Over the years I've learned to. It hasn't always been the case, but I have made conscious efforts to experience these different things. I thought it would be interesting to have a group sexual experience that was intentional. That we would go into it as a sacred act. What is more common is that someone has a party, and some people start to make love, and one thing leads to another, and pretty soon you have a room full of people who are making love. It's quite nice and it's an orgy and everyone has had a good time, but it was not an intentional spiritual act—a ritual.

I wanted to play with that ritual aspect, see what it would be like. A group of us were sitting around one day laughing, and I said, "Let's do it." We invited people, and fourteen came. We held hands, sat around in a circle, and talked about the fact that we wanted to free our souls. We wanted to free our *selves.* We wanted a theater to really be ourselves. That meant that we might have sex or we might not. The possibility was open for it to happen. It would be a healing not a threatening thing. If anyone didn't feel safe, there were safe places and spaces to go to. Then we started to party.

We did the usual ritual type thing of calling in the directions and chanting white light into our bodies. We didn't use a strictly Wiccan or ceremonial magic approach because everyone came from different traditions. We did a healing visualization where we brought in white light through the tops of our heads and sent it out of our bodies to the room. We were kind of glowing with a spiritual white light before we even started. Then we did some drumming. It seemed like drumming and dancing shook the shyness away, which is a very empowering way to get things going. Pretty soon people were making love, and it was a wonderful, wonderful night.

What surprised me most of all was my fear that came up about the whole thing. I didn't have sex that night with anyone. I became a voyeur. That intrigued me because I had certainly been looking forward to the possibilities. In other group sexual activities I have been very active.

What do you mean by "fear came up"?

I pay attention to my emotional responses, and I just had *fear.* How my body feels, what it tells me is a very good way to establish a boundary line. This is safe and this isn't. This is where I can go and this is where I can't. Enormous waves of fear came up, and since then I have explored why that might have happened. I used Re-evaluation Counseling, a type of peer counseling, to explore that. It's a type of counseling where you learn to express emotions and discharge them. When the fear came up, I knew that the orgy had triggered something from the past, and for me that can mean the past in this life or in other lifetimes. I wasn't going to question where the fear came from, but when I triggered the emotion in a counseling session, I just started screaming at the top of my lungs. That has come up several times since then. It is a lot of fear around being persecuted.

I am a nurse, and I have terrifying dreams and images of senators pointing their fingers at me and calling me a Witch and satanic. Why the orgy triggered a year of counseling on these kinds of issues I don't know. I went back to feeling like a Witch who had been burned at the stake. I realized that in past lives I had been tortured by male priests, doctors, men in authority positions. I don't know why that came up, but it has unleashed an enormous amount of healing work for me. As I let the emotions come up and I scream and I cry for that one hour each week, I have been able to go forward in my clinical practice with a great deal of confidence. I think it will all become clear to me at some point.

What was the result of the ritual for the others in the group?

Everyone had wonderful and growth-producing transformational experiences. I'd say that out of the fourteen I can think of two or three people who had some kind of fear or inhibition that came up for them. Most of the people experienced a kind of ecstatic high. As a matter of fact, many of the people who were there usually take a hallucinogenic drug when they do group workings, and I didn't permit that. They all mentioned that they felt as high as they had on hallucinogens.

In the wee hours of the morning, when we calmed down from the sexual activity, we were reading poetry to each other and lying on each other and touching, and there was a lot of processing going on. I was pretty aware of what had gone on for each person. I considered myself a priestess in that situation.

I've had requests for more of these rituals, but I don't do my sex work unless I am inspired. It has to be ecstatic and spontaneous and inspired or I won't do it.

Why should a person consider doing this kind of activity?

All paths lead to the same place. Tantra is the internal union of opposites. It's another path to the Divine.

If more people became involved in this activity, what do you think the implications for society would be?

It's not an activity so much as it is an orientation. It's a mindset. It's a willingness to say, "I'm in charge of what I do with my body. I'm not going to go by prescribed behaviors. I am going to explore and investigate." As each one of us unleashes that block, those chains, it will profoundly affect the world. As each of us becomes freer, we unleash freedom. That spreads. It's contagious.

There is a wonderful gospel in the Nag Hammadi texts under "Thunder Perfect Mind." It says, "I am the darkness, I am the light. I am the barren one and many are my children." It's a feminine voice that goes through all the opposites, "I am the virgin and I am the whore. I am the feminine. I am it all conjoined." She finally says, "I am the utterance of my name." That is what each of us has to speak. Our own true will. My name is D'vora, and it rings clear. My path to getting there has been to work sexually.

I work with people who have been raped, who are victims of incest, and who are very frightened of their bodies. I hurt for them because I know how beautiful it is to be inside your body and really enjoy it. It means a lot to them and to me that I can discuss those issues without shame.

Anything you would like to add?

Practice safe sex. At the orgy we had everything available that the individual might want to use: condoms, plastic gloves. Pay attention, know when you are safe. Listen to your body and to the fears that come up. Don't act on something that appears dangerous.

I would not recommend this for everyone. As you become more adept at working the energy fields, you can read the messages. Listen to your dreams and your visions, your voices. This is not just "fucking." Each person has to make their own boundaries.

ANNIE SPRINKLE is a highly controversial performance artist, lesbian, Tantrica, and sacred prostitute. A one-time porn film star, she has some two hundred X-rated films to her credit. More recently she has made and been the subject of many documentaries, docudramas, and workshop films and videos, including *The Sluts and Goddesses Video Workshop, or How to be a Sex Goddess in 101 Easy Steps*. Author of *Annie Sprinkle, Post Porn Modernist*, she now works exclusively with women, guiding sacred sex workshops and creating sex magic rituals. She was interviewed by phone on April 2, 1994.

Are you a Pagan?

I've never really studied Paganism or Witchcraft officially, but after talking with you I guess that I am. Certainly, when I do my performances and my workshops there is a strong Pagan element. It just sort of happened naturally, somehow.

What does the word "Pagan" mean to you?

It's one of those nebulous words like "Tantra"; you can't really quite put your finger on it. Everybody has a different definition for it, and every book has a different definition. To me personally it would mean someone who practices ritual and is interested in the well-being of the planet and who is sex positive. I don't really know for sure, but I like that I don't know. I don't *have* to know.

What religion were you raised in?

Unitarian. Part of me still thinks of myself as Unitarian. I've gone through phases off and on. A few years ago I started to go to a Unitarian church again once in a while. I like it because it incorporates everything, and it's very humanistic. They do Pagan rituals on occasion, depending on the church. They are very open minded. Mostly I would say that I follow the path of Tantra. I feel very much connected with the legends of the ancient sacred prostitutes; that's really my religion.

I got into mainstream prostitution when I was eighteen. I always had a sense that there was more to it than people thought. It was something that fit my needs. I didn't just want to go to college; I was looking for adventure, I was very interested in sex, I needed money, I needed to be touched. I was a very insecure person, and I needed to be told that I was sexy.

I also felt that it was a very important job, that I was a kind of pleasure priestess and a healer. I decided to follow my muse and go with what was happening; it could have been something karmic. It could be that I was just born to be a sacred prostitute.

There are sacred prostitutes, and there are what are called profane prostitutes, both of which are equally important. I have a performance piece about my personal sexual evolution, which I travel all over the world doing. It starts out where I am a porn-star bimbo, a naive, profane kind of prostitute, and I develop into a more powerful and mature, spiritually minded, strong woman whom I call Anya.

I have three characters in the piece. I start out as Ellen Steinberg, which is who I was born as. She is very insecure, thinks she is ugly, and has low self-esteem. She then becomes Annie Sprinkle, who is a porn star, prostitute, and stripper. She is an outgoing, fearless slut. Then I develop into Anya, who is more of a teacher, a healer, a more mature and a wiser woman with more experience. You could say that she's a Pagan.

Most people have an idea of what a profane prostitute is—a woman who gets money for sex. But the idea of a sacred prostitute in our culture is unknown. Can you go into that a bit more?

Actually, both kinds of prostitutes may receive money for sex. In my performance I have brought back the legends of the sacred prostitutes through doing a ritual of the sacred prostitute. It is partly based on my own creation and imagination and partly on what I have read about the sacred prostitutes in ancient times. I explain how a long time ago it was a great honor to be a sacred prostitute, but that sex was really different then. In the temples of the sacred prostitutes the main elements of a love-making session were prayer, ritual, healing, and meditation. Then I describe those beautiful temples and talk about how they devoted their life to learning about the art of ecstasy. It was understood that when you were in sexual ecstasy it was the best time to connect with the Divine, the best time to make your prayers, the best time to create a miracle or get a vision. I have to say that has been my experience.

Then I light candles and make prayers. Each candle symbolizes a prayer. For example, I was just in Austria, at Hitler's birthplace. A few days before I got there, in this small town of seventeen thousand people, a woman had been stabbed to death for telling a guy she didn't want to have sex with him. He was a seventeen-year-old boy, a total stranger to her. This happened right in front of the theater.

So I lit a candle in her memory and made a prayer for a safer world for women. I then made a prayer for myself, and the audience members were given candles to make their own wishes. I evoked the spirit of the sacred prostitute and the Tantric and the Taoist masters and all of the greatest sex teachers to help us find new ways of expressing our sexuality in the time of AIDS and other sexually transmitted diseases. Then I lit a flame in a beautiful pyramid-shaped Agni Hotra bowl [a Hindu fire-purification ritual bowl]. I called on the spirits of the Earth and the Sky, who are two of my favorite lovers, and who are so filled with sensual delights and who make me so happy. I invited them to make love with me.

I gave everyone in the audience a rattle—sometimes I do this with four hundred and fifty people; it builds a *lot* of energy. I've learned so much from doing that, and I have done it all over the world. Then I put oil all over my body, and I brushed my skin to stimulate it. I put tiger balm on sensitive areas like my nipples and my anus in order to wake up my body. I also did breathing and undulating and stretching exercises, all in front of the audience.

So I got in touch with my body, and I started making pathways for sexual energy. Then I took a vibrator and vibrated all of my chakras. I vibrated my clitoris, and then I used a dildo, and I ejaculated and went into sexual ecstasy.

My whole goal in this is to feel whatever is there while in a state of sexual ecstasy. Sometimes I will have orgasm, sometimes I won't. Sometimes the energy is very low, and other times it is the most powerful and amazing experience.

What is the audience supposed to get out of this?

On a good day I've had women break into spontaneous orgasm. I've had people cry—that happens a lot. I invite them to have an experience, and I hope that they get something from it, a thought, a feeling, or a vision, perhaps some new energy or a new idea. It's really a meditation for them. It's whatever they want it to be, and quite often it mirrors what they feel about their own sexuality and about masturbation.

On a *really* good day, when the energy is very high, it's a very powerful experience for the people in the audience. Quite often at the end people will come up to me, and I become the Goddess, people see the Goddess in me. They often throw their jewelry at me! They take off their jewelry and give it to me.

At the end when it's all over, I just gaze into people's eyes. I stay very present and meditate, and I sometimes trance out. So this is all about using sexual energy to experience the Divine or, one could say, the lack of the Divine.

Sometimes people get angry. Sometimes they are totally healed or they are totally inspired. It's the most important thing that I do, I think. It's also the most difficult thing.

It has taught me so much about ritual and about energy and about life and about sex. You know what? It's working. It's sex magic. Amazing things are happening in my life which I feel are a direct result of the sex magic in the ritual. I know that it has changed some people's lives in a very deep way.

What else do you do? Do you have a mundane career?

No. I've never had a mundane career. I make videos; I have a video called *Sluts and Goddesses Video Workshop*. My video is an all-women video, and it has been played at all of the best museums and festivals in the world. It is considered art, and it's also sexually explicit. It's a lesbian classic, although it's beyond lesbian; it's a pivotal women's classic, I would say. I've been in two hundred regular porno movies, but those don't count; that's more of the profane prostitute kind of thing.

What would be the point for Americans in the nineties in what you are doing. How could your path affect American culture?

Part of my message with the legend of the sacred prostitute ritual is that sex is more about energy than about bodies coming together. That we need to have more of a focus on sexual energy because of all the sexually transmitted diseases. Also that people aren't utilizing anywhere near their potential as far as their sexuality.

My message is that sex is sacred, that it is spiritual, and that it is a path to enlightenment.

Do you see any connection between the violence against women in our culture and the fact that sex has been repressed?

I think that when a man commits a rape, there is a lot of energy there. All the fear and adrenalin builds up a lot more energy than you have in regular sex. If they can learn how to create a high erotic state in a much more positive way, they won't have to rape to experience that energy. That is just one part of the puzzle.

People can be taught to experience high states of ecstasy. Most people don't know anything about it, and they don't get very far and they feel unsatisfied. I think much of the violence against women is at the core a lot of sexual frustration. When people are sexually satisfied and having wonderful orgasms, they aren't so violent; they are happy and satisfied. This could have tremendous implications for world peace. My motto is, "Let there be pleasure on earth and let it begin with me."

Our sexuality has so many gifts for us. If we were to use them more, we wouldn't be so frustrated, miserable, unhappy, and violent and cruel to each other. I don't think we'd pollute the planet if we saw the Earth as our lover and enjoyed Her sensuality more. We would treat Her more like someone we were in love with. I think this work has ecological implications.

The image of the sacred prostitute is beginning to take off in a big way, especially for sex workers. Sex workers are women who make a living through sexuality. They are creating more healing and holistic environments for their work. The red wallpaper is out, and fresh flowers and aromatherapy are in. They are creating a whole different aesthetic around prostitution, and they are owning the fact that their work is important. This is a small group of really privileged women, talented and bright women.

These are the kinds of things I'd be thinking about if I wanted to be a prostitute: I'd be afraid of encountering a violent man and of being expected to have sex with somebody that I was not physically attracted to, maybe even found repulsive. Have you ever encountered those kinds of situations?

Sure, I've been in prostitution for twenty years. I wasn't an alcoholic or a drug addict; I have always had a choice in what I did. This is a gift. I think that there are women who are able to share the gift of their sexuality with a person who is needy. It's an ability. Not everyone has it. It's a very generous thing and a very loving, caring thing. These are the privileged ones. In fact, many of them are Pagans.

Obviously, if you are a street prostitute, you are risking violence. Being a taxi driver, you risk violence; being a convenience store worker, you risk violence. Many jobs are dangerous, and certainly prostitution is. Especially because it's illegal, which does not help things at all. I'm on the steering committee of the Prostitutes of New York, and in fact next week I am doing a benefit for Coyote. These are prostitutes' rights groups. There is a big movement to de-criminalize prostitution globally.

But what I am talking about is the re-emergence of the sacred prostitute. There is a school in San Francisco called the Body Electric School of Erotic Spirituality. One of the many things they are doing is training men how to be sacred "intimates" or sexual healers.

Is this a good idea in the time of AIDS?

Being a sacred prostitute doesn't mean that you have to have intercourse. Much of it is erotic massage. My girlfriend in California is a sacred prostitute. She does erotic massage; she never has intercourse or oral sex. AIDS is, of course, a big issue, and there are certainly ways to work safely. There are also prostitutes with AIDS. Some of them have it and are working. Hopefully, they are having safe sex, but it is a fact.

Do you get mostly men or mostly women coming to your shows?

I'd say it's fifty-fifty. My best audience is women. The best show I ever did was in Northampton, Massachusetts. It was an all-women audience. The all-women shows are the best. That's because I am a woman, and it's a woman's story, and I'm appealing to women. I relate better to women anyway. Men are welcome to come if they want.

At the end I open myself up, and I go into a high state of sexual ecstasy without a man. A lot of men get upset over that. I also reveal a certain amount of female power. If I'm having incredible multiple orgasms from the depths of my cunt, up and out, it looks pretty intense and it scares men. It can scare women too, but I think it's important that people see it.

A woman who is really sexually knowledgeable, who is super orgasmic, looks a lot like a woman giving birth. She really goes into her breath and her animal energy and her power, and it shows. That can be empowering and inspiring to watch or it can be scary as hell! That is why prostitutes, and especially sacred prostitutes, have been really supressed. They are arrested, they get no support, and everything is done to squelch their power. The men in the system, the patriarchy, don't want women to be more orgasmic than them. Women are capable of being much more orgasmic than men. They have more sexual power and a higher capacity for experiencing ecstasy.

There is a sad side; there are many women out there who are suffering and on drugs and who are being exploited and are miserable. But sex is a healing, nourishing force, and I would like to see us honor and give more support to people who give pleasure. That's their job, to make people feel good. And they are very much persecuted for that. I believe a woman has a right to control her own body—to have an abortion if she chooses—and I believe that a woman has a right to take money for her sexual favors.

Things are changing. The fact that I go and do my show and I talk openly about having been a prostitute and a porn star and I do the ritual and I douche on stage and I show my cervix to everybody and I go into sexual ecstasy—the fact that I can do that without getting arrested is a miracle. There is controversy along the way, but we have come a long way, that's for sure.

I feel that I have saved lives and I have made people feel more pleasure than they have ever known in their life. I've given them their most blissful moments, and that's a beautiful thing. Over the years I have helped teach people more about their own sexuality through my workshops, performances, and sex work.

My own health is remarkably good, and I think that's because I allow my sexual energy to flow freely. It keeps me emotionally cleansed. I consciously use my sexuality as a healing tool, as therapy. The benefits are abundant. Money is coming in, I have love. There are great benefits, but you do have to pay a price, as with anything.

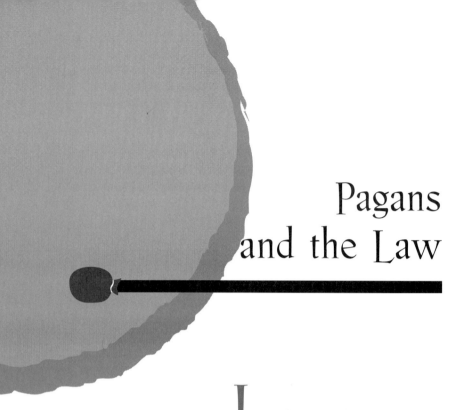

Pagans
and the Law

Intricately entwined with the need for freedom of expression is the all-too-human fear of the unknown. What is new and exciting for one is cause for fear and prejudice for another. So the human experience is sometimes gridlocked with intricate systems of rules and laws that are designed to guide and protect.

With laws come law enforcers, armies and police, and all too quickly the line between protection and violation of one's human rights can be blurred. Still there are those law enforcers who live up to the true meaning of the Sanskrit term *Shanti Sena* or "peacekeeper," and in this chapter we introduce two such remarkable people. The fact that they are working toward the same goals in spite of being polar opposites in their approach, and more fundamentally their beliefs (one is a Pagan, the other is a Christian), is a testament to the true spirit of diversity.

PAUL TUITÉAN describes himself as a Wiccan solitary; he is not a member of any one group or belief system but is following his own path. He is a member of the Guardians of the Fourth Face, a Pagan, fraternal service organization loosely inspired by the North American Plains Indians' Dog Soldiers Societies. Their purpose is to develop a network of competent and experienced personnel to provide the organizational infrastructure and emergency service backup at Pagan gatherings needed to ensure the safety of all attendants. They are also interested in helping to develop communications and informational resource networks specializing in Pagan security issues for concerned, responsible community leaders. He was interviewed by phone on February 9, 1994.

Have long have you been a Pagan?

I've been a Pagan as long as I can remember. As far as being Wiccan, I got involved with that in 1981. I had my first "vision quest" when I was fourteen. I did it all by myself.

After that I started looking at other nontraditional spiritual paths, technologies, and sciences. I also started studying the history of religion. I met people who were overtly Pagan in 1977 or '78 at a War Gaming Shop. That's a place where they play war games. I also started meeting some at science fiction conventions.

I am not comfortable with a lot of people, but these were people who had something in common with me, the war games and the interest in history.

In 1981, just for the hell of it, I joined a basic Wicca class. I then found out that many of the teachings of Wicca were similar to the thought forms and mindsets that I had all along. For example, the belief in the wholeness of the Universe. The idea of Gaia, that the Earth is a living being.

Are you in a Wiccan coven?

Currently, no. I am a solitary. My current practice is eclectic, a mix of Gardnerian and Native American practices. Also, because I live in Minneapolis, where there is much Norse influence, that comes into what I do.

The Minneapolis area has a lot of people from the old country, Swedes and Norse. The ecology is also very similar to Scandinavia. The mindset of people is very similar to the people who live in the northern areas of Europe. When I use Norse Runes, Norse Gods and Goddesses, and Norse ways of doing things, I get better results up here than I do when using Greek ones, for example.

You are involved with something called the Guardians of the Fourth Face. Could you talk about that a bit?

It is a Pagan organization developed to provide safety and emergency services for Pagan gatherings. We put it together around 1988 because many of us had seen too many almost blunders and near misses at gatherings when it came to security and emergency services. So we got some people together who had police experience, military experience, and medical experience. A good number of us have EMT experience as well.

Do you go to all the Pagan festivals?

No. We only go to a few; we only go when we are asked. There are about six festivals that we do regularly, and they tend to be in the western and midwestern portion of the U.S. There are many Pagans who don't understand what we are trying to do, and they get upset with us. Also, since everything we do is on a volunteer basis, both in time and money, there is no way we could get to them all.

Do you go incognito?

People know we are there. That is important to us.

You don't ever just invite yourselves?

We *have* to be invited by the festival organizers. We sit down with them before the festival starts and figure out what boundaries they want us to cover, how they would like certain things handled. One of the trickier things we've had to deal with in the last few years has been the drug issue. The way we handle that at each festival is determined by the festival organizers. We've seen festivals where people have sold highly illegal drugs darned near in the open. We've been to festivals where they don't try to hide their usage of illegal substances. The problem with that is that in the last few years the police have used it as an excuse to confiscate property and arrest people.

You said some Pagans have problems with what you are doing. What do you mean by that?

There are Pagans who have problems with authority figures, with what they see as militaristic figures. They have problems with "cops." We've had people verbally assault us on occasion, but we have never had a physical fight of any kind with anyone.

Can you talk a bit about the kinds of things you have done to help people?

The reason for our starting the organization was something that happened at a festival. A person who was working in a halfway house brought three of her mental patients with her. One of them was an extremely dangerous manic depressive with psychotic tendencies, and he did not bring his medications. We ended up babysitting him for twenty-four hours until we could get him out of the festival. The nurses and others were afraid that he was going to lose control. He was six foot four and weighed three hundred pounds.

One of our normal procedures is that around four o'clock in the morning we will do a major sweep of the festival grounds looking for people who have fallen asleep and did not mean to. One year we found someone who had apparently been drinking at the main fire, and who had staggered back to the other side of the camp. We found him asleep next to his campfire. It looked like he had fallen into the campfire and rolled through it. He was sky clad [naked] and snoring peacefully. He had burns and frostbite. We carried him to the medical people, still asleep.

Do you go to the Rainbow Gatherings?

No. One of the things on our agenda is to get in touch with the people who put together the Rainbow Gatherings. We would also like to contact the women who do security at the Michigan Women's Music Festival, just to compare notes. Another one of the goals that we have is to develop procedures and mindsets appropriate to Pagan gatherings.

Most of the mindsets we would like to develop have to be different because our people are not belligerent. I've rarely seen any bad drugs at festivals; we've rarely run across a situation where we could not talk to someone. We just had to figure out how to talk to them.

Thirty-six-hour shifts are not common anymore, but they are not unusual. There have been festivals where there was a fire watch all the time. People had to be up for the entire time of the gathering. We normally have people up at all times, but we try to keep it down to one person.

Most of our style of dealing with things is "a stitch in time," because if we can get to something before it gets to be a problem, it can be diffused much quicker. So we always have someone walking around, feeling the energy of the festival, locating potential problems, so that if one occurs we know where it is.

Lt. Ed Maxwell is a former police officer, investigator, and instructor covering crimes of ritual abuse. He is a co-author of *Occult Awareness,* a handbook for law enforcement officers. He is unique in the context of this book, for he is the only non-Pagan (non-Wiccan) interviewed for this project. This interview may leave some readers with the uncomfortable confrontation of their own prejudices against law enforcement officials, as Lt. Maxwell's refreshing open-mindedness shatters all the stereotypes of American police. He was interviewed by phone on January 27, 1994. Further reading material and resources are listed in the endnotes for this chapter.

Are you a Pagan?

No. I am a baptized Christian, but I have studied with Pagans and worked with them and attended Pagan rituals in order to learn about the different beliefs that the Pagan community holds.

Can you describe the police work that you have done with Paganism?

In 1985 I was assigned to a detective division as an investigator in child sexual abuse. Most of the cases were intrafamily sexual abuse, but within a one-year period we got two cases with multiple victims, mostly young girls. In one case they claimed they had been raped by the Devil, or raped in a ritual situation where candles were used. In the course of investigating the cases, I discovered that there were adult male perpetrators who were utilizing occult-related activities—rituals, robes, pentagrams, candles, books—to convince children that they were all-powerful and that they could control them. They told the children that if they would submit they would be given magical powers. I quickly understood that I didn't know a whole lot about what these adult perpetrators were talking about. In 1985 there just was not a lot of information available to nonpractitioners.

There was a group of people in Virginia who had started a group called Bothered about Dungeons and Dragons, but they had an agenda. The information that they gave out was slanted. The Maryland State Police put on a seminar because they were seeing an increase in criminal activity involving children where the adult perpetrators were saying, "I am Satan" or "I am a Witch." Then someone from the Pagan community in Delaware reached out to me, one of the members of a Druid organization. He said he had heard about me as a result of some talk shows. He liked the fact that I was open-minded, and asked would I like to hear their side of the story? The Druids were afraid that they would be caught up in the hysteria that was starting to take over. At that time Geraldo and Sally Jesse Raphael were all picking up on this. So I met with him and discovered that there are two distinct patterns of occult involvement.

There is a legitimate group of people who are involved in the worship of the Santeria Gods and the Pagan Gods—a whole world that someone who was brought up as a Christian would not be familiar with. Then I felt that it was incumbent upon me, knowing that there were people out there who were protected by the first amendment and not breaking any laws, to at least let my department know about this.

The state police wanted information, and local colleges started coming to me, and the whole thing snowballed. A local Wiccan group came to me and said they would be happy to teach me anything I wanted to know. I was accepted by the community and allowed to attend and photograph the rituals. Out of all that I put together a two-day course for the University of Delaware that I call Occult Awareness. It was designed to instruct people who were in the throes of hysteria that just because someone doesn't pray to "God," they are not doing something illegal.

Cops were coming across the Afro-Cuban religions because of the influx of immigrants from El Salvador and Haiti. They were coming across people who were sacrificing chickens in their basements, and their neighbors were going crazy. I come from the position that you have the right to do whatever you want as long as you don't break the law.

What are the kinds of things that a person who is new to all of this, or a police officer, might look for in order to distinguish between "authentic" Pagan activity and "pretend" Pagan activity?

That is a distinction that I don't even want my officers to make. You can pretend to be a Pagan. You can pretend to be a Satanist, as a lot of the kids we get involved with are doing. What I'm trying to do is ask officers, teachers, school principals, and social workers if a law is being broken or if someone is being harmed. If not, then let people be people.

The Pagan community here was being very open, and they were doing their rituals on public park land so we were getting calls. Invariably anything that had to do with the occult was immediately seen as Satanism. That was the big word on everyone's mind, that there were Satanists sacrificing a baby in the park. You'd go over there and find out that it was a Wiccan group doing a Summer Solstice ceremony. Everybody was having this mass hysteria because of the media mostly.

One of the pamphlets you sent me about your work said that for a Satanist the highest object of power is the blood of a male baby. In several other places it said that there has not been one case of satanic ritual murder that has ever been proven in the United States. Those two statements seemed a little contradictory.

You have to look at where those statements are coming from. The course that I teach is designed to stimulate thought on the subject. It is not meant to give people ideas. The information I hand out is from practitioners and from the people who are fighting the practitioners. The comment about the blood from a male baby comes from Aliester Crowley's book. The passage that says we can't prove that there has been a single sacrifice is from FBI statistical evidence. You have writers who purport to be occult experts saying, "This is what we do." From the law enforcement viewpoint, if you don't break the law you can worship whomever you want to.

I have an acquaintance in Allentown who purports to be a high priest in the Church of Satan. He is very open about that. He always says that he won't break the law, he won't take blood with his knife. The pamphlet is attempting to show what the left wing and the right wing are saying. Each person has to find out where they are comfortable down the middle. . . . There is material that is written for adults that is being interpreted by children. A child, a teenager of seventeen years, will read it and get all hepped up. He might not read the next page, where it says, "But of course you cannot kill anybody." What if he stops there and doesn't go to the next page?

This is what I am trying to get the investigators to look at. If they have a problem, if someone is sacrificing cats, they might have someone who has taken a few books on the occult and read one chapter out of each one. Now they have their own pseudo-religion. To a true believer that would not be a Pagan. It also would not be a Satanist. But in the perpetrator's mind he is actually doing something valid.

Keeping in mind the fact that the FBI has never found a case of satanic, ritualistic murder, isn't it true that there are thousands of people coming forth at this time—it seems like it's more all the time—who are claiming to be ritually abused?

You have to keep government censorship in mind. This is only my opinion, but when you look at the time when most of this was coming out, 1987 to 1992, you find that the FBI did not want to get involved in investigating religious crime. It's a government agency, and the first amendment stands smack in their way. So for them it's easy to say, "Overlook the religion and just go after the crime." It's semantics, but then they are not fueling the hysteria.

Are you saying that there were cases of satanic ritual crime going on?

There were cases of ritualistic murder. I have films of ritualistic murders. But even though the person that did it says they are a Satanist or a Pagan or a Wiccan or a Druid, would Anton LaVey [author of *The Satanic Bible,* Avon Books 1969] agree? Who gets to say who's the Catholic and who's the Presbyterian? I can call myself anything I want. I can call myself the worshipper of a door.

You have met a large number of Witches, Druids, and Pagans. Have you seen any evidence that Witches, Druids, and Pagans are prone to violence or kidnapping or the kinds of things that the popular stereotype of "the Wicked Witch" would have people believe?

Not the ones that I have met and known. I have complete trust in the ones that I have dealt with. They believe that they have a religion. They are practicing their religion, and they have a creed, "Do as you will and harm none." They really believe that. If you were a person who did break the law, would you allow a law enforcement officer to be part of your group? However, there are people out there who are rogues. Look at the Son of Sam. Look at the Nightstalker. These guys made up their own rules. Obviously, they do not fit the mold. They are not "good" whatevers . . . . They called themselves what they wanted so that the media would pick up on it.

I am firmly of the belief that Wiccans, Druids, and Satanists have a right to exist in society. I say that a lot, and that is why I'm not very popular in many places. What a lot of people of Judeo-Christian background want to hear, and most cops are of a Judeo-Christian background, is that Satanism is evil, so we have to stamp it out. I go in and tell them that if they find an altar in the woods, just because it isn't a Christian altar, there is no reason to tear it down. That just because people are worshipping in the woods, that is no reason to put them in custody. But I also tell them to be aware that there is a group of self-styled nuts out there that do what they want and disregard the laws. Some of them may say that they are practicing occultists, and they give the occult a bad name.

I notice that you have mentioned Pagans and Satanists and Druids all in the same breath. Do you feel that Satanists and Druids, Pagans and Witches are all in the same group together?

As much as I feel that Jews, Catholics, and Hindus are all in the same group; they all worship the One Deity. I do see a distinct difference between Satanists and Pagans. To be a Satanist you have to believe in a Christian God. To be a Pagan you don't. If you don't believe in the Christian God, you can't believe in Satan. Satan is an entity of the Christian religion. Pagans are dealing with the Earth spirits, the embodiment of the life that surrounds us. I know a lot of Pagans who don't pray to Gods. They pray to the spirit of the Gods.

That's a tough concept for Judeo-Christian groups to understand. I have to emphasize that point because everything on the media makes it satanic. After the murders in Matamoros, Mexico, CNN spent three days talking about Satanism. It had nothing to do with that. Satan sells newspapers.

What was the cult that was responsible for those murders? Can you go into that a bit?

It was an offshoot of a Cuban religion called Palo Mayombe. They use a blood sacrifice of animals, but they don't believe in human sacrifice. This guy just took it one step further through drug-induced manipulation. He said if it was okay to kill a chicken or a goat, why not kill a human?

I read that for their altar they need a human skull and other bones?

Yes, they do. That's not to say that the bones have to come from someone who is alive. They usually get them by digging up graveyards. That's illegal here, but it's not necessarily illegal in Africa. This is where my force comes in. We routinely get graveyard vandalism calls. If you have a little bit of knowledge, you can look at the grave and how they did it, and you have a good chance of identifying who did it and why. They are practicing a form of black magic. They are different from Santeria. The difference would be the difference between Christianity and Satanism. It's the dark side and the light side of the same church.

Santeria is closely attuned to Paganism in that it is polytheistic, with different Deities having different responsibilities. The difference there is that the Deities of Santeria have more control over day-to-day activities, and they appreciate and demand blood worship. If you go to the Yoruba church in Philadelphia, they will go crazy if you say that, because they don't use blood worship anymore. They worship with fruit and trees. That's what they do in the United States because they are not allowed to kill animals. If they were allowed to kill animals, they probably would still be doing it.

I thought that the Supreme Court just passed a resolution saying that they were allowed to sacrifice animals?

Now they are, yes. But the SPCA would probably still try to arrest them for cruelty to animals. Even though the Church of Babalu-Aye in Florida took it to the Supreme Court, and they won.

Cops need to have this knowledge. They don't have to be afraid of every Pagan group or Wiccan group or Afro-Cuban group that they come across.

In your experience, is the prejudice against Pagans, both among the police force and among the general public, growing, or is it easing at this time?

I think it's easing exponentially. I think I have worked myself right out of a job. At least with the police and the social workers around here. I used to get twenty reports of hysterical sightings, but now I won't get something unless there has been a crime committed with it. It used to be that when the local Wiccan group had a ritual in the park, people would want you to go and shut them down because they were Satanists. It used to be that people thought I was a Satanist because I would tell them that you can't arrest somebody for believing that Satan is God. You can arrest them for abusing a baby or for raping a woman, but you can't just do it to someone who believes something different than you do.

America is basically a Christian community. People have been brought up believing in God and country. Satan is seen as the ultimate evil.

I've heard that a lot of people believe that the child abductions and missing children are the work of Wiccan cults who take the kids to do nasty things to them. Have you seen any evidence of this?

No. The numbers of 55,000 missing or dead children each year are inflated numbers. They are inflated by the way that law enforcement takes reports. It's not intentional. If Johnny Jones runs away on Monday at nine o'clock at night and he returns at ten o'clock, that's a missing child report. If Johnny Jones runs away one hundred times during the year, which some kids do because they are chronic runaways, that becomes one hundred missing children. Yet there is only one child creating the statistics.

I think that when we are looking at government agencies who are investigating "religious organizations," we have to keep in mind their charter to investigate. We don't investigate religion, we investigate crimes. That is what my goal in teaching this course and in giving out this message has been.

We should not be the oppressors. We should be the investigators and helpers. We are charged to help everybody equally. We have to stop categorizing people by what they are. It's what they do that counts.

We have cops who are lay preachers, and sometimes they are not enforcing the law—they are preaching. The churches do a lot of instructing on Satanism. If I go to a class that is being instructed by an evangelical minister and he's teaching about Satanism, he's teaching from an evangelical viewpoint. If you go to a lecture on Wicca and it's being given by a Druid, you are going to realize that it's Wicca as seen from a Druid viewpoint. It might not be, say, a Gardnerian viewpoint.

You have been hanging around with Pagans for about six years now, has anything interesting happened to you?

Well, they tried to teach me magic. I teach my people that magic happens if you believe magic happens. I really believe that people believe that magic happens.

Have you ever seen any magic happen?

Nope. But I do believe that I have the rudimentary ability to read auras now, color changes mostly. When I am lecturing, I can see the people who are turned off; they are icy white or stone blue. I see the guys who are really mad at me, and I think, Uh-oh, this guy must have a real heavy religious background because he is glowing bright red. Then I see the people with a nice ethereal green, or sometimes it gets more interesting with some purple around it. Those people are really interested.

I tell people in my class about one incident, because it illustrates the hysteria that people feel about the occult. I was with a Druid group that was led by a not very threatening-looking type. He was with his wife, who is very small and had her baby with her. There were four other Pagans present. They were in garb, but it wasn't anything very threatening. It was an open ritual for Lughnasad [Summer] out in a park.

Two "Pagan"—not as in Pagan religion—motorcyclists, who are from a fearful gang here on the East Coast, outlaw bikers, pulled up about one hundred yards away. I said to myself, "Uh-oh, this is not going to be good." I happened to be filming the ritual with the Druid's permission, and I was hidden behind some trees. The bikers didn't see me.

All of a sudden the bikers left, and I said, Whew, because I had thought they were going to wreak havoc on this poor little group of mostly women. About twenty minutes later these two burly outlaw motorcyclists came crawling through the woods. They were afraid to stand there and watch because they were afraid of the magic.

Wow, that's real power!

I've seen people walk by not knowing what's going on and all of a sudden they will realize that it's an occult incident. They don't know *what* it is, so they grab their children and run because they are afraid that someone is going to be sacrificed, human sacrifice in the middle of the county park.

Another time the Druids applied for a permit from the parks department, which they were given. Then the county parks department called us and said, "They said they weren't going to kill anybody, but we know they will because they are all like that. Get over there and stop it." We said, "If you thought they were going to kill somebody, why did you give them a permit?" People just have so many preconceived notions.

Television just kills the ability for the occult religions to mainstream. Movies, too, all the grade-B movies that are about witches, devils, warlocks, and monsters. They are all evil. You never see a good Witch on TV.

What do you think that Pagans have to do to turn it around?

Pagans seem to be afraid to "out." Even here in my county. I know that there are four Alexandrian groups; they just won't even talk to me. Total secrecy is one of their tenets. So people don't even know that they are there, and then when they trip across them, it scares them. If Pagans can become confident enough to know that they have a right to a first amendment religion, that they can tell people what they do, it will help a lot.

The first group that really comes out like that is going to get hurt probably. I believe that if you are the CEO of a Fortune Five Hundred company or on the fast track to become one, and you come out and say, "Yes, I believe in Satan instead of God," they are going to ostracize you quietly somehow.

That has to be fought. They did it to women thirty years ago when they said they couldn't be management. Through court cases they have broken the glass ceiling and taken their rightful place. They did it to blacks, and now blacks have come up. They did it to homosexuals, and now homosexuals are coming up. I see the Pagan community moving up the ladder, it just hasn't chosen when to get on the elevator. What I have seen in Delaware is that there is a lot of acceptance because they have become very public. They go on TV, they go on the radio, they have open rituals, they explain what they are doing.

Pagans and the Politics of Persecution

It would seem a ridiculous notion to be opposed to any group whose basic principles include the preservation of a healthy and whole planet, the right to a peaceful life, and the freedom to choose one's personal religious beliefs. Yet people who use such words as "Pagans" or "Witches" to describe themselves are often placed in positions of defending not only their beliefs but also their very lives.

The next three stories are about the problems Pagans have faced due to their identity and beliefs. Only by education, communication, and identification ("coming out") will the problems ever be solved. The path is long and hard and filled with dangers, but it is essential, as these people have discovered.

TERRY RILEY is a Celtic Wiccan, songwriter, metaphysician, and poet. Terry and his wife, Amanda Riley, are cofounders of the Southern Delta Church of Wicca Aquarian Tabernacle Church (ATC). In June of 1993 they opened up an occult shop in Jonesboro, Arkansas, in the middle of what is described as both the Bible Belt and Klan Country. Their troubles began almost immediately, and their plight made international news coverage. Many Pagan legal defense organizations came to their aid, including The United Council of Pagans Network, Lady Liberty League, The Aquarian Tabernacle Church, The Southern Delta Church of Wicca (a branch of the Aquarian Tabernacle Church), and The Universal Life Freedom Quest Society. Terry Riley was interviewed by phone on February 3, 1994.

What religion were you raised in?

I was raised as a Baptist, but it wasn't a strict rearing. I was taught the Christian teachings, but we didn't attend church regularly. I have two uncles who are Pentecostal ministers, and I was taught the Pentecostal faith when I was growing up.

When did you become interested in Paganism and the occult?

In 1979 I began doing some reading—self-help books. One of them changed my life; it was called *The Magic of Believing* [by Clyde Bristol]. After that I found out that they were teaching courses in San Antonio, Texas, at a place called the Concept Therapy Institute. From there I went into in-depth personal study for about four years on reincarnation and higher knowledge. I spent every day from one o'clock in the afternoon to midnight studying at the library and at home.

Finally, about four years ago I ran into *The Complete Art of Witchcraft* by Sybil Leek. I then realized that she was talking about the same things I had been studying all that time. I had been raised with all the propaganda about Witchcraft and Satanism from the Christian point of view. Once I read that book, I realized that I had been a Witch for fifteen years. I finally had a label for what I was. My philosophy, my beliefs about Nature all applied to Wicca. That got me really excited. I started some in-depth study of Wicca. My wife and I read about it for two years; we talked to any Pagans we could find.

One day some friends of ours were at the local coffee shop, and some other people came over and sat down. We were talking about the subconscious mind and the power of suggestion, and they used the word Celtic somewhere in the conversation.

I said, "What do you mean Celtic?" and they began to talk about Celtic mythology. Then I found out that they were Druids. We began working together, and gradually a few more people got involved, and eventually we had a group of ten people who were working together.

Two years ago some of the group fell away, and some others came in. We now have a coven that is tax exempt from the IRS and we are about to open up the First Church of Wicca.

How is a Celtic path different from other Wiccan paths?

Most Wiccans that I meet are eclectic. They take bits and pieces from different traditions and different mythologies and don't follow any set pattern. If you are following a Celtic style, you use a particular tradition. Our coven uses the Irish Celtic tradition, and we also follow Druidism. We follow the mythology of the Tuatha De Danann, the Children of Danu. Our Gods and Goddesses come from that line.

That sounds an awful lot like Keltrian Druidism.

That's basically what it is.

So what is it about Paganism, what is the essence of it that keeps you involved in it?

The Goddess worship. The aspect of bringing the feminine back into Deity that the other religions of the world have left out or don't acknowledge. Before I was ever a practicing Wiccan I was a firm believer in the male and female aspects of creation. You can't have one without the other. It seems to me that most of the other religions of the world have left out the feminine aspect. I just cannot comprehend how they can have any creativity without the feminine.

I understood a long time ago that as far as the conscious and the subconscious minds go, the conscious mind represents the male and the subconscious mind the female. If you want to get an idea, since the subconscious mind produces everything in your life anyway, you get the conscious mind or the male aspect to plant a seed in the subconscious, feminine mind, and from there it brings forth the manifestation. That's the way I see it anyway.

Has your group held public rituals in the past, or is this a private, secret group?

We held some public rituals while we had a shop. We opened an occult shop in June of 1993. We were the first Wiccans in this area to come out in public with our religion. Most of them around here are pretty secretive because of the persecution and oppression you get when people find out that you are a Witch.

What was it like to open an occult bookstore in a place like Jonesboro?

Well, it was pretty exciting. There are about three hundred Pagans that we know of here in this corner of Arkansas. We were discussing the fact that since most of them practiced in secret and there weren't any occult shops around here to get supplies like incense, candles, cauldrons, you had to drive over to Memphis, where the supply was very limited. We decided that it would be a good idea to open an occult shop in Jonesboro specifically for the Wiccan religion. We took eight hundred dollars and rented a little shop. Our plan was to help the local Wiccans save some money since we could order in bulk. We had candles and books, Tarot cards and incense and talismans and necklaces, crystals, and things like that.

We opened on June 21, the Summer Solstice, and the landlord who had rented us the building, a cheap little building behind the bank, said not to worry about being a little controversial because anything you do in this area is controversial. He said that as long as we gave him his three hundred dollars a month, he didn't care what we did with the building.

So we opened the Magick Moon, and two days later the landlord appeared with two Christian ministers. They told us that we were going to have to vacate and that they had decided to tear the building down. I said, "What do you mean tear it down? You just spent seven thousand dollars to remodel it." He said they had decided to do other things with the property and that the rent was due July 10, which was two weeks away, and he'd just as soon that we be out of the building by then and tomorrow would not be soon enough.

After they left I got really angry, and I went to the local newspaper. I told them that I felt I was being discriminated against because of my religion. I said that if they forced me to leave the building, I was going to sue them. The next day the newspaper had a big story about it, and that led to the papers in Memphis picking it up and then the papers in Little Rock and then the TV stations in Jonesboro and Little Rock. By then there was a big uproar.

Finally on July 2 six local ministers called a press conference in Jonesboro and got on the local TV station. They said they wanted to see my shop run out of town. They called me a Satanist and said that I posed a threat to local children. They urged everyone in the community who was a Christian to deny me the rental of any town facility for the practice of Witchcraft or any occult activity. As a result of all that I filed a $260,000 lawsuit against the six ministers for violating my right to operate a business. That suit is currently about to go to court.

After they had their little press conference, the only way I could think of to respond was to get hold of some covens in Memphis, Tennessee; Little Rock, Arkansas; and Springdale, Missouri. That amounted to about one hundred and fifty individuals. We formed a Freedom of Religion march that we held on August 1. We marched three miles down the main streets of Jonesboro in front of seven prominent Christian churches in protest of the shutting down of the shop.

The media kind of went crazy over this. CNN covered it; we were on the *700 Club;* Pat Robertson had us on. We made the front page of the *London News*. Japan and twenty-nine other foreign countries covered the march. It just kind of went crazy after that.

Pat Robertson had you? He's a born-again Christian; how did he treat you?

He said that because of the Witches' march and because of the occult activity in the United States, God is lifting his hand of protection and that is the reason we are having all of the natural disasters, the earthquakes, the floods, the hurricanes, and the tornadoes. I kind of went crazy when he said that. I put together a news clip, and I sent it to every Wiccan church that I could find in the United States.

The Japanese were doing a documentary at that time on Satanism in the United States, and they had seen us on *Inside Edition*. They contacted us and then came to the shop two days before we were closed down. They interviewed us and took it back to Japan and made a one-hour television special where they showed the difference between Satanism and us.

According to the Japanese, Christians and Satanists are the same thing. I told them we feel the same way, that you can't believe in Satan unless you are a Christian; therefore, you can't be a Satanist unless you are a Christian, either. The Japanese believe in the power of the Chi [Life Force], which is the same thing we believe in. They were fascinated that Wicca was so close to their philosophy and religion. They devoted about five minutes of their show to us to explain the difference between Satanism and Wicca.

We had to close the store on August 10. We got a thirty-day extension after I found an attorney who would talk to me. According to Arkansas law, on a month-to-month lease you have to give thirty days notice before you kick somebody out.

My wife and I and our entire coven searched the city of Jonesboro, and we were denied thirty-one different buildings. Nobody in town would rent to us. I'd call and ask if the building was available, and they'd say it was. I'd ask how much the rent was, and they'd tell me. I'd ask if I could get a lease on it, and they'd say sure. Then I'd say, "This is Terry Riley. I want to put the Magick Moon Occult Shop in there," and the excuses would start to fly.

Some of them just hung up on me. Some just flat out told me that they didn't agree with my religion, and they would never rent to anybody like me. One lady declined to rent to me because she didn't think she could get fire insurance on the building if I was in it. Another lady took my check for the deposit and then two days later sent it back because she was advised to sell the building.

Have you contacted the ACLU?

Yes. I think they were kind of scared to take the case. The first excuse they gave me was that because it wasn't a city official or a government agency that was denying me my rights they couldn't help me. After Pete Pathfinder from the Aquarian Tabernacle Church called them, they reexamined the case and came back and told me that they just didn't have the money to handle it at this time.

Who is Pete Pathfinder?

He's the one who is chartering our church right now. When we started this whole thing back in June, we had the telephone number of the Lady Liberty League, which is run by Circle and Selena Fox. We called her, and she gave us Pete Pathfinder's number in Seattle. We got hold of Pete and told him about the problems we were having. He immediately started sending us literature and giving us advice and help. We've been in close contact ever since.

If people are having similar problems in the future, who should they contact?

Pete Pathfinder or myself. My wife and I have created the United Council of Pagans Network in Arkansas. We are affiliated with Selena Fox, with Pete Pathfinder, and with just about every major Pagan organization. The first month we had a $900 phone bill because of all the Pagans we were contacting.

Are there other Pagans in the United States who are facing similar issues?

There is a lady in Oklahoma who went to court to get a divorce. She and her husband are both practicing Wiccans. As soon as they began to file the proceedings, her husband suddenly turned Christian and tried to use the fact that she was a Witch against her in the custody battle over their children. This young woman, who was nineteen at the time, went into court and represented herself. A county social worker who had examined all of her books on Wicca got up in court and stated that she could find nothing wrong with this religion. The lady won the custody of her children. She said, "It felt so good to go into court representing myself and beat my husband in the hometown of Oral Roberts."

There was another couple down in Fort Polk, Louisiana. He's in the army, and they had put an ad in the paper to try to connect with other Wiccans in the area. They got a study group of about twelve people together. They found that their house was too small, so they decided to go to the chaplain's office at Fort Polk and ask to use one of the rooms there to study and have services in. The chaplain said, "Sure, no problem." He took them through and showed them a room they could use and said they could have their services in the courtyard. So they put an ad in the paper advertising that they were going to hold Wiccan services at Fort Polk. Then the fundamentalist Christians started raising a ruckus with the chaplain until he withdrew the offer. He told them that they couldn't hold services or do anything at the Fort.

Then they called Selena Fox and the Lady Liberty League, and Selena gave them our number. We put them in touch with Pagans who were working in an army chaplain's office in California. The California Pagans started sending letters to the chaplain at Fort Polk informing him that the military has recognized Wicca as an established religion. The last I heard they were able to hold their services on the base.

There was a lady in Virginia who we were just told about last week who had a little occult shop. A man and his grandson used to come in there all the time. The grandfather ordered a book called *The Witch's Bible Compleat* by the Farrars. After they ordered the book, they didn't come in to pick it up. The woman also drove a school bus on the side, and the little boy who would come in with his grandfather was riding her school bus route. When the book came in and they didn't appear to pick it up, she simply handed the little boy the book as he got off the bus one day to go home. She told him to give it to his grandfather.

They came down and arrested her and put her in jail for distributing pornographic material to a minor. That was because there were nude pictures inside the book [some Witches like to do their ceremonies "sky clad" or nude]. She has yet to go to trial over that incident. All because she passed *The Witch's Bible* to a little boy whose grandfather had already paid for it.

What do you think would be the best course for Pagans at this point in American history? What do Pagans need to do to break this cycle of misunderstanding?

It took a long time for my wife and I to come out in the open where we live. I think if more Pagans, especially here in the Bible Belt, stand up and proclaim their religion to the public and get out more information, educate the public, they will begin to erase the propaganda and all the lies that have been put out about us.

It's also a war that will have to be waged in the political arena. The Pagan religions are still considered "alternative" religions. Until we have the same stature that the other religions have, the equal respect that the other religions have, we are still going to be persecuted.

We went on the Jane Whitney show in October to tell our story. We told them that we were licensed, ordained ministers of Wicca. They also had a little reverend on the show from Jonesboro, from the United Christian Church, who was in opposition to us. When the show was aired, they listed Gary Taylor as Reverend Gary Taylor. They called us "self-described" Witches. When you are licensed and ordained as a priest and priestess of Wicca, the generally accepted idea is that you are a reverend. As long as they call you "self-proclaimed," they put you in that secondary classification. Then you will never get the respect and the equality that the other religions enjoy.

Who gave you a license to be a priest?

The state of Arkansas. Pete Pathfinder ordained us; he has a tax-exempt, established church recognized by the United States federal government. He sent us our ordination papers, and we took them to the county courthouse. They say that I am a Wiccan priest, with ministerial credentials. I can do funerals, weddings, and baptisms just like any other minister. And so can my wife.

We have a lot of things going on in Arkansas lately. Two weeks ago a man in a town twelve miles from Jonesboro shot and killed a woman. He confessed to it, and he said he shot her because he believed she put a hex on him. He believed she was a Devil worshipper, and he was God's emissary who had to do what was right to get rid of these people. They only set his bail at $200,000. That means that for ten percent of that he can get out on bail. It seems strange to me that a man can go around and kill someone he thinks is a Witch—she turned out to be a Christian, by the way—and they don't set the bail too high.

Meanwhile, they have three boys on trial who are being accused of an "occult crime." These three teenagers are accused of killing three eight-year-old boys. The authorities said they belonged to a satanic cult that ate the hind legs of dogs. They were given no bail at all, no possibility of getting out. They are on trial right now. One of the boys confessed, and the other two pleaded not guilty, but they wouldn't let them out on bail at all.

I was raised with the propaganda just like everybody else. I believed that if you were a Witch, you had sold your soul to the Devil and you went around on a broomstick and you cut up babies. Until I picked up the book by Sybil Leek I still had that notion in my head.

NOTE: On April 4, 1994, the six Jonesboro ministers filed a summary judgment against Terry and Amanda Riley. The court ruled in favor of the ministers, stating that the ministers have the right to speak out against anything that goes against biblical scripture, and the case was never brought to trial. The Rileys were prevented from introducing any evidence. The Rileys now plan to appeal to the Arkansas state court.

LADY SINTANA is a high priestess of English traditional Wicca and a former star on the burlesque stage with the Minski troupe from New York City. She is founder of the Ravenwood Church & Seminary of the Old Religion, in Atlanta, Georgia, and owner of the House of Ravenwood, a Pagan shop. The early years of the Ravenwood shop were filled with opposition that was often violent, to the point where all-night vigils were held and intruders were surprised with guerilla "peacefare" techniques. Hers is a colorful story of perseverance in the face of persecution. She was interviewed by phone on February 19, 1994.

Are you a Pagan?

No. I have never considered myself to be a Pagan. Twenty-five years ago the terms were different than they are today. We are dealing with a lot of new terms now. When I started in traditional Wicca, [its practioners] did not consider themselves Pagan at all. To our understanding Wicca was a religion within itself, and [its clergy was] the clergy of the Pagan people. The Wise Ones of the Pagan people.

So what was the tradition that you were predominately trained in?

English traditional Wicca. What sets us apart from other traditions—for example, Gardnerian Wicca—is that Gardner is relatively new. His tradition really caught on in the early 1950s. In traditional Wicca there is no nudity; they are all robed. There is no sexual initiation. There is no fivefold kiss, though in some aspects there can be a fivefold anointing. That's part of the mystery teaching.

Can you imagine a Witch out on an English moor naked? It's ludicrous. Our whole concept of our sexuality, our sensuality, our sexual life and being is one that reveres that act as so sacred. We do not believe that the height of spirituality is the sex act as is symbolic in individuals fornicating! We believe in a much higher experience than that.

We have no scourging, we don't believe in self-punishment or punishing another like that. There is no binding like cord binding to induce altered states of consciousness. We believe those states are achieved through the mental work that one does and through spiritual work. We refuse to use drugs as well.

How did Witchcraft affect your mundane life, or did it?

I happen to think that being a Witch is a full-time thing. It's a daily act of mind and faith and spirituality. It's the composite of the entire individual, so of course it affected my life.

If somebody had told me a month before I ended up with Ravenwood that I was going to do that work, I would have laughed. I was making exorbitant money. I was living a very jet-set life. I had it made. My queen was Lady Circe in Toledo, with the Sisterhood and the Brotherhood of Wicca. I got the old House of Ravenwood originally for her to come to and have her shop in, so she could move here from Toledo. When we opened, I put my money into it, and then we were both immediately arrested. They sent us to jail because she was doing Tarot card readings. That was in 1975.

It was quite horrendous, and to make a long story short, she left. She wanted nothing to do with Atlanta, and I got pissed off at the way we were treated. We were sentenced to a year in jail, in less than twenty-four hours. The judge refused our attorney even being briefed on the case or spending time with his clients. I was found guilty for running a business without a license, which in Georgia has always been a little yellow slip of paper and you had thirty days to comply. I was sentenced to a year in jail and a $500 fine. We were held in jail for hours because we were "lost" in the system. Supposedly, they didn't have us in custody so we didn't get out of jail until ten o'clock that night. When we got out, I had contacted my media connections. We walked out into the hall and there were flashbulbs everywhere.

Eventually the case was dropped, after two years of battling on my part. All of this set a pattern in motion. I became absorbed with the fact of how few civil human rights we actually had. I cancelled my contracts, and I never went back to the theater from that day forward. I took a vow of poverty. I got a 501-C3, tax-exempt status. It wasn't hard to do because we qualified. We were perhaps a test case for our religion. We were open to the public; we had a sign in front. We lived for ten years with night guards.

Were you ever harassed or threatened?

Almost every night. They burned crosses if they could get near enough, and they would come with Molotov cocktails. They would come with pickup trucks, shotguns, Doberman dogs, and gas cans. The lighthearted ones would come to do a little initiation experience like the Georgia Tech football players. They would try to piss on the Witches' porch. They would throw rocks, bottles, coke cans, fire on the sacred circle where we did our rituals.

Was anyone seriously hurt?

Nobody was seriously hurt, blessed be. At the time it was horrendous, but later it all seemed very funny. Today we can laugh about it. It seems as though Spirit gave us the greatest protection you can imagine.

Some very uncanny things were happening at that time. People would come to do damage and we'd be running after them, and all of a sudden a police car would appear on a robbery detail. They had seen the guys running, they would pull in, do a *Starsky and Hutch* turn around, and a helicopter would appear over them. Needless to say, the troublemakers never came back.

The Fulton County police and the Atlanta police were absolutely wonderful with us, for many, many years. But we made sure we had our own protection. We taught our women archery and quarter staffing. The women guarded as much as the men.

There were no guns, but we were very innovative, and we did a lot with chains, rocks, bottles, slingshots, and big boards with spikes driven through them, which we placed in the driveway in the dark. When the cars would pull in and try to pull out real fast, we had them. We caught them all the time and then we'd call the police or talk to them and let them go, depending on the situation.

I was put in jail a few times. We had a city solicitor here who really wanted to get me. He was a religious right-winger, and just the fact that I was this notorious Witch in his area gave him a heart attack every time he thought about it.

What were you put in jail for?

I went through two jury trials for throwing a glass of wine on this woman who pinched my boobs. I happen to be rather well endowed. She had done some really malicious things to some of my membership, so I went up to her shop to have a talk with her about it. I had a glass of wine in my hand because I had just come from the pub where we were talking about it. We decided to go as a group and have a talk with her. We walked over to her shop and began to discuss the problems we had been having, and I became a bit emotional. She reached over and tickled my boob and said, "Oh, aren't you melodramatic." Well, she ended up wearing the wine.

She said it was assault. I turned around and snapped my fingers and said, "So be it. Whatever." And we walked out. She then called the police. By then the police didn't want to come anymore to arrest me. So I went down myself and went through the finger printing, the mug shots, and two jury trials. They wanted to sentence me to a year for assault with a glass of wine. I admitted to throwing the wine on her, and the first jury was a hung jury. We have people almost killing each other here in Atlanta, and they don't bring them back on a hung jury. But with me they did.

The second time around it cost us $30,000. I would not plea-bargain because what they were trying to do was to criminalize me, make me into an unsavory character. I would not buy into it. We ate potato soup to pay the attorney and defend ourselves. Their strategy was to try to wear us down. They put us through eight hours of depositions. My lawyer had to be there for the whole thing, and he had to get paid. The stenographer had to be paid.

Later, in 1979, when we filed for property tax-exempt status (as a church), we won it, but they kept appealing. It went all the way to the Georgia State Supreme Court.

How has the community been treating you lately?

We've had a tremendous amount of media through the years with all of the court cases. In 1985 my health became bad, and we sold the old house. I had an adrenal tumor, which, being a Witch, I didn't need anyone to tell me why I had gotten it. I lost an adrenal gland, and they didn't think I was going to do very well, so we went semi-underground. We kept our public classes and our teaching going. In eighteen years we have never missed a moon for our people.

In 1989 we moved to Decatur, Georgia. Everything was going very smoothly after that until just this last summer. My neighbor became very fearful for some reason. We do everything out of doors, all outdoor circles. The black robes really terrified her. It took her four years to do something about it. She finally got a senator to listen to her and brought a lot of problems on us for a while. The senator and my neighbor had a big demonstration; three hundred and fifty people showed up. They had gotten a neighborhood organization all up in arms about the "Satanists" who lived in their area. They said that we had tombstones in the backyard and that we were killing animals. The senator insisted that I was of the Devil.

He had no knowledge of who Lady Sintana was. He was very new. If he had bothered to check, he would have found out. As it was it became a media circus; nineteen articles were written in the Atlanta area in thirty days. Every columnist picked it up, and they were supporting me. It made Dekalb County look rather foolish. It made the senator look very foolish because they really came down on him.

The one thing I have found in being a public person is that you really have to be better than anyone else. You cannot have any shades of gray in your life at all, or it will come out. Everything I was doing was above reproach. There was nothing they could do.

You have been doing some interfaith community outreach with Christian clergy?

I've done work with the Columbian Seminary and with Morris Brown at Spelman College. I've been teaching them what Wicca is and what it is not. I've been talking with the young seminary students who are getting ready to go out into the world and minister to their congregations.

The consciousness is changing rapidly. At the same time, there is this religious right-wing backlash. Some of the young ministers are becoming more and more frightened by the New Age phenomenon, by the higher consciousness of people. They are becoming more adamant that this is against God's work.

In 1979 you put on the first southern Psychic Seminar, and Sybil Leek was there?

Years ago they used to have these wonderful things called Elders' Meets or Witches' Meets where traditional Witches would get together once every year or so. With the Witchcraft explosion and the Paganism that ensued, a lot of the elders just got fed up and disgusted with what they were seeing happen in the name of the Craft.

A lot of our Witch Meets got taken over by the young ones who were coming up who had no real respect for eldership, ancestry, roots, or authority. It was my attempt at that time to try and bring together elders and people that I felt I wanted my young students to meet and know on a personal basis.

Sybil Leek [author of *Diary of a Witch*] used to come and visit us, but it was always very private. She was full of wisdom. I don't really know what she espoused at her seminars because I didn't attend too many. When she was with us, she was at home, and we spent most of our time in and around the kitchen.

Isn't the English traditional Craft very hierarchical as opposed to some of the other traditions?

Yes, we are. We are also matrilineal, though we do have high priests who can be coven leaders. We believe in the male-female balance within the group. But the hierarchy comes from years of work and dedication; it isn't achieved overnight. The Ravenwood group has been together for nineteen years, and we have only eight third degrees. It takes from nine to thirteen years to attain that degree.

If a person says that they are a third degree in your tradition, what kinds of things does that mean they have accomplished?

They have fully accomplished the balance of the personality and the emotional systems. They have balanced the elements—air, earth, fire, and water—within their personalities. They are absolute servants of the people from that point on. Their life is dedicated not just to Wicca but to humanity and to nature. Those things are the primary focus of their life, over relationships, careers, or anything else.

There is a controversy that is brewing in the community these days, which has to do with people getting paid for the services that they offer. You mention the third degrees as servants of the people; does this mean that they don't get paid?

How are they supposed to live if they don't get paid? What are our people supposed to do? We have a very educated lot here at Ravenwood—scientists, biochemists, lawyers, doctors, teachers, educators. But at the same time, some of us have to do this full-time in order to keep it going. I am the full-time member at this moment and have been for the last nineteen years.

At the same time I have been under a vow of poverty. I would never, ever suggest that to another person. When Selena Fox [of Circle Sanctuary] wanted to go off her vow of poverty, we helped her. I would hate to see one of my daughters of the Craft or one of my sons of the Craft get taken the way I did. I was under the false assumption that because I had worked and made a certain amount of money in my life, I had security. Lo and behold I find that I do not. There's no trust fund or anything for me in my old age, and I am fifty-seven.

Do you think that's wise?

No, it's not wise. That's why I tell them now, "Don't do it." Ravenwood has existed for years on pledges and donations. How do you maintain properties, how do you maintain places? You *have* to have resources.

How do you think we should go about getting that money?

It can be by pledging or by tithing. In the last twenty-five years I have seen that those people who come in and refuse to give anything don't get anything out of it. They are here today and gone tomorrow. Easy come, easy go.

Ravenwood has a very centered group that has been together for eighteen years. Some of our high priests and priestesses have now formed their own groups. A few have stayed with us because they are teachers here, and we have full-time work for them. They get nothing for what they do, but the money supports the place where we have our public meetings; it supports the things we do during the year, and it supports the property.

We have never put down for a property tax exemption on the property where I live. We do our public outreach and our classes elsewhere. We are so large that we are at the point of institutionalization. Ravenwood is at a point where it has to break off, spiral away from the charisma of myself into its own. It has to do that so that if something happens to me, the group can go on. The group is strong enough at this point and our teaching is so structured that it can live past me.

You talk about honoring elders and honoring tradition. How do you feel about people whose practice is eclectic, who incorporate Native American and a little bit of Celtic and some African shamanism and then throw it all together. They read a book by Llewellyn, and they make up a different ritual for every season?

If you want to start your own tradition, then name it. Generally, people do that because they have never learned a qualified system. They pick up a little bit here and a little bit there, and generally those groups don't stay together for any amount of time. They all want to be high priestess and high priest, but they don't want to serve the people. They don't want to be responsible for the classes, the Moons, the Sabbats. When you are a high priest or a high priestess working in this field, you can't be sick all the time and just cancel events. Or do them only when the mood takes you.

Ravenwood has never cancelled a Moon. How do you cancel a Moon? How do you cancel a Sabbat? You *have* to serve your people, and it isn't always convenient. I think people ought to think of these things before they start taking on students. This is something you devote your life to. It's a hell of a responsibility. A lot of them want the titles and the recognition, but they don't want to do the work.

SAM WAGAR is the founder of the Pagans for Peace network and is chair of the National Council of the Congregationalist Witchcraft Association. He describes himself as a Pagan, environmentalist, feminist, peace activist, and former anarchist. The CWA is Canada's national Witchcraft church with a similar structure to America's Covenant of the Goddess (COG). Its membership consists of autonomous congregations from different traditions and a minimal set of theological and ethical agreements.

Wagar also publishes *Pagans for Peace*, a bimonthly, left-wing, feminist-inspired Witchcraft journal, as well as the *Directory to Canadian Pagan Resources*, the most complete directory to Canadian Pagan resources. The *Directory* includes gatherings, newsletters, and groups.

Of particular interest, he was a candidate for election to the province of British Columbia's legislature until the knowledge of his religious beliefs became known. The controversy surrounding this is detailed in the following interview, conducted by phone on February 24, 1994.

First, are you a Pagan? And when did you first discover that you were?

Yes, I'm a Pagan. I guess I knew it when I decided that I was a Witch. The two came at about the same time in 1983. I thought of the two things as being synonymous for a while, but I have since come to realize that there are quite a few Pagans out there who aren't Witches. I don't think there are any Witches who aren't Pagans.

Can you describe the difference between a Pagan and a Witch?

Paganism is a Nature-centered, Earth-centered religion. That includes everything from what the Diné people [the Navaho] to ourselves practice. Witchcraft is, if you will, a denomination within this broader Earth-centered spiritual loop.

What religion were you raised in?

I was raised as an Anglican, that's the Episcopalian church. I became an atheist when I was eleven. Christianity just didn't make any sense to me anymore. I had real difficulty with the sexual mores, the way that they treated women, the division between spirit and our everyday lives, the hierarchical setup of the church, a whole bunch of things that just didn't ring true to me.

When I was eleven, I said, "This doesn't make any sense to me, and I'm not going to go to church anymore, Mom." She was not happy, but that's the way it was.

Paganism is obviously a religion. How did you go from being an atheist to being a Pagan or a Witch?

It was sort of a conversion experience for me. You know that famous saying that people just sort of realize that their religion has a name? In my case I was an evangelical atheist. Then when I went to university I became a Trotskyist, a member of a Marxist-Leninist political organization. I still have a strong Marxist tone to my understanding of the world. I was militantly atheist for quite a few years. Then a friend of mine died, and I went to his funeral, the standard Roman Catholic funeral, and the priest spent all this time talking about how great it was that my friend Larry was dead, because now he could be with Jesus.

It just made no sense to me at all because I felt some sense of my friend's continuing presence. I felt that he was still there in some ways, and I wanted to be able to connect up to that feeling. I felt a need then for spirituality. Something went snap, and I felt I needed a spiritual path that made sense to me.

I looked up a friend who was a Witch, and I asked her to tell me something about this Witchcraft stuff. There was no way I could have anything to do with the patriarchal religions; there were just so many things that were wrong, for me, with the way that they viewed the world. So she told me about it, and she gave me some books to read, and we did some stuff together for a while; and it made sense, and it has kept making sense ever since.

So what was it about Paganism that drew you to it?

I've always been strongly feminist, and the fact that there was a strong Goddess component was very appealing to me. The immanentist aspect was really important too, that our Deities are here and now, and we can do and be and see ourselves as embodiments of them in some respects rather than seeing God "out there" somewhere and ourselves as mere worms underneath his feet.

I also like taking my clothes off with my friends. I like the valuing of the senses. It's very important to me that you can find enlightenment through pleasure and enjoyment and through acting. That you don't have to sit and contemplate your navel, but you can act in the world, and that action can provide you with a source of enlightenment and understanding.

What tradition were you trained in?

I received a very small amount of formal training. Every group that I have ever been in I led. I received about four or five months' worth of formal training from a priestess with the Wiccan Church of Canada. Then I continued on my own for about two years after that, having some really remarkable experiences that confirmed for me that there was something going on here and that I should consider myself an initiate of some sort.

So over the years you have been active in the peace movement, and you have been doing political work; can you talk about that?

When I went to university, I decided that I was going to become a student radical. That was in 1975. I joined a small Trotskyist organization, basically because their politics were less repulsive than the Maoists or the Communists. So I ceased being a Communist, but I continued as a leftist. I was an anarchist-Communist, active in the extreme left for about ten years. I participated in some direct actions like jumping over the fence of a nuclear power plant and helping to set up a peace encampment on the steps of the legislature in Toronto. Shortly after I became a Pagan, I set up the Pagans for Peace network.

What does Pagans for Peace do?

Basically, what we do is connect up people who are active on the left in the peace movement and in other social change movements with one another. We try to articulate a coherent theology that includes political activism. We think that you can't divorce your spirituality from the rest of the world and that when women are being raped and discriminated against, if you are in a Goddess movement, you have to politically act to address what's happening to people in the real world. By the same token, if you have a forest being cut down somewhere and you are in a Nature-oriented religion, if you don't do something about that forest, you are being hypocritical. Exactly what you do is up to yourself, but you can't simply say that you will act on the astral and not in the world of here-and-now reality.

Didn't you just run for political office?

I've rocketed to the right so far that I'm now a member of the Democratic Socialist political party. It's called the New Democratic party. It's somewhat further left of anything you have in the United States. It's sort of like a Labor party.

I've lost some of my altruism. Anarchism works great if you think that when you destroy the state, all of the oppressive relations between people will just evaporate. But if you look at what happens when the state *has* been destroyed, you see things like Bosnia and Lebanon, where warlordism has become the norm. Then you realize that a bunch of guys with guns are going to go and set up their own little oppressive relationships. So personally I am now a strong believer in the power and effectiveness of the state in solving social problems as well as in just keeping people safe on the street.

Basically what happened is that about six years ago I joined the New Democratic party, which in Canada is a mass political party. We have members in most of the provincial legislatures and in the federal parliament. We have received in the vicinity of 15 to 20 percent of the vote in every election. We are a significant, major, respectable political party.

I served in provincial riding associations. A riding is what you would call an electoral district. I have been living here for some time, and the person who was representing this area in our provincial legislature quit so that the leader of the conservative political party here could run for election and she could enter the legislative assembly. Because we have a parliamentary system, the person who commands the largest number of votes in the legislative assembly is the premier, the head of the government. There is no separation between the executive and legislative branches here. So it was important for the leader of the conservative party to be in the legislature.

So we were sitting around at the New Democratic party office talking about this by-election that was going to have to happen to fill this seat, and a couple of members of the executive said, "Sam, why don't you run?" I am fairly articulate, I know the party's policy pretty well, I am a reasonably good candidate. So I thought it over for a while, and I decided to run, and I was acclaimed as the candidate, following all of the party's procedures to the letter.

Here I am, I'm the candidate in this by-election, which I have no chance in hell of winning. About a week later this enterprising reporter with the local newspaper did a check through their computer to see if my name turned up. And, by golly, it turns out that I was on the front page of the largest newspaper in British Columbia and of other Canadian newspapers for being a spokesperson for Witchcraft organizations for many years.

So after about five minutes he had a dozen newspaper stories, and he called me to see what was going on. He asked me, "What do you think your chances are?" I said, "Oh, I think it's too early to tell." Then he asked if I was upset about running against the head of the conservative party and so on. Then he said, "I did a background check, and I ran across this Samuel Wagar in connection with the Covenant of the Goddess church, the Congregationalist Witchcraft Association, and Pagans for Peace. Are you that Samuel Wagar?"

It had to come out, I said to myself, and I said, "Oh yes, that's me. Let me briefly tell you what my religion is about." So we all have our thirty-word or less summary, and I gave him mine. I said that it was my religion, and that it had absolutely nothing to do with the political issues that I wanted to talk about in this election. I said I'm very concerned that the free trade agreements are going to damage a lot of our farmers' livelihoods—both NAFTA and GATT.

It happens that the New Democratic party which I belong to is the governing party here in British Columbia. They have funded abortion clinics and addressed women's issues and other issues that have been neglected by other parties. So I gave this guy my little spiel, and I said, "By the way, let me get your fax number and I'll fax you the press release that was put out when I became a candidate."

Then I took a deep breath, and I called the party. I hadn't bothered to tell them I was a Witch because my religion is my business. As a matter of fact, it's part of the party's constitution that if someone is a candidate for the nomination, the provincial executive will check them out and give their stamp of approval before they accept their candidacy. I assumed that at some time or another they must have done that. And if they didn't, it is their problem, not mine. So I called my campaign manager and told him that I belonged to a small religion with about five thousand adherents in Canada. That's the figure from the Canadian census, which asks people their religion. I said, "Let me give you my thirty-word summary, and if anybody calls you, here are a couple of books you can read so you can answer their questions." Little did I know what kind of storm was to break over my head.

Then I got a phone call, this was on the 12th of January, 1994, from another reporter. This guy says, "I just talked to the provincial secretary of your party, and this fellow has said something that amounted to the fact that your religion is a reason to reconsider your nomination and that you should have told your executive what your religion was." An alarm bell went off in my head, and I said, "I'm sorry, I can't talk to you about that. I'm going to have to call Mr. Reynolds and talk to him." So I then phoned my wife, who is a lawyer, and I asked her what the problem was. She said not to worry about it, your religion is your own business, it is a constitutionally protected and guaranteed right, you can have whatever the hell religion you want to. Let's not worry about it.

I said, "Thanks for the reassurance," and I phoned up Mr. Reynolds. I said, "Keith, what the fuck is going on? You shouldn't be undercutting your candidate. You especially should not be making a big issue out of something that is not an issue. My religion is my own business. It has nothing to do with my political choice, and it had nothing to do with my candidacy." He said, "But I think it does have something to do with your candidacy." I said, "You are wrong. If you make it into an issue, you will have the issue being 'Major Political Party Discriminates against Candidate on the Basis of Religion.' That is not an issue that you want." He then said, "Well, I think that it is an issue, and it is of concern to me, and you should have told us what your religion was." So it went back and forth like that. I then told him I had talked to my lawyer, and that she said it had nothing to do with anything. He asked when I had talked to my lawyer, and I said it was just that afternoon.

The next day, Thursday the 13th of January, I was on the front page of the two major newspapers in British Columbia, and I had three television interviews by the three networks in the morning. Radio, TV, the local press, major papers across the country, and CNN picked up the story. I spent at least nine hours on the phone or talking to reporters. The story went national instantly.

The initial story from the first reporter who contacted me was a "backgrounder" story about the guy with the weird religious preference running for the New Democratic party, which was what I thought the story should be. Every other story since that point has been about the guy with the weird religious preference being discriminated against by a major political party on the basis of his religion. They dropped the weird reference real quick. So the story became a major national story for at least two weeks. There was a major national story because a member of a minority religion, my own sweet self, was being discriminated against by a major political party. The head of our party, who is the premier of this province, said, "Some might call this a cult. What kind of Witchcraft is this guy practicing? It's a real concern to me." He said this not just to a reporter or in the shower. He said this in front of a whole bunch of cameras and a whole bunch of reporters. So I spent a lot of time trying to pull the party's chestnuts out of the fire, because I wanted to be the candidate.

I spent a lot of time making the points that our party had a seventy-year history of fighting for the underdog and of trying to bring people into the political arena, of working for the rights of minorities, of endorsing lesbian and gay rights, of being active in antiracist work for many years. And that it was utterly unthinkable that our party would discriminate against somebody on the basis of their religion.

On the 14th of January I was informed by the members of my local executive that in fact they had reopened the nomination. Remember that I was acclaimed as the candidate; there was nobody else who wanted the job of being sacrificial lamb this time around. They reopened the nominations, so that I had to recontest my nomination. They effectively took my nomination away from me. A party loyalist out here who has a strong sense of ownership was thinking that I had embarrassed *her* political party, and she ran against me for the nomination. I got fourteen votes. She got sixteen. One of our members of Parliament who is openly gay—the only openly gay member of Parliament—came out and endorsed my candidacy. He said he thought that the party had discriminated against me, and that it was really horrible. So the party is quite split around this issue.

I'm now a human rights complainant as opposed to a candidate. The day after the second nominating meeting, which I lost, I told the party brass that either they were going to apologize formally and completely to myself and to the other Witches of British Columbia and make undertakings that they would never allow something like this to happen again, or I was going to sue their ass off.

I then spent the weekend talking with members of my religion here. I tried really hard to make sure that even though I had not been formally nominated as their spokesperson, that what I was saying was in fact what I should be saying.

We have the equivalent of CNN here; it's something called NewsWorld. I had a live interview with them already scheduled. I hadn't heard anything back from the party so I went, and I had the mixed pleasure of announcing to the world on a live national TV interview that I was going to the Human Rights Council about this to lay in a complaint.

Thus far the party has been completely unresponsive. I have a complaint against them for discriminating against me and for encouraging others to discriminate against me, naming the premier of the province and the provincial secretary of the party and the party in general.

You'll have to let me know how this all turns out! Can you talk a bit about the Congregationalist Witchcraft Association and what it's trying to do?

My coven joined the Covenant of the Goddess in the 1980s because we wanted to find a group of people that we could network with and share theology with. It's hard when you are a little group to really develop your theology and your understanding beyond a certain point. We also wanted to get some legal status in Canada for a congregationalist approach.

COG seemed pretty good except they weren't doing anything in Canada.

So we began discussions with groups around the country. Those discussions went on for about two years, from 1989 to 1991. We had a fairly wide-ranging group of people involved—from Alexandrians to Dianics to Pagans for Peace and eclectic whatevers. In 1991 we formally chartered the thing.

It's a federal nonprofit religious corporation. Our objectives are to provide a home for those Witches who agree with our basic statements of theology and ethics. Basically, what it boiled down to is that we are group oriented; we restrict voting membership to groups. We don't pretend to represent all Witches, but we hope to serve those that we do represent well. We think that people should not be able to sell the Craft at all.

Does that include not having paid clergy?

You can pay clergy as long as you don't require people to pay for the clergy. Groups can support whoever they want to, but they can't charge students a specific fee for taking classes; they can't charge for membership in their groups; and they can't charge for initiations into their groups.

If you want to perform Tarot readings for money, that's your own business. But you can't charge for teaching the Craft if you are in the Congregationalist Witchcraft Association. We also do not allow discrimination on the basis of sex, race, and so on. Groups who are all female or all male can join, but they have to behave reasonably towards other groups inside the organization.

What are your "ethics"?

Our ethics are "An ye harm none, do what you will." We specifically approve of all sexual orientations that are noncoercive. It's not like we tolerate homosexuals or tolerate straights; we enthusiastically approve of sexual orientations. That is an ethical statement. Not charging for the Craft is included in our basic ethics. All groups and individuals must agree with our basic ethical statement in order to join.

The basic theology statements are your standard Wicca stuff. We say that you can worship the Goddess alone or the Goddess and the old Gods, substantially the same as the COG statement. The one difference I think is that we specify that we are purely for groups. That individuals can join, but they cannot join as voting members.

Are you international?

At this point we are barely national. We have members in six provinces around Canada, but we are still a tiny organization.

In 1987 I realized that there wasn't any kind of a directory to Canadian Pagan resources. I thought, Gee, there really should be. So I started publishing the *Directory to Canadian Pagan Resources*. I've published five editions thus far, and the sixth one is in the works. It comes out about once a year.

What is your vision for the future?

I think the Craft is undergoing a process of "denominationalization." The eclectic and New Agey folks are getting together on their own. The more traditional and congregationalist folks are getting together on their own. Those who want to form big churches just like all the other churches are doing their thing.

I don't think that in ten or twenty years we will be calling ourselves the same names anymore, and I think that's a healthy thing. I think that for far too long we have pretended that all of those folks who have the same roots to their spirituality are in fact doing the same thing. That just isn't so.

We're also having a new wave of leadership coming up. That's what your book is about, and I think it's quite sensible. Some of the people who have been around for quite a while are going to continue being around and doing things, but the new wave of leadership is inevitably going to come up, and it will be expressing a different sort of vision.

EDITOR'S NOTE: As of August 1995, Sam Wagar reports that the Human Rights Council has recognized his complaint and will schedule a public hearing in the near future.

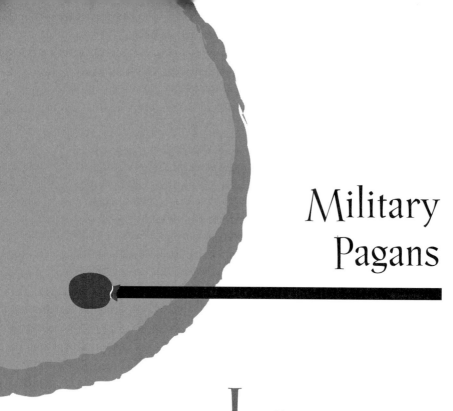

Military
Pagans

I t would seem to most people that the military world would be the antithesis of the Pagan community. Where the military is regimented, with rules, conducts of behavior, hierarchy, and a clear mission of defense and persuasion by potently violent means, the Pagan community has its basis in consensus, cooperation, shared responsibilities, and a fundamental belief in peace through unity. These generalizations do not represent the total views of either group, and yet both groups probably consider the other a less than desirable bedfellow. Yet they do coexist and even, as in the case of the next three gentlemen, cohabit. There are no clear numbers of just how many Pagans are currently serving in the United States Army, but the army is aware of their existence and is even quietly tolerant of them. The army has published a handbook for chaplains that explains the religious requirements and practices of "certain selected groups," including Wiccans and Pagans.

In spite of these more liberal views by today's modern army, the inevitable conflicts between duty and spiritual integrity for a Pagan soldier must arise. Each person deals with this in his or her unique way.

KEITH GREEN is a Native American from the Seminole/Tuckabachee nation. He is a former corporal with the U.S. Army and served as a member of the Presidential Honor Guard. His tour of duty included active combat service in

Panama. He was interviewed on July 30, 1993, near Leesburg, Virginia, at a Wiccan Lammas gathering.

Do you consider yourself to be a Pagan, first of all?

If Pagan means non-Christian, then I am. When I was really young, I was told by certain people that Indian beliefs and Christian beliefs were all the same. I was taught to believe in God, in a superior Jewish Jehovah, but in my teens I started questioning that. People who were a big influence in my life showed me that it wasn't even similar to Native American beliefs. They were two different worlds. Our beliefs have been passed down forever, and Christianity is only a few thousand years old.

Do you equate Native American spirituality with Paganism? Do you think they are the same thing?

Some things are similar, like the drumming. But we do different drumming for different things in the Native American tradition. In Paganism it seems to be a kind of therapy thing, a raising-energy kind of thing. But we actually do different kinds of drumming for different ceremonies.

Any other similarities?

Dates, harvest, things like that. Earth worship, you know, respect the Earth, respect Nature. With the Native American beliefs it's really strict . . . like this is the way, this is how it is done. Where in most of the Paganism I've seen, they just kind of go with the flow. But we have a set way of doing things. We do it one way only. I have seen some Pagans who do things in a structured kind of way, however.

How about the orientation to the Earth?

That's one of the first things I noticed. Earth energy, the way they pull energy from the Earth. It didn't seem the same as when we do it, but later I realized that it actually is.

How did you first meet Pagans? How did you become involved with Pagans?

I moved to Springfield, Virginia, and I lived in a group house. Some of the people there had Pagan friends. It's a really big Pagan area. Just living out there I kind of got integrated into it. It seemed like everybody I met was a Pagan. After you meet a few, they stand out. Then you can pick them out. I have friends that I went to the science fiction conventions with, and while I was there I met more. Then I started coming to Pagan events.

I met some Witches back years ago, but they were Satanists, into the dark stuff. That's what my first thought was when I met those people in Springfield, when they said they were Pagan and everything. Then I got to know them a lot better and found out what they were talking about. They were open to tell you what their beliefs were. That was probably four years ago.

Obviously you are hanging out with Pagans, so what is the most important aspect of Paganism for you? In other words, what has given you the most positive benefits? What causes you to keep hanging around?

I had moved away from where my council, my family is, in Oklahoma, twelve hundred miles from here. Paganism was the closest thing to a spiritual kind of activity I could find. It's like you're doing something real. It's not the exact same thing, but it's something. Because I am living twelve hundred miles away from everything I know of my spirituality and beliefs, it's good to find something similar close by.

There are a lot of Native American people who are into Native American ways, why aren't you hanging out with them? Why are you hanging out with Pagans?

I do go to some powwows and stomp dances. But when you get down to the religions of the different tribes, it's like mixing Catholic with Baptist. They are whole different worlds. There are many similarities, but there are also many differences. It's really hard, because if you didn't grow up in a particular council, you can go to their dances, but they won't bring you into their inner circle. You're still an outsider because you're from another tribe, another council, another family.

But you haven't found that with Pagans?

Not to that extent. Nowhere to that extent. I was surprised to find that there are different kinds of Pagans. I just met my first Druids at the Free Spirit Gathering [a yearly Pagan festival in the Washington, D.C., vicinity]. I got to talk to them and find out how they are different. They're more open, nowhere as closed as the Native Americans are.

Can you talk about why you enlisted?

I wanted to be out of Oklahoma. I had a lot of reasons. I was very rebellious, and because my dad didn't want me to be in the military, it was the first thing I did. I enlisted, and I went to Fort Benning. I went through my basic training, infantry school, and then got assigned to an infantry unit. I spent eight months there until I got orders to come to Washington, D.C., to be in the Presidential Honor Guard.

What is that?

It's just a ceremonial position. Everyone is above six foot two. Everyone has less than a thirty-two-inch waist. You're hand picked. You have to have a clean military record. They pick out the "All-American" soldiers, basically.

What was your function? What did you do?

[Laughing.] Basically, crudely, we were "show-offs" for the army. We went to the White House. We did military funerals at Arlington Cemetery. They sent us to the Pentagon when foreign dignitaries or military officials would come. We were bigger than life, bigger than average people. Every service had them. Everyone was six foot two up to six foot eight. You were just there to look good so when foreign dignitaries would come, this is what they would see of the United States Military. All these big guys . . . thin, big, the whole deep-chest look.

Before I was in the Honor Guard I was sent to Panama to Jungle School for thirty days. From Panama they sent us to Puerto Rico for a week of down time. Then they called us in a day early, packed up all our stuff, and we got on a plane. Six hours later we were jumping onto the airport in Panama.

You mean in the battle, in the fighting?

Yes, for Operation Just Cause. We were there for twenty-seven days.

You saw active combat?

Yes. The first week was the worst. After that it was just sporadic. I lost a lot of faith in the government then for the simple fact that no one said what really went on down there. I can't say what did actually happen. I'm just saying a lot of stuff wasn't right. I've seen some inhumane stuff go on. That's all I can say.

You can't give details?

No.

So, that made you want to leave the military?

Yes, that's what started it, plus a few other things.

The army is predominantly a Christian organization, and I'm just wondering what it was like for you, both because of your Native American background and because of your Pagan leanings. What was it like to be in the army?

I had a little problem with that, because everything was Christian based. In my first year or two, I had problems with it because I was around a lot of really hard-core Christian people. By that time I had learned enough about Christianity, about discrepancies in Christianity. After a year a lot of people got to know me, and they knew not to say anything around me for the simple fact that they couldn't argue with me. The harder-core ones, it opened up their minds a lot.

The army has really changed. It's in a big transition right now. Especially with the whole gay issue.

Both the Native American tradition and the Pagan tradition are traditions where the Earth is sacred. I wondered if that was a difficulty being in the army?

Not anymore, because in the last five or six years, the army is really trying to clean up everything, clean up its act. I was an army brat when I was younger. When I used to live on military bases, we would go around to the ranges and pick up live smoke grenades, live bullets; they were everywhere.

But the army is really trying to make a difference. They're recycling now. They started doing that when I came in. Everywhere we went they said, "Take everything we brought here. Leave nothing here that wasn't here before." If it didn't grow there, we took it back with us.

What about Panama?

We left a lot of stuff there. [Laughing.] That was different. That was the war. You dropped something, and if you had time you picked it up. If you didn't, you didn't even care. We left a lot of trash.

Your father was a three-times enlistee in Vietnam, yet he didn't want you to serve?

The politics of the military is why. He got disgusted with it. After Vietnam he just got fed up. Maybe I can see why. You can't articulate what it is like to sit in a war zone like Panama. To be running and have someone shoot at you . . . the sounds, the smells. To hear bullets going past you. It's just this real distinct sound when a bullet passes you.

We jumped in that first day. We were in a plane, a C140, and it was loud, really loud, and it was cold. You'd go out, you couldn't hear anything. You could see the lights of the runway as you were falling. You weren't really thinking. When you jump out of the plane, you hear, but nothing really matters because it's kind of cool to be flying through the air. All of sudden reality kicks in. Those little flashes of light are guns shooting at you on the ground.

You get this weird sense of reality. Nothing can compare to that. I like slam dancing for that same reason. When you're out there, everything is right there, right then, nothing else really matters. It's an alternate reality, I guess. To explain it . . . you can't . . . there's no way to talk about it.

Your senses are more alive maybe?

Yes, you feel everything, you hear everything.

And that's what causes people to re-enlist?

We have some police action every three years somewhere. I would say that's what causes people to re-enlist now. When you go to military infantry school, they keep talking to you. The school is brainwashing you because everywhere you go, you have to scream and holler, "Kill." What you actually do in combat is a whole lot different; it takes on a whole different perspective.

What's it like when you've actually done it?

The first day we were there, we were in the underbrush beside a city park. A guy threw a grenade at a tank, at a Bradley that was coming up the road. Actually, there was a whole line of them, that's what we were waiting on, we were just making sure they got up there all right. It was weird, you know, I kinda pulled up and shot. I didn't see him fall. It wasn't real, it was like watching a TV show. After that everything was numb . . . I still think about it. I feel bad because I didn't feel remorse. I didn't feel anything, everything went dull after that.

Some people were bothered a lot. Some people weren't bothered at all. I always wondered what it would be like. It was like watching TV, I guess . . . like watching war movies. It wasn't real, everything was just happening. I had played so many war games. When I think about it now, I wonder why I don't feel anything.

The next interview is with a highly decorated major who is currently active in the U.S. military service. For reasons of his own he prefers to remain incognito for this interview, calling himself **KOKOPELLI**.

Are you a Pagan?

For about six years I've been explicitly calling myself a Pagan. Before that I was probably more of an atheist and before that a Roman Catholic.

When did you first discover you were a Pagan?

Getting exposed to the Pagan scene. My wife was a Witch for many years, and she started getting more active in the Craft, practicing with other Pagans. At about the same time or just before it I started calling myself a Pagan. I started meeting more people as she got more active, and discussing the ideas, and it just sort of jelled for me—the worldview, the ideas, the connectedness of the people in the community.

What is the most important aspect for you? What is it that keeps you interested?

I think it is the community and the people, because it has given me some of the deepest friendships I have had. It's almost an extended family. In my work I travel a lot, and I have to uproot frequently. It's important to be able to establish community anywhere with my fellow churchmen. It makes me connected again, and it's company.

You said you used to be an atheist. How does this compare to being an atheist?

I was brought up Catholic, and I rebelled against that, and then I was just a nonbeliever. Then I started to get systematic about reading books by Ayn Rand, the whole worldview of individualism and the view that an individual is responsible for himself. My whole upbringing had been that God was going to save you or is an outlet to gain forgiveness for sin, etc. I was taking a tack that I was seeking self-responsibility and I didn't need a God to grant me salvation or bless what I did or save me or put me into an afterlife afterwards. I rejected that.

Is Paganism the same or different?

It's different from the other theology because Paganism itself doesn't forgive you, doesn't have some omnipotent Deity to forgive you for your sins. Nor can you absolve yourself of responsibility by getting a baptism or putting it all on the blood of Jesus. You're still responsible for yourself under Paganism. When I saw that this religion didn't have those kinds of leaps of faith in that regard, how it was very compatible with the individual-responsibility aspects that I'd integrated into personal philosophy, I warmed to it even more.

Are you still an atheist?

No, no, not at all. First of all, I've come to look at the world and all the wonders and beauty of it and feel the Gods and the presence of the Gods and the Goddess embracing me. I accepted that as opposed to a world where it's just the world out there and nothing else. I've become more aware of the connectedness and interconnectedness of things in this world. I look at that as part of what is called the Gaea Hypothesis. We're the self-aware presence on the earth.

I started working and getting more training as I did guided pathworkings [guided meditations used for instruction and exploration]. I made some personal breakthroughs where I felt touched by the Gods, by something that I hadn't experienced before. It was beyond the rational.

What is it like to be a Pagan in the military?

I don't wear it on my sleeve. I am in a pretty high-profile position. My judgment is really looked upon to guide general officers' decisions and multimillion dollars' worth of projects. I have some serious decisions to help them make, and I need them to not question my judgment. I'm not saying that I'm secretive. I just don't socialize a lot with other people in the military such that I would have to explain my religion. My boss knows that my wife's a very active Witch and Druid because of articles written about her that I've shown to him. I generally tell my immediate supervisors. I don't want them to be blindsided.

In my previous job, where I was a battalion staff officer in Pennsylvania, I had talked with a few of my coworkers. One particular devout Catholic was having problems with a Satanist cousin or something. We had talked about my religious interests, and he was concerned that in my Paganism there might be some relation to Satanism. He was worried about his cousin, and through my explanations he was shown that there is a difference between Paganism and Devil worship.

Another thing that happened was that we had bumper stickers on the car about magic and "The Goddess is alive and Magic is afoot." Later, when I was in a field exercise away from my typical duty station somebody confronted me by saying, "I hear you are a Satanist and make sacrifices to the Devil." It was in the middle of stuff and came out of nowhere, but it came from a higher-ranking NCO and someone I respected. So I wasn't about to brush it off. I basically said that's not what I believe. I don't have any truck with the Devil, and I don't even believe in him. I have nothing to do with sacrifices like that. That's not what I'm about.

I didn't really have time to get in depth about what I *did* believe, but I took time in that busy schedule to seek out a chaplain who was not a strict fundamentalist but was definitely a Christian—almost a holy roller Christian. He was a military chaplain in the army reserves. I took him aside and we walked in the woods, a great place to talk, and I told him about what I *did* believe and how people were coming up to me and saying things about this which were different from what I believed.

He said, "I've read about these things, and if this ever comes around to the battalion commander, and if he's gonna refer it to me . . . I've got you covered." What he did was he had gone and found the military chaplain's reference manual, which had the American Council of Witchcraft and Gardnerian Wicca described in detail, and it was fully compatible with military service. He gave me those references so I could actually have copies of them. He said, "You're covered. This is what we're talking about here, and there's no problem with this."

I also talked with him about the devout Catholic who was concerned about his Satanist cousin. It was fortuitous that we had talked about this because later in my own office there was starting to be some gossip. They would say things like, "Hey, that guy's got some weird ideas . . . we hear he's into Devil worship," and the Catholic came up and—he told me this later—interceded with those two other guys and said, "Oh no, he's nothing like that. He's a Pagan. He believes in the Earth Mother and Nature worship and stuff." So by having talked to the Catholic, that took care of other stuff that was creeping up in my office behind my back. He squelched it just because I had talked about it with him, and he felt a kinship with me just on a religious basis.

I was in a rock and roll band, too, on the side. And that was wacky enough, in terms of giving me a reputation, although our band used to play at the unit functions, so they were used to it. I had sort of an around-the-edge kind of reputation there, and so they didn't put Paganism past me.

As a result, there were positive things out of that just because of the way I was able to work with the chaplain's core, the chaplain there, and my coworkers to head off problems which could have happened. But it never came back to reflect on any of my ratings. My boss never confronted me with it.

When I came to the new location and higher rank in the general staff, I would talk outright with my boss because you don't like to get the bosses blindsided. They don't want to get caught by surprise. It's easier to front load them even with the hard news.

Anytime you have something bad to say, and this wasn't anything bad, it's just that they'd rather hear something out of you than get it from a third source and have to come to you with it, and then you have to defend yourself. It's easier to go and talk about it with the supervisor and explain it.

The military is obviously a very hierarchical and structured kind of body, and the Pagan family is almost the exact opposite, nonhierarchical, nonstructured. How do you reconcile those two realities?

I look at my Pagan time—although I try to live all my life in Pagan time— when I am off duty and with Pagans in a Pagan environment, as less structured. It's time off. It's away from the structure, it's away from the hierarchy. It's vacation. It's free time. I can feel freer and enjoy that time. Although in some cases I use my skills as an organizer and as a hierarchical person that can work with hierarchies if I need to organize something with my Pagan comrades. I'm more adept at that than some of them are, so I can use my skills with Pagans. But there's no real conflict as such.

My job requires bureaucracy because there is a huge organization, and it needs it. I don't know how else the military can operate and do the mission it needs to do. But with that all in mind, and all that structure, I've found the military has been really receptive to ideas of how to do things differently. They'll let you use your imagination to get the mission done because what's important is the mission and the timeliness. And particularly in a combat situation, you have to be creative.

I don't have combat experience, but I do have experience in problem solving and new projects in the military that I've come up with. New ways of working on things where all I had to do was show that they could work and after they did work, show them what I did. They were more accepting of creative solutions within the hierarchy, within the structure, because what they wanted was the mission done. It allowed for the freedom to operate. So I don't feel, even though I'm a Pagan and have a sense of freedom myself, that I am constricted in a military environment.

Have you met other Pagans in the military?

Very few at my immediate work site. But I've come to certain Pagan festivals and come across other Pagan military people . . . they are sort of a point of reference, there's sort of a "club." They'll post fliers on the bulletin board about the military Pagan network or something. I touch base with them in that way.

Also, if I go to a large city, an open event, and meet a lot of different people, I find, particularly in the city I'm in now, that there are a lot of navy Pagans. I don't run into as many on the job, because I wouldn't have any occasion to know what their religious preferences were.

Do you find, in general, they are afraid to reveal themselves because of some consequence?

Generally, yes, most of the military people I know are pretty close to home about their religious preferences. They don't need grief from their supervisors, and in some cases they would be less than favorably regarded, whether it be in evaluation reports perhaps, or duty assignments if they revealed what they were. This is thirdhand from people who were talking about it. They almost universally would prefer not to discuss it with their bosses.

Some people say how can you be a Pagan and be in the military?

Well, the military itself is concerned that you have an allegiance to it because they count on you, they pay you good money, and they expect you to respond, particularly in an emergency situation. And there are people's lives at stake at times. I have high rank and command authority for people, for large budgets, for equipment facilities that are worth millions of dollars. I have a commitment to the taxpayer, to the government, to watch over those. They are in my care. I take that as a personal responsibility.

I'm fortunate in that I volunteered for the military. I wasn't drafted. A lot of the drafting ended by the time I got into the military. All the oaths I swore, at that time as an atheist, I swore to my convictions that I was going to uphold my word, my sense of personal responsibility. That I would fulfill my commitments due to my rank and position. That hasn't changed now that I have allegiance to Gods and the Mother Earth, because I still accept my responsibilities in this organization I've been committed to and I feel an important part of. I'm going to fulfill those responsibilities because I'm entrusted.

My authority is derived through law that was passed in a republic. Part of what we're defending is also our liberties, and, personally, I feel strongly about the right to freedom of religion. This is the freest country on earth. I would prefer not to have Nazis or militarist Japanese over me. The fact that we have a country that is free and defended allows us to practice freedom of religion and worship the Gods as we choose.

During Desert Storm some things were written in Pagan journals like all humans are children of the Earth Mother and that it is wrong to bomb and kill and desecrate the natural environment the way we were. Some people would say that warfare is incompatible with Goddess worship because the Goddess is often thought of as saying, "All acts of love and pleasure are my rituals." I was just wondering if you had any comments about that?

Throughout history we find the Gods invoked on behalf of various military enterprises, and I'm not going to defend those. Just because there was Paganism in the past doesn't preclude them from being warfare societies . . . not withstanding the myth, the theory that there was a Goddess religion in the past which may have had a peaceful society. Nobody knows about that for sure.

I'm not privy to all the information the president had during Desert Storm to say why he had to go in there at that time. It tears you when you have to think about going to war, about what the awesome responsibilities are. I had to face it—I didn't go, but I had to renew my own commitment to stay in the military and support it in the face of what was going on there.

If you look at the history of our foreign policy, we've been supporting Israel, supporting other countries in the Mideast. In a way, I can say we got ourselves into it by building up Hussein to where he was. Now we're having to fix up something we put in place. What comes around is that we get our own boys' lives lost in having to do that.

And women.

Our own people, whichever, and their people, too, suffered. The destruction that comes out of it, whether the oil fields or pollution. They dumped a whole lot of oil in the oceans trying to clog up some water distillery plants. It tears you. I like to think that we didn't choose to do the polluting. Those other guys blew up those wells, those other guys dumped the stuff. We attempted to contain that kind of thing.

We were involved in bombing attacks, and it was cruel. I have to share in that karma too. In another respect, in the overall sense, that lesson was something the country had to learn about payback for the mistakes it made, whether it be the foreign policy of Israel, of building up a Hussein in the first place. Perhaps in the overall sense, the way that particular war was waged could have been worse. It could have been something that was left festering, and it could have been, in a long-term sense, a religious situation where we'd be worried about Islam, etc.

In my magical community we did some workings about the war. We were really torn about how we were going to approach it. Were we going to say Goddess, end the war! or Peace at all costs or whatever? We were really thinking through how to do it, and we just came down to, "Goddess, you have to let this develop. If it's a bloodletting, then we're going to *learn* from this." I mean, that's not nice, but this is the lesson. Whether it be the horrible military incursion that the country would be involved in such that the reaction of the people would be one where they would turn away in horror from such military action in the future.

I'm not going to apologize for the faults of elected leadership to hold to the people's will. Then again, the people have the elected leadership, and the elected leadership is over the military. We're responsible to the people through them and the orders they give us. We're also responsible for acting legally and ethically within the confines. We can't say, "I was only following orders." That's not an excuse. You only have to follow a lawful order, and that's important when you are carrying out a military duty or assignment, even in the heat of battle. I don't have experience in the heat of battle, but even in the high-pressure situations I'm in, you have to do the right thing. You have no excuse.

You can go to jail. Whatever the highest penalties are for not doing the right thing, that's part of the national legal fabric of the military, too.

One important aspect of my job which makes it really fulfilling for me in the military is that I am a facility manager and an environmental manager on a regional basis in the United States. My responsibilities include training and awareness of environmental problems and responsibilities as well as the proper way to care for things like hazardous materials and hazardous wastes at various military installations where they conduct maintenance services and dispose of oils and lubricants and handle these day to day. I alluded to the army's open ideas; they didn't really know what they wanted to do. I've been able to implement my ideas and get this done really well such that they asked me to share those ideas across the country. That makes me really happy to be in the service of the Goddess for the military and for the U.S. taxpayer.

Can you give a concrete example or an anecdote about the green movement in the military?

Just the fact that we now have environmental orientation tapes to give to every soldier that is in training. He can't just take a can of oil and pitch it out in the woods somewhere. They have to dispose of it through certain channels. He or she is responsible and will be held accountable for waste. They will be prosecuted. It'll be dealt with in the military, and heaven forbid that civilian authorities catch them, they'll hold the whole military responsible; but [the military] holds the individual criminally responsible. The army has taken it to heart.

So my contribution is in the training, the orientation. Not only the orientation of basic soldier skills, but for the guys who are doing maintenance everyday. We send them to forty-hour hazardous-material-handling courses. The military has produced these kinds of training courses to get them to be doing the right thing, handling wastes and hazardous materials in accordance with the EPA standards.

What about the large bases that have basically been operating above the law, that have been ignoring EPA standards?

All bases are having to get tested, and where they are finding hazardous materials or hazardous wastes, they are having to put them on what they call the National Priorities List of the worst-contaminated places in the country, and they're going to get dealt with whenever there is a cleanup.

But practices that led to that are being shut off, and commanders and people responsible are getting prosecuted for doing this kind of thing. It's hard to deal with people who were errant in the past. It's history now. Now it's the taxpayer's, everybody's responsibility to clean up.

We used to build with asbestos and use lead-based paints. We had underground fuel storage tanks which could leak and get corrosive. We're taking a lot of steps to remove underground storage tanks and replace them with above-ground storage. Getting asbestos out of there. Doing Radon, doing other kinds of environmental cleanups of facilities, of motor pools, of equipment, to make them less polluting and cleaner. Generally a lot of housekeeping tasks are getting regimented in the military to keep them from being careless and negligent and polluting, and we are putting the teeth of the military behind enforcing that.

So that's kind of like imposing a little bit of Pagan values onto the military system?

Exactly. It's really satisfying to use the system to clean up Mother Earth.

DON TWO EAGLES WATERHAWK is a Native American of the Cherokee/Tsalagi nation. He is a medicine toolmaker who has been very active at Pagan festivals and continues to do outreach work with current and former Pagans who have served in the military. He is a former policeman and Vietnam veteran. While on active duty he served as a sergeant E5, a Green Beret, and a Medic. He was interviewed at Starwood, at the Brushwood Folklore Center near Sherman, New York, in July 1993.

Are you a Pagan?

I understand that Pagan *(paganus)* means "person of the land" in Latin. Since my concern and my love at this point is with the planet, being a Pagan is very much what I would call myself. My heritage is Tsalagi, which is Cherokee. The original pronunciation has been bastardized to "cherokee," and is now pronounced that way even by the Cherokee.

I'm a Pagan, I'm a Pagan being, because I found that Pagans don't necessarily put walls on things, they live life a little bit freer. They pass less judgment and certainly impose a lot less control.

As far as belonging to a particular tribe or association, I'm a native of the planet, instead of a native of a particular tribe. I don't go to powwows, simply because there's a lot of control at those things, and I'm very eclectic.

I don't pass judgment on anyone, no matter what their religion or culture is. For me that seems to be what Paganism is all about. It's a coming together of all philosophies, all cultures, all groups. It has no control-through-fear. It's the freedom, really. That's what it's all about, it's the freedom of it.

Were you raised in a traditional way?

No. Originally, I was baptized Lutheran. My mother divorced my father. My father was full-blood Cherokee. My mother was Austrian. Then when my mother got divorced and remarried, I went to a Christian Science church.

After Christian Science I was always questioning, why, why, why? I went to Episcopalian churches, Protestant churches, Catholic churches. I just wanted to know why. It bothered me that instead of giving me an answer I was always told either "because" or "you just simply have to or else this will happen to you," back again to being run by fear.

At a very early age, I think probably about thirteen or fourteen, I decided this was just too scary, I couldn't imagine someone that was supposed to be filled with love that would not accept my problems and therefore threatened to hurt me if I did anything wrong. So I just left organized religion and followed my own path, using a little bit of everything.

I believe in parts of the Ten Commandments; there are parts of Christianity that are very dear to my heart, but the only part I don't like is the satanic part, the sin part, the evil part, the control through fear. I left that behind; there was no need for it, and I saw that early on. I teach my children the same way. I don't go to a church, but I tell them, "Go for it." They've been to fundamentalist Baptist churches, they've been to a Catholic church, they've been to a synagogue.

At what point did you decide that you were a Pagan, or how did that happen?

I was probably a Pagan somewhere around when I was thirteen or fourteen. I think I decided officially four years ago. I was a cop for thirteen years, and then one day I was on the job about forty-five minutes, running radar on an interstate, and all of a sudden I decided white man's law wasn't for me anymore. There were too many injustices. Meaning that the laws were not created equally for everybody. There was a lot of . . . I don't want to say "big corruption," but I would say that, being a police officer, you have to subvert your principles, your honesty, and your truth a lot. That's just not what I wanted to do. It was starting to affect me. So right then, I quit. It was very scary. I just quit! I called on the radio and said, "I quit! No two weeks' notice!"

Then, I got home and thought, "Gee, what am I going to do?" So I went up to the reservation in New York, the Seneca Reservation at Grandma Twyla's, and I did my first Inipi, which is a sweat lodge ceremony. Something happened there . . . I opened up something I had kept closed, and even to this day I'm not sure what it is. But something simply happened, and I realized that, Hey, there's something else for me that I can do. Instead of just simply doing it for my family, I can do for the good of all. I can become a bigger part of the bigger picture instead of a small part in the containment of just my family. That happened October 13, 1989.

You started studying the Seneca tradition with Twyla at that point?

I started studying the Seneca tradition, but I don't want to say I just jumped into it and that's all I looked at. I had studied Oriental philosophy for about twenty years. I liked it because it involved a lot of honor and respect. It was very detailed. It was very creative.

Which Oriental philosophy?

Oriental philosophy in general. When I went to Vietnam, I got a chance to talk to a few people in my busy time there. I spent some time in Hong Kong, spent some time in Osaka, learning from a few elders. Certainly not a large amount of time but enough time to become interested in what they did. I enjoyed that. It also was more of an Earth-based way of seeing things. The Oriental philosophy to me at that time was probably the closest I got to Paganism.

After I quit my job, my wife, Cathy, gave me a book—this was before I did the sweat lodge. Cathy has been following the Red Path for about twenty years. She gave me a book called *The Medicine Wheel*, which was really a story about four elders . . . biographies, I guess you could say. I remember staying up all night reading this book, and I remember watching the sun come up in the front window.

I closed the book, and I told myself, "You know, I'm going to write a book one day and the name of the book is going to be *All This Shit's the Same!*" I know that's rather crude, but that's what I felt. I realized then that the Native American way was the same as the Oriental. The Oriental was the same as all of the others. It's just that there were little glitches and changes made. All this stuff's the same. So that's what made me decide to not pay any attention to being part of one particular group or culture, or philosophy, but to take bits and pieces of everything and make it fit me personally.

Everybody is different, and I didn't want to follow behind anyone. When I give workshops, I try to empower people to be their own teacher. I say to them, "Hey, if you follow behind somebody, when they shit, you're going to step in it too! So why not walk beside them or make your own path?"

What do you do to make a living these days?

Probably the best description of what I do is that I make spiritual tools—not saying that they work. I don't believe that they have the "magic," or the "power," or whatever word that you want to use that people might associate with them, but they are focusing tools.

Can you talk a bit about your experiences in Vietnam and about being a warrior in a Pagan context?

Well, I enlisted in the army. I was a medic. To be a medic you have to enjoy helping people. I got a high from that. I didn't realize at that time, but I now know it was a spiritual high—having that much control to be able to help people at the point they were ready to cross over to the other side. I was very good at it, but it also came to the point where it became ludicrous because so many people, friends, were dying around me. I felt the pain of losing so much that I shut down totally. I became very callous. Life didn't mean a lot to me.

There's an old Vietnam vet saying that's very crude and very simple. It says,

"Fuck it, it don't mean nothing." That's the attitude you have to take in a very intense type of survival situation. That's the kind of attitude you have to take when you are fighting for survival twenty-four hours of the day.

It taught me a lot about freedom. I think right then, without knowing it, I was looking for the Pagan society. Because the Pagan society involves freedom. Freedom of religion, freedom of *being*. You can't find that in any other type of society or organization. Paganism has no real organization.

When you are in the military, you are so controlled, so restricted. You have absolutely everything taken away that has anything to do with individual freedom. Here you have the exact opposite part of the wheel, which is absolute freedom . . . "Do what ye will, and ye harm none." The military is just the opposite. They teach you to harm all! The military experience was one that I needed. I needed that point where I lost everything, my identity, my personality, my freedom. I look back and I say Thank you, because I had to go through that part of the wheel to see this part of the wheel.

Do you have any contact with vets now or people who are actively Pagan and actively in the military?

What I've done in the Pagan community is reach out to veterans in certain ways. If you notice by my booth [at Starwood] I have a POW flag, and I put that up not only in honor of the MIAs and POWs but also as a way of saying, "Hey, I'm a vet, and if there are any other vets around that are Pagans, come on by! I'd like to talk. We have something in common."

We were warriors . . . which is in the past. We no longer need to be warriors. We're in a new type of world now. The Indians call it the Fifth World. We've left the Fourth World, which was the world of man and it was the world of control, and aggression, and domination. Now we're in the beginning of the Fifth World. There's no longer a need for the warriors, but there is a need for people who understand what the true aspect of being a warrior is all about. That we can tell other people about who have not been placed in that situation.

In Khesanh there was a huge battle where literally hundreds of troops were slaughtered because they couldn't get out. Someone, a Marine, had scribbled on this C-ration box, this cardboard box, "Life has a flavor that the protected will never know."

That struck me. See, we tend to take life for granted. We tend to feel we're invincible, that we're not vulnerable at all. So warriors who have been in that need to tell the people, "You know, there's a lot more pain than you can possibly believe. Instead of doing things as an individual, you have to start doing things for the community."

In the outside world there's so much separation, and in Paganism that's not what it's all about. Paganism is community, and we depend upon each other to survive—much like the veterans in Vietnam. We could not separate ourselves. We had to depend upon each other for simple survival.

Like you said, you enlisted. Our general perception was (and I was one of those people out there demonstrating) that people had enlisted because they wanted to fight. They wanted to go to Vietnam. The people who did not want to fight went to Canada. We've grown and learned a lot since then. Our perception at that time was that you had chosen it, that you wanted it, that somehow it was a macho thing and you wanted it. You know, we couldn't bear it, it was awful!

I can't say why I wanted to go. I truly did. Everything that I went into was voluntary. I was a Green Beret. We were considered the killers of Vietnam. Granted, I chose to be a medic, but nonetheless I went through the training. My dad, who was totally against the war, was in so many protests, was just so dead set against it. He said, "Don, I'll take you to Canada. I'll make sure you have money to survive. I don't care how long it takes, how long you have to live there, it's no problem." But I didn't want to live there. I wanted to live here. So I knew I was going to survive. I can't tell you how I knew. I just knew it was going to happen. And yeah, I had to spend three years of my life, but I figured three years was better than the unknown many years that I wouldn't be able to live in this country, because I'd have to run.

So I chose that particular path. The lessons that I learned there, the traumas that I went through . . . it simply made me who I am today. Without that I don't know where I'd be. Who knows, I might be in jail, in a penitentiary for some stupid robbery. I don't have any idea. So I can't look back at it and say, "Gee, what if?" I look back at it and say, "Thank you." There is not one thing—and Paganism helped me understand this—there is not one thing I can say about my path, especially the military, that I can't say now, "Thank you, I'm glad," because it taught me something. I did some things that were shameful, but I did it in a war, you know. I mean I was nineteen years old. I had to do those things to survive. I'm not crazy. I don't take psychotropic drugs. I've never been in a psychiatric institution. I've been able to work out all my issues. Through it all I learned a lot, and now I'm able to teach other people.

I don't look badly at the protesters. I just think, "You people didn't *really know* what was going on." It was sad when it was blamed on us. But I'm glad that happened. I don't look back at it with any animosity toward the protesters. What I had to go through coming back from Nam was incredible. My first twenty-four hours back here were more terrifying than the eighteen months I spent in combat in the Bacmamh Mountains of Vietnam.

Why?

When I landed at Cleveland airport . . . I mean I was plucked out of the field, and we had just gotten hit badly the day before, and two of my good friends were killed. The next day I was taken to Bien Hoa; then we flew from Bien Hoa to Osaka. The plane went from Osaka to Hawaii, Hawaii to Washington. As soon as we landed in Washington, we were told we were going to get a free meal. Welcome home, Vietnam vets! The free meal was a stale hot-dog bun and a cold hot dog because we landed so late the kitchen was closed. We were all tired from twenty-three hours of flying. We were immediately hustled into a warehouse where loudspeakers blasted us, "If you have any contraband, this is the time to get rid of it now . . .," any explosives, guns, weapons, ammo, drugs, anything like that.

I was strip searched because I still had on my jungle fatigues, which had blood spots all over them. I had a three-day growth of beard. They figured, "Wow, this guy, he's got something."

They strip searched me. They took away all my unexposed film. They squeezed all my toothpaste out of the tube. They emptied all my shaving cream . . . making sure there was no contraband in there. They took me in a room and had a dog come by and sniff my ass. It was like, wait a second, I was supposed to be welcomed home as a warrior type of thing?

Then they put us on a plane; the plane went to Denver, Denver to Chicago, Chicago to Cleveland. I got out of the plane at Cleveland. I live thirty-two miles from Cleveland. It's a straight shot down the interstate. It took me three and a half hours to get a ride. Nobody would pick me up.

You were hitchhiking?

Yeah, I was in uniform, and I didn't have any money.

They didn't give you money?

Yeah, they gave me money. It was a check, but where am I going to cash a check? It took me three and a half hours to hitchhike thirty-one miles. Finally, a trucker gave me a ride. I was really pissed. It was hot, July 1 when I came home. So I decided, "Well, I'm gonna go to a mall . . . get in some air conditioning." So I go to a mall, and I notice they have a movie playing, and I make the mistake of going into this movie and sitting down and watching it. It was *Easy Rider*. Nothing like a little fueling the anger! So I came out of the movie with my duffel bag, and I went across from where the theater was to Gray Drugstore, and I went up to the woman at the counter, and I said, "I want a pack of Kools." She looked at me and said, "Could I see your ID?"

And I lost it. I tore the entire counter apart, smashed the cash register on the floor. I snapped. Police came and got me down on the ground. They called the manager, who wasn't there; he was at home. He came. He asked me what had happened, and I told him. He refused to press charges. He fired the woman on the spot. His son had died in Vietnam. Of course, he couldn't believe that here I am in full uniform, with ribbons all over my chest, and she asked to see my ID to make sure I was 18. She was wearing a peace symbol.

The cops decided not to press public disturbance charges. They let me go. I walked down to the end of the mall to get out to the entrance to catch a cab to go home, and two flower children came up, and one of them spit on me. And all of a sudden I felt this incredible calmness. I was very angry up to that point, and then I felt this incredible calmness. I remember looking at these two very pretty young ladies, and my first thought was that right then and there I wanted to go back to Nam. I didn't like it here anymore. There was no friendship here. There, at least I knew who the enemy was. Here, I didn't know anymore. My own people were the enemy. My first thought after that when I looked toward these girls was, "You have no idea how easy it would be for me to kill you. And I wouldn't blink an eye, and it wouldn't bother me."

All I could do was to think, "Today is Tuesday, I can get down to the recruiters office, re-enlist in the service and get right back to Vietnam." Because there I was loved. I was respected. And I was honored. I had family twenty-four hours of the day; I had family. I ate, slept, and died with these people. I didn't have that here anymore.

I got into a cab, I gave the cab driver whatever money, whatever cash I had left at that point, and I said, "Take me home." I went home, walked in the front door, and my mother backed up from me, because she had been watching all of these things about the war on TV and she figured that I was psychotic, that I was going to hurt her. When she backed up, I just turned around, walked out, went to the Holiday Inn.

I stayed there for three days, never left the room. Didn't eat, just drank water. All I could think about was, "I got to get back, I got to get back, I got to get back to my people." I was against everybody in "the world." We called *this* "the world." I was against everybody because nobody knew what the hell was going on. They weren't my friends. I didn't do anything wrong. My family didn't want me there. The people didn't want me there. I realized that I didn't want to be there. I couldn't believe that any God would allow this to happen, not only what was happening in Vietnam but what was happening here!

It was just very traumatic. But after the third day, I decided I needed to get out of the hotel room. So I called my stepfather, and he was gone. I knew where the key was. He was out of town, so I brought my duffel bag and went in.

I would only go out at night, when there weren't many people around. In combat, where we were, I was a night fighter. So I was very comfortable in the dark. I would go to the worst sections of town, because one of the things that combat vets had was an addiction to adrenaline. You know, you had to have that excitement! All of a sudden we were cut off from it. So I would find the worst parts of town and walk in at night and say, "Go ahead, mess with me. Do something. Somebody pull a gun on me. Anything!" I was invincible at that point. I knew if I could survive eighteen months in Nam, nothing was going to bother me here.

This went on for almost a month, and then I met Cathy. Now that would have been August 3, 1971. I've been with Cathy ever since. So we're coming up to a quarter of a century. She was the exact opposite of what I was. I was aggressive. I wasn't *dangerous*, but I was not about to take any shit. I trusted absolutely no one. I did not trust her at the time. It took me a few years to even trust her. I would always sleep very lightly with her, figuring that she was going to do something to me! Here this gentle deer of a woman! But what she did was that she taught me that I indeed had another side. She helped me get through all of this.

She was a Pagan *then*! We didn't associate the name with it, but she's the one who helped me with this transition.

So where does the Pagan world fit into all of this?

The Pagan people here at this festival, we're *united*. Even though we're of hundreds of different cultures and philosophies, we're united! Outside it's not; it's all done through fear. "We're the best people. We're the only people. All you people are wrong, and all you people are going to go to hell!"

You don't see Pagans do that. The people in the military saw the extreme; we lived that extreme. So we knew that there had to be that opposite. We knew directly or indirectly through spirit. We knew.

There are a lot of Vietnam veterans, or veterans, who are not Pagans, or are not involved in the Pagan community, but in their spirit, they're Pagans. They're tired of passing judgment. They're tired of living in "control through fear," and that's what the military is.

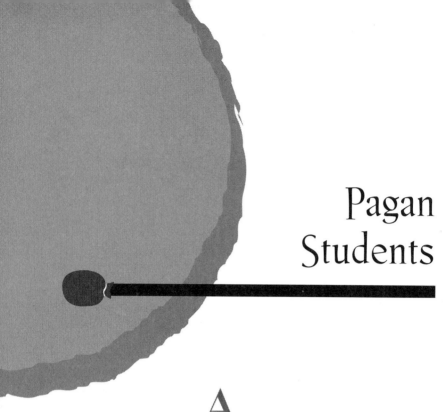

Pagan
Students

As Paganism is accepted and has become more popular with the general public, a number of Pagan student organizations have been springing up on college and university campuses across the nation. So it is not surprising to find that at a campus the size of the University of Massachusetts, there is the University of Massachusetts Pagan Students Association listed alongside the institution's Science Fiction, Hang Gliding, and Outing clubs.

We talked with two students and two graduates from separate institutions to find out how a Pagan lifestyle and worldview interacts with a modern higher education.

WILL HOWITT is a working scientist, electrical engineer, designer of analog and digital circuitry and software, Tai Chi teacher, drummer, and MIT graduate. He is a member of the Earth Drum Council and the MIT Pagan Students Association. The MIT Pagan Students Association has recently become a member of COG, giving it important benefits. Howitt was interviewed by phone on February 17, 1994.

When did you first realize that you were a Pagan?

It first occurred to me in about 1986, while I was a student at MIT. That was at a time in my life when

I was still trying to be as devout a Catholic as I knew I could be. Religion had always been important to me but I was becoming increasingly dissatisfied with the Catholic faith.

There seemed to be a very large gap between the precepts and the tenets of the faith as presented and the way the people who called themselves followers of that faith ran their lives.

So how did that lead to Paganism? That's quite a jump.

There is a Pagan students' group at MIT; it has public rituals from time to time which are announced and advertised. People who are new to Paganism are invited to come and see what it's all about. I believe it was Samhain [Halloween] 1987 when I attended my first ceremony.

I didn't really know what the word "Pagan" meant at that time. The advertisement had included a picture of a ring of people dancing on a hilltop. It looked vaguely ominous to my eyes because I was not used to such things. I have to admit that the real impetus in my going was a friend of mine, who was a big fan of heavy metal music. When he heard that there was going to be this ritual going on, he decided to attend because he expected to see a goat sacrificed or something like that.

We both attended the ceremony, and it was certainly quite different from what he was expecting. He was not a particularly religious person; he was mostly going for the thrill factor. I knew that I was looking for something, but I wasn't exactly sure what. I didn't experience an instant shock of recognition, but there was a certain amount of recognition after the ritual was over that the kind of thing they were doing and the way in which they were doing it was more appealing to me than what I was doing as a Catholic.

My friend wandered off, bored due to the lack of goat sacrifices. I hung out with the people afterward, and I liked what I found. Soon after that I began thinking to myself about the things I had done when I was young that I would not have understood as religious at the time, but which would have fallen within the limits of Pagan activity. For example, I used to make little altars with stones and sticks in the backyard. I understand that a lot of Pagans report the same thing. Many of them describe this sense of something that they felt or knew all along but just didn't have the words for. I also read a lot about Native Americans when I was young. We never played cowboys and Indians; we just played Indians.

The MIT Pagan Students Association held ceremonies at Samhain and Beltane only and not at the other holidays. Once in a while they would have a get-together, which was basically the opportunity to make homemade ice cream. By hanging out with these people I started learning more about Wicca, of its many branches and forms.

There were some Alexandrians in the group, some generic Witches, and a few Discordian types. When I use the word "Wicca," I mean a follower of any faith that is oriented primarily toward Western European agrarian, pre-Christian tradition. That may be a bit too broad, because there are a number of people who only consider the word "Wicca" to be applied to followers of Gardner or of the people who followed after him, rather structured organizations.

The people who call themselves Discordians are distinguished by the fact that they don't fit into any other category. They honor the Goddess Eris. She was the one who shook things up at a party Paris was attending in ancient Greece. She tossed in the golden apple that pitted the Goddesses against each other because they each thought it was theirs. They turned to Paris and said he would have to pick which Goddess it belonged to. Eventually this led to the Trojan war. Rather than having a lot of structure, the Discordians have a tendency to see their role as foil or prankster in relation to other people's organizations. Although I understand the appeal of wanting to upset apple carts, I feel very little attraction to that sort of philosophy as an explication of a way to live one's life.

I'm tempted to bring up the subject of chaos theory. Do any of the MIT students make a connection between that and the Goddess Eris?

No. I would wonder if any of them did. I don't really see the connection. There is something that is common among the Pagans at MIT that you won't find among Pagans in other situations which is that everybody at MIT is pretty much a technophile in a pretty big way. They are familiar with mathematics and the general notions underpinning most of the sciences. They have a tendency to view humanisms with a little bit of disdain.

When the word "chaos" is used in the sense in which it is used in mathematics, it is not the same notion as the philosophy one would describe of a person who would toss an apple into somebody's party. Systems which are chaotic in the mathematical sense are not unpredictable. This is perhaps one of the things that many people don't understand. It's not the same thing as randomness or uncertainty. It is in fact entirely predictable and deterministic.

Okay. So you are sitting with these people at MIT making homemade ice cream. Where did it go from there?

From much discussions with these people and from reading a few books, I got a clearer idea of what people meant when they used the word "Pagan." I began to feel that their notion did not encompass everything that could have been included. They concentrated on the solar cycle for the calendar of holidays, but it has become clear to me that the concentration on the solar calendar comes from a tradition that is from an agricultural society, from people who were farmers. We at MIT were not farmers. I began to look at that, and I began to suspect that there had to be more to it. Another thing was that while most of these people were turned off by the Christian faith in general, they were assembling a church and a structure and a regimen that seemed to be based upon the model of the Christian churches.

The notion of a priestly cast, the idea that you have to go through certain training, wear certain clothes, adhere to certain ways of doing things, that you have to use certain words in a certain order. The idea that if you don't do all those things, it won't be "right" somehow began to feel like it wasn't entirely what I was after either. Although it was closer than when I was Catholic. So I was still wondering where I was heading.

Several of the books I got my hands on mentioned shamanism, but they didn't pay much attention to it. I began to seek out texts on shamanic practice rather than what I term "Wiccan" religion. So while still attending the Witches' solar holidays and still appreciating the solar calendar, I felt the need for a religious structure that was oriented toward the personal, human growth development that I was feeling myself go through. I found shamanism to be much closer to what I was looking for than these "Witchy" traditions.

Most Pagans, I think, would consider shamanism to be a slightly different category. You can take Michael Harner's course on how to be a Shaman, for example, pay thousands of dollars to go through it, and you would not necessarily consider yourself to be a Pagan. Nor would Pagans necessarily consider you to be a Pagan. So what makes you a Pagan?

What I think I understand as Pagan is a religious viewpoint that focuses upon the human condition as being part of the environment of the earth both physically and spiritually. One cannot consider what it is to be human separately from what it is to live and work and be well in the environment we find ourselves in, which gives us sustenance. There is a reverence for life of all kinds in the environment we find around us.

You will see that definition is quite broad. As a matter of fact, it does not exclude Christians. I still follow many of the ideals of Christianity even though I am Pagan. I do not think that the two are necessarily exclusive.

Do you celebrate the eight Pagan festivals? Or do you revere any of the Pagan Deities?

Yes I do, if by Pagan Deity you include most of the descriptions of the Earth Mother and the Sky Father. The primeval male God and the primeval female Goddess appear in almost all of the religions that I would call Pagan. Sometimes there are many of them. Sometimes there are few.

Can you talk about the fact that you are a scientist and that you went to MIT and how it's possible for someone who is trained in Western rational scientific thinking to be simultaneously holding the idea that the earth is female and that the earth is a Goddess and that the sky is male and a God?

It certainly is possible. I'm almost tempted to say, "What's wrong with it?" The difference between science and engineering is that science is oriented toward discovery of natural phenomena around us, and engineering is oriented toward using knowledge of those phenomena to build things.

Science is a process; there is very little dogma associated with it. There are bodies of knowledge which have been developed using science such as chemistry, classical physics, quantum physics, and so on.

This process is not at all incompatible with religion in general. In fact, it is not at all incompatible with Paganism in particular. Paganism distinguishes itself from the Messianic religions in that it's a do-it-yourself kind of religion. It doesn't have much in the way of fixed dogma. That leaves a lot of open questions that you need to answer on your own. So you can consider Paganism to be entirely compatible with the scientific approach.

There is a German mathematician by the name of Kurt Gödel. In about 1930 he proposed a startling theorem and then proved it. What the theorem says is that a system of mathematical logic can either be complete, that is it covers all of the phenomena in the field of study, or it can be consistent, that is, the rules do not contradict each other. But it cannot be both.

He proved this using very rigorous mathematics. It really set the mathematical world on its ear at the time because using math's own rules, it demonstrated that there are things that math can't do. Mathematics as we have structured it is very strictly tied to self-consistency. Therefore, by this theorem, which is proved in consistent logic, it cannot be complete. There must be unprovable truths, things which are true but which will never ever be proven.

There goes your scientific hypothesis.

It doesn't necessarily go. All that it means is that if you are using strict logic, in the sense that we understand it, you are not going to get everything. Mathematical logic, which derives from the strict logic of the classical Greeks, is very carefully and strictly self-consistent. Therefore, it cannot be complete. There are other philosophical systems which are certainly intended to be complete, which one will find if one studies for a while, that seem to be inconsistent. There seem to be a lot of contradictions. That's just the way it is.

You can use the scientific method and simply observe phenomena and hypothesize all you want to. The scientific method is not invalid. The scientific method says, "Look at this phenomena. Come up with a theory, an explanation of why it should be. Make a prediction based on that theory. Test your prediction."

There are phenomena in the world which do not fall within the purview of our mechanistic viewpoint. The notion that a scientist should not be religious doesn't make a whole lot of sense if one comes across at least some data that seems to indicate that there is stuff going on that your logic can't deal with.

I have encountered both internal subjective phenomena and external objective phenomena that lead me to believe that the techniques, which for lack of a better word I will call magic, are not completely groundless. They are not simply people fooling themselves or just playing around.

Can you give an example of that?

Yes, I can. I have seen weatherworking in action. Probably the best example I can give of that was at the Rainbow Gathering in Vermont a few years ago. The central ritual of the Rainbow Gathering is a vigil which is held from dawn to noon on the Fourth of July. I joined that circle between eight and nine in the morning and stayed in prayer until noon. The weather had been disturbed all morning long; there was a layer of roiling clouds above us. Those clouds just stayed that way and didn't seem like they were going anywhere. At noon a single-syllable chant started for a brief period of time. The chant was simply "Om." As it built into a crescendo, it ended up in a huge howl. Six thousand people roaring.

At the moment in which our chant built up into that crescendo, the skies directly over us parted. The sun shone down, and there was a perfectly circular rainbow around the sun. There were still clouds all around us, but we were under this patch of perfectly clear blue sky and a rainbow.

I was there. I was about one row away from the central fire, and I was weeping.

I was too. I didn't have anything like a camera to record the phenomena. It is possible that it was coincidental, you can always say that things like that are a coincidence, but for that to have happened at that precise moment seems a long stretch to be seen as coincidence. I actually heard a couple of people complaining that there seemed to be people at the site who were playing with the weather and they weren't entirely happy about it.

MARTY HILLER is a Hedge Witch and a Doctor of Computer Science and Electrical Engineering. Her Ph.D. work at MIT was done in computational neuroscience, the study of the brain. She was interviewed May 8, 1994, in Belchertown, Massachusetts.

When did you first discover that you were a Pagan?

A friend of mine back in Minnesota knew someone who was a Witch. Another friend of mine apprenticed herself to a Witch and later married him.

My family wasn't very religious. I got my spiritual sense on my own, and mostly from experiences in nature. I got a lot of comfort as a child from going out and climbing trees or watching the sunrise. I never experienced in a religious setting until my friends started talking about Paganism and Earth worship and the four elements and that kind of thing. It really connected in with that sense of peace and comfort that I had always gotten from nature.

So you were a Pagan before you went to MIT?

Yes. I call myself a Hedge Witch. I haven't apprenticed in any formal tradition (other than science), and to some extent I am antagonistic to formal teachings. I really don't like the hierarchical sense that I get from some of the apprentice-ship-based traditions. I practiced on my own and made things up long before I worked with other Pagans. I basically derive my sense of religion from my internal sense of right and wrong. If it makes sense to me, if it connects within, then it's right. Doing things in a manner that is dictated by someone else has never made sense to me. The reason I have mellowed on that a bit is because as I practice longer and longer, I realize that there are certain basic skills that can be learned which are independent of the details of ritual.

When you are working with spiritual energies, there are natural ways that they flow and ways that they don't flow. If you are doing a ritual and you put things in the wrong order, it won't work. For example, if you don't ground and center before and after, it's going to be chaotic, and it will affect other parts of your life in ways that it shouldn't.

How did you encounter the MIT Pagan Students Association?

I saw this ad that said "Let's start a Pagan student group," and I thought that sounded pretty neat so I went. That was the first time I connected with any community of other Pagans. They seemed very open to the way that I thought about things. The initial core group worked very well together. We were a lot like what I would call a coven, rather than a social network, which is what PSG seems to be these days. We did a lot of ritual together, and we met twice a month.

We did seasonal celebrations and new and full moon celebrations. The first Spring ritual that I remember really well was at the Equinox in 1985. It was totally impromptu; we had expected to be doing a different ritual, and then it looked as if it wasn't going to happen so we decided to make one up. Since it was spring it made sense to plant seeds, and someone suggested doing the tree of life meditation. We dug up some dirt from one of the gardens and someone found a pot, and we planted our seeds and charged them with our hopes for the coming year.

The tree of life meditation is very widely used. You start by centering yourself, and you build up a core of energy to send down to the earth. Then you use that connection to draw energy up from the earth and send it out through yourself to the other people. I am not sure why that ritual worked as well as it did, but it felt very cohesive and very magical.

Does the general student body come to these rituals?

A lot of people do come to the Samhain ritual.

Would you call yourself a scientist?

Yes.

When most people think of a scientist they think of a "rational" person who uses linear logic. Can you talk about how it is possible for a person trained in rational thinking and linear logic to be a Pagan involved with spirits and with the Otherworld and polytheistic Deities and so on?

The thing is, science really doesn't have very much to say about religious experience. I've known a lot of amateur scientists who are rabidly antisupernatural and who believe that science proves they are right, but it's actually difficult to prove anything beyond a doubt using the scientific method. A negative result to your experiment doesn't necessarily mean that the thing you are looking for isn't there; your experiment may simply be faulty. And I don't really think the energies I work with are "supernatural" anyway; they are part of nature.

Part of what I have learned from my scientific training is that what we are really doing in science is making models. We don't actually know what the real world is like though we have some working models. That is an approach that is used widely in science and in engineering. Each model is accurate in certain situations, and it breaks down in other situations. So whatever model you are working with, you need to be aware of the limits of its applicability.

I have extended that so that religiously I am very much a pluralist. I think that depending on what you are trying to learn about the world or what phenomena you are interested in, the model you use is different. For some aspects of reality a model that involves spirits *works better* than a model that involves electro-magnetic phenomena or mechanical or chemical interactions. Especially when you are talking about consciousness and about subjective experience, mecha-nistic models of the world just don't get you very far.

How do you think that Paganism could affect American culture if more people were aware of it and its values?

Pagans have been forced to become very accepting of diversity because we are such a diverse group of people. Pagans are letting go of the concept of absolute right and wrong, good and evil, of the idea that we can be so sure about everything because some authority is going to tell us what is right and wrong so we don't have to think for ourselves . . . that kind of reliance on outside authority leads to violence between groups of people.

I would not say that this kind of thinking is nonexistent within Paganism, but it is certainly much less acceptable there. There is much more of an acceptance of the idea that different people have different ways of looking at things. I think that the mainstream culture would benefit from a healthy injection of tolerance right now.

Are there any problems in the Pagan community?

There are a lot of people in the community who are acting out and working through personal problems. Partly because it is such an open and accepting culture, it is very easy to do that to excess. I don't think that alternate or open sexualities or drug use is inherently a bad thing, but there are people who have a very hard time with those aspects of their lives, and they come in asking for trouble.

Because it's counterculture, there is a lot of self-consciousness about being different. There are people who really get off on being "unusual," and that makes me uncomfortable sometimes. People can get overblown in their self-presentation, putting on airs and pretending to have a lot of powers that they don't have. I think that gives us a bad name because there are people claiming to be able to do things that they can't do.

There seems to be a lot of tension between the feminist Craft and the traditional Craft. There have been times when I felt I was under suspicion within the feminist community because I am a scientist. And there have been times when I have felt very uncomfortable with some of the sexual dynamics. There are people who are more aggressive with their sexuality than I like.

On the other hand, in some ways that kind of thing is even worse in mainstream society. If a guy is coming on to me there, he is usually pretending that he's doing something else. He's pretending that he wants to get to know me, or whatever. In Pagan circles someone is much more likely to come and make an explicit proposition. If they want to have sex, they are willing to admit it instead of going through all of the round-about pretense. That sometimes makes me uncomfortable, but I also think that when it's out in the open, sexuality is a lot easier to address.

If someone says "I'd like to sleep with you," it's easier to respond directly than when someone says "I'd like to get to know you better." And I do feel safer in Pagan circles, because if I'm not interested I can come right out and say so without feeling like the whole world is going to come down on me for turning this guy down. I'm allowed to say no. And I'm allowed to come on to them, too, if I want to. Maybe some women are a bit more respected. Or maybe it's just because sex is more out in the open.

Can you talk a bit more about your conflict with the feminists?

There is a part of the feminist community that is very separatist [and] matriarchy oriented. I don't think that they are the majority, but they are quite vocal within the feminist Craft. Going to MIT and being trained as an engineer, I sometimes feel like I'm seen as having sold out to the patriarchy. Of course, I've also been called a man-hater by the other side!

Some of the ways that Goddess worship is played out in the community do disservice to women because a lot of the images of the Goddess are very traditional—mother, lover, and Amazon. Even Amazon is seen as nature-woman. She's not allowed to be techno-woman.

I'm much more of an equal-rights feminist. The thing that attracted me to feminism in the first place was the idea that I could do what I wanted to and that I didn't have to follow some socially prescribed gender role. I've always been good at math and science and I've always been interested in them, and that is something that women aren't supposed to do according to *anybody's* traditional gender roles, feminist or otherwise. So the appeal of feminism is the freedom to follow my own heart, to do what I am interested in doing. What I have done with my own images of the Goddess is that I've looked for Deities that I identify with and which have really fleshed out the aspects of the female archetype that correspond to my experience, like Brigid [the ancient Celtic Goddess of Smithcraft, poetry, and healing]. Brigid is the Goddess of technology, right? Smithcraft was the high technology of that age—not to mention art and medicine.

Is She the Goddess of computer scientists?

I've known several Pagan women at MIT who were drawn to Her. A former president of the Pagan Students Association also had Brigid as her matron Deity. She did the Brigid/Candlemas ritual every year at MIT, and as a consecration of tools. People would bring in the tools of their craft to be consecrated. I brought my computer keyboard one year. A friend of mine brought his pager. Someone else brought her dance shoes.

STEPHANIE KERKOW AND DAVID CARRON are the copresidents of the University of Massachusetts Pagan Students Association. Both are psychology majors at the University of Massachusetts in Amherst. They were interviewed March 31, 1994, in Belchertown, Massachusetts.

Stephanie, are you a Pagan?

Yes. I consider myself to be a Norse Pagan. That means that I have given my life and my troth to the Norse Gods. I have professed that they are my Gods. I believe that there are other Gods, but my Gods are the Norse Gods.

What religion were you raised in, and when did you discover that you were a Pagan?

I was raised Protestant. My uncle had been Wiccan for a long time, and when I said I was interested in Paganism, he got me involved in Wicca. I was initiated in my freshman year of high school. I didn't like the Christian teachings; I thought that subjugating yourself to a God was wrong. I was first attracted to the magical side of Paganism. I liked the idea of "bending energy to your will." After that I got interested in the religious side of it. I guess that at first I thought I needed power, but then it turned out that what I wanted was spirituality.

When I joined the UMass Pagan Students Association, I found that I wanted to be a Norse Pagan. I had a friend who was a Norse Pagan, and I am part German, so I wanted to explore my heritage.

David, are you a Pagan, and if so how did you become one?

I am a Pagan, and I am Asatru, more commonly known as Norse Pagan. I was raised Jewish. Culturally, I am still Jewish; you can't escape being what you were raised as, but my religion is Asatru.

That's quite a jump to go from being Jewish to being Asatru, isn't it?

Not really. They are both tribal religions, and they are a lot closer than you would figure. The family is very important for Asatru. The community, the people are bound together.

If they are not that different, then what was it that made you want to change religions?

Asatru clicked; there was a calling inside me. I first found out about it in elementary school. I found a book, Delandro's *Norse Myths*. The Norse Gods were just so vibrant and alive and attractive. I must have been seven years old at the time.

I am sure you know that the Germanic people did some serious trashing on the Jewish people. Does that ever come up for you as an issue?

Well, my family wasn't terribly happy about my decision, but I didn't expect them to be happy about any religious conversion. I don't see it as that much of an issue because the Norse came a long time before Hitler.

I understand that there is a group of Norse Pagans that is only accepting people that are 100 percent Northern European. That's the kind of thing that I think people are afraid of when they hear of Odinists or Asatru. Can you talk about that group and how you feel about it?

Stephanie: The Asatru Alliance came out of the Asatru Free Assembly, which broke up in the seventies. The Asatru Alliance was nonracist until last year, when at the Allthing there were three kindreds who said anyone who is not Northern European cannot practice this religion. They even said that homosexuals should not be considered Asatru at all.

How do you feel about that?

I think it sucks. My kinswoman is half Brazilian, and she would not be considered Asatru even though she is one of the most religious Asatru that I know. In their eyes she would not be considered a member of the religion.

How is Asatru unique? How does it differ from Wicca, for example?

David: Asatru is polytheistic. We have many Gods and many Goddesses, and we take them from the Scandinavian myths and the Northern European myths. There are technical details of how we are different from modern Wicca—the way we create sacred space for example.

Are there female Deities as well?

Stephanie: The sun is female, and the moon is male. That's a big difference from Wicca. I know Wiccans who couldn't possibly imagine the sun being female because the Moon Goddess is a big symbol with them. In the North the sun is a good thing. It nurtures and brings fertility to the earth.

Can you talk a bit about the UMass Pagan Students Association?

David: It was started in the fall of 1987. The first major action they did was a demonstration that they staged. A Christian group had sent out a flier to every person in Amherst. It was a full-color, impressive flier. The flier insinuated that Pagans had a hand in murdering people. They also said that local Pagans in the area were kidnapping children. The Christians had a big convention to tell the story of debauchery that Pagans were engaged in. The UMass Pagan Students picketed this.

Have you seen a copy of this flier?

David: Yes. We have it in the office.

Stephanie: So we've been active since then. In the beginning a lot of "goat slayers" showed up. These were people who came just to see if we were going to make sacrifices, or people who were looking for a sacrifice to kill. Those people eventually left when they found out that the UMass Pagan Students Association is an ecumenical group, religious based, and into the study of Wicca and Asatru and any other religions that people might be interested in.

We don't turn away people who are just curious. We've had Christians come to find out what we were about. People have done reports; there have been a number of articles written about our group in *The Collegian*, the local campus paper.

We have between ten and twenty members at any time. We celebrate all of the major holidays that fall within the year. We recently started going up to a cabin that belongs to the UMass Outing Club. It's in New Hampshire, and we hold a May Day festival there. We have a Maypole which is currently displayed in our office, and we have a library with a lot of Pagan publications. Anyone can join the library for $2 and read the information we have. We are a registered Student Organization on campus. UMass is fairly liberal about the kinds of student groups on campus. There are over two hundred of them at this time.

Do the students that you go to class with know that you are doing these things?

Stephanie: Oh yes. I have a poster on my door that says UMass Pagan Students. I wear a hammer, a sign of Asatru, around my neck. Sometimes I wear a pentagram. We also have information tables where we do fundraisers, we do Tarot card readings. We poster on campus extensively so that people will know that we are there. We have an office.

Can you describe one of your events that you have hosted and what it was like?

Stephanie: We did a Samhain ritual which twenty people attended. We had a Dumb Supper, which is a ceremony to honor the dead, generally dead relatives. You try to avoid contacting unsavory or crazy dead people because you don't want to attract that energy to yourself. A Dumb Supper is a way of contacting a dead relative to say "good-bye" when they have passed on. It's very cleansing because if you were on the other side of the country when your father passed away, you might never have gotten to say "I love you." This is a way of saying that and of sharing a meal with those who have passed over. It's a time to honor and respect and reflect about those who have passed on. When you pass the chalice, it's totally silent; you keep silence in respect for the dead and in hopes that they will join you. You sit and you eat and you give them the proper respect. Then you say good-bye and close circle, and afterward you take whatever food is left over from their plate and yours and you libate; you leave it near a tree hoping that the Gods or the spirits will take their share.

The Church of
All Worlds

The Church of All Worlds (CAW) promotes and fosters experiences with the environment and community that awaken people's sense of the planet, each other, their own potential, the spiritual, and the Divine. CAW has between three and four hundred paid members. The larger community is estimated at about fifteen thousand. In the Bay Area of San Francisco there are twelve hundred affiliated people. Along with its founder, Oberon G'Zell, CAW publishes *Green Egg*, a magazine of Goddess and Nature religion.

OBERON (FORMERLY OTTER) G'ZELL is the primate of the Church of All Worlds. Oberon's wife, Morning Glory, is an active partner in CAW and has an amazing collection of Goddess statues from many cultures, with which she travels and does workshops. Oberon was interviewed at Starwood near Sherman, New York, in July 1993.

When did you first realize that you were a Pagan?

I've been a Pagan, like most of us, for all of my life without necessarily knowing it. I identified myself as a Pagan when I first really saw the word in context as applied to the pre-Christian indigenous religions of Europe, which would have been in 1967.

How did the Church of All Worlds begin?

The Church of All Worlds had been inspired by the book *Stranger in a Strange Land* by Robert Heinlein. It began as a "water brotherhood," which was a closed and secret society not accessible to the general public. Everybody knew we were there, but we were very selective about who we invited in. It had grown to about a hundred people in five years, and we decided to become public and incorporate and do the "church" thing.

When I began working on bringing it out, the first question people asked was, "Is this a Christian denomination, or are you Hindu, or what are you?" We had never really thought about it. Then I realized what we were was Pagan. That was because of our fundamental affinity with the Nature-based ancient religions, the indigenous folk religions of the world, that had natural cycles and all that stuff. This was implicit in Heinlein's book, the concept of "Thou Art God" and "Thou Art Goddess." And that all the universe is sentient. It's animism, really.

My first interest in Paganism really began with myths and fairy tales. When I was about three years old, I read the Childcraft Books put out by *World Book Encyclopedia*. Eventually I realized that it was all Pagan—the fairy tales, the legends, the lore, the customs, all the things that I had grown to like so much. And I thought, That's obviously what I am. There really was never a time when I was not interested in these kinds of things. I always had a feeling that this was where my heart was.

You have been a Pagan for about twenty-five years now. What is it about Paganism that has kept you interested, and in which religion were you raised?

I was raised in white-bread Protestantism. I was very active in the church. I was always very religious, and I had a perfect attendance record in Sunday School through high school. I was a junior acolyte, I was the narrator for the Christmas pageant, and was really into it. I went to all the retreats and study groups.

It's just that at some point I outgrew it. It just did not include any of the things I was interested in. It didn't include nature, it didn't include the myths and the legends, or dinosaurs, or space travel, or astronomy or geology and the sciences in general, which have always fascinated me. It didn't include much of history other than biblical history.

At some point I began to realize that the history they were giving me was not the history of my people. I'm not Jewish, and all the history we got was of the Jews. But where was ours? I mean it's great if you happen to be Jewish, but my personal history would be Celtic and Teutonic, and none of that was included.

Somewhere along the line I had a sense of being not who they were talking about. And of being "a stranger in a strange land." That was it. I went searching for my people, my culture, my religion, and for my roots. For my tribe.

So what is it that keeps that inner spark that you have found in Paganism alive? That light that sustains you?

It's a level of reality, I guess. It's real on a level that none of the other spiritual teachings are. It deals with the Earth, the Goddess. It deals with nature and with people. It includes all of that—love, sex, nature, blood, death, life, birth, and the cycle of the seasons.

There's also this phenomenal love and joy that you find in the community, in the tribe. I'm constantly overwhelmed by that alone. It doesn't mean that we don't have our quarrels and disputes and some things that I get disappointed with or upset and pissed off about. But that happens in any family. What we have is a real family, a real tribe. Our entire history until the Industrial Revolution was the tribe. When you talk about "traditional family values," it was the clan.

Can you tell an anecdote about how being a Pagan has affected your life in terms of your career, your married life, your friendships, personal ways that you have benefited from being a Pagan?

There is really no aspect of my life that is not permeated with being a Pagan. It's the whole perspective. It's hard to pick one thing. My choice of vocation has simply drawn me deeper into more and more commitment to serving the Goddess.

Which Goddess do you mean?

Mother Nature. On some ultimate level when I speak of the Goddess, I really speak of Mother Nature. My first introduction to the Goddess was in Walt Disney "true life" movies, where they always talked about Mother Nature. They never talked about God. They would say, "Mother Nature paints the landscape in the fall with beautiful colors." Well, Mother Nature made sense to me. It makes sense to everybody! When you talk about Mother Nature, you don't even have to argue, everybody knows what you are talking about.

When I had my great "theagenesis" revelation that led to the Gaea thesis back in 1970, it was a matter of Her tapping me on the shoulder and revealing her face to me.

Are you saying that you invented the Gaea thesis?

Yes.

What about Lovelock and Margulis?

They came around about three years later.

Had you communicated with them or published anything about it?

No, I didn't know who they were, but I did publish it in *Green Egg*. Also in half of the other Pagan journals around and in several books that were published before they came out with it. Their very first thing was in October 1973 in *The Journal of Atmospheric Biochemistry.* There was an article by James Lovelock about Gaea as seen through the atmosphere, or something like that. He looked at it from the outside in, I looked at it from the inside out.

Can you describe the Church of All Worlds, what the purpose of it is, and how it's working, and how it's currently evolving?

I'll try. It's very hard to describe. As Margot Adler said in *Drawing Down the Moon*, CAW is hard to pin down because it's so all-inclusive. It was inspired but not really based on Heinlein's *Stranger in a Strange Land*. A lot of the ideas Heinlein put down, his metaphors and terminology, were very applicable, but the story is a story. It's not our story; it's a fable. And you could say the same thing about the founding story of Christianity; that's not the history of the church. The fable of Christ and his disciples has nothing to do with the history of the church at all.

It's the same thing with the Church of All Worlds. The story of *Stranger in a Strange Land* is a fable, it's a myth. It's a creation myth that has a lot of interesting stuff. But the interesting thing about it is, at the end of the story all the pieces are sort of wrapped up and the people who had been involved in the story are left to carry on. That's what makes it interesting. It's open ended. And we are the sequel.

What we've done is we have carried on. Having been given these teachings, these ideas, these concepts, we've continued evolving with them for thirty years. What we have done is to create a large enough tapestry that all kinds of threads can be woven into it. That is the great benefit; it's not a limited paradigm. So we have woven in the threads of all aspects of cultural heritage, lore and customs, folkways, legends, music, art, fable, and visions. Lots of visions.

One of the most important things about CAW is that we have our roots deep in the past, in our cultural heritage. We also have our roots deep in the earth, and like a tree our branches reach up to the stars, into the future.

I think that future mythology is a very important concept that we haven't had much in the world before. Most mythology has been backward looking, harking back to a Golden Age long past when everything was nifty, like Atlantis or Camelot. But we aren't living back there, in the Garden of Eden, the primal paradise. The idea of trying to reclaim that kind of thing is missing the point, because we are going forward, and I think it's crucial that we develop myths of the future.

Star Trek, the television show, is an incredibly important phenomenon. It offers us a future vision that is influential. You have to have something out there as a beacon to draw you toward it. That's what science fiction can do. Science fiction has its roots in utopian novels and visions and fables throughout the ages.

CAW is deliberately revolutionary. We embrace science, evolutionary theory, and are continually evolving, changing, and growing. We are antidogmatic; we not only tolerate diversity, we celebrate it and revel in it! We are very inclusive of ethnic, economic, social, age, and sexual orientation. Every kind of diversity we can possibly find, we like to bring it in. Everytime we find a new kind of flower, we want to plant it in our garden.

You yourself are not going to be on the planet forever . . . excuse me, I think I made an assumption there! But what is your personal vision of where you would like to see CAW go, and what would you hope would be the implications for American and world culture?

Well, part of our mission statement for CAW is to evolve a set of myths and experiences and practices which will provide a context and a stimulus for reawakening Gaea and uniting Her children in a global family based on responsible stewardship. That's a synopsis. We feel that what religion needs to be doing is to bring the whole family back together. There has been this fragmentation.

Theologically one could say that there had been this great divorce between the Mother and the Father a millennia ago, and it was a real messy divorce. He was abusive, and some of the kids went with Him and some of the kids went with Her. What we need to do is to bring the whole family back together. We need to have a reconciliation. We need to recognize that we are all children of the same Mother. That's part of what we are out there doing.

CAW within the context of the Pagan community has always been a force for community building. One of our major vehicles for that has been *Green Egg*, which has always been a real interlinking of the many aspects of the community. We were the first organization to be founding and promoting ecumenical alliances. The very first one was the Council of Themus that we formed back in 1970. The United Federation of Pagans is the latest attempt in that direction.

The term *pagan*, applying that to the community, was in essence one of those things. Once upon a time Benjamin Franklin was asked what his greatest invention was. He said, "Americans." Because up until his time, until he started using that word in his newspaper, people thought of themselves as Virginians and New Hampshireans or Protestants, Puritans, Catholics, Irish, German, or whatever, but they did not think of themselves as Americans. He united them, and he came up with the term *American*, and suddenly people were together.

I did the same thing with the word *pagan*. When I began associating with other groups, I found Witchcraft groups over there or Greek and Egyptians over here, Norse groups, and everybody doing their own little thing. There was nothing that united them all together.

If you could influence American culture or world culture how do you think CAW would do that, or how would you like to see it happen?

I think we would be promoting a paradigm shift away from the concept of the inanimate clockwork universe that has been with us since the 1660s and the "Scientific Revolution," and we would attempt to "re-ensoul" the concept of nature so that people perceive a more animistic and pantheistic world around them. They would see they are part of a living universe and not separate from it.

As far as our specific contributions, I trust we will continue to be a catalyst. So many elements of the Pagan community today—rituals, chants—originated in the Church of All Worlds. The very theology, the Gaean theology, is something that we originated. Being able to put out seeds and have them grow and be adopted by people is part of our contribution.

We are trying to find ways to create a club that we all can belong to, so that everybody is on the same side. We are providing a model for what is possible, showing that some things can be done even if they look impossible, such as polyamorous love relationships. It is a concept that was so hard to talk about because there really wasn't even a word for it. People talked about polygamy; that means marrying many people. Polyfidelity meant being sexually exclusive among several people. But there was no word to discuss the common phenomenon that people actually encounter of people simply loving more than one person. It was unthinkable, but it was happening all the time.

Because there was no word for it, people could no more deal with it than a generation ago people discovering that they were gay and not having any way to integrate that because there was no model. There wasn't even language for this that was not pejorative. You could possibly discuss nonmonogamy or say some kind of put down thing, but there was no formal concept. Polyamory means loving more than one, loving many. I am sure that there are people who don't have any capacity for that, who are only capable of one love in their life and that's it. Or only one love at a time perhaps. Although serial monogamy is a kind of strange phenomenon because it usually means that when somebody falls in love with a second person, they feel that this ends their relationship with the first person.

This doesn't have to be anymore. When you have a child, you love that child, and then you have another child and you also love that one. You might have several children, and you love them all. Having a new child doesn't mean you have to stop loving the one you had before. The same thing is true for relationships.

This is what people constantly experience and constantly wrestle with. They fall in love, and they think their marriage has to be destroyed. Our immediate circle of friends includes, right now, four couples who are celebrating their twentieth anniversary of being married to each other. We are all going away to have a big get-away together. So I think there is a basis for real stability in the type of relationships we are doing. I don't think that the standard dyadic, monogamous marriages demonstrate this very clearly.

In your polyamorous union with all these couples do emotional issues come up like favoritism or the desire to be primary with one particular person, or is the affection equal all the way around? How does that work?

The same way any friendship works. Some people are closer to each other than others. They just are. It's not really an issue, particularly. I guess it is when you are a school kid and you are wondering, "Who is my *best* friend? Are *you* my best friend?"

Yes, but it is in human nature—at least my experience of human nature is people feel insecure sometimes. Humans want to feel that they have someone—do you know what I mean?

Well, the issue of security is crucial. Security is the basis for feelings that lead to jealousy and a lot of the problems. We address that very intensely, and we even do workshops on this. We've created models that work. Part of them are based on fundamental commitments and really making sure of the security in relationships. It's the first priority.

So do you all live in close proximity to each other, like in a neighborhood? Or do you live in the same house?

Now we live in close proximity in a neighborhood. We have a fundamental triad: Diane, who is the editrix of *Green Egg*, lives forty feet away from us in the next house. We have been together with her for ten years, which is about half the length of time that Morning Glory and I have been together.

How do you think this has affected the kids?

The kids are, I think, incredibly healthy, happy, and fulfilled by this stuff. They are constantly comparing growing up in our contextual family with other kids that they have known, and they are very pleased and proud. They bring their friends around, and their friends all think that they have a great situation.

What would you say are some of the problems we are facing as a movement right now, as a religion?

We are facing the problems that Pagans have always had. The problems of insular tribalism. We are tribal by nature, and there's this tendency to turn inward and to not form alliances very well. We tend to be suspicious or hostile to other groups, and we pick each other apart.

What is the vision you are holding for the future of Paganism? Where would you like to see it go in the next twenty years?

Well, the growth is exponential, and this explosion of growth will continue. As it does, we will have larger numbers of people and proportionately fewer people to train them effectively. Over half of the people identifying themselves as Pagan in the surveys that I have seen consider themselves to be solitary. Most people complain about the difficulty of finding a group to associate with. The most common structure of the community is the coven structure, which tends to be limited in size. It is usually closed and simply cannot accommodate a huge number of people. We have to find ways of dealing with that, because we will be getting more people all the time.

As we grow larger and older our second generation will be growing up, and we will be having a third generation of people who have grown up entirely in a Pagan context. The kids who are playing around at the festival here will some day be taking their role as priests and priestesses. So we need to be thinking about their education, their training, preparing them for life both in our community and in the world outside of it.

I feel that acquiring more land will be an important fact for the future. What we have here is wonderful; this is Pagan-owned land and it's so magnificent to have our own country. We've been a diaspora of the souls, where our people on some soul level have been scattered throughout the earth without a country, a tribal territory, or a homeland of our own.

We've been finding our tribes and finding our way back to each other. We are like gypsies. Every acquisition of Pagan land that comes is a step in the direction of having our own country. Someday there will be entire Pagan villages and communities.

That's already happening in the New Age community.

Right, and it will happen in our community, too. In the cities there will be Pagan apartment complexes. In the country there will be Pagan communes that will grow into villages. The seeds of this are already in place. As we acquire land, we will build temples and places of worship that will be meaningful.

In the future we will interact more and more with the mundane community. We will have open meetings that people will attend, like New Moon New York. A couple of years ago they did a Beltane [May Day] gathering in Central Park with seventy-five people. This year there were three hundred people and three Maypoles. They anticipate that next year it will more than double and they will have five or more Maypoles. Anybody can come.

Afterwards what do they do with all of these people? Suppose five hundred people say they want to come to their meetings? How are you going to fit them into somebody's living room? Where do you go from there?

We have now reached a critical mass in some odd way. We've been like the mycelium under the ground of a mushroom colony. We are an underground phenomenon in spite of our efforts to be as public and available as we possibly can, with our books and all the outrageous stuff we do. The general public doesn't know we exist. People, academics, are still writing books where we aren't mentioned at all. We are usually not invited into the dialogues that go on between the world religions. They will send them to the Dalai Lama or to Rolling Thunder but not to us and to our people, even though we have this huge community. Even though we have over five hundred publications, which is a staggering phenomenon in itself.

We haven't solved this problem, and maybe right now it's just as well. A couple of years ago the *San Francisco Chronicle* put out a survey of its readership asking people questions on religion. They didn't ask what religion you were, they asked questions on belief. One question was, "Do you believe that the earth is a living creature with a will and consciousness of its own?" Fifty-two percent of the respondents agreed with that. That means that fifty-two percent of the readers of the *San Francisco Chronicle* are basically Pagans by our lights without knowing it.

Someday soon the world will suddenly discover us. It will discover what this word means and what it stands for. That it stands for people who are Earth-loving, tree-hugging, Nature worshippers. When that happens we will experience a phenomenon that we are at this point ill-prepared to cope with.

ANODEA JUDITH is a past president of the Church of All Worlds. She is the author of *Wheels of Life: A User's Guide to the Chakra System* and *The Seven-fold Journey: Reclaiming Mind, Body and Spirit Through the Chakras*. She is a frequent contributor to *Green Egg* and other publications. The interview was conducted at Starwood in 1993.

How long have you been a Pagan?

I would say since 1975 consciously. I finally found some writings that spoke to what I had always believed. I'd been a Pagan all my life, but I didn't have that model to apply to what I felt and believed, what my spiritual values were until then. In 1975 it was through Z. Budapest's *Feminist Book of Lights and Shadows* that I finally connected. A friend came to me, and she was all excited because she had been reading about Witchcraft and she wanted to tell me all about it, and she wanted to do a ritual. That was when the mental model, the reality of the experience, and the feelings that I was having came together.

Can you give some examples of being a Pagan from your childhood?

I have always loved nature. I was always happiest in nature. Whenever we went to Grandma's farm, I was just ecstatic to play in the hay and climb the apple trees and walk in the fields. I always sensed a distinct power in nature.

I was raised in different religions, among them Christian Science, which of the Christian religions has some overlap with Paganism in that the concept of healing is a mind-influenced one. That you can influence reality with your thoughts, which is very much a kind of magical thinking.

Does Christian Science honor nature in any way?

It doesn't specifically speak to nature. It does say that everything is God. It has a bit of the duality of mind and body or mental and physical, that polarization, which I don't.

Christian Scientists tend to deny that matter is real. Their basic statement is that there is no life, truth, substance, or intelligence in matter. All is Infinite Mind in its infinite manifestation. If something is going wrong in your life, it's because of an error in your thinking or your worldview. You work on that. I think that there is a lot of truth in that.

How does Paganism express that? You said they were similar.

The sense that we are a part of reality and we can influence reality. That the mind and the outer circumstances of the outer reality are interrelated and intercausal and, even though Christian Science doesn't speak to nature, where we are at physically has to do with the manifestation of our reality.

How do you put that into your Pagan spiritual practice?

I believe that the state of my inner consciousness and how I conduct my own inner state, which means what I eat, how I take care of myself, my actions, my interactions, have to do with my reality. As I clean up my own space, my interactions with other people are cleaner. As I ground my own self, my life becomes more grounded. I work with other people to get them grounded. Their financial situation usually gets better as they get more grounded.

I have worked with the chakras a lot of my life. A chakra is an energy center within the body that is a meeting point of mind and body where we assimilate and express certain kinds of energy. For example, when I work with someone's heart chakra, their relationships get better. It's the interface between the inner and the outer world. They really aren't different; they are intercausal.

You have been a Pagan for almost twenty years. What would you say is the central truth, the juicy bit that has really kept you hooked all this time?

There are several juicy bits. One is the concept of Divinity as female. Female *and* male but including the female, which the other mainstream religions do not do. As a woman and as someone who honors balance and totality, that's essential. The Goddess as a Divinity, as an archetype or however you want to put it, has definitely touched me in my life and filled me with Her presence and brought me many gifts and joys.

Part of it is also the connection with nature. The honoring of nature as a living Goddess. As something that is alive, that does respond, that has intelligence. To me nature is the most profound statement of creation. It expresses organization, intelligence, beauty, harmony, completion, totality, essence, in the most profound sense.

The third thing for me is the sense of community and the juiciness of the ceremony. I find that good ritual brings me all the way there. I am totally engaged. It's the closest I can come to the meeting point of all realities. Mind, body, emotions, the physical, mental, political, psychological—all these aspects come together. They are all threads that we weave. This is probably most true when I am leading a ritual, which I seem to do more often than being a participant these last few years. It feels like putting one's hand into the pulse of creation. That is very exciting to me.

I feel sorry for people who don't have community. People who grow up isolated with a few friends here and there. The Church of All Worlds community has been there for me for seventeen years. I am now going to graduation ceremonies for people whose mothers I knew when they were pregnant with them. That sense of continuity is there. We don't have a lot of turnover—some, as in any group, but most people seem to stick with it and stay together through thick and thin. If anything happened to me, my community would be there. There are many people I could turn to and many who turn to me. I couldn't have done some of the things I have without the support of community.

How has being a Pagan affected your ability to make a living, your relationship with your biological family, the aspects of your mundane life?

My mundane life isn't very mundane. It never has been. I've worked as a healer, as a therapist, as a massage therapist; I had a private practice for fifteen years. I have a master's degree in clinical psychology and a license in acupressure massage. I have studied many of the mind-body therapies.

How do Paganism and psychotherapy relate?

Paganism works on healing the world, and psychotherapy works on healing the individual. One does not happen without the other. Paganism is constantly addressing the imbalances that have occurred in the world, and sometimes in an individual therapy works toward healing and balancing in the same way.

When they are done well, they are both spiritual experiences. They are experiences of the spirit expanding and coming into balance with itself.

Have you ever been openly Pagan in a clinic?

Always. I don't grab a loudspeaker and say, "Hey! I'm a Pagan!" but I have never hidden it. I let my clients know, and occasionally I get somebody who says they couldn't work with someone who believes in that, and I say fine. They don't have to believe the way I do.

If it's relevant—for example, a woman who is trying to find a sense of the Divine within herself—I will share with her that there is a Goddess and there are people who believe in a feminine form of Divinity. That can turn light bulbs on for them. But I don't bring it into my therapy if it's inappropriate.

Where is your path going now?

I'm trying to make an influence on the world to heal it and bring it into balance. I'm trying to address the root causes of the pain that people experience. As a therapist I have heard about this pain over and over again. I have heard about people's parents and the way they treated them, about the child molesting and the alcoholism and the abandonment and all the deep wounds that people have and that they carry and pass down because they are not healed.

I'm at the point now where I can't just fix those wounds without addressing the causes. The causes get down to many theological implications and the imbalance of the patriarchal takeover and the loss of the Goddess.

What do you mean by "patriarchal takeover"?

There was a time when the Goddess was worshipped as the main religion of the planet. There was a period about six thousand years ago where that changed. We went from a more matrifocal—which doesn't mean matriarchy but more feminine-centered—sense of theology to a patriarchal one. It really is a patriarchy because it is men dominating women. At that time there was much brutality toward the Goddess religions and those who practiced them. They were driven underground, and in that process, through generations after generations, we lost all the values that were connected with it.

Those values that we lost are part of the imbalance that enable people to molest their children or abuse them or drive them to alcoholism. It's that emptiness of soul, that big hole in our psyche that people don't even realize is there because this happened so long ago. That's what I am addressing at this point in my life.

Does this have anything to do with the work of the Church of All Worlds?

Yes. CAW is trying to address that same psychic split, the divorce between heaven and earth, between male and female, between mind and body. Those three especially, and there are smaller ones that fall under those categories, divided a totality. They need each other. Heaven and earth need each other. Men and women need each other. Mind and body need each other. Addressing that split is a way of healing and bringing it back together. When we do that on an archetypal level, it will also happen politically and psychologically.

How do you do that?

You start by understanding the archetypes, what they are, how they are brought into awareness, what to do with them. As we work with the archetypes, we evolve them. An example is that we perform the Eleusinian mysteries every year. These are the mysteries of Eleusis, the rites of Demeter and Persephone going to the underworld. In doing that we embody those Deities, sometimes for a whole season. That doesn't mean every minute, but we are always aware of that thread. If someone is to play Persephone, then they really go into the underworld. They go into it in their psyche for the whole winter, and they work with the concepts of the underworld.

As a modern woman does that, she actually evolves the archetype. I played Demeter for a season, and I worked with Zeus, accusing him of being the absent father who gave away his daughter without even asking. I raised her and he gave her away, what is this? We worked that through in the ritual. Then I found that in the clients who came to me who knew nothing about this, who were not a part of the ritual, these same archetypal patterns were healing. When we do these rituals, we get into the workings of the universe. We rearrange the relationships and things get a little bit better. I'm not saying that happened all over the world, maybe it only happened in my sphere. But even so it's worth it.

Can you describe some of the principles that CAW stands for?

The mission statement of CAW in essence is that we are trying to foster the coalescence of consciousness. We are trying to foster experiences with the environment and community that awaken people's sense of the planet, each other, our own potential, and the spiritual, the Divine. We help others to recognize their community and their purpose in harmony with Mother Earth. We help them connect to that in a way that helps them evolve to their next stage.

What is your relationship with Oberon G'Zell?

He is a brother, he is a lover, he is a compatriot. We believe we have known each other in other lifetimes again and again. We are twin souls in a way. We are both Sagittarians, and we have a kind of innate understanding of each other. We are both visionaries, and we are both doers.

We built the Church of All Worlds together. He built it before I came along, and then I helped. We have been mutual supports for each other, we have provided intellectual stimulation for each other, we have been lovers. I have been lovers with his wife, Morning Glory, too, just as long, and I have a deep connection with her as a soul sister. He's a soul brother.

I have observed open marriages over the years, and in most of the ones that I have observed the marriage eventually broke up because one partner or the other would find someone that they preferred, whether that person had more worldly accomplishments, more money, more interest, more spiritual compatibility, whatever. Invariably the marriage split up. Can you talk about how you have managed to keep a marriage intact in the face of all of that?

It takes a deep honor and commitment to the sacredness of marriage. My husband and I really feel our marriage is a sacred blessing. That is a value that we hold above everything else. If push comes to shove, he's more important to me than someone else. He is my primary partner. We have what we call a sacred marriage, which is a marriage of the God and Goddess.

We feel that we have been put together to do divine work together in the world and to balance each other in that. And we really love each other. Neither one of us wants to be monogamous, because you become a closed system when you are monogamous. Then there is no new energy coming in and it gets into this binary back and forth, back and forth, same old thing, and you are not growing and you are not new. When other people come into the relationship they bring something new that we both experience. I think one thing that is important about doing it successfully is utmost honesty. You cannot have secrets or lies. Everything must be above board.

Someone may prefer not to hear about certain aspects just because they don't want to hear about exactly what kind of lover somebody is or something. And that's fine. But you don't have secrets. You don't lie and see somebody on the sly.

I wouldn't sleep with or see anybody who wasn't checked out ahead of time, someone that my husband didn't feel good about, or somebody with whom I was having an issue. It's never happened, but if my husband didn't like someone I'd respect his wishes and vice versa. I wouldn't be comfortable with him sleeping with a woman I disliked or didn't trust or who was dishonest herself.

I think the other thing that is important is inclusion. When he sees someone else, I don't feel like it's taking something away from me. I feel like it's bringing something additional to me. Even if he goes there to see her, because he comes back full of a new kind of energy that we can share and vice versa, so it's not an either/or situation. We frame it as inclusion.

I also always enjoy being alone. If I have a night alone, that is a blessing; I can stay up and read in bed and not worry about keeping anybody awake. It keeps our relationship open and fresh.

We are committed to each other. Even if someone were to come along that really stirs my passion, I still hold that commitment, no matter what. The people I know who do this stay together.

What about the issue of disease? We're living in the time of AIDS . . .

It's very real. What we do is we have something called a condom commitment. Because we are married and are primary partners, we don't use a condom with each other. I've had my tubes tied, so I can't get pregnant. But if we were to sleep with someone else, we would use a condom.

There are certain people that we will allow inside of the condom commitment who become regular lovers, who then also have to use condoms with anybody else. There is another man whom I have been lovers with as long as Otter—seventeen years—who I see quite frequently. He's on the inside of the condom commitment with us. But with anybody else he's with he has to use a condom.

So we know exactly who the germs are circulating among. Now it's just the three of us. I would not allow someone on the inside of the condom commitment who had not had an AIDS test. If somebody doesn't want to use a condom, they don't sleep with me.

How has a polyamorous relationship affected your children?

I have a son who is eleven who has grown up in CAW. I was doing rituals when I was pregnant with him. It has never been an issue for him; it is very natural. His father is also polygamous, and so are most of the people he sees around him. He doesn't have that model of jealousy.

I can only spread my energy so far, and so I am very very picky about who I sleep with and probably keep to myself more than a lot of people because I only have so much time and energy. The only thing that he would object to is if I spread my energy to other people to the point where I was neglecting him, which I will not do. It's never been an issue. It's not some blatant thing where we sleep with anybody who comes through; it's not like that at all. There is stability in our marriage.

Where would you like to see CAW go in the future?

CAW is growing. It used to be that I knew everybody, and it's not that way any more. I come to festivals, and I meet CAW members whom I have never met before because we are growing so much. I would like it to grow to a place where it's really coherent and respected in the outer world as a viable religion with something important to offer.

The administrative level is our weak point right now. We are visionaries, we are revolutionaries, we are spiritualists, and the administrative level is difficult for us. That mundane plane of balancing the books and typing things in triplicate and keeping the files and all that is the plane we are working on. We need a solid inner structure.

We don't go out and recruit. We are not "trying" to expand. It's expanding all by itself, and we can barely keep up with it. We have "nests" popping up all over the country, small worship groups, and we need to take care of the nests. People tell me, "We are out here in Timbuktu, and church central doesn't talk to us very often." Church central can barely return the phone calls that we get. They come in all day, and we have jobs and we do other things.

We need more people at a higher level of experience and initiation so we can administer to the new people coming in. Consolidation of the nests, dissemination of information, getting the information out that explains our beliefs and how we practice, giving inspiration and structure to people who want to grow, this is what we need to work on. I see it as a big net where we support each other and we weave together. The stronger we weave, the stronger the net gets and the more it can hold. A strong net will support people in the work of changing the world.

You have a full-time job and kids, too. It sounds like your job would be a lot easier if you were paid clergy.

You bet! Money is earth plane. It's another one of those divorces that has happened. The idea that you can't be spiritual and be reimbursed for your efforts. I think that money is part of the earth plane and part of the Goddess, and when we support a religion and its events and its clergy, we are supporting the Goddess.

I live my life on a shoestring budget, and I've done amazing things with very little, and I have gotten very stressed out in the process. I'm at the point where I have cut way back on all my activities because I couldn't do all that was asked of me and still survive. I was paying with my body and my health. I'm sort of in retreat mode.

I would do more if I could be paid. It would enable me to do what I do better. But the community is very resistant to that. Yet that doesn't match when they expect services. They say, "Why should I pay for this?" but they also complain when a phone call isn't returned right away.

Where do you think this resistance is coming from?

From having grown up in other religions that required their money and gave them very little in return. There is also the belief in Paganism that everybody is a priest or a priestess. Why should I pay you to do it when I can lead a ritual? It's not really about leading rituals, it's about how much time you put into something. It's one thing to lead a ritual because it's your turn that full moon. It's another thing to counsel people, to spend time on the phone, to be fostering ideas together, to participate in interfaith dialogues, to go to the religion conferences, to make it your life. It's really a profession.

Don't you think that a lot of Pagans think that if someone paid them to do that full-time, they would love to have that opportunity? I think that most Pagans are deeply spiritual and committed people who would like to be full-time clergy themselves.

No. It's amazing how few people actually want to go through all the requirements to become clergy. Maybe if there were a price on it, more people would be inspired, but I think there are very few people who feel that level of calling. I think there are very few people who could maintain it at that level.

But I think there would be more of them if we supported them, and I don't think it would be a bad thing. CAW has six active clergy right now and four hundred members. All six clergy are in California, and there are a few in the wings just finishing their requirements now. This means that we are really stretching ourselves thin.

What are the requirements to become clergy in CAW?

There is a long list of things. We have something called the Emerging Network Training System. It's a nine-circle system where you get progressively more involved in the religion, in the community, and in the church. As you do, you take on magical training, you help the organization run, you study counseling, ritual design, drama, philosophy, theology; you do a solo vision quest in the wilderness for nine days, an extensive research paper, several essays; you spend a minimum of three years in the church. Usually, it takes people about ten years before they are actually ordained.

You have to prove yourself to the community. We won't ordain someone that the community won't support. If the community isn't ready to see someone as a person they respect and that they are willing to come to with a problem and are excited about being in their ritual, then we won't ordain that person.

Are there any other issues that you see as potential problem areas for the Pagan community?

One is that the community is like an organic being that is growing and is at an adolescent stage. It's just starting to feel its power, and it doesn't yet have maturity. One thing that has been fundamental to the Pagan revival as it has come out of the sixties is that people have been focusing on breaking down structures, learning to pull the stops out, and learning to break the barriers that previously held them in. That is a process, a stage of taking the defenses down. Until a new structure takes its place, this is a very tenuous place to be in. I think that we are in that fragile place right now.

Everyone is really into freedom. When I receive an essay from someone that isn't well written or well researched and I send it back, they complain about it and say, "What is this authoritarian shit?" So they are still reacting to that. The more mature attitude is that it's not "authoritarian shit." We want it to mean something and for it to be good.

We have opened up a lot of things, and the opening has been wonderful and exhilarating. Once opened, you realize that there are more dimensions to it. Sexuality is one of those. One of the things that many groups are looking at is how does open sexuality work with children being around it? Everyone has agreed that sexuality between children and adults is not okay; in fact, it is harmful. But how do you define that? Does it mean that an adult does not be naked around the kids when nakedness is part of our belief in the sanctity of the body and being natural? How do people perform with each other when children are in the background?

We have a crop of girls reaching adolescence right now who have grown up in our community, and it's a real question. What do we teach them about sexuality? We have never taught them that it's evil or that it's to be avoided. They are gung ho to just jump right in, and we are saying, "Wait a minute! You are too young." And they say, "What do you *mean* we are too young?" We are wrestling with a lot of these issues.

I see internal self-discipline as a real issue. If we don't want an external authority, then we need to be internally disciplined. Someone told me a story last night about a previous Starwood gathering where someone was drumming really late and there was some trouble with the neighbors and they were told to be quiet, and they said, "What do you mean be quiet? This is the only time I get to make noise, and you can't tell me what to do!" That is not being mature or responsible to the fact that what we have is very special, and if we are going to protect it, we will need to sometimes put limits on it.

A lot of people are still in the phase of just learning to be free. "Don't tell me to shut up—I am just finding my voice!" This has to go! I'm in a different phase of it because I've been in it longer, but I can see where ten years ago I was in the opening-up phase, and I wouldn't have wanted anyone to tell me to shut up either. I feel a bit like a mother in that sense, watching the children mature. If we are going to be respected, then we really need to have inner integrity.

There are a lot of jobs that need doing to further the movement that people have no training in doing. Accounting—boring and mundane stuff. We have people in our church, for example, who volunteer to take on the membership program who don't know how to type. Or people who want to be treasurer but who never took an accounting course.

There are a lot of amateurs doing jobs around business and administration. They don't have an aptitude or an interest or even a vision for that. They are artists and spiritualists who are doing it because it needs to be done, but they are not doing it well. We need to be developing our mundane feet. Nobody wants to do that because it's not fun or exciting.

Circle
Sanctuary

Circle was founded in 1974 by Selena Fox (high priestess). Fox and her partner, Jim Alan, and a group of friends began meeting at the Fox-Alan home in Sun Prairie, near Madison, Wisconsin. In 1978 Fox decided to devote herself full-time to the Wiccan ministry. That same year Circle Sanctuary was incorporated as a Wiccan church. A forced eviction from their Sun Prairie home in 1979 by a prejudiced landlord led the group to eventually settle on what is now the Circle Sanctuary site. The land serves as the base for a nature preserve, organic herb farm, and church headquarters. In 1984 Alan left the community and Fox to devote himself to a writing career. By 1986 Fox had married Wiccan priest Dennis Carpenter; he and Fox serve as high priest and priestess of Circle.

Circle serves as a clearinghouse and networking center for people involved in Wiccan spirituality, Druidism, tribal Nature wisdom traditions, pantheism, animism, neo-Paganism, Goddess spirituality, ecofeminism, and related forms of Paganism. The community publishes a directory, *The Circle Guide to Pagan Groups*, which is updated periodically. They also publish *The Circle Guide to Pagan Arts*, *Circle Network News*, *Circle Bulletin*, and the *Pagan Spirit Alliance Newsletter*. They have a special friendship network, for people who want to start forming friendship bonds with people of similar ethical values, called the Pagan Spirit Alliance. The annual gathering of Circle members is the international Pagan Spirit Gathering; it is one of the largest Pagan festivals in the United States, and it is held in Wisconsin every June.

SELENA FOX [pictured here with Dennis Carpenter], high priestess and founder of Circle Sanctuary, was interviewed at the Ecumenicon conference in Washington, D.C., on July 17, 1993

When did you first realize that you were a Pagan?

My earliest experience as a Pagan happened when I was a very young child. I'd go out in nature, which often was the backyard of my Arlington, Virginia, childhood home, and spend time with the trees and with the birds. I'd sit quietly with other life forms in nature.

I didn't call it Paganism then. But clearly the mystical experiences that I've had throughout my life were full of other dimensions and species. As a young child I also had a variety of inner-vision type experiences, prophetic dreams, astral projections, and a variety of different experiences that now as an adult I can look back at and understand. I was making contacts with the spiritual dimensions of reality.

I was raised as a fundamentalist Southern Baptist. I was not raised Pagan. But within my Southern Baptist upbringing I got a very deep commitment to working on behalf of others. A sense of service. A sense of love and the importance of love as part of spirituality. A sense of building bridges and of having a direct connection with the Divine. So while that was not coming directly out of Southern Baptist teachings, my process of development in this life clearly wove together some Christian mysticism with my early Pagan experiences. It wasn't until I was a teenager that I acknowledged that there was a difference between my Pagan theological leanings and the religious underpinnings that I'd been raised in.

It was at the age of seventeen that I started calling myself a pantheist. I no longer felt that I fit within the circle of Southern Baptists, or of Christianity. I was female, I felt a calling in the ministerial direction from a very early age, and it was not an option for me to be a pastor of a Southern Baptist church.

I allowed myself to connect with a wider circle of spirituality, and that's when I more fully embraced Paganism. I had studied the classics throughout junior high and high school. I was an honors student in Latin and the classics. I went on to the College of William and Mary, where I continued my study of the classics, although my major was psychology.

I led my very first public Pagan rite when I was twenty-one. It was a Dionysian Rite of Spring with ecstatic dance, Greco-Roman cultural underpinnings, and it had the full blessings of the classics department. I was the head of Eta Sigma Phi, the classics honor society, and I really felt that in addition to discussing the ancient Greek and Roman literature, we needed to do something more experiential. Hence this idea for the Rite of Spring enactment. It was wonderful.

My college years were back in the late sixties and early seventies when there was a lot of social change happening on college campuses, and I was very involved in those processes. I now see that my Paganism started taking a more public form then. As I look back, I realize that I was serving as a priestess at that rite I was leading along with some of the professors. It really laid the ground-work for some other things that unfolded.

That summer I worked on an archaeological dig and connected with a woman who was a family-tradition Witch who had roots in old Prussia. I realized that there were other people who had a religious orientation very similar to where I was coming from. That basically opened the doorway to my involve-ment with contemporary Paganism.

So that was how you began. What has kept you interested?

I was born in October of 1949. I am forty-five; it's been a little over twenty years. Since the 1960s I've been involved in building bridges of understanding and connection amongst people of different paths, cultures, races, and reli-gions. I see that Paganism works well in that way because it has a multicultural aspect. Within the circle of Paganism, which I often refer to as Nature Spiritu-ality, or Nature Wisdom Ways as an even more encompassing term, I am able to grow as an individual as well as a priestess and follow what I feel is my life path.

I also see that Paganism, unlike some other religious forms, has a lot of room for creativity, and it also has, as a central focus, the communion with the Divine in nature. That is something that has been with me since the earliest days.

Can you give some specific examples of what you mean by multicultural?

In my form of Pagan spirituality I design rituals that focus on some common-alities in terms of connecting with the beauty and the Divinity in nature. I design the rituals in such a way that people from different racial and ethnic ancestries that also are connected with Nature Wisdom Ways can be part of the circle of sharing, can be part of the ritual and contribute from their own experience to the ritual form.

I'm very involved with interfaith work and have been in the public sector in that regard. There are people connected with the Circle Sanctuary community that come from a variety of backgrounds. Some have Native American ancestry, some are Mexican-American, some are from mixed backgrounds, there are a few Asian-Americans, we have African-Americans, Euro-Americans. We may have different ethnic roots and we may blend different ethnicities and cultures, but we have circles of sharing that allow people to honor their ancestors. We build bridges across cultures to bring rich folkways from each person's personal experience and weave it into the rituals.

Some rituals are much more focused on a particular cultural orientation. Sometimes we do invocations in different languages in our ceremonies of connectedness with Mother Earth. We might have someone speaking in Spanish because their roots go into ancient Mexico as well as this country.

I know you have a degree in psychology. Did you ever have a practice? How does that tie into your Pagan ministry?

I've been doing counseling work, and I've had ongoing training for twenty years. I am a psychotherapist and a counselor. I am presently doing my counseling under the spiritual counseling or pastoral counseling realm as a minister.

Is there a school of therapy that you are particularly fond of?

I've been developing my own model over the years. In my training I've had the opportunity to have my professors critique my model. It's a holistic and integrative one that has as its framework working with the elements of nature and with the sacred circle. I do not say that this map is for everyone, but it works for me. In terms of doing my psychological practice I certainly have woven in things that I have learned from Gestalt therapy, from psychoanalysis and psychodynamics, cognitive-behaviorist, and other training. If I were to put myself in any of the categories in terms of my personal model, it would most likely be transpersonal psychology.

What I call "green psychology" or "eco-psychology" incorporated within a psychotherapeutic practice works to see that the people are in balance within themselves, with others in their support network and their community and also with the rest of the community on planet Earth, as well as with all of the other life forms. I see that as central.

My psychology, my teaching, my reading, my priestessing, my work in all of its many forms, my nature preservation work, are all leading me to look at human wellness in terms of interacting with other life forms in addition to looking at the subconscious, at life histories and work histories and educational experiences. I see all of that stemming from my Paganism and also feeding my Paganism. That is the essence of my priestess work now.

What is Circle Sanctuary. How did it get started?

I started Circle in 1974. I got the name and the logo, twelve circles around a central circle, in a vision just before Samhain in 1974. From the earliest germ of an idea, it was an organization that was to be a place for people from many different paths to come together and share and grow and learn from each other.

For the first few years it took a form of networking through my writings and some music. Jim Alan, who helped found Circle with me and with whom I performed and traveled, eventually collaborated with me on a songbook, after which it was apparent, due to the great response we got from people about Paganism and Witchcraft, that something more needed to evolve. People were writing not only to get a copy of our songbook so that they could incorporate our chants and songs into their rituals, but they were also asking how they could get in touch with other Pagans in our area. Out of that I founded Circle Network in 1977. This is the networking branch of Circle.

Circle Network has grown from a few hundred people in the seventies to thousands of people, groups, other networks, a broad-based Nature Spirituality networking ministry.

We are probably best known as a contact service, resource center, and clearinghouse for Paganism. People can call us up or drop us a letter. We publish a directory, the *Circle Guide to Pagan Groups*, which we update periodically. We also have the *Circle Guide to Pagan Arts*. We have a special friendship network for people who want to start forming friendship bonds with people of similar ethical values called the Pagan Spirit Alliance. We have a variety of different publications. *Circle Network News* is the best known of all of our publications because we have it in countries all around the world.

It's the number one, most widely distributed Pagan publication in the world, isn't it?

Probably. We've been publishing it since the late seventies and in newspaper format since 1980. We have contacts in more than fifty countries. Yes, there are Pagan readers all around the globe and in every state in the United States and in all the provinces of Canada. We're primarily working with people around the world who have some expertise in English.

We have *Circle Network News* in Russia, in the former Soviet Union, and in places most people would not think about Paganism being present, such as the Middle East. We see *Circle Network News* as not only a place where news of the Pagan movement can be shared but as a journal where people can exchange ideas in a scholarly way, as well as in an experiential way. We try to cover a wide range of material.

Circle is also a church. It has a healing branch to it. We do absent healing for people who have sent in requests. We do some direct healing for those that come, and we do planetary healing work. We also have my telephone psycho-therapy/counseling practice as part of the healing work. For some people it's a regular session, and for others it's brief therapy.

We also host gatherings through our center. We sponsor the international Pagan Spirit Gathering (PSG) every year. It's a week-long gathering focused on intentional community within a Pagan natural setting. It happens at Summer Solstice time, and people from many places and paths come together as a means to celebrate the Summer Solstice and to put into action principles of living in harmony with each other and the rest of nature. It tends to be rustic, as we are camping outside. Some people do bring campers, but we are in a natural park area and we celebrate the Summer Solstice.

Circle has Wiccan underpinnings. We celebrate the eight Sabbats. But rather than focusing on a particular pantheon from a particular culture, we have more of a multicultural focus.

We are listed as a church in the church directory that comes out every

Saturday night in the Wisconsin *State Journal*, and we occasionally have people from other religions and traditions who take part in our celebrations.

We have a two-hundred-acre nature preserve that we are caretaking; another branch of our work is nature preservation. We're caretaking the land not only as a nature preserve but as what I call a sacred nature preserve. It's more than preserving habitat or the creatures of the woods and the wetlands and the meadows. It's a place where people, who are also aspects of nature, can hopefully connect in a spiritual way with the rest of the biosphere.

We are located rather close to a state park. People can go there for recreation. But to have land set aside for sacred purposes is something that I feel is an ancient tradition that needs to happen in greater frequency on the planet today. I see Circle Sanctuary as a place where the sacred land function is very important, and we have encouraged other people to establish other sacred centers across the U.S.A. and other parts of the planet.

I feel that it's vital for the growth of Paganism to have some "safe" places in natural locations for people to have their rituals, and I feel that it's necessary for the good of the planet as a whole. Humankind needs to have some places that are safe to go to where one can do spiritual rituals and connect with the spiritual essence of the planet. Connect with the Ancient Ones in contemporary forms.

When you were in the process of getting the land, you ran into some legal problems. Can you share what happened?

What happened that year was that Paganism's festival movement was starting to blossom, and I was involved with helping to organize a gathering that took place in Indiana. Somehow the national media got hold of the fact that this gathering was happening and showed up there. We ended up getting mentioned in the article because of a wedding that I had done. Coming out of being mentioned in *Time* magazine, I received all sorts of media requests to talk about Witchcraft. I realized that there might be some fallout from being so public, but I decided to do the interviews. Public television did a documentary. It was all positive. It accurately portrayed what we were doing—being in touch with Nature and Witchcraft—as something benevolent, not something to be feared or exterminated.

The word *witch* and even the word *pagan* really upset some people. I don't think the person who threw us off of the farm we had been renting even saw the publicity. He just heard that *witch* word. While we had rented that property for four years and had what we thought was a good relationship with this person, he became so frightened by that "W" word and the fact that our religion was getting this visibility that he sent an eviction order out.

We didn't even have a lease. It was a farm in the country owned by a farming couple, and we decided that rather than try and contest it we would just move on and start our sanctuary project a decade earlier. We lost the farm because of our religion. I spoke with the landlord after the eviction happened, and he thought we were devil worshippers because he heard the word *witch*.

So we lost that farm. During that time we started raising funds. We tried to purchase some land to establish a center. That took about four years. Once we began the purchase of the land, which was only a few miles from where we had been renting, we thought we had done enough legwork and that we had checked out the area and that the people were used to us. But shortly after we signed the papers, we started hearing rumors about "Witches." There was fear and misinformation. We got a call from some local clergy who were investigating what was going on. We spoke with them and tried to allay their fears; however, there was an unwillingness to have something religiously different in their area.

When a minister said, "Don't even come to my church" when I suggested an ecumenical exchange, I knew that there were some real problems. So there were a series of rumors going around. There was a group of people who had a history of driving other religious groups out of the area that we later found out about.

It never occurred to you to move to another area that would be more friendly? I know of people all over the United States who are setting up communities here and there, and most don't run into this kind of opposition. You don't hear about it anyway.

I was guided to the Circle Sanctuary land through a dream. We had invested our financial resources in the land. We were not in a position to be able to leave. Even more importantly, I really felt that it was the place that we were supposed to be. I had a very specific vision of the land; I had gone there, and it was the place I had seen.

During the time of intense conflict I did do several guidance quests. I prayed for guidance regarding that very question: "Is it better for us to give up this battle and move on to some other location as all the other religious groups before us had done, or do we stay?" On each occasion, whether searching alone or working with the other people there, direct messages came that indicated *stay*. Often these took the forms of actual artifacts from the ancient native peoples that once lived on the land literally popping up out of the soil. Essentially, I would put the prayer out, go out, and I'd find an ancient Indian spear point or other artifact in my path. All the indications we got from Spirit as well as from a political point of view were that the best course of action was to stay the course. We did not want our struggle to negatively impact the movement. After four years we finally did get zoning recognition as a church on the township and county level in 1988. The good news is that more understanding came out of it.

In 1985 Jesse Helms attempted to pass legislation at the federal level that would define the Wiccan religion as satanic and take away tax-exempt status for Wiccan churches. Circle was very involved in fighting that piece of legislation. We became very publicly visible in that, and I personally got very involved.

Since 1985 and the period of our zoning battles, our work at Circle has taken another turn. In addition to all of our other work we moved to the forefront of religious freedom networking. A week does not go by when our center does not get a call or a piece of mail from someone who is having problems dealing with mainstream society because of their religion. What we do is not to fight everybody's battles for them. But we now have a networking branch called the Lady Liberty League. There is a network of people within Circle who are willing to help others who are having problems because of their religion, on a volunteer basis.

Are there any politicians, congressmen, or senators that you have been working with?

Most of the Pagans who are involved at the federal and state and local government level are not at all "out" about their Paganism. They are concerned that it would adversely affect their ability to be elected to office. There are people up on Capitol Hill, and there are people in state governments around the United States who are Pagan. In fact there were so many government workers at one of our gatherings a few years ago that a Pagan Civil Servants Support Group was formed! People came together to talk about these issues. Pagan bureaucrats!

Can you give a specific anecdote about someone you know who has faced prejudice?

A woman was running a battered women's shelter, and it was common practice at that office to photocopy personal stuff if you paid for it, and she had photocopied some Pagan rituals. One of the discarded copies ended up in the waste can, or somehow someone found out that she was Pagan. She was fired from her job because she was a Witch. She was affiliated with our network, and we gave her support in her case. This was in Mississippi. It went to a federal court, and she won the job discrimination case.

Another one was a woman who had her altar confiscated at a publicly funded college in the South. Although she did not have to go into a court situation, there was an attorney who was part of our religious freedom network who did some communication work with the college officials about civil rights in this country that basically restored the woman's rights.

There have been a number of different instances. There have been people with Pagan and metaphysical supply stores who have experienced attacks. There have been smashed windows, even fire bombings. It has happened over the years in a number of different places in the United States. There have been a number of cases of parents denied custody of children because of their religion. There was a man in Canada who had to deal with this issue. Our center gave him support, and some others gave him support. Fortunately, he did finally regain his rights to visit his kid.

But not all of these religious-freedom cases go so well. There was a woman who had her well poisoned. She made the choice to leave the area as a result. One of the more famous cases that got national attention was a group of people who were doing a Summer Solstice ritual in Florida who got shot at. Fortunately, nobody got hit.

Because of these things that have happened, a lot of people are reluctant to be visible about their Paganism. But I really need to balance what I have said about persecution with the great advances that I see happening. I see myself as a religious activist. I have been doing some education with law enforcement, with chaplains in the military, in the prison systems, in hospitals. I do informational exchanges with people in the American establishment. I work sometimes with doctors as well as psychologists and psychiatrists. I work within academia. I am trying to do education to help eradicate prejudices, but I'm not out to convert anybody.

The idea is to get out some basic information. I do not claim to try to represent all Pagans everywhere, but what I do try to do is give enough basic information about the Nature-centered focus of the religion and its benevolent focus. That we are basically coming from a place of wanting to work for a better environment, for a better world. We want more love, peace, and harmony. We put that message out so that people can know that the vast majority of people who use the word Pagan to define themselves are coming from that place.

I've been on the *Today* show, *Donahue*, *Sightings*, *Sally Jesse Raphael*, *Larry King Live*. All of these national media things have been a learning experience for me. I have in each case prepared myself by looking deep within for a way to connect with the essence of Paganism and for the way to hopefully be the vehicle for tolerance to unfold.

What's the vision that you are holding for Paganism as a movement?

That Paganism achieves public tolerance and understanding as a religious form. That our people do not have to hide. That people in public service do not have to hide their Pagan affiliations because it will be a political liability. That the intolerance, the bigotry, and the hate crimes will stop.

Also part of my vision is that there will be more places set aside all around the planet for people to do spiritual work, communing with the Divine in nature. Some of those centers may be called Pagan, but I am less concerned about the label they may have put on them and more concerned about the process.

Can you give some anecdotes about magical or mystical things that have happened to you on the land?

I think that one of the most recent things that has happened to me was while I was giving a tour of the land to some people as part of our Beltane festival. One of the people was from Russia, another had some roots in Europe, and it was a very eclectic, small group. We went to one of our meditation spots that we know has been used by ancient Native Americans, and I've done meditation work there in the past. I'd just been up there a few days before. I was in the process of talking about the ancient ways and how part of my work as a priestess was to teach respect for the ancient ways that were practiced here long before Europeans came on the scene. Just as I was finishing talking about that I had a very strong energy surge happen within my body. I had a sense to look down at my feet. Right between my feet was a perfect, ancient arrowhead point. I picked it up and had a strong sense that I had made contact with something very ancient and powerful.

That has only happened a few other times. This was the first time that a point had appeared when I wasn't in the middle of a zoning crisis. I took it as an affirmation of what I was saying, that in terms of being in harmony with the land it had to be not only in its present state but with ancient times as well.

Having that kind of interaction with the forces on the land can be a very powerful thing for people. At our Lammas ritual several years ago, just as we were giving thanks to the quarters and focusing on continued prosperity for our fields and gardens and in our lives, a gentle rain started sprinkling down. Then it started raining more. As we came down the hill, there was a huge double rainbow across the sky.

We've had some very wonderful and beautiful things, natural phenomena, happen in connection with rituals. I'm not implying a definite causal effect, but basically to be in a ritual space in nature and to have on top of that some added bonus like shooting stars, northern lights, rainbows, a bird flying by, is awesome.

DENNIS CARPENTER is a former school psychologist, and is editor of *Circle Network News*, co-administrator of Circle Sanctuary, and high priest. He holds a Ph.D. in psychology.

How long have you been a Pagan? When did you first realize you were a Pagan?

I first realized it in 1983 or so. It was through a philosophy professor friend of a friend. I was a school psychologist at that time. My best friend was a bass player in a rock-and-roll band, and his wife had this friend who was a philosophy professor. I was staying with them during the summer because I wasn't working, and we'd go to magical book stores. He'd pull a book off the shelf and say, "Here, read this." One of the first books he ever pulled off the shelf was *The Spiral Dance* by Starhawk. I read that, and there was this feeling that a lot of other people report, like, Oh, this is me, this sounds like what I believe.

Then through those same people I ended up going to Pagan Spirit Gathering in 1983, sponsored by Circle Sanctuary. I had this quite incredible experience, where I was connecting with people of similar interests. It was all very new and different and exciting, and there was a real pull to it. This was in Wisconsin. I happened to live about four hours away from Circle, so for the next year I attended events sponsored by Circle.

I was not fitting in very well in the public schools at that time. I did not really like being in them, because I didn't have interests similar to those of the people I was working with. I was single at the time, and the social structure in the schools was not fitting where I was mentally. I then realized I was kind of at a midlife crisis.

I was starting to not believe in the system that I worked in. I was required to test kids and place them either in special ed or not in special ed, and there weren't a lot of resources available in the public schools to do anything about it. It was a very nonrewarding job, writing reports and sitting on cases and going on to the next one with a minimal amount of direct working with people. There was very little of seeing any results of what I was doing other than fulfilling this bureaucratic role.

I realized that I'd been in schools for twenty-five years or so, since I was five. I went straight through graduate school into working in the public schools. Here I was, thirty years old, I had worked in the public schools as a school psychologist for five years and taught at a university for two years, and I simply needed a break. Then this job opportunity came up to work at Circle Sanctuary. I had been editor of the state school psychologist newsletter for a few years, and I had worked as a yearbook advisor in one of the high schools I worked in, so I had some interest in publications work. When an opening came for an editor of *Circle Network News*, I thought it would be perfect. I could take a break, do something different, and see what happened.

So I took the great leap of faith and moved to Circle and started working there. Then Selena and I became romantically involved and ultimately got married, and I moved into the position of running the organization with her.

So what is the most important thing about Paganism for you personally? What is the essence of it?

I would say the essence of Paganism really does center on the relationship between humans and the rest of nature. From a belief point of view it's a religious system that has a view of Nature and the Divine that's consistent with my beliefs, in contrast to the views of mainstream Christianity that I was raised in. I started studying Paganism as part of my doctoral work, so it had become very much a part of my job and my studies, my livelihood.

Has it helped you to live your life in any way ?

Well, you know, that's really hard to say because life changes happen over a period of time. You grow older, things happen in your life, and you go on. I'd say from a spiritual point of view, experiences in nature come closest to experiencing a sense of the Divine that I can say that I've had. For me it doesn't occur as much in formal rituals and that sort of thing as in just walks through the woods. I can't think of examples where I've walked out in the woods and had a 3-D technicolor vision of the Goddess or anything like that. It's more kind of a diffused sense of oneness with nature.

I really started focusing on my doctorate in Paganism because it was a subject I have great familiarity with, and professors I was working with, and still work with today, were encouraging. I first set out to survey the research that had been done on Paganism, because I'd go places and people would make statements about what Pagans were. I just went in and played the straight academic role of asking what research had been done on Paganism. There's been kind of a switch since the early days. In the seventies the research that touched upon it was coming out of a sociological perspective and trying to look at ways in which Pagans were deviant. How they were part of the youth-of-the-sixties culture.

Some of the sociologists of that time were keenly interested in what drives people to the occult and to esoteric subjects and that sort of a thing. Later on some of the doctoral dissertations that were done were focusing on the social structure of groups, Wiccan/Pagan groups, circumstances by which people became involved in Wiccan groups, and some of the characteristics of Pagans and Wiccans.

I tried to pull it all together and make it all as meaningful as I could. It seems that in a large part Paganism is a baby-boom-generation phenomenon, in that the people who are considered leaders of the movement were all born during that time period. They are better educated than the general public, with great numbers holding advanced degrees. The one thing that came through was that, even if Pagans had not elected to go the traditional academic realm, they were very well read and versed on what interested them. Some of the studies that I've done did show that compared to the general population Pagans earn less money than you would expect from their educational background.

Do you think Pagans are smarter than the general population as a whole?

That's a difficult one. Being a school psychologist and having spent years of my life in testing kids with intelligence tests, I'm pretty well versed on what that construct is. My guess would be Yes, that Pagan people are very bright. I can't really say how they would compare to the general population—whether it's a matter of being brighter or it's a matter of choosing to do something with the brightness that other people are scared to do or haven't had the life circumstances leading them to a point where they felt like they could do it.

I think the one thing people really need to understand when they look at Paganism and the people involved in it is these people are deeply spiritual people. Many of them have had intense experiences since childhood. Mystical experiences. And they lacked a framework within mainstream Christianity or whatever religion they were involved with at the time to make sense out of those experiences. Those experiences have led them to feel an intense calling, an intense ecological calling, an intense commitment to various social issues such as feminism, and that was inconsistent with the religious cultural context within which they were raised.

I'd say ecology and feminism are the two most important issues. The sexual imagery surrounding Deity [the Judeo-Christian tradition imagines Deity as the Father, Son, and Holy Ghost] and it being an exclusive male phenomenon have caused a lot of females to gravitate toward the Goddess and Paganism. The whole biblical set of notions regarding the relationship of humans to the environment and the relationship of the Divine to the environment is, for the most part, inconsistent with this sense of oneness and unity with all that comes through the kind of experiences that Pagans have had. When one interprets why people are involved in Paganism, they have to really look at the spiritual experiential level of their lives.

How many people did you interview?

For the purposes of my study I had to interview sixteen people. These were randomly selected people from Pagan Spirit Gatherings. Plus I did a set of questionnaires with another set of fifty-six randomly selected people. They reported having life-changing mystical experiences that influenced their choice of jobs and especially their level of committment toward trying to do something about the ecological well-being of the planet.

So these are numinous experiences in the Jungian sense that completely transformed these people's lives?

Yes, that was commonly reported. The kinds of experiences ranged from this sense of oneness with the whole of nature to 3-D technicolor numinous experiences. Some did report walking away from those experiences with their life totally transformed.

What other data have you come up with regarding Pagans?

The process by which people become involved with Paganism is kind of interesting. I look at 1979 as a really pivotal year in Paganism.

What happened that year?

The books *Drawing Down the Moon* [by Margot Adler] and *The Spiral Dance* [by Starhawk] emerged, and there was the real birth of the current-day Pagan networking activity, through the publication that year of the first edition of the *Circle Guide to Pagan Resources*. While Circle was formed in 1974, other groups saw a real explosion in 1979.

I think that books and periodicals are really the big factor that leads people to find out that there are people like them out there. Twenty years ago there weren't many books. Now you can go into bookstores, and there are whole shelves of them. If you ask people how they became involved, books played a very important role in those kind of chance occurrences where you stumble across the information that resonates with what you believe.

I feel that in sitting with you and talking about generalities, I really went out on a limb, because I know that the first time that something like this gets printed, there are going to be a whole host of people saying, "No, that's not the case."

Paganism is really a classic example of postmodern spirituality, and by postmodern I refer to people like Charlene Spretnak and David Ray Griffin and people who have talked about postmodern spirituality in a general way. David has published through the State University of New York press and Charlene has the book *States of Grace* that talked about postmodern spirituality and listed several of its features. When I read that, I was really struck by the way that Paganism epitomizes what they were talking about.

The first thing is this holistic notion that everything is part of an interconnected whole, often described as this interconnected web of life, going beyond some of the dualistic separating features of other religions. This notion that the Divine is immanent within everything rather than transcendent. The notion that all of nature is alive and animated and ensouled and that humans aren't the only focus of this spiritual Divine force of energy includes the re-enchantment of Nature. Coming back to the realization that all of nature is alive and the Divine energy is laced through all of nature, not seeded in certain locations, as in the human or in a transcendent sky god. The notion that the Divine is not something out there separated from the creation.

Paganism really does offer a radically different spiritual worldview than that of contemporary Christianity, and I think that it really has the potential to play a role to try to bring about a greater balance between humans and the rest of nature, but that remains to be seen. Because it remains to be seen whether a different worldview is going to translate down into different politics and economics and all those other things.

The Covenant of the Goddess

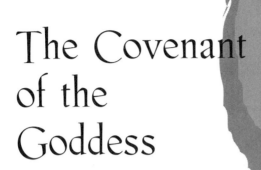

The Covenant of the Goddess is a confederation of covens that was founded in 1975 and has been growing and functioning ever since. In 1993 it cosponsored the Parliament of the World's Religions in Chicago. Its members gave presentations, held panel discussions, and even organized a full-moon circle.

The following interviews make it clear that they are a very diverse group with many individual options.

JUDY HARROW is a "Gardnerian Heretic," and is public information officer and former first officer for the Covenant of the Goddess. She was interviewed on January 20, 1994.

When did you first discover that you were a Pagan?

In the mid-seventies I dated a man who was involved with science fiction. Through him I met some people who were Pagans. It was the typical thing. I discovered that there was a name for the kind of values that I had been holding all my life. I attended my first circle at Samhain, 1976. If I remember correctly, I had been reading Pagan- and Wiccan-oriented books for about a year before that.

What was it about Paganism that attracted you?

The nature orientation primarily, and secondarily the feminist orientation. As a child I was sent to summer camp, in the country, not far from New York, and the camp that I went to emphasized camping—cookouts, nature hikes, sleepouts, woodcraft skills. There was a great deal of exposure to forests and to nature studies. I was seven years old the first summer I went there, and I went for six years. I later became involved with the Girl Scouts and maintained that interest in being in the woods. These were the northeast deciduous woods from the New York area. The love of the forest was where it all started for me.

When I began to learn about the threats to the environment, that all the things that I loved were becoming threatened, my feelings became more intense. To find people who based their worship around the natural cycles and the budding and leafing and changing of the trees was a very meaningful thing.

It's also clear with hindsight that I was looking for the Goddess, for an empowering spiritual model for myself as a woman. I was raised Jewish, but my family was not very enthusiastic in their Jewish practice.

If you were a reader of this book, and you were completely unaware of what Gardnerian Witchcraft was, what would you need to know to understand Gardnerian Wicca?

It's a tradition of Witchcraft that started with the work of Gerald Gardner and his immediate group. We know that other members besides him contributed to it. He was the high priest and the individual who gathered these people together. He also wrote the books. It's characterized by a symbolic structure that has now permeated most of modern Witchcraft. It's the worship of both Goddess and God in a circle, with the four quarters representing the traditional four elements and other things that correspond to that four-way scheme. Our ritual year is divided into eight Sabbats. The lesser Sabbats are the Solstices and Equinoxes, and the greater Sabbats are the cross quarters, which fall approximately midway between them.

Where did Gerald Gardner get this from?

That's a matter of great controversy. He said he was initiated on the full moon of September of 1939. Some of us believe that he was initiated into a preexisting coven. Some of us believe that the initiation came directly from the Goddess.

You are a Gardnerian Witch. You have been described as a Gardnerian Heretic. Can you explain what an Orthodox Gardnerian is and what a Gardnerian Heretic would be?

It's very complicated because both sides of that particular controversy are claiming to be orthodox. The way Gardnerians work is that you are brought into a coven, you are trained, you are initiated, you are elevated to second and eventually to third degree. It's reasonably normal that when a person becomes third degree, they begin to teach and gather a circle of their own and do what we call "hiving off." The term is modeled on nature—bees leave the hive to form a new hive. It's also reasonably normal when someone hives off that they might do things a little bit differently from the way they were trained. As you mature you begin to have your own perspective on things and your own experiments that you want to try.

From my point of view the way our tradition has always worked is that the new young priestess would go to the priestess who had trained her and say, "I want to do . . . ; make the following changes . . . ," whatever. The priestess who trained her says it's all right and why not go ahead and try it. Or she might suggest that it's going a bit too far. We call this the "check-back."

When I hived, I wanted to make some changes. I went to the priestess who trained me and I got her approval. But there were other people who were "cousins" who were from other branches of the Gardnerian family who felt that had *they* been my elder they would not have approved. So who changes the tradition? Who is the heretic? Did I change the tradition by the changes I made in the way my particular coven operated, or did they change the tradition by trying to override a long-standing procedure for providing the tradition with both change and continuity—that is, the check-back procedure.

Both sides are claiming to be traditional, and we know that we have two different perspectives on what it means to be Gardnerian, but we have never come up with a set of names for those two perspectives. The Jews have come up with the terms orthodox and reform, for example, and everybody is comfortable with those terms. But we have yet to come up with terms that everybody can agree on and that no one will be insulted by.

Have you ever thought of just breaking away and doing your own thing?

Oh yeah. I've wound up having to do something somewhere halfway between that is very difficult to communicate. Some of the people that have hived from me no longer wish to call themselves Gardnerians. They feel that they don't want to deal with the politics of it, that the people who are criticizing us for being too innovative are stifling. They just want out.

Some of them insist on calling themselves Gardnerians because they look at Gerald Gardner's own practice, which was quite experimental, and the practice of Gardnerian Wicca in the British Isles, which is also quite open to experimentation. They point out that American Gardnerians have always used the check-back procedure, and they say, "Damn it, we *are* Gardnerians." And that is my position, also.

So I have within my family a sizeable group of people who have hived from me. The one thing that we know is that we are all family to each other. We had to take a name for ourselves that included those of us who are Gardnerians and those of us who prefer to reject their Gardnerian roots. The name we chose was the name of my original coven; we are Proteans. I announced the existence of Protean Witchcraft in 1991. I am the founder of the Protean tradition.

But the important thing is to think of it as something that in philosophy is called Venn diagrams. That is to say that you draw a circle and say that everything within the circle is Gardnerian and then you draw another circle that is part in and part out of the first one, so that there is a large part that is within the Gardnerian circle and a crescent that is outside it—that is where the Protean tradition lies. We did *not* declare independence from the Gardnerian tradition; we kind of straddled the border.

Being for the Protean tradition is being for change. Proteus is the Greek God of change. You go to him when you have a question about change. He changes his shape; he is a fish, he is a bird, he is a flame, he is a tree. If you can stay with him and hold on to him through all the changes, you will get your answer.

Protean is a word in the English dictionary that means many formed, many shaped. We need to be adaptable; we don't need our religion to ossify into rote repetition or a particular set of words and gestures. We need to stay with the inspiration of the moment, with the voice of the Goddess that speaks from within. We need to let our shape change while our essence stays stable. To open a channel for creativity because creativity is the voice of the Gods.

A lot of Witchcraft traditions seem to place a value on not talking about things, on secrecy. Can you explain what the purpose and the value of that secrecy is?

There's more than one value to it, and there are different things that we tend to keep secret. I've been doing a lot of thinking about this recently, as a matter of fact. One thing we keep secret is the personal confidentiality of people, which we have done because of religious discrimination. People have lost their jobs, people have at times lost their homes if they were renting. People have lost their children in custody battles. In a more subtle way, people have not received promotions. I personally was refused admission into a training program in clinical hypnosis.

That is only half of the equation. The other half is the secrecy of the ritual materials. For example, the contents of the initiation. The simplest reason is that the initiatory experience is one of deep psychological and spiritual change. Some of that depends upon the element of surprise. If the details of what is in the initiation become too widely known, and this is the reason I rewrote mine, the element of surprise is lost. Boundary maintenance is another reason for secrecy; having certain things that are just ours lets us know our own.

You are involved with COG, can you talk about that?

I am currently co-public information officer. I have been on the board of directors for COG off and on for several years. I was national first officer in 1984.

The Covenant of the Goddess is a confederation of covens that was founded in 1975 and has been growing and functioning ever since. It seems to attract those covens that are willing to be a little more public and that are concerned about our rights. It exists as a legal church, and we do a tremendous amount of public education. We go out and speak, not to proselytize but to show that we are normal people with normal jobs and that we aren't marching around under some kind of mind control. We are "normal" people, who worship the Goddess. We are hoping to dispel some of the misconceptions and prejudices and secure more of our rights.

COG was recently cosponsor of the Parliament of the World's Religions, which was a *major* ecumenical event held in Chicago during the summer of 1993. We were there to represent Goddess worship and Wicca.

We had put in an application for a park's permit to do a full-moon circle near the hotel. That permit was denied for fairly specious reasons. We got the ACLU and the Parliament to help us, and eventually the decision to deny the permit was reversed. We did hold the circle one day later than we had originally planned.

Meanwhile, some of the Orthodox groups, not all of them, decided to leave the Parliament because they felt that they could not be in dialogue with Pagan groups. As a result of both of those things, instead of being lost in the shuffle of this huge multireligious event, we ended up having attention focused on us. We became the hot topic. We became what the grapevine was buzzing about.

When we finally got to do the circle, there were five hundred people there, along with a great deal of media. There were stories about it in newspapers all over the country. There was a wonderful article in the *Detroit Free Press* that was probably the best of the articles. The *New York Times* and the *Boston Globe* and all the major city newspapers ran stories.

How do you think Pagans were received at the Parliament?

Very well. We did the five hundred–person circle. We did two "What Is Wicca?" panels that both overflowed the room and had to be moved, and various of us did specific presentations and speeches. It was very well received all across the board. I need to say that there were four Pagan groups there. COG, Circle Sanctuary, the Earthspirit Community, and the Fellowship of Isis. The Earthspirit Community in particular did a wonderful job of arts presentations. Their choral group MotherTongue is superb. If a picture is worth a thousand words, what they did with their performance was the picture and the feelings, while COG was supplying the words. Our presentations complemented each other perfectly, and MotherTongue led the chanting at the circle in the park. There was *no* competition there; it was cooperation right down the line.

What is C.O.G. focusing on now?

Following up on all the opportunities that the Parliament opened for us. We just did a Yule ritual in New York City in cooperation with one of the local Unitarian Universalist churches, and we filled the church again. About five hundred people turned up, and the Unitarian minister was the high priest for the circle. That also generated some very nice articles in the *New York Times*.

Was the Unitarian minister a Pagan?

Yes, he is involved with CUUPS [The Covenant of Unitarian Universalist Pagans].

You said that what attracted you to Paganism was the relationship with the earth, yet you are living in New York City. How do you maintain that focus on nature when you live in New York?

That's a good question. The natural cycles *do* happen here, and the wheel of the year does manifest in the streets of the city if you are open to it. You can feel the changes in the air and the light and in the way people act and react to the seasonal changes. I once wrote a Beltane ritual about spring coming to the city, about people being out with their boom boxes, washing their cars, being out on the steps, on the block.

Do you think Paganism is experiencing any problems at this time?

Sure. They are growing pains. The hot controversy right now seems to be about paid clergy. I am very much opposed to that idea. I think that it would change the nature of what we do; I think it would destroy the intimacy.

My current coven has six members. They could not support a clergyperson. When we get together, everybody knows everybody else. There is a high level of trust, and we can work very deeply on our issues.

Do you have a vision of where you would like Paganism to go in the future?

I am moved by the example of the Quakers, who have never been very large in number but for three hundred years have been a presence. They have a very clear sense of who they are and what they are about. Most Quaker groups are still small and intimate. Most are, three hundred years later, without paid clergy. They sit together in silence—their religious style is just about the opposite of ours—and they believe in the inner light. They believe in the spirit within; they listen for that guidance that comes from within. At the heart of it they are really quite similar to us. Their theology is one of immanence. For three hundred years they have focused on social justice. They believe there is that of God in every person, so every person should be treated decently.

I believe that Mother Nature is in a life-threatening crisis. She needs advocates, healers, guardians of all kinds. She needs her people around Her with all their various talents and capacities. In the way that the Quakers have been about social justice, a respected yet tiny minority, we could be in the same way the advocates for the earth.

PHYLLIS CUROTT is a lawyer and current first officer (president) of COG. She is also a high priestess of the Minoan tradition. She was interviewed by phone on February 26, 1994.

So when did you first discover that you were a Pagan?

I discovered it through working in the circle into which I was initiated. I actually began working with them without a full intellectual comprehension of what was going on. I had been undergoing a series of extraordinary experiences. I was in my final year at law school, and my psyche spontaneously shifted to balance the almost over-development of my rational logos mental faculties. I had been a philosophy major at Brown University, and I was at NYU, which is one of the top law schools in the country. I was working as a law clerk as I was going to school.

In 1978 I had a kind of epiphanal experience. I experienced a connection that year between my self and the center of my being, my soul, and another aspect of reality, which I now call spiritual. This was not a part of my upbringing or my previous experience. It was very physical and visceral, and all of my senses were affected. I was at home when it happened the first time. I was doing some Yoga, which I had been doing for many years, and I suddenly "broke through" to another level of consciousness. Once that happened, a series of events began to occur. I developed a photographic memory, which I had never had before. I started to become somewhat precognitive. I was having dreams where I would hear what someone was going to say before they said it. I would know that the phone was going to ring before it rang, and I frequently knew who it was on the other end of the line.

Now when I look back, I see that I was experiencing two very specific archetypal energies. The first was Pan. When I speak of it poetically, I now say that I heard Pan piping and I followed the sound. I experienced a yearning for companionship with that kind of male, erotic, creative, rebellious energy. I found myself pursuing it in its various cultural expressions such as the movies of James Dean and the music of Bruce Springsteen. The other was that I began to hear the name Isis over and over in my mind. I decorated my bedroom in Egyptian motif; I kept going back to the Metropolitan Museum of Art to stand in the Egyptian collection, and I felt very serene when I was there. Eventually, I was led to a poem by Coleridge, "Kubla Khan."

I would never have ended up where I am today from any rational choices. It was like being given signposts along a road. I said to myself that either I was having a schizophrenic break or there was more to reality than meets the eye. The way that I was experiencing things was corroborated. I would have a precognitive flash, and then something would actually happen. Or I would have a dream, and then what I had seen in my dream would come true. That told me that it wasn't that I was suffering from too much stress and flipping out, but rather that there was more to reality than met the eye.

Being a materialist, I needed some kind of explanation, so I started to read books on New Age physics. It was fascinating to me, because it began to shift my thinking about the nature of the universe and how things worked and the relationship between time and space and the mind. I was simultaneously getting all this Dionysus stuff and this Isis material. But it wasn't California weirdness or something. I hadn't done drugs. I was part of the political counterculture not the drug counterculture.

I didn't have a Carlos Castaneda, Esalen, alternative framework in which to place all this stuff. It was New York City. There was no Open Center in New York back then. There was nothing. At the time, I was managing a rock and roll band, The Dates, and working as a lawyer. I was working for a foundation fighting organized crime in trade unions by day, and by night I managed the band. I met a woman who was working as a management person for a record company and who was bright, capable, and very interesting. The only thing idiosyncratic about her was that she was a Witch. We became friends, and one evening I went to her place. She said, "Let me charge your ring on my altar."

So I took off my ring and put it on her wand, which she placed on her altar. We crashed, and in the morning she asked me if I had ever had my Tarot cards read. I told her that I had never had them read for me, though as a teenager I used to read them for other people at parties. She told me there was somebody she wanted me to meet, but before we did that we went back to the altar for the ring. She took it off the wand, handed it to me, and I put it on my finger. It felt as if I had stuck my finger into an electric socket. It was tingling, and it literally shocked me.

She then took me to The Magickal Childe, which is a famous bookstore. We went to the back of the shop, and she introduced me to Lady Rhea, who read my cards. I told her that I was trying to find my path, and her response was, "The path lies within." So I said, "How do I get there?" and she said she would read my cards. She was right on with some very small details, very psychic. I was very impressed. At the end of it she said that she was running a women's group that met every Sunday, and would I like to come? She felt I might find some of the answers I was looking for in that group.

So I went the following Sunday. There were about forty women there, of all ages—black, white, all different kinds of occupations, all physical types, interesting, bright, offbeat, and mainstream. We met in the temple room, which is a huge room in the back of the store. And I wasn't quite sure what I was doing there. A lot of the women were talking about "the Goddess," and I wasn't exactly clear about what they were talking about. I just knew that I loved the women that I was meeting, and each week they invited me back.

Each week there were fewer and fewer women. At each of the meetings they would do a little bit of ritual. They would address the four quarters, do a libation, and maybe invoke the Goddess. It made me a little uncomfortable and a little self-conscious, but I liked the poetry of it. After about two months there were ten of us left. At that point they said that they were putting together a coven. This was the first time I had heard mention of that word. They said that they were high priestesses of the Minoan Sisterhood. They explained that the Minoan tradition was an offshoot of and a reaction to Gardnerian Wicca and Italian traditional Wicca.

They had felt that the Gardnerian tradition was too narrow in its restriction requiring that you had to work opposite gender in initiations. These two priestesses were lesbian and bisexual. They were a couple, and they wanted to do an all-women circle, which in 1979 was unusual. They were not radical Dianic Witches. They were Gardnerian basically, but they wanted to work with all women. So, with a fellow who happened to be gay and trained as a Gardnerian and in a Welsh tradition, they started a new tradition. They were unable to find many lesbians to be in their circle—the group I was in had four gay women and six straight women—so they made the decision to work with straight women. The Minoan men's tradition remained focused around gay men and has only recently restructured itself to include straight men.

The circles that I lead now have women and men working together. We work with the Greek pantheon and some Egyptian Deities. We also work with the Divinities that Gardnerians do. The Minoan Sisterhood's version of the work is very Gardnerian in many respects. Our training is basically the same. Our high priestesses, Lady Rhea and Lady Maiu, have always been quite adamant that the tradition is Gardnerian.

When they created the tradition, it caused quite a stir in the Gardnerian community. People questioned whether our initiations were valid and so forth. But the Gardnerian tradition requires the presence of a high priestess in order for initiations to be valid, and Lady Rhea and Lady Maiu contended that it was not necessary to have a high priest to create a Gardnerian high priestess.

How does the Minoan tradition relate to the earth?

We work with both lunar and earth-related cycles. We meet once a week, always at the full moon and at the dark of the moon. We are trained in drawing down the moon, and we meet at the eight Sabbats. The first circle that I was high priestess of was a women's circle. My second circle is a mixed circle of men and women.

How is it different having men and women as opposed to just women?

The men and the women meet separately, and then we meet together, so we do both. I have a high priest working in my circle who is a third-degree Minoan brother. The thing that characterized the early Minoan work was the exploration of polarity and energies across the entire spectrum. We would go from Aphrodite to Artemis and explore a range of energy from maiden to warrior, from rational to nurturing mother to seductress. We were able to fully explore our power and women's mysteries. It was very liberating. We are still in the process of discovering the effects of having men in on this. It's a challenge for a lot of women, because they feel that they need a safe space for them to be truly open.

I have found that a lot of women are drawn to the Craft out of a need for safe harbor, for a place of their own, for a place to explore their fears and their gifts. The presence of men to some extent was felt as a little threatening or a source of constraint. So the challenge became how to create safe space, how to confidently open ourselves and explore women's mysteries in the presence of men, who have been unfortunately experienced as oppressors.

It's been the same for some of the men because they have felt that the Craft does not welcome men. One of the primary reasons that I started to do circle with men was because there were wonderful men who were being drawn to the Craft who couldn't find a place to work. It seemed to me that men who were drawn to the Craft should have a place to work where masculine energy would be honored.

So the men meet separately in order to explore men's mysteries, and then we all meet together. We challenge each other and we honor each other and blend and exchange the energies, and it's very exciting.

Can you talk about COG and what its goals are and what you have been trying to do in it?

I got involved with COG because a woman came to me as a lawyer and asked me for assistance. She had been trying to register as a clergyperson in order to perform legally binding marriages in New York City. The city clerk who was under Mayor David Dinkins at the time was refusing to allow her to register. She knew that I was in the Craft, and she knew that I was a lawyer with a background in civil liberties. I called the New York Civil Liberties Union, because I had been an ACLU member and I knew that we would need some additional firepower. We took on the city, and we won. The battle went on for quite a while but Dinkins backed down because he knew that they would lose. Judy and other folks from her coven were then able to register.

That made me aware of the existence of COG, and I thought that what they were doing was very important. I've always had a political sensibility; I have been involved in progressive issues. So in 1987, when the women I was training were about to get their third degrees, I took my circle and we joined COG. In 1990 I ran for first officer of the New England local council of COG and was elected and did that for a year. In 1992 I went to Merrymeet, and a bunch of elders from COG approached me and asked me to run [for first officer of the northeastern regional division of COG].

I went through a dark night of the soul where I didn't know if I was really up to it or if I had the capacity to handle the responsibilities. Finally, I decided I would do it, and I am now in my second year in that office.

What does being a first officer involve?

Basically running the organization. Last year it involved some extraordinary responsibilities that were unique to the office because of our participation in the Parliament of the World's Religions. Last year I was charged with taking the Covenant public in a way that it had never been before. That meant preparing professional press materials, doing a lot of interviews, and being tremendously public. I went to the Parliament and conducted a lot of workshops. I did an interfaith workshop with some other incredible women from different religions on the Goddess. I did the "What Is Wicca?" workshop. I gave a speech talking about the environmental crisis as a reflection of a spiritual crisis. I circulated as much as possible.

How many people are in the organization?

I don't know. We have ninety covens now. We also have about fifty solitaires, and depending on how the circles are organized some of them have people that are associated with them. My circle, for example, which at this point has eight people, has an outer court of about forty. We don't register individual members unless they are solitaires. The coven is actually considered to be the member of COG. We are organized like the Congregational Church in America. We are a Covenant of independent covens that have bonded together for mutual governance.

What is the purpose of covens joining together?

Legal protection. One of the most important things that we do is that we are a legally recognized church. That means that our members who are elders are clergy. They are legally recognized with the power to marry people. They can go into prisons, they can gain access to Pagans in the military and provide services for them.

The Parliament was a perfect example of the importance of COG. By all of the covens being joined together and having a structure and money and resources that they had pooled over the years, there were funds available and people to help organize and to participate. We were organized. We had a treasury and a budget. We had people to call upon. I did very little legal work last year, and I virtually worked full-time to get COG to the Parliament. It was a *huge* project. A single coven could never have done it. They probably would also not have been recognized. It would have been difficult for them to obtain even the grudging recognition that we got.

We were a real presence there. I made a speech, and Andras Corban Arthen made a speech, and we did ritual and performance and we got a lot of press attention, probably more than the Dalai Lama. We were prepared for it. We had a press kit that had been put together by COG members who were professional press people and PR people. We had our act together, and we served the larger Pagan community by being there.

I am constantly getting calls from all over the country from people who are in legal predicaments and needing advice and support. COG serves an important function in terms of mutual aid.

There seems to be a trend with Earthspirit and ADF and COG and other groups to do public ritual. Can you comment on the tension between or the conflict between the traditional view of the Craft as being an intimate group of people who know each other and who trust each other implicitly and who feel safe with each other and do magic together, as opposed to this large outpouring of energy toward becoming more public and reaching out to the New Age and other groups?

They are both valid, they are both important, they are both necessary. I think that the practice of secrecy was a consequence of persecution. The Old Religion was not originally persecuted, because it was the religion that was practiced. It was a religion of techniques and practices, not a religion of dogma. It was predicated upon the individual learning and participating with the guidance of a teacher or the assistance of a shaman. There were always people who had a special calling and who devoted themselves to it. But the Old Religion was the religion of the community. I think that is an appropriate goal for us to have again.

People continue to be persecuted, and so each individual has a right to make a decision as to whether or not they will be public. Some people cannot be because of their jobs or child custody situations or whatever. It is not easy to be public, but it is ultimately essential to those of us who can be public to be public in order to make it safe for everyone else to practice.

As long as we are hidden, people can continue to project upon us their worst nightmares. When we are out and we are seen, when we are publicly visible and when we speak openly and freely, when we conduct rituals in the middle of Central Park and thousands of people can see who we are and the *New York Times* puts us on the front page of the Style Section, then people will see that we are not satanic. That we are not perpetrators of dark, heinous crimes. They will begin to learn the truth of what we are all about.

Why is that important? There will always be a mysterious mystical center. Every religion has that mystical core. Not everyone will walk the full path to that center in their lifetime. It is appropriate to maintain vows and initiatory practices.

DON FREW is a high priest of Gardnerian and NROOGD (New Reformed Orthodox Order of the Golden Dawn) Witchcraft. He is a former public information officer and former first officer in COG. The interviewed was conducted by phone on March 3, 1994.

Are you a Pagan, and if so when did you first decide that you were?

I am definitely a Pagan, at least as I understand Paganism. I sort of first experienced that when I was a kid. My parents were not religious; my mother was a lapsed Christian Scientist, and my father was basically a capitalist. When I was in sixth grade, I connected with a group of other kids who had read some occult books and who had a sort of coven going. I got involved with them, and the group lasted less than a year. Then I came to Berkeley, and I had a serious interest in the paranormal but no real conception of the spiritual path or the religious path. I was just interested in psychic phenomena.

That led to an interest in ritual magic, and through the process of practicing ritual magic on a regular basis and in a very experimental way I began wondering what would happen if I invoked Deities. Then in a very dramatic circumstance in which I was in the hospital and I was actually expected to die, the person who I most often worked magic with did a healing ritual for me and invoked healing Gods. That had a pronounced and remarkable effect. I healed overnight. The doctors were mystified, I was astounded, and I asked my friend what he had done. He laid out how he had adapted a sort of Pagan ritual form. That was when I said, "Huh. It looks like there is something to all this God stuff." So I started experimenting with that, and then I made contact with the local NROOGD community in Berkeley. I attended my first public Sabbat and thought it was really wonderful.

Thereafter, in the course of preparing for what I was still considering a secular magical ritual, I had a full-blown religious vision. I have never had anything quite like that before or since. I was in my ritual room, and my friend at the time was living in L.A., so we were doing coordinated rituals. We'd both cast a circle and do such and such an experiment at the same time and compare notes afterward. This one was on the night of the full moon, and the time we had coordinated for was midnight. I had finished my ritual preparations at about eleven-thirty, and I looked at the clock and said, "I've got some time to kill." So I started meditating. As I lay down on the floor to meditate, a chant that I had heard at the public Sabbat came to me—it was the "We all come from the Goddess" chant.

I started chanting that to myself as I was lying there. My eyes were shut, and suddenly the darkness in front of my eyelids parted, just like somebody drawing a curtain. I found myself staring at a sunlit scene that was as real, or more so, as the room I was lying in. I was in a field that led to some woods. There was a hill up to the right. Everything was green and beautiful; it was a summer's day. There was a path that led out from the woods and up the hill. I immediately recognized the scene and thought, "Gee, this is what the Summerland is supposed to look like." Then I heard singing, and it was other people's voices singing the chant along with me. I saw a group of people coming out of the woods. There was a woman with dark hair in a white robe, and she was followed by children who were also in white robes, and they were all singing the song.

They approached me, and, ever the scientist, I said to myself, "Huh. This *must* be the Goddess. I wonder what I'm supposed to do." I racked my brains for something profound to say, and I couldn't think of anything, so as She approached, I stepped forward and bowed. I said, "Lady, would you watch over me in my undertakings?" She stopped singing and turned and looked at me and smiled and said, "Of course. Are you not already one of my children?" and She gestured back behind her. I looked back, and there in the group of kids was me at the age of twelve wearing a white robe and a white cord and singing the song along with the other kids. That was exactly the age I was when I was in the group in sixth grade.

I had been wondering for some time if I should consider that as being involved in the Craft or not, since it was just a half-assed kid thing, wannabe Witches. I was sort of astounded, and I turned to Her again. She had started walking on, and I got the feeling that it was finished. I stepped back, and the darkness closed just like a curtain, and I opened my eyes and I looked at my watch. It was just about midnight, and I went on with the working with my friend. It was only afterward that I realized that it was the same age I had been when I had this prior involvement. The white cord was what a first-degree initiate in NROOGD wears, which was the only group I had made contact with.

That seemed to say to me that there was really something to all of this and that I was already on the path. At that point I went to the people who had led the public ritual. This was Robin Goodfellow and Gaia Wildwoode, who together with Isaac Bonewits and Sally Eaton—whom he was married to at the time—were forming a new coven called FireStar. They were getting together a study group for that. I told them I was very interested, and they invited me to join them. I believe that was in 1979.

Because of the years I had spent studying ritual magic, I went through rather quickly and got the first degree and then worked in that coven and became a second-degree, which in NROOGD is an elder. After that I encountered Meredydd Harper, who was a Gardnerian Witch of the Bay Area. I wanted to study Gardnerian Witchcraft just because I wanted to learn what different Witches were like, and I got the three Gardnerian degrees from her.

Then through just the weird way the dynamics shook out, the high priest of that coven left, and I wound up being high priest. At about the same time, one of the elders left FireStar to form a new group, and I went with her and became high priest of *that* group, Black Oak. And so I was high priest of a NROOGD coven and a Gardnerian coven simultaneously.

Can you compare the two systems, NROOGD and Gardnerian Wicca? How are they different, and how are they the same?

I would say that the NROOGD practice was created in the sixties very consciously and that spirit of creativity has stayed with it. It is very vital, very dynamic. Its real strong point is the Sabbats, because from very early on they were doing public or semipublic Sabbats. The NROOGD Sabbats are, I think, the best combinations I have ever seen of something that feels like traditional Craft and yet at the same time is always new and different. The Sabbats that we do out here range from a hundred to three hundred people. There is a definite urge to creativity while still staying similar enough that we recognize each other as initiates. At this point the group is starting to get disparate enough that people are actually starting to say, "Those people don't look a lot like what I do." It's only just at that stage right now.

Gardnerian, on the other hand, definitely has roots. It has a central lineage of history and continuity. There is much more of an impulse, which I tend to fight, to do things the same way each time, to keep doing them the way that the people who went before us did. That's the way Gardnerian Craft in America is. It's a sense that "we're doing it the way it has *always* been done." And that has its own sort of homey feeling. It has its own strength and sense of support, a sense of roots. There's a special kind of tradition, and that's the best I can say for it. For some people that can be kind of stifling because they feel like their creativity is stifled. Similarly, in the NROOGD tradition some people wonder where the continuity is, where is the thing they can count on if it's always different?

So in my own personal practice, when I do ritual on my own, I will do a Gardnerian circle with a NROOGD banishing, and I will blend in some other NROOGD aspects. I find that they blend very easily; I don't find any conflict.

When I am practicing in a group, I am very clear about what's what. If I am teaching somebody Gardnerian Wicca, I make sure that they learn Gardnerian, not some weird Gardnerian-NROOGD amalgam. And I do the same when I am teaching somebody NROOGD. I have enough of a scholarly inclination that I want it to be very clear to people where the material I teach is coming from.

For my own practice I fundamentally consider myself to be a Witch. That's basically what I am. NROOGD is one set of tools to use to be a Witch, and Gardnerian is another set of tools. Depending on what the common language is of the people I am working with, I will work one or the other. The Witch identity is primary and the traditional identity is secondary.

What is a Witch?

I would say that these days the term "Witch" is applied to so many different kinds of things that the definition that COG came up with for membership is probably the closest you are going to get without disenfranchising people you don't want to disenfranchise. That definition says a Witch is a person who meets on a regular basis to observe the Sabbats and the moons in some way. They focus their worship around the Goddess and the Old Gods. They subscribe to something akin to "An it harm none do as you will." And, of course, the bottom line is, it takes one to know one.

Have you done some work with COG?

I was PI [public information officer] for three years. Then I was first officer for a year with Diana Paxton in 1988. I was the youngest person elected to COG's Board.

While you were first officer in COG, what was COG trying to do? What was the mission at that time?

When Diana and I were first officers together, COG had just gone through one of its worst times. That was over difficulties within the Southern California Council. That had caused COG to polarize. We had just gone through a Grand Council the year before that was really difficult. The mission that Diana and I had was to try to smooth things over, to consolidate and to get the membership back up, because we had lost a lot of members. We needed to get our financial base back together. So our mission at that time was one of rebuilding.

As a result of our efforts, and those of the national Board, membership hit an all-time high until this last year, when membership went even higher. We pretty much doubled COG's assets that year. Instead of being a largely hand-to-mouth organization, we ended up with enough money so that we could stick some of our savings into a CD and just have that as a nest egg. That pretty much started the pattern in COG of building up our savings. Up until that point COG had operated on the basis of having just enough money to make it to the next year, and that's it. From then on COG has had the policy of building up its assets so that we can deal with unexpected events. A lot of the unexpected events were PI things, things like the Helms amendment that required mass mailings. Or the Eric Pryor Prayer Crusade fiasco out here that required lots of phone calling and mass mailing.

When the opportunity came to attend the Parliament of the World's Religions last year, COG was able to say that it had enough money to deal with it. That was exactly the kind of project that we needed to save money for. It was a once-in-a-century event, and it cost a lot.

COG is now at sort of a difficult crossroads, coming out of the success of the Parliament and wondering where to go from here. There are definitely a lot of different views. I'm being a little cagey because I represent one very strong voice for a particular way that COG should go.

What are the two points of view? What is the debate about?

The way I see it, it's about how does COG move into the religious mainstream. This is what everything I have done, as PI and as first officer, has been about—how to enter the mainstream. As I see it, there are two ways to do it. One is to try to be like them, so that they welcome us as one of the club. The other route is to educate the mainstream so that what they consider to be mainstream encompasses more things, so that it grows larger. The latter is the route I support.

I think it's a very difficult issue for the Craft right now, because I think that the inclination to be more like mainstream churches is a very natural one. It's very easy to understand. That's the way that people were raised, and so that's what their model of religion is. A "real" church has buildings and a paid clergy and all these other things. It operates by democratic vote or by a board of directors or whatever.

There's this sense that a lot of people have that, because we are growing up, we need to act more like them because they are grownups. They are "real" religious groups. There are a few people out there—they are probably in the minority, unfortunately—who are saying, "Wait a minute. Pagan religious organizations were *never* like these churches."

I think that the best approach is the one that COG has taken, to say that we're here to deal with the government and that sort of thing. The spiritual authority is handled by whomever your coven has chosen, and that's your business. I think that's the best way to keep it. Not to centralize the power. I think that centralizing power is something we should avoid like the plague. We've lived for a long time as a grassroots organization, and we should stay that way and continue to grow. The hard part of that is that periodically the Craft and Pagans in general go through periods where people come to us in droves. That happened after the Joseph Campbell program on PBS, for example. Now we have more people coming to us than we have teachers, and the teachers are getting burned out. The response on the part of a lot of people has been to say that we need to create a laity, a lay organization to deal with all of these people. I think that that's the worst possible solution.

One of the distinctions that I see between "Witch" and "neo-Pagan" is that people say, "The Craft is a religion of clergy." I don't think that the Craft is either a religion *or* clergy. I think that Paganism is closer to being a religion. Within it there are many specialties. There are people that you go to if you want to go to a Sabbat, that's the NROOGD people out here. For example, if you want an initiatory process of relationship with Deity, you might go to the Gardnerians. If you need a healing, you might go to a shaman. Depending upon what kind of need you have, you go to various specialists.

The specialists are either a specialized priesthood the way that the Taoists were a specialized priesthood, or they are people offering different mysteries like the way the ancient Eleusinian mysteries would have been offered. You have many specialists working within a single context, and that is our strength. I would like to see us keep doing it that way. I think that when we think of the Craft as a "religion," or when we think of ourselves as clergy in the sense of having to learn pastoral counseling and having to take any student that comes to us, I think those are all big mistakes.

The way people are responding to the huge influx of students is largely coming out of their Christian upbringing, where whichever church they were in was the "one universal and catholic church." The result of being the only way to Divinity was that you had to take *everybody*. You had a moral obligation to take everybody. But Witchcraft is not the only way to Divinity. There are lots of different ways to Divinity out there. There are lots of different neo-Pagan ways to Divinity out there. I don't think that we are under any obligation to take anyone. If there are more people coming to us than we can handle, the best we can do for them is to turn to them and tell them to do what we did. And that was to get together with friends, read books, and start a group. It worked for us!

Unless we encourage that kind of individuality, that kind of approach to Divinity, we will start down the same path that the Christian church did. We'll set up a pattern where we become the intermediary between these clergy and the Divine. Sooner or later, and probably sooner, those people will start looking out for their own interests, their own survival. Because we will be paying people just to be clergy, we will be replicating all of the same problems that people are rejecting now.

Because most Pagans come from a Judeo-Christian background and because they are unconscious of other religions, there is a constant social pressure for them to replicate the process of the mainstream churches. That way lies doom for us. I think that this will be the biggest challenge we face in the next ten years.

Can you briefly talk about the police work you have been doing?

The way police function is that they go a lot on first impressions. If they pick up somebody who has just killed a cat and says they are a Witch, when another Witch steps forward and says, "I'm a Witch; Witches don't kill cats," all the cop will think is that people always deny their crimes and that the person must be covering up something. Whereas if the first person they talk to says, "Hi. I live in your community, you may need information, I have a group, I am someone who is an official liaison person, I just want to introduce myself. If you want any information I'm here to answer questions," then when they pick up the kid who says he's a Witch and he's into killing cats, their impression will be that this kid says he's a Witch, but he's not anything like this completely nice person they have known for a long time, so he must be lying.

All I did was put together a manual for people that says this is how you go to the police, this is how you establish a relationship with the police before there is a problem, before there's a crime. You go to the police and you say, "This is who we are. We are here to help. We are concerned citizens, and we want to help." My experience has been that they will be really open to it. They are really friendly.

Is your public relations work related to what you just described, or is it something different?

I initially was doing that as public information officer for COG. I am no longer on COG's board, but I am known in police circles as someone to contact. And I'm a consultant for the police on ritual crime on a regular basis.

You have been doing some interfaith work as well?

For the last ten years or so I have been COG's representative on the Berkeley Area Interfaith Council, which COG has been a member of since 1975. It consists of representatives from all the religious groups in the Berkeley area, which I imagine is one of the most diverse groups in the world.

We have an interfaith Thanksgiving service, which Pagans are always part of.

We do tree plantings up in the hills, and we also participate in larger events like the Parliament of the World's Religions.

It's essentially the same kind of thing. It's going to people who may have heard something weird about us and just being there in person. More often than not, the image that Witches kill people or eat babies or whatever is also tied up with an image that they have warts and scuzzy teeth and green skin and the whole bit. When ministers meet someone who is dressed completely normal, who speaks relatively intelligently, and is nice, most of that just goes out the window. It just vanishes.

Do you think Witches should make an effort to dress normally rather than in black with heavy eye makeup and jewelry and that sort of thing?

I think you always have to balance being true to yourself with being true to the people you are representing and getting your message across. The first thing that you learn doing public relations is that what you know to be true is not necessarily what other people will understand. Wearing a black robe and dying your hair red may be how you practice the Craft. But the person you are talking to may be looking at your weird hair and not listening to what you have to say. And if the point of your communication with the other person is to get them to understand who you are, they may not understand it because you dress that way. It's a matter of communication skills and learning how to get the message across, of learning how they communicate and how they talk, learning their jargon. Not to try to masquerade that you are being like them but to make sure they understand who you are.

Is there anything else on your mind these days?

Yes. I think that there's a serious danger facing us now, and that's that most of us still learn our practice from books. And most of the books that are out there have been sanitized for the public. A growing percentage of our movement don't know a lot of basic things about magic. They don't know about competent use of sex for ritual. They don't know about competent use of drugs or how to deal with spooks that they may encounter, about hauntings and things like that. They don't know how to defend themselves.

Things that should be a part of our basic knowledge are getting completely lost because that stuff doesn't go into books for public consumption, and that's where most of our people are getting their training. We need to make a concerted effort to preserve the esoteric knowledge we have and to make sure it at least gets passed on even if it never gets used.

AIDAN KELLY is a doctor of theology and a poet. He is one of the founders of the New Reformed Orthodox Order of the Golden Dawn and of the Covenant of the Goddess. He is the author of *Crafting the Art of Magic, Book I: A History*

of Modern Witchcraft 1939–1964. Kelly was interviewed by phone on January 19, 1994.

Aidan, do you consider yourself a Pagan?

After I founded the NROOGD in the late sixties there was a weird loop in my path. In September 1976 I realized that I was an alcoholic. At that point I did what was then the obvious thing to do, and I joined AA. I became therefore the only sober Pagan that I knew. At that time there wasn't *anyone* else in the Craft or the neo-Pagan community who was in a twelve-step program, and there wasn't *anyone* in the twelve-step program who knew anything about Pagan religion. It was just an impossible situation.

I was used to being in circles where I would go to quietly drink, have fun, and then pass out. I continued to try and be in the Craft for six months and not drink, and that was very painful. So I stopped going to Pagan meetings, and I started going to AA, and that was like living on a diet of sand. For my first AA birthday my wife and I discussed what religion we were going to be if we were no longer going to be Pagans. I had heard that there had been a lot of changes in the Roman Catholic church, so I tried going there.

It was a very high experience. I was able to hear a message of real hope, but there was about a three-foot-wide section on the left wing of the church where I could be comfortable and be Catholic and use *that* theology to work the twelve steps and stay sober. I tried doing that for about the next ten years, and it got more and more difficult to do. The territory that I was standing on kept getting narrower and narrower. It finally got to the point where I was actually starting to have a physical breakdown because of the stress.

What was it about Catholicism that was actually giving you trouble?

The fact was that I blamed the church for the way I had been abused as a child and the fact that they condoned the abuse. The other part of the problem was that the Roman administration still owned all the machinery of the Inquisition. It has never been abolished. They changed the name to the Sacred Congregation for the Doctrine of the Faith; it's usually called the CDF. Joseph Cardinal Ratzinger is the head of it. He is the prefect of the organization. He holds the office that was once called the Office of the Grand Inquisitor. They changed the name, but they didn't change any of the roles. So this was all part of a process with my second marriage blowing up and reconnecting with the Craft. That was in late 1986.

Where did you first encounter the Craft?

In books. The first book that I read was by Theda Kenyon called *Witches Still Live* and it was published in the 1920s. It was about Leland's *Aradia*, and it also went into a lot of folklore, and it talked about the persecutions. This was a real eye opener for me as a teenager because it was something that the church had never mentioned. That opened my eyes to look out for books. Over the next fifteen years I found Gardner, I found Graves's *The White Goddess,* but I had never run into any Witches or any type of organization.

In the fall of 1967 a good friend of mine, Sarah, with whom I had often talked about this stuff, was in a class on ritual taught by James Broughton, poet and filmmaker. The class assignment was to create a ritual for everyone else to come to. She asked me if I could put together some kind of Witches' Sabbat out of the information that I had, and I said I'd try. I started working at getting it written, and she went around recruiting people to help work on it. Pretty soon we had, guess what, thirteen people working on this project!

In the course of this we came up with a name for ourselves, the New Reformed Orthodox Order of the Golden Dawn—with tongue firmly in cheek. We put on the ritual for the class, then we did nothing for a while, but the group of friends who had worked on this became a kind of occult study group. We did the ritual again; we did a wedding for some friends, and it worked a little better. Lammas 1968 was the first one where we really did it up with an open ritual. We raised enough energy to get stoned; we just blew ourselves away. It was wonderful. After that there was no backing out.

It wasn't until three years later that we ran into other Witches. So twenty years ago there was starting to be a national network of people. In 1973 we met our first Gardnerians. The first official Gardnerian coven in California was led by Dagda and Athena. Athena was elevated by Lady Theos.

By this time, 1973 or 1974, there started to be national communication between Witches of various traditions, and national organizations started to pull together. Gwydion [Pendderwen] and I started working on the idea of getting some kind of national church to happen, and we were able to pull the Covenant of the Goddess together in 1975. I wrote the original COG charter and bylaws. I think some of the feminists have a hard time with the fact that a man wrote all that stuff. There were a bunch of people who worked on COG in the beginning, who served on the board of directors, but Gwydion, Alison [Harlow], and I were the ringleaders. The original idea was mine and Gwydion's.

We had been working with some other neo-Pagans in California about creating a generalized Pagan church, and even though people worked on this for years, it just wasn't happening. There wasn't enough common ground. People didn't agree on a basic philosophy or a basic organizational structure. Neo-Pagans are just too diverse. All of a sudden it occurred to us that maybe we should have a church that was just for Witches. At least the Witches could agree on who they were, and something could get organized.

Do you have a mundane job? Do you do some kind of work?

Yes, I've been working in publishing for thirty years, editing science textbooks for the Scientific American Library. Much to my delight, I have worked with a great many famous scientists who are my heroes.

Has being a Pagan affected your work, or has your work affected your life as a Pagan?

Probably the effect is that in the publishing world you are expected to be an eccentric individual, and you are not punished for it like you are in academia. I knew all along that I wouldn't function very well in academia, even though I have taught college and university courses for the last fourteen years. No one has *ever* offered me a full-time faculty position—not even when I was doing my best to look like a Roman Catholic.

Is the NROOGD still alive and kicking?

Oh, yes. It continued to be an organization until May of 1976, at which point the Red Cord Council, the assembly of the second-degree initiates, decided that it was getting unwieldy and another level of structure would need to be created—something like an executive committee. The members simply rebelled against having that much structure, and they dissolved the organization.

The members decided to declare it a Craft tradition with each coven being autonomous. If they wanted to get together to celebrate Sabbats, that was their own business. At that point there were several hundred members. The council had gotten to the point where in order to have a full quorum there needed to be at least thirty people. It has continued on since then. There are many dozens of covens, mostly in northern California.

How does it differ from other Witchcraft traditions?

What was unique about it was that it began as a project of reinventing the Craft for ourselves.

Doesn't everybody do that?

Not quite the same way. At the time there was very little information available in books. I was able to go through the fragments that I had and with creative writing fill in the gaps and create something that worked. What I saw about the Gardnerian rituals was that the basic structure of them was fine, but Gerald Gardner was probably one of the worst poets of the twentieth century—even worse than Crowley. In order to be a good Gardnerian, you have to have bad taste and a tin ear.

I was trained by the best poets in the world, like John Logan and Wright Morris. I knew Robert Duncan, James Broughton. I spent ten years being trained in writing poetry. Poetry is really my path to being creative. I was trained to go into a certain type of altered state of consciousness in order to write. As John Logan commented to me one time when we were crossing 19th Avenue dodging traffic, "When you are writing down stuff you already know, that's prose. When you are writing down stuff and you don't know what it is until it's on paper—that's poetry."

When you use poetry in ritual, does the poetry flow through you at the moment of the ritual, or is it something that you get down beforehand and then you present it?

You have to do it beforehand. You couldn't possibly be creating good poetry under ritual conditions. Preferably, the material should be memorized rather than read in a ritual. The better the poetry, the better a spell works because it is working on many more levels. Something that people fail to realize, and it's one of the simplest things to understand about poetry, is that it doesn't mean only one thing. It has to mean at least *two* things in order to be poetry, and there has to be an interesting relationship between those two things. If it means three things and there are three interesting relationships, that's even better. It's even more powerful.

One of my favorite examples is the opening words from the Gospel of John, which are usually translated as "In the beginning there was the Word." But what the Greek also means, straightforwardly, is, "In the foundation is rationality."

Do you think that Paganism has any problems today?

Oh Lord, I tend to say a lot of things that make me unpopular. . . . One of the things that I liked about being a Roman Catholic of the modern liberal variety was that I didn't have to believe any kind of historical metaphysical bullshit. A lot of people don't understand that modern theology doesn't compromise your integrity, you don't have to believe in nonsense and bullshit. My stance is that if I didn't have to believe in nonsense and bullshit in order to be a Christian, I am certainly not going to believe in it in order to be a Witch.

A great deal of what people in the neo-Pagan movement believe these days is bullshit. For example, the invention of the great matriarchal age, which is myth not history. I have no problem with it being a myth; I have a problem with people not knowing the difference, because that's childish. There's the great Gardnerian myth of the secret covens that preserved all the information for centuries up to the twentieth century when they emerged from under a rock; again this is *not* history.

The neo-Pagan movement overall, the bulk of which is the Craft, is hitting a population size of about half a million. And it needs to grow up and face the theological and philosophical problems that any religion has to face, such as being able to live with the ambiguity between myth and history.

The story about Moses on the mountain is a myth, a very meaningful myth. And when Judaism was founded and when that story was written, everybody knew that it was literature, that it didn't really happen. That information can be found in Jewish scripture. But with time people forgot, and they are trying to claim the myth as history. Ditto for Christianity as far as the myth and the history.

If Paganism is going to be an adult religion, it's got to live with the fact that the Gardnerian *Book of Shadows* was not preserved; that's a modern creation. Every religion has done this, and Paganism is just showing parallels in the evolutionary process. But as long as you don't know the difference between myth and history, then you don't understand either.

One of the structural problems that's coming up is that between Wicca and the Gardnerians and the Craft as a whole; there is this problem of it splitting into liberal and orthodox wings. It is very much reproducing the history of Judaism. There are a number of Gardnerians and a number of others who call themselves things like British traditionalist and so on, who really believe in practicing the Craft by the book. What they mean is the *Book of Shadows,* and they really want to believe that the core of the book was passed down traditionally to modern times and that it really does have this kind of antique authority. The *Book of Shadows* is like a liturgical manual; it has the script for initiation rituals. Gerald Gardner put it together first, and then Doreen Valiente worked with him and wrote it into the form that it's in now. She has admitted this in her own writings.

This book was brought to America by Ray Buckland, who brought Gardnerian Witchcraft here. Ray founded the Long Island coven which became the center of Gardnerian Witchcraft in America and proceeded to inspire a lot of imitations.

The NROOGD was an imitation, and we admitted it from the start. There are a lot of people who are Gardnerian imitations who don't admit it. They claim they got it from their Grandmother. I'm just not impressed by the fact that Grandmother managed to channel the exact wording that Doreen Valiente came up with in 1966. I mean, Grandma was certainly talented, but there is another explanation.

The fact is that the vast majority of the Witchcraft movement in America is Gardnerian officially or by extension. There are only a few strands of pre-Gardnerian Witchcraft that have merged, and *they* are all similar to one another. Victor Anderson would be an example of that type of tradition—the Faery Faith. Victor while working with Gwydion proceeded to adopt the Gardnerian stuff wherever it looked useful, but it wasn't that important to what he did. His work was very eclectic; it was not a preserved pure tradition. If something was useful, they used it. If it didn't run fast enough, they stole it. As T. S. Eliot said, "Poor poets imitate and good poets steal."

What does it mean to be a Gardnerian Witch as opposed to the Faery Faith? Can you go into that a bit more?

A lot of it is a difference in style. The Gardnerian style always deals with the *Book of Shadows* and the degree of adherence to it. At least the Orthodox Gardnerians do it that way. The Liberal Gardnerians take the attitude that Gerald rewrote all the rituals, and if you truly want to follow Gerald, then *do what he did,* rewrite the rituals. They feel that the religion has to keep evolving, and that it's not a Chinese opera performed exactly the same way every year.

The Faery pattern is much more improvisatory. Gardnerians can tell if you are one of them by whether you followed the same script in your initiation. The Faery emphasis would be much more one of asking, "Did the initiation work? Did it produce the kind of effect that it was intended to produce?" If it didn't produce that, then it was the wrong initiation, and it's better to redo it in order to get the right effect.

What contribution do you think neo-Paganism is making to American culture, or has it made any?

It is making a contribution in that it is encouraging a much freer, organic style of worship and a way of integrating your life and your faith instead of being a "Sunday-only" Christian, for example. Or a "Sabbat-only" Pagan. I see a lot of this in neo-Paganism and particularly in the Witchcraft community, that you are aware that you are trying to live your life according to certain spiritual principles and that it takes paying attention and ingenuity to figure out how to apply them to your life regularly. That you live according to your ethics. That you remain open to spiritual reality. It's very much the same kind of thing that you get in the twelve-step program, where, having had a spiritual awakening, you try to practice the principles in all of your affairs. It's also the kind of thing that a Muslim means when he says that someone is a Sufi. He's not just mechanically doing the Five Pillars of Islam, but he is in fact trying to live his entire life on a spiritual basis, to always be compassionate, to always reach out a helping hand to people who are in need.

The Pagan movement has the advantage of doing this in ways that the established churches cannot. It appeals to precisely the people that the mainstream churches are failing to appeal to at all. It's possible to be a devout atheist and be a Pagan, because those are two different levels that don't really contradict each other. It's possible to still be Jewish and become a neo-Pagan, because the membership in one community doesn't involve forswearing the other. This is significant because even though there are now female rabbis, Judaism historically has not given women as equal a place in their society as men. In New York City, which is one-third Jewish anyway, the Craft looks like a Jewish subculture because so many of the members are Jewish in their background and because so many of the priestesses are Jewish in their background. They are able to be religious in a way that even being a rabbi wouldn't allow them to be.

One funny thing about the Craft and Paganism is that Witches in general are about twice as likely as in the general population to be Jewish, but there isn't any great difference in proportion between Protestants and Catholics. The myth that the Roman Catholic love of ritual makes good Pagans is not real. Of Pagans overall, about 6 percent are Jewish in background, and the general population is about 3 percent Jewish. Pagans are twice as likely as the general public to be Jewish. Pagans are also six times more likely than the general public to come from a non-mainstream background—Christian Science, Mormonism, etc. They are six times as likely to have parents who were into something a little "strange." What has happened is that the neo-Pagan movement is pulling together all of these strands of earlier attempts to create new religious communities that didn't work. And the Craft is doubling in size every two years.

Can you give an anecdote or an example of something that happened in your experience that was truly magical?

In 1973 the NROOGD had just gotten to the point that it had several autonomous covens functioning, and we had, therefore, the Red Cord Council to run the administration. The covens had usually been meeting for the Sabbats robed. We decided that now that we had three or four covens, we could really proceed to have a skyclad Sabbat to see how much energy we could raise like that.

That morning Alison called because Victor Anderson had been taken to the hospital, and he was in intensive care with a massive bleeding ulcer. He was due to undergo surgery, so she asked if we could send some energy.

At midnight Eastern time, nine P.M. here, my wife, who had been scheduled to be the green priestess in charge of the healing ritual, was in the middle of the circle·naked. We were dancing around her, raising the cone of energy, and she said that all of a sudden the gates opened up, and this energy came through kind of like a psychic battleship. She just stood there and held the energy as long as she could, and then she *threw* it, saying, "Victor, catch!" and she just dropped, crash.

We got the rest of the story from Victor later on. He was in the hospital when he felt the energy hit, and he immediately started feeling very much better. The doctors came in toward morning to prep him for an exam, and when they went in with the instruments and looked, they couldn't even see where the wound had been. There was nothing there. Surgery was unnecessary, and they sent him home.

The other man who shared the room with Victor in the hospital came from a Hawaiian background, and he said to Victor as he was leaving, "Tell me if I am being too nosey but where did all that manna in the room come from?" Victor just totally cracked up.

ROWAN FAIRGROVE is a Wiccan priestess and "electronic elder." **RUSSELL WILLIAMS** is a Wiccan priest. Both are former co–first officers of COG. They were interviewed on April 15, 1994.

Rowan, when did you discover that you were a Pagan?

My mother was an archaeologist, and so I was lucky enough to be exposed to the beliefs of many lands as a child. Although my upbringing was Christian, my mother's brother was a Yogi, and my father always joked that he was a reform Buddhist. One of my mother's cousins was an Ozark herb woman, and she taught me farmcraft and kitchen magic.

At about puberty I began to spend a lot of time in the jungle and, when we moved back to the U.S. later, in the woods. I had an affinity for storms, and once during a windstorm in the woods behind my home I danced with the winds and then went back up to my room and played a song on my guitar. I could hear words to it in a language I didn't know, and I saw myself dancing in the wind on the edge of a cliff with water crashing below, and I knew that I was a priestess in that vision.

My girlfriend and I started doing rituals on a beach after that, using Homeric hymns, Norse Eddas, and what came from inside of us. I later got involved with what would probably be called a magical lodge, although they considered themselves to be practicing Witchcraft.

In early 1973 I visited a friend in San Francisco who was aware of the Goddess and who was later a member of Starhawk's Compost Coven. I went to the Mystic Eye and bought a copy of Farrar's *What Witches Do*. But the big breakthrough for me came in the winter of 1973 when I was visiting with my folks in San Diego.

I borrowed their car and drove off to find Z. Budapest's shop. When I found it, we hit it off and I found myself in circle with them that night. But even more important was what I took home with me—early issues of *Green Egg* magazine. I started writing away for more information and contacted Alison Harlow and Margot Adler among others. I also answered all eighty questions in the original questionnaire for *Drawing Down the Moon*.

Then I started visiting the Bay Area every year and circling with various folks. This let me be around for some of the early days of the Covenant of the Goddess even though I lived far away, in Tallahassee, Florida, at the time. After that, some people in Florida came to me for training, and we started a coven together. I also started attending the festivals, and it just kept growing from there.

How has being a Pagan affected other areas of your life such as your mundane job or parenting?

My job is as a librarian, which I consider to be right livelihood. I preserve and disseminate knowledge, as a village wise woman might have in the days before the printing press. I know how to find a variety of information in many forms—books, electronic sources, knowing whom to phone, and things like that. I am also a Tarot reader, mostly by e-mail, and many people come to me for other kinds of advice. I find the two vocations quite similar.

Parenting is a hard question. I am not a custodial parent, and so some of the day-to-day issues don't touch me directly. But helping to raise a Pagan child in a world that disbelieves in us, with a co-parent whose parents would freak, is hard. I recommend Ashleen O'Gaea's book on Pagan parenting [*The Family Wicca Book*] as a resource for anyone concerned about parenting questions.

What kind of work have you been doing in the Pagan community?

I take part in the presentation of the NROOGD Sabbats. I teach. I read Tarot. I take an active role in the Northern California Local Council of COG, and I make myself available on the Internet for questions and readings. I see myself as an electronic elder. There are lots of college students on the net who are just exploring Paganism, and I think that having experienced folk to talk to is a good thing.

What role do the arts play in your path?

Artwork is very important in my work; working with the hands is an important part of creating magic. One of our covens in particular, MoonDragon, does a craftworking as well as a Sabbat magical working each Sabbat. At Brigid [or Imbolc, celebrated February first or second] this year we got unscented white pillar candles and *wachsfolien* (wax sheets) made by a company called Stockmar from Germany. The wax sheets are very thin and come in eighteen different colors, including gold and silver. We decorated our candles with symbols of what we wanted to bring into our lives in the coming year. We had a big selection of cookie and canape cutters in all kinds of shapes, including neolithic Goddesses and a Pan, along with hearts and stars in various sizes and two different cats. Lots of cookie bakers in the coven, I guess.

An amazing, wonderful, creative group of candles emerged from that—all lovely and very evocative. We then broke for a potluck supper and then we did a circle to raise energy to bless the candles with our intent. It was really intense. We did a couple of candles on behalf of people who weren't there—a friend with cancer and a coven member who was away on another continent. I had about six different essential oils on my hands by the time we were done, and I could hardly taste cakes for the smells.

At Ostara [Easter] we do Pysanky eggs. At Beltaine we do a well dressing by creating a flower petal mosaic around a hot tub. At Lammas [generally August 1, a harvest festival] we bake, of course, and at Samhain we carve pumpkins. Here is the blessing of the pumpkins from that ritual to give you the flavor of how we weave art and ritual:

> In elder days the folk carved turnips to light them on their way through cold winter nights. In this fertile new land we have found a vegetable that is much easier to work with. Yet still we carve and remember those who went before us. We carve the face of old Jack in many guises on our pumpkins to provide light and protection in the dark time of the year. Jack provides the sacred flame that watches our homes, our sidewalks, and our streets. His flickering light turns away all enmity and provides a beacon to the friends and ancestor spirits coming to visit for Samhain. Old Jack is the keeper of the knowledge of death and the Otherworld. He is the symbol of the psychopomp who guides those who journey between the worlds. We invoke him into these newly carved pumpkins to guide and guard our homes and to show us the pathways of knowledge.

That is really lovely. You call yourself an electronic elder, could you talk a bit about the Information Highway in the context of Paganism?

One of the really interesting things that I see in the future of the Wiccan community is the growth of electronic networks. One of the problems for seekers in the Pagan community is geographic isolation. In the 1970s a number of magazines arose to serve the far-flung community. Festivals began to be held which allowed people to gather and learn from each other and find traditions and teachers. But often the magazine or the tape of Pagan songs was a small drop in a very large sea of isolation. I remember how when I lived in rural Florida it was so exciting to get a new issue of *Green Egg* or *Circle Network News*. We were the only Witches we knew of within hundreds of miles. Joining with others for a Sabbat meant driving to Atlanta or Jacksonville or even Miami. Telephone calls were expensive and just not practical as a way to keep in touch.

In the 1980s I was fortunate enough to move to the Pagan-rich San Francisco Bay Area. Still, except for the festivals, I mainly knew only the people in my own area and people who networked through COG. Then about four years ago I joined the electronic revolution, and now I regularly correspond with Witches, Pagans, Asatru folk, and other earth religionists all over the world. This has been a wonderful broadening of my priestesshood. I read Tarot and teach over the Internet. I share and learn and do virtual ritual with other Witches—some old, some young, some new to the Craft, and some who are elders. We are all connected by electronic mail and newsgroups that span the globe.

One of the really wonderful things about the electronic world is that you are not judged by how you look, your disabilities, or your income level—you are judged by how articulate you are and, in the groups where I hang out, by how caring you are. I'd like to share with others how to find this wonderful electronic world, but one of the characteristics of the electronic frontier is that things are constantly changing. So I can give pointers, but the paths and nodes and access modes will change over time.

Some networks such as Usenet are fairly stable, and the newsgroups propagated there will be there in the future. Thus, I can recommend that a new electronic seeker check out alt.Pagan, alt.magick, soc.religion.shamanism, and know that they will find them. In addition, the commercial services like America Online and Compuserve have chat rooms and bulletin board areas devoted to some magical topics.

There are also mailing lists which generally have a higher level of discourse—they are limited to the list participants and are generally more civil and focused. Just by way of example, I belong to a mailing list for women Witches started by a woman in Sweden. We have shared tips on herbal remedies for menstrual cramps, discussed the ethics of magic, given each other tips on making sculpted Goddess figures, shared poetry and ritual, comforted each other in times of trial, and celebrated each other's successes. So women Witches in Europe, America, and Australia are sharing our lives daily in e-mail.

Another way that Pagan folk are connecting electronically is by Internet Relay Chat (IRC), a real-time conversation method. IRC channels such as #wicca offer a Wicca 101 class, currently on Tuesday nights, 10 P.M. EST. It offers sympathetic others to chat with, although I have found a much higher percentage of young, untrained people there than in other electronic groups. There are other channels like #magic, #asatru, #pagan, and others. I find IRC frustrating because people tend to talk one sentence at a time, so you don't get the depth of discourse that e-mail or newsgroups can give you.

Another resource for seekers is anonymous FTP sites. These are computers which allow log-in over the Internet by anyone. They hold documents and materials for people to download to their own machines using the File Transfer Protocol (FTP). There are a number of sites that have Pagan or Wiccan material and/or achieve postings from alt.pagan and other newsgroups. The advantage of FTP for a teacher is that you can put up material for many others to find. The disadvantage for the seeker is that there is a lack of quality control.

I recently downloaded a group of postings on the history of Witchcraft. Some gave the author's name, some did not. All were from wildly varying points of view and levels of sophistication. Here are some of the FTP sites:

SITE	DIRECTORY
ftp.lysator.liu.se	/pub/magickand/pub/religion/pagan
ptero.soar.cs.cmu.edu	/occult
slopoke.mlb.semi.harris.com	/pub/occult
quartz.rutgers.edu	/pub/occult
ftp.uu.net	/usenet/alt.magick and alt.pagan
wiretap.spies.com	/Library/Fringe/Occult

As time goes on, the frontier nature of the Net will be tamed. Already organizations like COG are beginning to set up anonymous FTP sites. People will be able to find out about the organization, download its publications, contact its officers—all electronically. Currently, the members of the COG board of directors are reachable by e-mail; submissions may be made to the newsletter electronically; and this connection will keep on growing as more people have online access. I think that the electronic frontier is where the next great explosion of Pagan thought and consciousness will come from.

So, Russell, how did you first discover that you were a Pagan?

I followed the typical pattern of discovering that there were others who felt as I did about nature and Divinity, rather than experiencing a conversion to Paganism. In my women's studies classes I saw glimpses of greater possibilities in books such as Rosemary Ruether's *New Woman, New Earth* and Elizabeth

Davis's *The First Sex*. When I moved to California in 1978, I used my women's studies connections to search for a Witchcraft study group.

What kinds of work are you doing in the Pagan community, and how is what you are doing different from what others are doing?

I've focused on three areas in my community work. First, I've worked in many open rituals so that the community—especially those who can't find a coven or who choose to work alone most of the time—can share our religion.

One of the reasons for this is that I have worked in the NROOGD tradition of Witchcraft for over a decade. A key element in that tradition has been providing open Sabbats to the Pagan community. In the 1970s NROOGD Sabbats were one of the few opportunities many in the San Francisco Bay Area had to experience a Pagan ritual or meet other Pagans. Now there are usually several open Sabbats every major holiday.

Second, I've worked with COG for many years, serving as assistant, editor and publisher of the newsletter, and holding various local and national board positions, including co–first officer with Rowan. I've participated in various COG projects, including its attendance at the Parliament of the World's Religions. The Parliament involved quite a variety of tasks: press interviews, serving as a priest for the ritual we did for hundreds of members of various religions and the media, chatting with an Imam from the Iowa State Islamic Association, and rewriting, editing, and typesetting COG's official information pamphlet in the week before the Parliament. Keeping any organization running involves much of the same kind of not particularly spiritual work; I've done my share of it.

Another major focus of my spiritual work has been sex. For instance, I have researched the history of sex negativity in Western culture. While the Christian attitude has traditionally been, "Sex is basically evil, but it's okay under certain restricted circumstances," the Pagan view is that, "Sex is basically good, but some restrictions are necessary." The Christian view has defined that of Western culture until the last few decades. Other influences on Western culture, such as the Jews', have fallen somewhere between the Pagan and the Christian, but the Christian view has remained the dominant one. While the Pagan community's handling of sexual issues has not been flawless, its attitude toward sexuality and the relationship between sexuality and spirituality represents, I believe, a large, positive step.

I have also done sexual healing work—not verbal counseling, but sex in a healing context. I should emphasize that this has always been done according to certain ground rules: It is always by explicit request; emotional and spiritual boundaries are clear; I never work with a student or anyone else who might think I hold authority over them. We always agree on safer-sex practices, and I always work with the blessings of my mate, Rowan. The key thing that differentiates sexual healing from other lovemaking is that my primary goal is the healing. This sounds obvious, but what it means is that my goal is *not* my own sexual satisfaction, or even having sex—sometimes what's needed turns out to be just physical closeness. Unconditional love, openness and acceptance, and the ability to manifest Divinity are healing. Sexual pressure and demands are not. I've been making notes about the techniques I use and may eventually publish them or share them privately with others who do this kind of work.

How do you see your path in relation to the earth?

I hold pretty typical Pagan beliefs: that we are part of the web of life, not special beings given dominion over the rest of it, and that humans have gotten out of balance with that web. Where I may part company with some others is that I believe it's possible to live a high-tech, information- and resource-intensive lifestyle without being out of balance with the earth. While I've found satisfaction in planting trees for the weekend, and I would like to see life changed to give us all more opportunity to feel our connection with the rest of the living world, I don't want to become a hunter-gatherer and give up my job as a software engineer or the access to experiences and information that modern technology provides.

You are an urban Pagan. How do you maintain your contact with nature while living in the city?

The bottom line for me, as an urban Pagan, is using various magical and mundane techniques to maintain a connection to the cycles of life around me. I do occasional hands-on work like planting trees, and I frequently write letters to politicians. I send checks to organizations such as the Natural Resources Defense Council, Planned Parenthood, and Zero Population Growth.

What is your personal vision for the future of Paganism?

I believe that Paganism will be an increasingly relevant spiritual path as many people feel the need for an underlying balance rather than a mere series of technical fixes to ecological problems. I believe that many will seek a path that does not retreat from all sexuality out of fear but values diverse forms of loving relationships.

Our challenge as a community is to help these people find their spiritual path using the resources available to us: our festivals, Pagan books and magazines, electronic communication, and our traditional forms of teaching through small classes, study groups, coven training, and individual instruction.

The old ways of teaching are still needed but are no longer sufficient. Electronic communication is particularly promising because access to computer networks is provided or required by an increasing number of colleges, and college is just the time when many are eagerly seeking new possibilities, new religious ideas.

We will take increasing political action to support our values of religious tolerance and diversity, and of recognizing the inherent worth of the natural, the feminine, and the sexual.

The Earthspirit
Community

The Earthspirit Community is a Boston-based Pagan networking and service organization with a national membership of approximately two thousand. Andras Corban Arthen and Deirdre Pulgram Arthen are the spiritual directors and founders of this group. While Earthspirit encompasses Pagans of many faiths, the governing body is made up of members of the Glainn Sidhr order of Witches, a traditional Scottish order founded by Corwain Ardwulf Cunningman in 1975 and based on the core teachings and practices of the traditional "lare" of a Scottish family of Witches.

DEIRDRE PULGRAM ARTHEN is the author of a children's book: *Walking with Mother Earth*. **ANDRAS CORBAN ARTHEN** and Deirdre Pulgram Arthen have released the tape *We Believe*. *MotherTongue*, a group consisting of Earthspirit members, has released the tapes *All Beings of the Earth*, *Firedance!*, *This Winter Night (A Celebration of the Solstice)*, and *Wheel of the Year*, *MotherTongue Live* (Available from The Earthspirit Community).

The interview with the Arthens was conducted in Medford, Massachussetts, in the fall of 1993.

What are some of the problems facing today's Pagan community?

Andras: I think that Paganism has an incredible potential for causing very important and positive changes in the world and that the Pagan movement as it exists today has a long way to go to get there. The movement in general tends to work against itself a lot of the time.

One thing that happens with Pagans in general, and certainly with Witches, is that because it is a very alternative practice to the mainstream models that we have in our society, it doesn't have the same kind of structure that other spiritual paths may have. It doesn't have a centralized authority or a very defined set of beliefs or dogma. On the one hand, this makes it very accessible to anyone. But that accessibility by its very nature means that anyone can join the Pagan movement and in a short time make any number of claims or profess any ideas that may or may not be valid.

There is no standard by which to gauge those persons' claims. It is not uncommon for someone to read a couple of books and start calling themselves a Witch or a Druid or the high priest of a coven. The question is, "What do those terms mean?" If anyone uses those terms, at what point do they have any kind of valid meaning? Unfortunately, there is a tendency in the Pagan community for people to want to "live and let live" and not challenge people's claims, their credentials, their experience, their authenticity. The result is that there are people who can range from the legitimately sincere but naive to the downright fraudulent and deceptive.

People can claim to have degrees of initiation or twelve years of training. This has happened so much that I think it is important that people be judged on the merits of who they are, not who they set themselves up to be. Within the Pagan movement, because we don't have a Bureau of Pagan Standards, or a Bureau of Witch Credentials, people must find out about the networks that exist that are fairly public and that have been around for quite some time. These will be reputable in the sense that they have lasted. Yet even within those there is a lot of room for disagreement. The important thing is for people to not take any claims that are given at face value. To not commit themselves to something until they have really gotten to know the people that they are getting involved with.

Deirdre: I would recommend that people start by going to one of the big festivals. At the festival they should take as many workshops as they can and ask a lot of people for recommendations. If the same name starts coming up over and over from people who you feel inside are trustworthy, check that person out. Attend some of their workshops or try to find them and talk to them alone. The festivals that exist now are so big that they are a great way to start your search.

This naturally leads us to the question of the community that you both founded—the Earthspirit Community. Can you describe what the Earthspirit Community is, what its mission is in the world, and what it is trying to accomplish?

Deirdre: Part of what Earthspirit has always tried to do is to communicate the Pagan worldview. One way we have done that is through the arts. We have always tried to have music and theater and artistic expression be part of the way that we communicate our ideas. For example, MotherTongue, a singing group, has developed because a number of us decided that we wanted to put together the chants that we had developed in the community. We wanted to record a tape that we could put out to the community as a whole. So we got together some singers and some drummers. Colin Ashleigh was very instrumental in orchestrating us, and eventually we had a full-fledged chorus of some thirty-five members, including harps, recorders, dancers, and other performers. It has been very exciting to develop writing and music for the group. Colin does just about all of the arrangements.

MotherTongue is a powerful way that we have of reaching out as Pagans into the world. It's a very beautiful and nonthreatening way that people can accept and open themselves to without getting scared away. The performances that we do seem to have a deep effect on people, although some people are better able to hear us than others.

We did an urban First Night performance this past New Year's Eve, and one of our favorite comments that a friend of ours overheard was when one woman looked at another and said, "You know, I don't think they are Christian!" It was really wonderful because it was clear that something had come across perspective-wise, but they didn't have any particular label to put on it.

What we do is to try to put across the Pagan perspectives of ancient Europe, but we don't try to convince people to convert or anything like that. We have several tapes out now, and we are planning a video. We would like MotherTongue to be an outreach vehicle for Earthspirit. We don't expect, or want, to be the Mormon Tabernacle Choir, but we do want to be a true representative of Paganism in the world.

What do you see as the relationship between art and Pagan spirituality?

Deirdre: Spirituality translates often much better through art than it does through words, whether it's dance or music or visual arts, because those things one responds to at an instinctual and gut level. You don't have to think about it or intellectualize or process it; it can reach you more directly. To me communicating something that is spiritual is more effective that way.

It is very important that we find ways in the Pagan community to support our artists, the visual artists and other kinds of performers. When you think about the great music of the world, it tends to be church music. These pieces were sponsored by the church as being a vehicle for connecting with people. This beautiful music reached people in such a deep way that people wanted to go to church to hear it. It was uplifting, it was enlightening, it was exciting, and it filled people's hearts. I would like to see Pagan music do the same kind of thing. That's the way we can communicate who we are best.

Do Pagans proselytize?

Deirdre: I don't know any Pagans who try to go out and convert anybody. I do know plenty of Pagans who try to go out and educate and who go out to do interfaith work to help clergy-people in other traditions understand a little better what we are doing. To find the places where we have common ground and can work for a common purpose, particularly with the environment in mind. I don't go out and try to convert anyone, but there are some ideas that I feel strongly about that I want to share.

There is really nothing to convert to in Paganism. It is so flexible, and there are so many degrees of participation. It's not like a church, where you have to join and put money in. If you have some Pagan perspectives alongside whatever religion you are currently a part of, that is where you are. There is nothing to convert *to*.

Paganism is one of the Earth religions. Do you see Paganism as contributing to the future fate of the planet in any way?

Deirdre: That is if we have a future! To me one of the most important things that can happen is for our world population, particularly our Western culture, to make a real paradigm shift, to make a dramatic change in its perspective of the world. To understand that we *are* the earth, that there is not this separation of "let's save the earth," as opposed to "let's save us." That we need to acknowledge the deep connections between us and every other form of life, and move from some of the human-centeredness of our behavior to a more global consciousness. To make a real shift on a deep spiritual level that causes us to act from a different set of underlying beliefs.

When a religion is geared toward transcendence and leaving this plane of existence to go to some other place where "perfection" is, [people] may not recognize that perfection could be right here. I don't think it's impossible, but I do think it's hard from within those perspectives to make the shift.

You are a high priestess, and you are obviously going to be influencing a lot of people. What is the vision that you hold for the future, for the people that you may be advising or teaching?

Deirdre: I feel that all of the conflicts we have, whether they are religious or political are all based on economy—who has and who has not. In order for there to be peace in the world we have to make that shift. It can't happen just among the upper-class, educated people. We have to find ways to go beyond that to reach people who are disenfranchised and not empowered. I see this starting in small circles and needing to spread and spread.

In the history of the world there has never been a time when there was peace. Maybe my dream of a peaceful world is not actually my vision for what I think will really happen. But I'd like to see us move in that direction. I'd like to see us acknowledge that there are other life forms on this planet that we co-exist with. That they are not there to be just "resources" for us. They are there and they are valuable for their own sake, not just for people to get energy from by eating them or using their bodies, or even by having them there to look at. They are there because they need to be there.

It seems to me that in Paganism we find people who pride themselves on being "different," and they sometimes go out of their way to appear strange. They express this in the way that they dress or behave. Do you have any thoughts on that?

Andras: There are a lot of people who feel disenfranchised by mainstream society. The Pagan movement being accessible, very open, and welcoming, it creates a place where people who feel at odds with society wind up. Like it or not we end up with people who are very poorly socialized, who are very insecure, who have been very hurt in their lives and who haven't healed, who are very needy, and who, because they haven't worked out a lot of their issues, are rebelling.

One of the downsides of the Pagan movement is that these people come and check into the community, and rather than doing something productive to heal themselves they seem to wallow in the same thing forever. There is a very strange sense in the Pagan movement of feeling and acting like victims. Some feel they have been victimized by Christianity—that the ancient Pagans and Witches were victimized by the Christian Inquisitions. They identify with that, and it gets into a lot of self-pity. People wallow in their own insecurities instead of doing something about it. I personally choose not to feel or act like a victim, and I don't take too well to that kind of mentality. I think that spiritually the Pagan movement as a whole is incredibly immature.

But couldn't this be regarded as a strength? We are blessed to be getting some very original people, ones who are not afraid to go against the mainstream of society.

Andras: In some ways this could be seen as a strength. But the problem is that before people can find their strength they have to heal themselves from the hurt and the pain and all that they have been through trying to fit into a society where they weren't wanted for whatever reason.

The potential is always there for these people who don't fit into society to create new models, but that is not happening yet. We have many people rebelling against the idea of power, for example, because of the nature of power in our society in general. In our society people may have power not because of who they are as people but rather for what has been given to them or because of what they have stolen or grabbed from other people or whatever. It's a very arbitrary type of power. As a result, within the Pagan movement are those who don't want any kind of power no matter how organic it might be. They see anyone who is in any kind of authority position, perhaps because of their experience or their talent, as someone they resent or they mistrust.

As a result we have a movement that is lacking in leadership and that is not really going anywhere. The people that we do have in positions of leadership, who have a group that contains more than five or ten people, will be resented. Groups don't work by consensus that easily if you want a long-term, effective process.

Ideally, our whole society would work by consensus, but we are nowhere near that in practical terms, so people are rebelling no matter what the model of leadership. There is a sense of iconoclasm within the Pagan movement that turns into a lack of respect for people who have achieved something. There is a real lack of community, a lack of people pulling together. There is a sense of mistrust of other people, a very competitive attitude. Sort of the "big fish in the small pond" syndrome that is very destructive to any type of community development.

There seems to be a tendency for different groups and individuals to be very intolerant of each other . . .

Andras: There are people who claim to be in support of diversity. These people seem to feel that because they are not a part of mainstream society that somehow they are exempt from the patterns found in that society. They think by a simple name change, they now can call themselves a Witch or a Pagan, that this has effected a deep and thorough change in personality.

People say things that they pay lip service to. They really believe these things, but it isn't translated into action. I'll give you a personal example. We call ourselves Pagans and Witches, but we don't worship Deities. We've had people tell us that we aren't *real* Pagans or Witches because we don't worship Deities.

The question is, if you really believe in diversity, how far are you willing to take that? Yet if the Pagan movement becomes so diverse that it can accept anything, how can you call it the Pagan movement? These are some of the things that people have not yet really come to grips with.

I was at a workshop a few years ago at a Pagan festival, and someone asked, "What is a Pagan?" The workshop presenter answered, "Anything you want to be." What I am saying is that this is a problem of the Pagan movement. I think there is too wide a sense that we all really come from the same mold.

For diversity to be real it means that people have to be really different, and what is the common denominator that ties them together that allows for the differences? In the Pagan movement if you try to define the commonalities, you will be shut up from all sides.

So how do you define Paganism for yourself?

Andras: I would define Paganism as a way of life that comes from a European tradition that is premised on the Earth being sacred, and really living that.

When you say "coming from a European tradition," does that obviate Native American or African spirituality or other non-Christian/Islamic or Jewish traditions?

Andras: I don't consider Native Americans or Africans to be Pagans. They are Native Americans and Africans.

For a lot of people Pagan simply means not Judeo-Christian, nonmonotheistic.

Andras: I refuse to call somebody by a term that they don't use to define themselves. I think it's very arrogant to say that Native Americans are Pagans. They don't call themselves Pagans. The point is that the first people who had the word *pagan* to describe them were Europeans. For a very long time Pagans were a particular class of people in Europe. It was only later when the Catholic church came to power and its boundaries went way beyond Europe that other people began to be called Pagans.

Overwhelmingly, the traditions that modern Pagans embrace are at their root European. It's only been in the last eight or ten years that there has been this interest in hybridizing Native American traditions.

Where do you hope that Paganism will go from here?

Andras: Paganism has a potential to subvert society in a healthy way. The Pagan movement is not completely makeshift. There are some legitimately ancient traditions that we draw from, and we are manifesting those traditions in a contemporary setting. We have some things in our religion that are truly ancient and which have lasted across time. We also have the ability to adapt them and to create with them. So it really becomes a living tradition.

One way to look at it is you inherit this house, a wonderful house with a lot of character. It may not necessarily fit your needs, but if you had to start from scratch, what would you build? So in many ways we have these ancient foundations that are very solid and very strong. The house that we build can be very strong because we have these wonderful foundations and we can give it the structure that we need for today. We can look at the things that need to be different and also at the things that we like about what is already there. We can assimilate the models that have worked for other people and adapt them to fit the needs of the present.

This is something that the Pagan movement hasn't really begun to do. I think that there is concern about what the legitimate ancient Pagans would have done. I don't really care too much about what people did two thousand years ago. In terms of what my life is today, it's a very different situation.

How do you see these traditions affecting the twentieth century and especially America?

Andras: By developing new models. For example, in forming relationships that are based on respect versus arrogance, that are based on community versus alienation. That are based on organic hierarchy rather than arbitrary authoritarianism. That are based on a sense of kinship and community with everything that exists. That are based on living in balance and setting priorities. The mainstream Christian society has contributed so much to the destruction of the planet that we need alternatives. That is what Paganism can do.

When did you first become a Pagan?

Andras: I guess I actually became a Witch before I became a Pagan. I always feel uncomfortable with the terminology because people mean different things by it, but I guess being a Witch is the same as being a Pagan.

What first caused you to become interested in Witchcraft or Paganism?

Andras: For me it wasn't something that I had set out to look for, although once I found it, there was a sense of this fitting everything that I had been looking for. I had not been aware that the things that I had been looking for in my late teens, in terms of life direction, could all be somehow combined into one heading. I was unaware that it was there or that it had a name.

It happened through a series of what some might call coincidences. I met a couple who were adopted members of a Scottish family of Witches. I had a marginal interest in the occult because I had broken with the church in my early teens.

Why did you break with the church?

Andras: It was actually kind of ironic. I was born in Spain and came to the U.S. when I was about twelve. I was raised and educated mostly by Jesuits. A Jesuit education is a really great education. It was very stimulating intellectually, so that by my early teens I was reading authors like Albert Camus and Sartre and other existentialist philosophers.

The more that I read the more questions I asked. The more I asked, the less satisfactory answers I got. It came down to a time when a professor said to me, "It's a matter of faith. You can't understand these matters by reason." So I guess I decided that I didn't have faith.

Since I was a child, I always had a strong sense of something beyond. I had what could be called psychic experiences when I was quite small. Between the ages of four and nine or so I would have these periodic fevers that would appear and then simply go away. While I was in delirium I would see things and talk to people and see these little people who would come and play with me except when there were grownups around. When I would tell my parents, of course there was the sense that I was hallucinating. But I always felt that there was something that went beyond the world as we knew it.

I guess that when I lost the faith, I was looking for something else that would address that feeling that I had. I tried a lot of the Eastern practices like Zen Buddhism, Sufism, and Yoga. They each had much to offer in terms of perspective and inspiration, but these practices were so steeped in cultures that were alien to mine that I felt as if I were playing at those things. Even things like Native American religion.

I felt that I was a person of Caucasian European descent; I was not Native American, I was not Chinese, I was not Hindu, I was not Japanese or Muslim, and in some ways I felt as if I was doing a disservice to those traditions.

By seeming chance there was someone where I worked who knew these two Witches. I had the same misconceptions and stereotypes that most people have about Witches. Yet when I met these people, they were very "normal" people. They were intelligent, funny, accessible, and the first time we met I thought it would take maybe an hour, but we ended up talking for four or five hours.

I asked a lot of questions, and they gave me a lot of answers. The more answers they gave, the more I had the sense that this was what I had been looking for, even if I had no idea that it existed. So I apprenticed myself to them, and they made me a Witch.

Can you remember what some of those answers were that they gave you that made so much sense?

Andras: First of all, a sense that everything is interconnected. That all things are bound together in a very subtle yet very strong way. That there is a web that binds everything to everything else. Also, that there is a dimension beyond what our senses can perceive that is very real and very present if you learn how to gain access to it. They had methods for that.

They said the Earth was sacred, and was not just inanimate matter or organic matter in the sense that a biologist or a physicist would see it but was alive. We were very much a part of that life and we were interconnected with it.

The role of the Witch in that process was of someone who had the skills or gifts that enabled her to interact much more directly with the forces of Nature.

They said our culture programs us to shut off entire regions of experience. It forces our experience into a very limited range. "Magic" as they saw it was a way to break out of a rut and enable us to fully and deeply experience the world in ways that we normally don't have access to. The role of the Witch was not only to do that but also to serve as a vehicle for other people to connect with that too. To cross that bridge.

They said the world of matter as we perceive it is not separate but is also a part of that sacredness of Nature. Our bodies are as sacred as anything else. Things like sensuality and sexuality are very much a part of our lives and are to be experienced fully, and there is no taint or sin naturally associated with that.

What "magic" enabled us to do was to experience freedom in a way we normally can't experience it. It freed us from certain shackles we have. Most of the time we don't even realize we have them, so it's hard to get rid of them. They are invisible.

So, Deirdre, what was it that caused you to first become interested in Paganism?

Deirdre: When I first became interested, I was in my early adolescence. I believe I was twelve or thirteen years old, in the late sixties. The hippie culture was really getting going, and I was trying to be as involved in that as I could at that age.

Witchcraft was one of the things that came up then, in my valiant efforts to be radical. I ended up by scaring myself out of it. It was just too "ooky spooky" and too risky. It wasn't until after I graduated from college and I was working as a waitress that I got back in touch with it.

I had been on an intense spiritual search all through high school; I practiced zen meditation and Christianity, I did Buddhist things, I read and read. Yet nothing really clicked. When I was waitressing, there were a couple of people at my job who called themselves Witches. I told them that I had been interested in that a long time ago, and they suggested that I take a class. A woman was supposed to be teaching it, but instead it turned out to be Andras. All of a sudden, through the course, I began to feel like this was exactly what I had always believed. There wasn't a single aspect of it that felt alien to me or uncomfortable.

When the class was over, I approached Andras about continuing to work with him and his group, and one thing led to the other and I am still here.

Andras, you said that you were born in Spain. I too was a little girl in Spain. I now realize that I spent years looking for that mystery and the ceremonial aspect of the Latin mass and that is a lot of what I have found in Paganism.

Andras: When I was a little boy my fondest dream was to become a Catholic priest. While the other boys were outside playing ball in the streets or in the park, I would be inside in my room giving the mass. I would take long rolls of brown paper and draw priestly vestments down to the details and cut them out and put them over my shoulders. I would get the neighborhood kids to come and I'd give them Ritz crackers for the host, and I was really into it.

I actually spent most of my childhood in Cuba. There is an old tradition there that is most often called Santeria or Lucumi. It's a hybrid sort of practice that combines the West African practice of ancestral tribal religion with Roman Catholicism. It is the remnants of the religion that was brought here by the slaves, retained under a very thin veneer of Christianity. The Yoruba spirits or Orichas are given the names and attributes of Catholic saints.

My family was from Spain, so they were very Caucasian Roman Catholics who kept themselves separate from the Cuban people who were of a mixed blood. At the same time, my family was very well to do, so our servants, maids were black Cubans. At least one of them had a mother who was a priestess, a Santera. I had a couple of experiences as a result where I was directly exposed to that. I found it very fascinating, in some ways because it was supposed to be taboo, but also because of the rituals, the drumming, and the dancing.

My grandmother on my mother's side was originally from Andalucia in the southern part of Spain, and she was very steeped in folk traditions. Even though she was a church-going Roman Catholic, she would do things like have us kids pick up the palm fronds that people had left behind on Palm Sunday at the church, and she would weave them into little dolls.

In the Caribbean there are these devastating hurricanes. My mother would do incantations, sometimes alone, sometimes with her maid, to abort the damage of the storm. My mother grew herbs in her backyard, and she knew herbal medicines for a lot of conditions. I grew up with all of that. But if you had told my mother that she was a Pagan, she would have been very upset because she considered herself to be a Catholic.

Deirdre: I grew up Unitarian. I think that Unitarianism is the closest established religion to Paganism in its focus on tolerance and equality. It is very human-centered, however, in a way that Paganism is not. But in many ways the two are very compatible. The philosophy and worldview that I have now are very similar to what I had then. But there was no ritual in Unitarianism. In Witchcraft and Paganism I have gotten that transcendence.

You have also mentioned that Paganism is a spiritual path for you. What is your concept of the Divine in that path? What is Witchcraft as a path to the Divine?

Deirdre: I don't think that I have one concept of the Divine. I feel the sacred manifests in many ways. Rather than having it be something like the image of a God that manifests in lots of different ways, I see it more as many, many ways that the sacred manifests that are all connected in a web.

It is the web that provides the continuum rather than one sentient being. I don't see it as necessarily male or female. Male and female is a very human way of perceiving things. It's a specifically biological, animal perspective. I feel that the things which we call female are very present in all aspects of reality and in all aspects of the sacred. The descriptive words that we use for "female," and the same thing is true of "male," are present in all of creation.

I don't anthropomorphize Deity in any way. I don't worship "Gods and Goddesses" or the "Lord and the Lady." Sometimes I will use specific symbols of specific Deities that have been culturally established—the various archetypal Deity forms that people have used over time. I will use them as symbols and as a way of tapping into a particular kind of energy. But I don't pray to them as something external to myself. I don't worship them or ask them to grant me a boon.

To me a God or Goddess with a human form is a symbol that incorporates various aspects of reality and energy forms, ways of being conscious. The symbol holds that.

Andras, what is your concept of the Divine?

Andras: I would say I am a dyed-in-the-wool agnostic. And I have been since my early teens; that hasn't changed. At this point I expect to go to my grave as an agnostic. I don't presume to know what lies beyond our experience in any kind of coherent form.

This is something which struck a very deep chord in me from my original teachers. They said the worship of the Universe through the medium of anthropomorphic Deities that had human guise and personality was the ultimate arrogance. This was a way of taking something that was really indescribable and that transcends all human perception, and rather than acknowledging it and letting it be, we somehow try and fit it into a nice, easily digestible, human concept.

This was simply an effort of humans to mold the world in human terms. This effort was fruitless in the effort to understand the mysteries of the universe, and it was also misguided. When I heard that, I knew that it was exactly how I felt.

I don't believe in Gods or Goddesses or worship them. Certainly, in the teachings that were originally passed on to me that was not a factor at all in any of the things that those people did. There was no worship or naming or conception of Deities in what they called Witchcraft.

In the Earthspirit Community rituals I have seen the Goddess and the Horned God used as figures.

Deirdre: That is what I was talking about before. Those are symbols which we personally find powerful and which embody a certain kind of energy. By using those symbols in ritual, just as by using a pentagram, it evokes a particular quality of energy in the ritual.

This doesn't mean that we are praying to them. In the rituals we do, those symbols are often present, but we don't ask favors of them. We use the symbols to bring the energy up in the circle and for people to feel a connection.

Andras: Nor do we call them by name. We talk about the Earth, but we don't talk so much about the Goddess. We feel that it is more appropriate to have that be purposefully vague. That vagueness translates into a sense of mystery.

Humans often try, desperately, and even pathetically, to give the unknown a shape. I chose not to do that. I make it part of my daily spiritual practice to experience the sacred in a very direct fashion every day of my life. And every day of my life I decline to name it.

What is the most primal, core aspect of Paganism for you?

Andras: For me it is the sense of an underlying force that is the basis of creation. It is the force that binds everything together. That there is an unnameable power that manifests in many ways and that transcends human understanding and that nevertheless is very real.

I think that one of the things that translates out of that is an organic and sacred linkage. Everything that exists exists in community in some way. Therefore, everything and everyone is deserving of respect and dignity. From the most complex living organism to a grain of sand.

That sounds very Native American.

Andras: One of the things about Paganism is that these basic teachings are really universal. What was a major revelation for me when I first started out was that the Pagan traditions are the equivalent of many indigenous traditions throughout the world. In a lot of ways those of us who are of European descent are spiritual orphans.

We had traditions that were as vital and as sacred as those of the Native Americans, and we lost them. There was an invasion, and some would even say a rape, that occurred which left us orphaned. One of the things I feel very strongly about is a lot of white people of European descent, perhaps because they feel a longing for their ancient traditions, have turned to indigenous traditions such as the Native American not realizing that in the process of trying to assimilate those they are contributing to further rape.

European people have virtually destroyed the cultures in which those traditions evolved. By indiscriminately trying to adopt those traditions, they are contributing to that further rape. I think it's more appropriate for people of European descent to reclaim our own indigenous traditions. We need to respect the traditions of other peoples, learn from each other, and work with each other, but also to remember we have traditions which are much more authentically ours. We don't have to rape and pillage the spiritual traditions of others.

And, Deirdre, what is the seed, the kernel, the nut for you?

Deirdre: The word that I got when I was thinking was *relationship*. I feel the real essence of it is seeing myself in relationship with all of creation: other people, the planet, other life forms; feeling a part of the greater web, movement, force, energy that is never ending and immanent.

This brings us naturally to your principle vehicle for sharing these ideas. How would you describe what the Earthspirit Community is, what its mission is in the world, and what it is trying to do?

Deirdre: [In] Earthspirit . . . we try to provide services to the Pagan community as a whole. We create networking opportunities, we foster artistic expression, and we put forth publications, festivals, and classes which help people to develop a Pagan consciousness.

People can become affiliated with Earthspirit if they are interested in supporting the activities of the organization. We put out a newsletter for those who want to stay in touch with the organization and stay up to date on what we are doing: bits of news, clippings from the media, pro-Pagan press and anti-Pagan press from around the country and the world.

Andras: There was a pilot one time for a TV show that was originally to be called *The Craft*. It was all about a woman who fell in with a group of Witches who were going to make her baby their next leader. It was just a cheap rip-off of *Rosemary's Baby*.

There was this massive letter-writing campaign that involved Pagans all across the country; we were very much at the head of that. Not only in letting other people know about it but in writing to the producers of the show and the network, the FCC, and other authorities. Not only did this show connect Witches with acts of violence, it really became an issue of freedom of religion.

They eventually changed the name of the show, but it never went anywhere. The series was not aired after that.

A lot of people seem to lump Paganism in with the New Age movement. How does Paganism differ from New Age?

Deirdre: I don't think it differs completely. Some people say that it differs by "one decimal point" due to the difference in cost of Pagan events and the very highly priced New Age events.

One thing that is considerably different is that much of New Age spirituality is head based. In many ways it's intellectual and it's oriented towards transcending, as opposed to being Earth-oriented. In that way it is a very Eastern perspective with a lot of elements of Buddhism.

Paganism in contrast is much more Earth aware; it can offer a connection with the rootedness that we have in the Earth. When I read New Age literature, I sometimes feel that is what is missing.

Earthspirit also puts on some large festivals.

Deirdre: Earthspirit organizes and creates programming for four festivals a year. The largest one is Rites of Spring, the oldest festival; 1993 will be its fifteenth year. It's one of the longest-standing and largest gatherings in the country, and it happens in western Massachusetts around Memorial Day each year.

"Rites" started out as a much smaller two-day event with everybody scrounging for sleeping space in the Boston area and has become something that is a week long. It now happens at a summer camp with cabins, camping, and a meal plan for those who want it. There are classes, performances, drumming, and ritual, and there is a beautiful private lake, so we have swimming and boating.

Anyone is welcome to Rites of Spring. But it's not something for observers to come to. It is for those who are pursuing a spiritual path that will put them in touch with the Earth. Come there if you want to learn and participate. Come there to connect with other people; we get between four and six hundred each year.

The other large festival is Twilight Covening. That takes place on Columbus Day weekend at the same location. It's not so much a Pagan gathering in the sense of an open, celebratory event. It is more of a magical retreat, an opportunity for people to spend some time with each other in small groups, learning something in depth and experiencing what we hope works as a full weekend ritual where the ritual begins when people arrive and ends when they leave. The ritual has different aspects to it. Although people remain in their smaller groups, they can connect with the movement of the segments. The ritual is very scheduled and very specific in nature, and it's been very successful. Most people who attend have a very powerful experience.

In the summer we have a festival in Cape Cod called Suntide, which is a camping event that is relaxed and celebratory in nature. It takes place near the National Seashore. The biggest event of that weekend is a ritual by the ocean with a circle on the beach, a fire, drumming, and a big lobster bake, which is a lot of fun.

In the winter we have an event called Hearthfire, which focuses on the themes of family and community and all of the different ways that we manifest those concepts, the different ways that we can be together and nurture each other. We do storytelling, music, and craft activities that include adults and children. We focus on traditional indoor winter activities such as circle dancing and other ways of keeping ourselves going in the cold and dark.

How is Earthspirit different from the other Pagan groups that exist? How is it unique?

Andras: The way Earthspirit is run is consistent with the way that most large Pagan organizations are run. It is run by a small group of people, and it is not terribly democratic. Most large Pagan groups tend to be run by the people who started the organization. Unlike most other groups there is a sizeable core community at the heart of the organization. There are fifty-odd people at this point who form the core group, so that even if Deirdre and I are the directors, there is a large group that actually carries out most of the functions.

Much of our focus is on providing service to the community. The scope of what we do is very broad in terms of the services that we provide. Most Pagan groups tend to focus on one or two things as opposed to such a wide range. We do all these things because we believe that this is what creates community.

For sometime now you have had a dream about a land-based community. What is going on with that?

Andras: That is something that we are actively working toward. We've had several ideas about how to do it. What we hope will happen in the next year or so is to find a piece of land in the central or western part of the state. We hope to move there and to start the development of an intentional community. Part of our plan includes the development of a conference center for Pagan studies. We would hope to include a Pagan cemetery as well. Depending on what kind of site we get, this might also be a place where we can hold festivals.

The people who form the core of the Earthspirit Community tend to have the same magical perspective. We see each other all the time, we work with each other all the time; there is a real strong cohesiveness that we have that is very different from what we have seen in other Pagan groups. This gives us a certain level of stability, though we go through our changes like anyone else.

Earthspirit also does a lot of interfaith work, as, for example, when we helped to kick off the interfaith service that began the celebration of the twentieth anniversary of Earth Day in Boston. Out of the nine people that were in that committee I think that five of us were self-identified Pagans. Three others were into feminist spirituality. The last person was a Unitarian. We came up with this ritual that included a Muslim call to worship; we had a rabbi blowing a shofar, a Native American medicine man smudged with sage. But it had a very Pagan flavor to it. This was done at the Esplanade in Boston in front of two hundred and fifty thousand people. Any Pagan seeing that ritual would have identified with it. It may have been the largest Pagan ritual ever held!

The Covenant of Unitarian Universalist Pagans

The Covenant of Unitarian Universalist Pagans (CUUPS) was formed at the 1985 Unitarian Universalist Association (UUA) Assembly in Atlanta, Georgia, to enrich and strengthen the religious pluralism within Unitarian Universalism by promoting the study and practice of contemporary Pagan and earth- and nature-centered spirituality. Founding members included Leslie Phillips, Linda Pinty, Christa Heiden Landon, and Reverend Michael Boblett.

The work of CUUPS includes networking among Pagan-identified Unitarian Universalists, developing educational and liturgical materials on Pagan spirituality for UU congregations, encouraging thea/ological (Goddess-centered) inquiry into the Pagan resurgence, promoting inter-religious dialogue, providing support for Pagan-identified UU religious professionals, and working for the healing of the earth.

Unitarian Universalism is a merged denomination that came from a union in 1960 of the American Unitarian Association and the Universalist Church of America. The two groups had experienced parallel histories and had discussed a merger for well over a hundred years. Many of the differences between the two were sociological and liturgical rather than theological. Organized Universalism is a strictly American phenomenon. The American Unitarian movement is intellectually related to movements in Britain and in a number of Central European countries. The term "unitarian" was picked up because it had been applied to the early New England proto-Unitarians by their detractors, and it was used so much that it finally stuck.

JERRIE HILDEBRAND is a cofounder of the North Shore CUUPS chapter in Salem, Massachusetts, and a former chapter head for the Witches League for Public Awareness (WLPA) and the Wiccan Information Network (WIN), New England Branches. She is also the illustrator of *Walking with Mother Earth, A Storybook for Children*, published by D&J Publications. The interview was conducted by phone on March 16, 1994.

Are you a Pagan?

Yes, I am. I was raised in the farmlands of upstate New York where respecting nature, animals, and the earth were primary to who you were. The conscious awareness that there was a word for it probably happened about twelve years ago when I realized that there were so many things in Jewish/Christian doctrine that did not fit for me. Things like the Trinity, male authority only, separateness from being part of the earth, and that women were left out of ritual, leadership, and language in a demoralizing fashion didn't seem to make sense any longer. Also my own Native American and Pennsylvania Dutch roots, the ways my father taught me about respecting life and nature, which didn't seem to click with Christian teachings.

Anyone who knows the Pennsylvania Dutch knows that there is a lot of magic practiced amongst the people there, with Christian teaching mixed in. Some called it *Pau wauing*. You can see it in their superstitions, hex signs, the *pauwau* doctors [i.e., healers], and so on. It was all part of bringing their magical traditions in with their Christianity. They never let go of their old folkways. Knowing all that about my family background led me to wonder what the name for all of this was. Was there a name for it other than calling it "folk tradition"?

Then I happened to move to Salem, Massachusetts, because the man I married lived there. I found out that there was this word called "Pagan" and that it meant "country dweller." That seemed pretty easy to resonate with except I remembered all of my friends in Catholic church collecting money for the "Pagan babies," so in many ways it didn't make sense to me either. Were they collecting money for the country kids?

Knowing that language sometimes limits how we describe or express ourselves, I started asking questions and going to the library and reading. I discovered that essentially what my father had been teaching me when he taught me how to skin a deer and how to foster crops and things like that were old ways. The more I read, the European stuff sounded like the Native American stuff to me only with their particular cultural twist. So I kept on reading, and I decided that "Pagan" was really what described me, especially since I am a country girl at heart.

When I got to Salem I found out that there was a person here who was teaching classes. Her name was Laurie Cabot. I took her classes about nine years ago. Her Witchcraft One class was basic meditation techniques and ways to use parts of the brain that were very common sense to me. To some people it was a new thing.

Having participated in Silva Mind Control, the EST training, and other transformational workshops, I realized that her classes were very similar. So I thought that maybe there was something I was missing, and I decided to take her second-level class.

In her tradition when you finish Witchcraft One, you are considered what would be equal to a "first-degree" Witch. At the end of Witchcraft Two you were equal to a "second-degree," though there were no initiations up to that point. You just got a little card that said you were a member of the council, and it had her signature on it.

At the end of the second class it seemed like it was more of the same, practicing learning how to read someone's health by hearing their name, their age, and where they lived and consciously tuning in to that person, and so on. Some of it I was pretty surprised that I could do, especially with the health stuff. I thought it was not enough information to know someone. Out of the few people whose names I could practice on, I was able to come up with some pretty concrete things that were validated as accurate.

I did not go on to her third class. It was called "The Religion of Witchcraft." It seemed like every time I'd start to think about taking the religion class something would come up and I wouldn't take it. After a while I started to listen to that, and I just trusted that I shouldn't be taking that class. Since then I have realized that her religion class was the one she did her initiations from. I was clear that if I were to be initiated into a group that I needed to be sure my life's vision and mission were in alignment with that particular group. It was not only for my own magical energy but for the group too. For me this particular path would not have been appropriate.

Can we talk a little bit about the "Salem scene"? A lot of people associate Salem with Witchcraft, which I have always found very interesting because none of the people that were hung there were actually Witches. The only people who were accused of Witchcraft in Salem were good Christians. The people who were real Witches did not die.

Right. The one woman, Tituba, who was a real Witch, was never executed, only jailed. She must have been a very competent Witch!

So what is it about Salem that seems to attract so much attention?

It's Laurie Cabot and the media. She moved here, and modern Witchcraft began to be associated with the city of Salem. In the 1960s the volunteer director of the local Chamber of Commerce convinced Elizabeth Montgomery to come to Salem and film some episodes for *Bewitched*. He was interested in bringing tourism to the North Shore, and he began calling Salem "The Witch City," since everyone who came here was interested in the Witch hysteria.

Well, Salem does have a large Witch population, does it not?

Now, its fair share, yes. How large is up for debate. Being a Witch in Salem means different things to different people. It depends upon if you are approaching being a Witch from the point of view of a shamanic way of life or whether you are approaching it from participating in the religion of Wicca. I personally have learned there are distinctions between the words Witch, Wiccan, and Pagan.

The first book I read and which really inspired me was Sybil Leek's *Diary of a Witch*. She didn't go around talking about this ritual and that ritual, this spell or that spell. In the interviews I saw of her on TV and read, I never saw her acting the way that people around here seem to act. She seemed to be very calm about it all; she wasn't "acting out." What I see around here is many people dressed in black wearing a lot of trappings who call themselves "Witch." Technically, I don't know if that means "Witch." For me and how I have been taught since those earlier days in Salem, it does not.

To me Witchcraft is a very deliberate, conscious exploration of what it takes to transform one's life through one's will. It's not something that I need to broadcast to the whole world or that I need to capitalize on or that I even need lots of like minds around for. That is what caused me to withdraw from the Salem scene and spend some time by myself searching and listening to that inner self that is my guide.

Eventually, I missed having people around, and I began to look for community again. That's when I discovered the Earthspirit Community. They were hosting a Religious Tolerance Symposium here in town, and people at the local Unitarian church asked me if I knew anything about them. At the same time, I had become involved with Unitarian Universalism, where there are a lot of people with different religious and spiritual thoughts sharing together and being involved in interfaith conversation and dialogue. This was what I had always thought was possible beyond just being in a Pagan community, but I had not found it until I stumbled onto Earthspirit and Unitarian Universalists.

It seemed like Earthspirit and the Unitarian Universalists were fostering the same kind of dialogue. I liked the idea of a Pagan organization doing interfaith work. I knew in my heart that Unitarian Universalism and Paganism could fit together—I just didn't know how. It was a question I was willing to live with because I like to live my life inside of questions rather than answers. I think a large part of transformational work is a willingness to sit inside of questions.

Some friends told me about CUUPS, and I asked people at the First Universalist Society here in Salem about it. I thought it was really interesting that there was a Pagan organization inside the UUA. I began teaching a course at the church called "Cakes for the Queen of Heaven." There is a part of the course where you are invited to bring your local Witch in. All of a sudden I was getting invitations from all of these UU churches to come and speak, so I approached the CUUPS organization to see what it had to offer me and this community as an outreach program to the local Pagan community. Eventually, five people from the "Cakes" course got together, and we created a chapter.

What kinds of things does a CUUPS chapter do?

Each chapter is autonomous. Its activities are specific to the individual people who happen to come together to form the chapter.

What is the advantage to joining with the Unitarian Universalist church?

You are not seen as a fringe religious thinker; you are perceived as already established. The interfaith community will take you much more seriously, at least that's what happened for me in Salem. They began to see that Paganism was something different than what they were seeing every day in Salem. That it was more than people's clothing, physical presentations, and constant complaining that the word "Witch" was being used wrong.

Do you have a vision for where you would like NSCUUPS to go?

I see us a catalyst for ending the "turf wars" between the groups here in Salem. We allow anyone to join us in worship and play; we don't care what tradition they are from. We are non-Deity-specific in our presentations, specifically for that reason. We are not interested in being facilitators, but we would like to be that bridge.

You know as well as I do that Unitarian Universalist congregations can vary dramatically. A Pagan who is walking into a Unitarian Universalist congregation really has no idea what he or she will encounter.

Absolutely. It has to be done with much caution, responsibility, and accountability. I'm not saying that to be flip about it. It's no different than telling anyone else about being Pagan or investigating the variety of Pagan groups out there. You must be very diplomatic and give up the human need to be right. That one ingredient—the need to be right—has created more religious fighting and bickering than any other human way of being throughout mankind's history.

Our group is successful by what I call sharing and caring. Sharing about the various Pagan traditions of many different cultures and creating cross comparisons into the congregation's reality and caring about the congregation as people of this planet and not putting their way of thinking and their lack of education down. It is ultimately the lack of education that creates fear.

Our group and the Binghamton, New York, group are prime examples of CUUPS chapters that have done an incredible amount of work in the local Pagan community, where they act as a bridge between the Pagan community and the church.

They [NSCUUPS] offer a place for worship services to happen, for gatherings to occur, and things like that. That is what our organization could be on a national level. And I'm not sure that we are ready for it. It's a lot of responsibility for UU Pagans to be willing to integrate themselves into the Pagan community at large. It is, I think, as confronting as for a Pagan community to integrate themselves into interfaith dialogues with other organizations.

What is so daunting about the Pagan community if you are a Unitarian Universalist Pagan?

I think that UU Pagans are pretty heady people. Many of the rituals that I have been to in UU Pagan groups, with the exception of Salem and Wisconsin, pretty much are based on books and intellectual speculation. There is not much heart-centered experience. In many UU groups it is also very female-based conversation. Our group is very duality-based, not only in ritual but in teaching of even the "Cakes for the Queen of Heaven" course. We welcome men and women.

So what would be your recommendation?

Communication needs to open up between chapters in the organization and be fostered. We are our greatest resources, but at this time most of us don't even know where chapters are located. At the chapter and national levels we also need to start opening up the opportunity for Pagan dialogue to occur from Pagans other than just those who are writing books.

CUUPS chapters need to look into Pagan organizations in their areas and begin creating relationships with them. They can then begin to participate in the larger Pagan community and expand their worlds. They can also begin to support the larger Pagan community with their time-honored stand of religious freedom and respect for world religions.

BRIAN REDDINGTON-WILDE is a practicing shaman and trance dancer, minister, and armorsmith. He was for many years an active member of CUUPS and is a founding member of Ecospirit New England, as well as a former member of the Church of the Sacred Earth/the Wiccan Church of Vermont. He was interviewed by phone on February 21, 1994.

What religion were you raised in?

I was raised Catholic. I left Catholicism several years before I officially became Pagan. I was actually considering joining the Catholic priesthood and, having taken a long hard look at it, I realized that I couldn't be a priest or even a member of the religion. The major factor that contributed to that was that I disagree with Christian morality and their long involvement in military affairs throughout Western history. The Ten Commandments say, "Thou shalt not kill." There are circumstances where I believe I might kill, defending my life, my home, or maybe even my country. I couldn't belong to a religion that said "Thou shalt not kill" when I realized that there were times when I might. I also don't agree with the Catholic morality that says you should have children no matter what the circumstances, regardless of world population levels and our ability to feed and care for everybody.

A lot of people leave the Catholic church, and they don't necessarily become Pagan. What was it about Paganism that attracted you to it?

In the 1980s, when I was living in Vermont, I had already been aware of Pagans for some time. A housemate of mine started up a coven which eventually became the Wiccan Church of Vermont and later the Church of the Sacred Earth. I didn't become Pagan at that point because all I had been exposed to was Wicca, and I didn't identify with being a Witch or with being a member of a coven. I didn't have anything against it; it just didn't click with me. Later on, when I stumbled across the concept of shamanism and started looking into that, it clicked with me in a way that Witchcraft never had.

Shamanism is an approach to practicing ritual that relies heavily on ecstatic experiences. The form that I work with in particular is ecstatic dance. I see the priesthood as being a functionary of people working for the Divine and relating the views of the Divine to the people. Shamanism is the reverse of that. It is a functionary working on behalf of the people and representing their cause to the Divine.

Who trained you in this?

I am self-taught. A lot of the experiences I had prior to discovering shamanism led up to it. Once I found out about ecstatic dance and going into trance with it, it suddenly made sense of a lot of experiences I'd had while taking dance classes and doing performance dance. A lot of the training was just trial and error, looking into techniques used around the world. I do a lot of reading in anthropology and history of religions. I look for techniques that are used in a number of world cultures, figuring that those are ones that are likely to work in a variety of cultures including this one.

Ecstatic dance is common to a number of different cultures. The concept of using a trance journey to go to "the Otherworld" is a common one. You travel to the Upper World or the Lower World to meet the different Deities, usually with the aid of drums or rattles. The deep tone of the drum or the high pitch of the rattle can change your brain-wave pattern so you can get into an altered state.

How did you discover and get involved with CUUPS?

My wife had been raised as a Unitarian. After we were married, she became Pagan, and I became a Unitarian Universalist. It worked out very well because the two religions complement each other very well. Modern Paganism puts a great emphasis on experience, and the UUs place a great emphasis on analysis and critique. Each of them adds something that is missing in the other.

CUUPS was formed in the late eighties. One year at the UU General Assembly, the annual convention for Unitarians, people started talking about how it would be nice to form an affiliate Pagan spiritual group within Unitarian Universalism. There are a number of such groups within the Unitarian Universalist Association. There is a Christian Fellowship, a Jewish one, a Hindu one, and probably a few more. Of the three people who initially came up with the idea for the Pagan group, one was a person in Chicago, and the other two were from the Boston area.

Relationships at the Boston area church were a little bit rocky. We weren't entirely welcome there. It's a very conservative congregation, and they were charging us rent for the room. There were a number of prominent members of the congregation who weren't too happy with us being there, and there were conflicts over not being able to book the space when we needed it. Eventually we realized that most of the members of the group were also members of the Arlington Street Church in downtown Boston. So we moved the chapter from Cambridge to Boston. We were welcomed in by the Arlington Street congregation and immediately invited to present children's education classes, adult religious education classes, and even a Sunday morning worship service.

At that time the chapter started working on the United Nations Environmental Sabbath program. That was something the UN Environment Program had come up with, to encourage all of the world's religions to do something once a year to honor the environment. We put together a worship service for that, which we presented at the Unitarian Universalist General Assembly in 1989, in New Haven, Connecticut. We also presented it as a Sunday morning service at the Arlington Street Church in Boston.

Ecospirit New England was a group that formed after the New Haven General Assembly. Bob Murphy, a CUUPS member from Rhode Island, called us to announce that the Earth Day 1990 organization was getting started, and that they were interested in adding a religious component.

I contacted the Earth Day offices in California, introduced myself, told them about the work we had done with the United Nations, and I wound up becoming the New England religion coordinator for Earth Day 1990, developing inter-religious services throughout the New England states.

The largest one was here in Boston. We had about three dozen religious organizations represented: Baha'i, Buddhist, Christian, Jewish, Muslim, Native American, Pagan, Sufi, Unitarian Universalist, you name it. All of the folks that we worked with on that project wanted to keep going once the Earth Day offices closed down, so we incorporated Ecospirit New England to continue with the inter-religious environmental work. Since then this has provided the vehicle for a lot of inter-religious work being done across the country.

Are you still a member of CUUPS?

No. They weren't providing any services to individual members or to chapters. The newsletter would rarely come out; it was supposed to come out quarterly and may have appeared once a year. The way the General Assembly is set up, member groups of the Unitarian Universalist Association have so many workshop slots that are available to them during the General Assembly. There are three slots for each group over the course of the conference.

CUUPS being an official organization had three slots, but the national never allowed local chapters to use the slots. When the Boston CUUPS chapter wanted to present the Environmental Sabbath service, the national CUUPS was not willing to sponsor us. We got our workshop slot through the Unitarian Universalist United Nations office.

The CUUPS people preferred to bring in outside people to speak, like Margot Adler and Starhawk. People who weren't necessarily active in the Pagan community, but who may have published related works. That caused a tussle because we kept trying to convince them to set aside one of the slots for the chapter closest to the site where the General Assembly was being held, and they simply refused to do it. They wanted to have complete control over what was being presented and who was doing it.

The Arlington Street Church still has an active Pagan group, we just don't call it a CUUPS chapter anymore. It is now called Q-Moon because it meets on the Friday nearest the quarter moon. The group is specifically for people who are interested in exploring gender as sexual identity through ritual and magic. We have adopted the term "pan-sexual" as shorthand for gay, bi, lesbian, transgendered, other, and heterosexual. We are fully accepted by the Unitarian church.

The way that Arlington Street Church works is that there are two ministers who are called by the congregation. They handle the services at the church, rites of passage for church members, and the like. There are also ordained ministers who are just members of the congregation, about six or eight of us. We take it in rotation to handle rites of passage, marriages, and memorial services for people who are not members of the church who call up looking for ministers to do a service for them.

Did you go to Divinity School?

No. I was ordained through the Church of the Sacred Earth which is a legally incorporated church whose requirements do not call for a divinity degree. Even though I am not an ordained Unitarian Universalist minister, my ministry is fully accepted by the Arlington Street Church, and I do outside services in rotation along with the other ministers.

It sounds like a very tolerant bunch of Unitarians.

Congregations within the Unitarian church vary greatly. Just a few blocks away from the Arlington Street Church is Kings Chapel, which is very Anglican in its outlook, extremely Christian in its orientation. The farther west you go, the more liberal the congregations are, more so than here in New England. I would advise Pagans who want to get involved with the Unitarian church to check out the local congregation. There may be more than one within driving distance. Particularly in areas of the country where Pagans would be likely to face discrimination, being connected to the Unitarian church will give them a little bit more community recognition and particularly safety for children.

If you want to raise children in an environment where they will be taught a variety of religious traditions and liberal values and have a larger community of support than they would get from just a small coven, the Unitarian church can be a good place.

Can you talk a bit about the Church of the Sacred Earth?

It was originally called the Wiccan Church of Vermont. It was incorporated in 1985, and I was ordained with them in 1988. Most of the members are in New England. It is very much like the Unitarian Universalist of Pagan groups. We changed the name when we realized that there weren't very many people in the church who still identified themselves as Wiccan. It's a congregational church; member groups can define themselves how they will as a coven or a circle or a grove. There are members who do not belong to a congregation.

One thing the church does that's fairly unique is to separate the role of ministry from the role of spiritual vocation. You don't have to be in the priesthood in order to be ordained. We leave it up to individual members and member congregations to define who the people are who have spiritual vocations, priestesses, shamans, whatever.

The church as a whole recognizes the ministers, and the ministers are the official public spokespeople for the church. They are expected to have a ministry outside of the church, working in the larger community. In my case I do my ministry through Ecospirit New England.

The member congregations meet on the full moons or the Sabbats or whenever they decide. The whole church has a meeting three times a year. The meeting moves around, usually to some place where there is an active local congregation who will take it in rotation. There are about thirty paid members and a number of unpaid people who show up for events. There are probably about fifty people active in the church right now.

Anything else that you would like to add?

For people who are looking to establish connections with the Unitarian Universalist church: If they get started as a CUUPS chapter, the congregation will more readily recognize them as a part of the Unitarian Universalist Association. It will help to build bridges with the congregation.

On the other hand, what seems to be happening across the country is that member chapters are dropping out of the organization after a few years when they realize that they are not getting support from the larger organization. They find that they can make it fine on their own. But starting through CUUPS certainly helps to build the connections that are necessary to work within a congregation.

Most of my work has been in inter-religious work through Ecospirit New England and also through the Boston Clergy Breakfast. That's an informal group that meets once a month for breakfast and also does other projects on occasion. Every month there is a different speaker; they address a wide range of topics which relate to being a minster here in the city of Boston. People have done presentations on the homeless, on legal issues facing clergy, the history of minority religions, and other topics. This month someone will speak on the history of the Krishna Temple here in Boston.

What do you do for a living?

I get some money from Ecospirit New England which comes from grants. I also do armorsmithing. I build suits of armor for the Society for Creative Anachronism and other medieval reenactment groups. My business is called Goblin Tooth Enterprises.

I think it is worthwhile to let people know that there is a place for Paganism in inter-religious activities. I've been working very strongly at it since 1989, and it's been going very well. In working with other clergy I have found them to be much easier to work with than many Pagans would anticipate. I've developed some very close friendships with clergy from a variety of traditions, from Krishna to Baptist and everything in between.

Pagan
Artists

$\mathbf{M}$uch of what emerges from this book is the perception that, through all the many diverse pathways of modern Paganism, we are creating a new society and culture. No emerging culture has ever been created in a vacuum; it has always been influenced by the triumphs and mistakes of the past. The names for societal roles may change, but the needs remain the same. Every healthy culture needs its dreamers and artists.

Paganism is blessed with many exceptionally talented people, and in this chapter we spotlight a very small representation of its artists, musicians, and performers. The common thread that runs through all these people is that they hold their artistic work to be a sacred path and an integral part of their Pagan orientation.

ELSPETH AND NYBOR are Witches and Pagan artists. They are the founders of Haven, a loose-knit Pagan community in the Washington, D.C., Virginia, and West Virginia areas. Nybor worked for many years as a commercial artist and an illustrator in Minneapolis and New York, where he was known as James R. Odbert. Today he works in mixed media, using colored pencils, airbrush, watercolor, oil paint, and pastels against a black background. He has been published widely by science fiction, Pagan, and commercial book companies. Elspeth is a fabric artist who works in the medium of soft sculpture. They were both interviewed in Keyser, West Virginia, in July 1993.

Nybor, how long have you been a Pagan, and what religion were you raised in?

I was raised in the Congregationalist religion, the Protestant church. As a church they were very open, very liberal. They encouraged us to go to other churches and attend services and then discuss them in the youth group. Of course, the churches that they encouraged us to see were all in the Judeo-Christian tradition because that was all that was available. But it was fairly liberal, and nothing was totally rejected without scrutiny.

I suspect that I have been a Pagan all my life. That's primarily because I knew all my life that I was going to be an artist. There was never any doubt about that. Part of that is that a muse sits on my shoulder and drives me, and the muse is Pagan. So I can't really remember when I wasn't a Pagan because I have always had this muse.

When I realized this, it was not a blinding flash or a vision, it was just that as my work emerged, I found myself more and more drawn to the themes and the ideas which were embodied in Paganism as opposed to the themes and ideas embodied in Christianity. Hence I became a Pagan. But there was no cut-and-dried moment.

I visualize my muse as a person leaning on my shoulder, looking over my shoulder and saying, "Is that really what you want to do? Is that correct?" She criticizes and she leads me and guides me. When I don't work, she kind of sulks and gets mad at me until I do work. I don't actually see her; maybe someday I will draw her.

A lot of people ask me where my ideas come from. I get them from everywhere. The most beautiful and moving painting I have ever seen had a Christian theme. It was Rembrandt's *Peter Denying Christ*. I saw it at Expo '67 in Canada. I was moved to tears by it. But *not* by the theme. It was the incredible emotional content that the artist had put into it and the utterly marvelous technical rendition of the content.

I could always draw. I was a good artist very early and drew constantly, much to the dismay of my teachers in school. My schoolwork was always littered with drawings on the sides. I went to art school, and the first thing they gave me was a drawing class, five days a week, five hours a day. Drawing from the model.

They did teach me some fine points of drawing, but mostly what they were teaching was large-muscle control, so I could draw with my whole body instead of just with my fingers, and along with that a way of working so that I wouldn't have to *think* about drawing. I would think about the subject I was drawing, but I didn't have to think about the technicalities of how my fingers were drawing.

When you get good enough at that, you think, and it just comes out the end of your fingers. That frees you to think emotions, and they become implanted in what you are doing. Whether the emotions are planted in an abstract picture or a realistic picture, it doesn't really matter, they are there. This took quite a while for me to accomplish; it happened after I left school.

Now I was free to just think about things, and they would naturally just come out. What I thought about were themes related to Paganism—erotic themes, joyful themes, and beauty. Not the ethereal joy of ascending to heaven but the earthy joys of being with a woman here on the earth, the joys of a sunset, the joys of walking among trees and the shading that you get in the area between the forest and the field. The feeling that you get being between the light and the shadow. These are marvelous, subtle things.

These are to my mind very much Pagan-related themes because they involve the earth and the mind and the feelings and emotions, not on an intellectual level but rather on an emotional and gut-feeling level.

How has being a Pagan affected the mundane aspects of your life?

One way it has affected my life is that a long time ago I made a deliberate decision to remain childlike in my outlook on life. Not childish, childlike. It's a somewhat simple outlook, somewhat naive, but it enables me to look at things clearly for the art; it goes into the art and affects it. My friend Oberon G'Zell is very childlike in his outlook on the world. This is a very Pagan way of being, in the sense that we can find wonder and joy in what we see. A lot of the themes in the art work are Pagan themes—for example, there is a piece called *Welcome to the Wood,* which shows the Horned God, Cernunnos, the antlered God of the forest who dies every winter and is reborn in the spring.

We naturally find ourselves discussing these topics with the customers who buy our artwork. Some people come up to us at the Renaissance fair, and when they see a horned God they say, "Ooh! The Devil!" They want to know why we have painted a picture of the Devil. You can see that they have been misled by the Judeo-Christian thought that anybody with horns is a representation of Satan. So we tell them that it's not the Devil or Satan; it's a God from a different mythology than theirs.

Our personal lives are going to be affected when the Tarot deck comes out. A long time ago a man named Bruce Peltz, a big science fiction fan, decided that he would get a whole bunch of science fiction artists and have each of them do a part in a Tarot deck. I was one of the people he approached, and I did a card of the Three of Swords. This was just about the time I had learned to read Tarot. I began thinking that I should do a deck of my own. The Tarot is full of Jungian archetypes and other marvelous things, and no artist, in my opinion, can look at the deck for any length of time without thinking how *they* would do this or that card.

It took about ten years before his deck came out, and in the interim I started doing my own deck. I then realized that the idea of just doing the standard Rider-Waite deck in my own style was not really what I wanted. I was in therapy at the time, with a Freudian therapist—I wish it had been Jungian therapy, because I probably would have gotten more out of it, but what I did get out of it were my personal symbols. A lot of those went into the deck. I made the deck to reflect our society as it exists today instead of the society of the late 1800s or early 1900s which is what most Tarot decks seem to reflect.

I have a card for right-hemisphere brain function and a card for labor negotiations, concepts that did not even exist when the other decks were put out. Many people have told me that this is a watershed deck. I'm not all that certain that it is. Only time will tell. I hope the deck will be out before too long, but I'm not letting myself get too enthusiastic about its presence, because as our society contains some very heavy erotic aspects, so does the deck. Society doesn't like to have these areas exposed, and five publishers have turned me down.

How do your artwork and your personal spiritual path combine?

The artwork has clarified the spiritual path. I've recently done a piece called *She Who Was First*. It is a picture of a woman who became almost two opposite things, the symbol for Virgo and the Harpies from Greek mythology. She is Lilith. I like her a lot. There is not much written about her, but if you go to the Gilgamesh legend, she was the woman who was cast out. Innana replaced her. The tree that she lived in was made into a bed for Innana so that Innana could sleep with the male God. This was symbolic of the casting out of the matriarchy and the beginning of the incursion of the patriarchy. I find her so interesting that I may decide to take her as a titular Deity. This has all come about through drawing.

I'm a Virgo, and I have done a black and white zodiac set; some of them have appeared in *Green Egg*. I'm trying to find a male Deity that would make a pair with the female symbol of Virgo, which I have also used as Lilith. There just isn't any listed with her. The only one that is listed with her is not really a Deity, because she is mentioned in the Talmud as having been the first wife of Adam. Adam is not really a partner with her because she left him! She wouldn't want to be paired with him. She left him because he insisted on being "on top." She wouldn't buy that. I suspect that when she was first in existence as a primary Deity there was some male aspect arrayed with her, and when the Hebrews brought in their God as the top one she happened to be around and she got used for this position. But there is very little that we know about her.

This is one of the things that the art has enabled me to do because it has provided the foundation for the thought of it. One of the things that I think is so good about where we are in Pagandom is, particularly in the male aspect, we have been cut off from our roots, and Paganism is addressing that.

I disagree with most of the people who are doing a great deal of research and trying to rebuild Paganism in a scholarly way. I think there is much more value in building it anew for our society, rather than trying to bring it forward from a different culture. To do that you really have to twist it to fit our time.

For example, our society has no formal rites of passage for young men. I've been doing research into what these rites of passage should be. Not what did the Masai do, or the Australian aborigines, or the ancient Celts, but what is necessary in a rite of passage. What needs to happen to the person going through it, so that he gets something out of it and society gets something out of it. Both sides have to gain from it.

You do go back and look at past examples, but you don't look to see *how* it was done, rather you look to see what element was common in all the various rites across cultures.

Elspeth, when did you first discover that you were a Pagan?

When I met Nybor. I wasn't even aware that it was a religion until then, though I have since realized that in my own way I had been searching for it all along.

What about it attracted you?

It didn't involve buildings. Ritual was held outdoors, which I had always felt was a better place to reach the sacred. The people were truer to their own ideals than most of the people I had met as Christians. There didn't seem to be the hypocrisy. And there was no ruling factor, there was no "Big Daddy" to come and rescue you when you made a mistake.

When you commit a mistake in the Earth religions, *you* are responsible. Nobody is going to come along to absolve you of it. There is also no one who is going to come along and reward you. You are responsible, good and ill, for your own actions.

You are the founder of a group called Haven. How does Haven worship? What kinds of things do you do?

Haven is a very fluid thing. It's not even really a group yet. It is an amorphous, ever changing, extended family/clan/tribe. Frequently what we do as a group is very spontaneous. We have family circle every Saturday night wherever we are, and the people that feel attracted to be there are there, and what happens is determined by who is there.

We generally use the usual format of casting a circle, of calling the quarters [honoring north, east, south, and west and calling upon the guardians of the various directions]; other people do that rather than myself and Nybor. We may use four different traditions in one ceremony because we always try to include as many people as possible to participate in any ritual that we do. We then welcome the Lady and the Lord without calling them any particular name. This is not an effort to get away from using a name, it's just that we both feel that by not designating one Deity we honor all of them. Then we ask if there are any works to be done. We are frequently asked to do healings. We raise power in a number of ways. We discuss how the land project that Haven is undertaking is coming along. We share our sacred drink, which is a particular formula of ours, and cakes.

We are looking for a couple of hundred acres at present. Probably in southern

West Virginia or Kentucky, possibly Virginia. Hopefully, it will be close enough so that those people who don't live on the land, who work in the D.C. area, will continue to work with us. The core of Haven as we envision it will be no more than three or four families who live on the land full-time and primarily grow the food that will be eaten and do the things to honor the Earth and make Her healthy.

It is my feeling that one cannot own the land. It is not for us to "own" the Earth. She is a being. But by holding legal title to it, we can keep that small space from being further harmed and perhaps heal it. Organic gardening has been my focus for a long time. I envision an ongoing project of finding old strains of fruits and vegetables, the ones that are dying out, and planting and preserving them to keep their genetic qualities available.

Other plans are to have a space for Pagan gatherings, a place for small groups and individuals to come for retreats, and an opportunity for everyone, whether living there or not, to get their hands dirty. Everyone will do something physical depending upon their area of interest.

I don't know anything about government or financing or any of these things yet, but I am learning.

They say that behind every strong man there is a woman. What has been your role with the artwork that you and Nybor are selling all over the country these days?

I've never quite thought of myself as being "behind" him. It's more like holding his hand and being beside him. I have been influential in his developing this particular technique that he is working in because I work with him on the color. He is color-blind. I also run back and forth to the studio that does the printing. I help with the naming as everybody else does. I try to see to it that Nybor does not have distractions when he is working on his art. I don't see this as subservient or as giving up anything. I see it as my half of the work. This is *our* work together.

For twenty years or more I have been a fabric artist and reasonably successful both creatively and financially. In 1991 when my neck was broken in an accident I felt that it was a sign that I was being called upon by the Goddess to do another work and I see that as teaching and building the Haven community. I tend to do the practical stuff. I've had to turn from being a fantasist and an idealist to taking care of the necessary things because Nybor doesn't like to do that. Other than that, we love each other, and I guess I support him in that way.

Can you give some anecdotes about what it has meant in your life to be a Pagan?

We've always had one or two young people living with us, in their late teens or early twenties, people whose lives are out of order and who have no place to go. I don't mean people who are psychologically disturbed or in trouble with the law, just young people without direction. We always need more hands to help with Nybor's work and with keeping the house and working in the yard.

These people come in, and they become part of the family. They stay about a year or two, and when they are grown and healed and ready to go, they go on. There have been six or eight of them so far.

We feel that we are here to help. When somebody tells us that they or someone they know is in trouble, our first thought is, "How can we help? What can we do for them?" This is what we are supposed to be doing. I don't know any better way to explain it. Of course, all of this caring and giving comes back to us. One young man in Baltimore was purchasing an original painting and paying us by the month, and I called and asked if he could give me two months at one time because we needed the money. He said, "Sure!" and hung up the phone. Six hours later he showed up on our doorstep with his partner and loads of food and a check for $900, which was the rest of the money he owed us.

People do this because they know that they have received love and caring and that we will always do for them when they are needy. Our house is always open for anyone who needs it. Even when we are not here. We tell people that if they need a refuge or a place to go, they can come here; just don't leave it any messier than it was and be good to the cats.

IAN CORRIGAN is a musician and vice archdruid of ADF. He is a cofounder of the Chameleon Club and the Association for Consciousness Exploration (ACE), the organizers of the Starwood Festival. He is also the author of *Portal Book*, *Symbols and Rites of Druidry* and *The Book of the Dragon*. His recordings include *Once Around the Wheel*, *Songs of the Wheel*, and *Ian Corrigan Live at Starwood!*. He was interviewed at Wellspring, a Druid gathering near Sherman, New York, in May 1993.

What religion were you raised in?

I was raised in a watered-down Protestant sect called the Church of Christ/Disciples of Christ. They were a sect that is now fairly liberal, but the church that I was brought up in was not; it was a rather stodgy Christian church. I basically blew it off as soon as I was old enough to think. I was fourteen or fifteen when I realized what I really wanted to do was find a coven of Witches and be initiated. That is what I understood as being Pagan at that time.

Fortunately, after some teenage experiments in the backyard, celebrating the Pagan holidays, and leaving a salt circle burned in my girlfriend's parents' back lawn, (we actually killed the grass in the shape of a pentagram), it took me about another five years to really connect with a circle of people whom I could work with. It was a noninitiatory Wiccan circle in Cleveland, administered by a Gardnerian coven, to the extent that we let them administer anything. It was called Moonlight Grove. That was probably in 1978. In 1980 I went to my first Pan Pagan festival. There were five hundred Witches and occultists there at a campground in northern Indiana. This was the festival where everything really took off. At this time North American Pagans began to be convinced that there was such a thing as a Pagan community. That oaths of secrecy and inflated egos wouldn't keep us from creating a community.

I was part of the group that founded the Starwood Festival, the largest Pagan-related festival in the U.S., which will be in its thirteenth year this summer. We are not a Pagan group; we're a bunch of hippie weirdos. There are a lot of Pagans and Witches in the group. It's called the Chameleon Club, and it runs the festival. Last year there were a thousand at Starwood, including about 120 kids. It happens at the Brushwood Folklore Center, near Sherman, New York, in the third weekend of July. It is always timed around the 23rd of July, when the Dog Star Sirius rises over the Nile Delta, signifying the beginning of the inundation [in Egypt].

In the early eighties through my travels out East, I ran across some old college Pagan friends of mine who had joined one of the covens of the Tuatha De Dannan in Providence, Rhode Island. I met some of the elders of that tradition who were at one of the early Rites of Spring gatherings in Western Massachusetts. They had brought their acoustic band and were doing Irish and English traditional music, which I had been doing for years. We hit it off real well, and before I could turn around, I was living in Rhode Island and taking my Wiccan degrees. After I took my third degree I couldn't think of any reason to stay in Rhode Island, so I went to Cleveland and ran a coven for a while.

I always had said to Isaac Bonewits that I would become involved in a local Druid grove when someone else organized it, I was just too busy. Some people finally said they would do it, and so I was willing to get involved and help them with ceremony. That became Stonecreed Grove ADF, where I'm still senior Druid.

So how is what you are doing unique in the context of Paganism?

I don't think that what I am doing is terribly different from what a number of other people are doing. I make an effort to blend scholarship and art. I think hard scholarship is important, and I think that speculation and experiment is the only way to turn the fragments of ancient tradition that we have into anything like a modern religion.

Most of my work in the Pagan community is, first, writing and either leading or directing ceremonies for our grove—I either write them or consult with the people who do write them—and giving workshops and lectures on Celtic culture, Celtic magic, or the mechanics of magic. Meditation, performance of ritual, trance work. When I go and speak or perform at a festival, I am usually doing three or four hours of workshops and teaching and maybe an hour of music.

How do your music and your sacred theater relate to your personal spiritual path?

My music relates to my personal path because it allows me, when the inspiration strikes, to craft beautiful things for my work. My path is very much the exteriorization of internal reality. I'm always looking for a better way, a verbal hook that will make somebody who doesn't really understand say, "Oh, there it is. I get it," and suddenly the meditation is working for them.

In art I am a utilitarian. I think that a decorated spoon is much more valuable than a six-foot-by-six-foot canvas. I prefer the *Book of Kells* to Chinese calligraphy. That carries over and makes me a sort of a high church kind of guy. I like ritual with a lot of tools and props and things I can display and hold up.

You are really a bard, aren't you?

Oh, yeah. On a good day. On other days I'm just a singer. I was lucky enough to have parents who, when I was eight, told me I was going to learn a musical instrument. My Pagan music interest rose directly out of my interest in traditional British and Irish folk music and Renaissance music. I have always loved vocal music, and there is lots of great a capella singing and harmony singing in the British Isles tradition. I still only play enough guitar to accompany my singing. I'm a decent songwriter. I'm inspired, but I don't have a large body of original songs. I am more of a performer and interpreter of songs.

As time has gone by I have become an adequate to good composer of ritual poetry. I don't write the kind of poetry where I express my inner self to the world or expose the guts of my humanity or any of that sort of stuff. I am interested in poetry as a voice for the Gods. Praise poems and trance induction are the facets of bardry that I work with.

There is no functional difference between a guided meditation where you walk someone through an inner-world landscape and story telling. I actually believe that there was *really* no functional difference in the ancient days when the bard would sit around the fire and recite the adventures of the heroes and the people listening were not just treating it like television. Especially when you hear about different stories being proper for different occasions and the luck that arises from hearing a story recited properly and on the proper occasion. So I have been making an effort to move in that direction.

My hero is Robin Williamson. He is the only person I would certify as a Celtic bard working today. There are wonderful Celtic singers and musicians, but they are really on the level of minstrel. They don't have the high spiritual angle that Robin Williamson manages to express. He has inspired me a lot to pursue recited pieces. As the result of not being able to play the harp and steal his version straightforwardly, I have been forced to work up my own version of the Spoils of Annwn.

So I really mostly consider myself an entertainer. I am glad that I have developed a store of ritual songs that I can use in worship, but I am just as happy to sit around with a bunch of people and sing five-part harmonies by the fire.

My Pagan work is really focused on the creation of ceremony, the crafting of magical techniques inside the Celtic Pagan aesthetic. I consider that to be as much an art as playing guitar and singing songs, if not all in all a higher art. It's more complex. It's like sacred theater. I've actually done some of that, scripted stuff where people take the parts of the Gods and walk them through and all of that. It's been interesting to move a little away from that.

In Druidic liturgy, which is what I work with now, it's more of addressing the Gods as spiritual beings, making offerings to them, and not being quite so ready to have them impersonated by members of the group. That is something we have never done in ADF . . . and maybe we ought to try it!

What is a bard?

A bard is a maintainer and transmitter of lore, a preserver of cultural heritage, an entertainer, to some extent the voice and conscience of a tribe. They used to say that the bard had the warrior's fate in his hand. It was the bard who was going to write the songs about that warrior before and after his death. He would determine how the warrior's memory would be held by the tribe.

The bard also had the power of satire, so he was also the conscience and expression of the group consciousness of the tribe. There are damn few of them, and I approach being one on a good day. I am still just a jongleur, a minstrel.

Okay, so you are a bard in training, a baby bard, and you are living in America of 1993. How does that fit into American culture?

It fits into the neo-Pagan subculture. To hell with American culture!

How do you see this Pagan subculture influencing American subculture? Do you carry a vision for the future? Where would you like to see all of this go?

It won't be long before we have public Pagan worship in most cities of the U.S., Pagan clergy involved in interfaith councils, a real understanding by the general public—or at least by the general public that reads anything—that there is this Earth-religion movement and inside of that the neo-Pagan movement.

I think the only real way we can do it is by example. We can do it by magic, but that will still be a slow process. Corporations have very powerful magic, after all. We are building a thought form, and they are building thought forms. When you own as many bio-survival tickets [money] as they do, then people believe your belief system very wholeheartedly.

DEBORAH ANN LIGHT is a performance artist, Hedge Witch, and member of the clergy of the Covenant of the Goddess. She received a Master of Arts in Religious Studies from Vermont College of Norwich University in 1985. Collecting poems from many sources, she pieces together verbal quilts to confront, commemorate, and comfort the realities of human life. Her performance pieces acknowledge rites of passage, and recognize the stereotypes of today's culture and revisions of history. She explores the pain and power of women's midlife and celebrates the eternal creation birthed in daily chores. Her performances honor the earth as she presents alternative creation myths. The interview was conducted by phone on March 24, 1994.

Are you a Pagan?

Yes, very definitely. I am a Pagan Witch.

When did you discover that you were a Witch and a Pagan?

I was fortunate enough to go on a trip to Ireland with Starhawk in 1982. The title of the trip was "From Megalith to Metaphor." On January 3, 1981, I was visiting friends in Tunbridge Wells, England. They were staying at a spiritual retreat house there that was run by the Church of England. There was a very ecumenical service every morning that it was considered polite to attend. So I was sitting there vaguely listening to all of this, and it was all "He, Him, Lord, King," and I thought, "Why is it He, Him, Lord, King?" Then my next thought was, "Why do I care?"

I discovered that I did care. And I started to explore whether there had ever been a female Deity. I'm fifty-eight years old, and when I went to college, which was in the fifties, women's studies didn't even exist, much less people like Marija Gimbutas [author of *The Goddesses and Gods of Old Europe* and other books].

Three times I saw the ad for this trip to Ireland. I knew that they had worshipped the Goddess in prehistoric times, and that this trip was going to visit sites in prehistoric Ireland. My grandmother came from County Cork, and I had always wanted to go to Ireland, so I went.

The first night fourteen of us gathered in a hotel room, and we went around the circle telling why we had come on the trip. There were two people from Australia and others from the United States and from England and Canada. It was a very mixed group. I kept hearing the word "Witch." The left side, the very conventional side, of my brain, went very rigid and thought, "My God . . . Witch?" and the right side of my brain thought, "This is going to be *very* interesting."

As I said, it was led by Starhawk, and there were some very powerful Witches on this trip, members of the group that is now called Reclaiming. We did ritual all over Ireland, except that we didn't go into the North and to no site that was closer to this period of time than 500 B.C.E. We were working with very ancient sites and with very ancient energies. There was a site in Kildare where there were several standing stones. We did ritual there, and I saw purple flames come up. Now it doesn't surprise me in the least that I saw this, but at that time I didn't believe my eyes.

I did my first trance work on the cliffs of Moher. I remember that trance as clearly as you and I are talking, and it was twelve years ago. A *wonderful* place to do your first trance work. The sun and the grass and these wonderful fuzzy brown caterpillars and the wind and the sea gulls flying . . .

When I finished that journey and came home, I knew that this was for me. It made great sense, and of course it was an extraordinary initiation. Every day started with a circle being cast, and we would then do a grounding with the Tree of Life and then everyone would discuss how they felt.

What was it like to work with Starhawk like that?

Well, you see, I didn't know who she was. It was quite wonderful and all very natural. Now Starhawk is a friend of mine, so she isn't as awesome, but even so, to work with Starhawk is still pretty awe inspiring. At that time it was just enchanting. I think Starhawk does the finest trance work of anyone I know.

After that I really wanted to get the Goddess exploration organized, so I came back and did a master's degree in an independent adult study program. As part of that I went to my first gathering. It was at the point where Reclaiming was just beginning. They had an apprentice program, which I did. That was in 1983 when they were just starting their Witchcamp in Mendocino.

So when people get to talking lineage, I say that I am an eclectic egalitarian as opposed to fam trad or Alexandrian or Gardnerian or what have you. My heritage is Reclaiming, because that's who I was trained by. They are my teaching elders.

Is that the style you work in now?

No. I am a solitary. You have an independence when you are a solitary. It's kind of like an adult degree study. There is a freedom, but you don't have the wonderful support that a coven gives you. On the other hand, you don't have to deal with all the "stuff" that can come up in a coven, too. I travel a lot doing the performance pieces, which is another reason not to belong to a coven; however, there are two covens that are gracious enough to consider me an elder. One is Foxwood in Laurel, Maryland, and the high priest there is Lord Orion. Then there is Circle Oak Haven, which is in Mastic, Long Island. But they are fifty miles away from where I live.

I have been extraordinarily lucky in that I've been able to go to many gatherings when I was doing my academic work and afterwards. It was after I got my master's that I developed the minor art form that I have with the performance pieces.

While much of those have been given to women's groups and to Unitarians, the most fun is to do them with Pagans. For one thing, they know what I am talking about. I always do them as a Witch, in my Master of Arts robe. I talk about the robe, and then I do my pieces, and then I say I am a Hedge Witch.

What is a Hedge Witch?

A Hedge Witch is a Witch who lives in the country. We collect things. We wander the roads and byways and gather what we find caught in brambles and under rocks and in the roots of trees. Then we gather people together and we spread out our pretties, and we say, "See? Let me show you this. Let me tell you what this said to me." I also collect poems. I put the poems together, and then I gather people together and "I muse as I meander in the meadows and metaphors of myth," says me, quoting myself.

One of the things I'll do is perform ceremony for those who ask for it. Someone once called me up and said she wanted a memorial service for her mother-in-law whom she loathed, and did I have any suggestions? So I said, yes, and then we talked about the basic framework of ritual, that the point is to get everybody involved and to use basic symbology that people may not entirely understand. But you can cast a circle with practically anything. You can do it in your kitchen and pull the symbols from there—the salt shaker, the faucet, the box of matches, and that sort of thing.

I used to use a lot of literal hands-on symbols, which was how the Hedge Witch thing started. I was really collecting symbols to stand for the elements and the Crone, and I had a series of dolls and so forth. Then I gradually, as my performance became more comfortable, dropped the props. Now I just do it verbally. Would you like to hear my generic circle casting? It came to me in the shower. Many people have heard it.

Sure!

You know that as Witches we can cast a circle anywhere and that we ourselves are the altar. You begin in the east with the air. Take a deep breath and blow. You see the air? Then we come around to the south, which is the fire, the will and the determination. To do that, clap your hands. Feel the sparks? And around to the west, the place of the emotions and the intuitions and the dreams that is represented by water. Where is your nearest, handiest water? Stick out your tongue! And around to the north, the place of the wisdom and the place of the purification of the body, spirit, and soul. Clasp your hands and know the unification.

That's how the circle is cast. We are now between the worlds! That really did come to me in the shower, and it's great because I never do a presentation without creating sacred space. You can do this with Unitarians, you can do it with the Hadassa, you can do it with anybody. Nobody is going to get uptight. It's totally nonthreatening, and furthermore they've giggled and you've got them relaxed. Their left brain has shut up, they are in a place to take in the poems and hear what I have to say. The poems go into the right brain because that's what poetry appeals to.

At the end when I'm finished, I will say, "The Earth, the Water, the Fire, the Air returns, returns, returns, returns." And then, "The circle is open, Blessed Be," and I take my glasses off. I lower the script, and generally they are nice enough to applaud. Sometimes there are those wonderful moments when they just sit there sort of awe struck, and that's great fun!

Have you ever had somebody walk out in a huff?

No, I haven't. But then I do this in fairly safe space. When I have spoken in Unitarian churches, I do a lecture called "Hecate's Wheel," which boils down to Witchcraft 101. It's a reduction of my thesis, which says what the Craft is and what we do and where we do it and how we do it. It goes through the myths of the wheel of the year and the Goddess and the God and so on. After that I might do "The Goddess Is Alive, Alternative Creation Myths." Those are poems starring the Goddess Herself, featuring Lilith and Eve, with Adam as a walk-on.

Then there are discussion groups afterwards, and that's where you get the interesting questions. You always get asked about Satanism. You generally get black magic questions about Black Witches. At that point I generally say, "We have Witches of all kinds, but we don't consider it polite to discuss their skin color." That generally shuts them up about that one.

Do you write poems?

I do, but I don't use them in performance.

Are you working with COG at this time?

I'm a member of COG and I have my clergy credentials from them, and at the moment I serve on the Interfaith Committee.

Is that how you ended up at the Parliament of the World's Religions?

No. I went to the Parliament purely as an individual spirit, as a solitary. I had many friends who were going, and I am very interested in comparative religion, particularly in ritual and symbology.

When I was there, the three organizations—COG, Earthspirit, and Circle Sanctuary—asked me if I would represent them in the assembly of spiritual leaders, because they were all sponsoring organizations of the Parliament.

Why do you think that they picked you?

I am of a certain age. I think I probably have a certain presence. They knew I wouldn't disgrace us; I know how to mind my manners as it were. Also, I didn't have presentations to do. All of those leaders, Selena Fox, and Andras and Deirdre Arthen, and Phyllis Curott, were very busy and very booked. Beyond that, I don't know. I was very deeply honored and said, "Oh, wow. Gosh. Of course I would."

What was the Parliament like for you?

It was a glorious adventure. It was the biggest, most magnificent festival you can imagine. It was full of color and sounds and music and dance and beards and hair and turbans and saris and crescent-shaped swords . . . the Sikhs wore crescent-shaped swords.

There were the magnificent robes of the Catholics. And the black of the Catholics. And there were the Pagans. Selena Fox had asked me if I would walk with Circle in the opening procession, where everybody was in high gear, where the Catholics were in their best bib and tucker, which is so beautiful as far as the colors go.

Somebody had an extraordinary sense of humor, because we met in rooms where they were putting all the groups together—the Buddhists and the Unitarians and the Zoroastrians. To get us all organized they had us meet in separate rooms with about ten religions to a room. There were signs all around the room giving the faith, the religious tradition. There was the sign for the Roman Catholics, and right next to it said, Wicca. So there we all were. That was wonderful.

It was very funny because at the beginning of the Parliament we didn't speak, we just kind of looked at each other. By the end of the Parliament we all mingled and chatted, and a lot of people had realized that we were all just people and nobody was out to "get" anybody else.

What about the Greek Orthodox? Did you interact with them?

I didn't. I heard about their leaving, but I didn't see it. At the beginning I was just a participant, just one of six thousand people.

What were some of the most interesting conversations that you had?

One was at the assembly, where we were in a very large and beautiful room and there were twenty-six tables with eight people at a table. The tables went from A to Z, and I was at table Z, which I adored. I swiped the Z; I have it.

You Hedge Witch!

Of course. Wouldn't you have? I also have this wonderful card that says "Reverend Deborah Ann Light, Neo-Pagan." That was how they dealt with us. The assembly met in the Art Museum in Chicago. We were bussed over there. On the second day we were waiting for the bus, and I was chatting with a Catholic priest who happened to be from Portland, Maine, and I said, "Oh, my secretary is from Rumford, Maine." We were talking about Maine and Maine winters as you do with people, and he turned out to be the bishop of Portland, Maine. So we are chatting away, and my friend the Indian, who was at my table, came up. The priest from Maine put his arm around me and gave me a hug. He was friends with the Indian gentleman, and he said, "This is my friend the Pagan, and she will have me a Pagan before we are through." I am quite sure that this was the first time that a Witch and a Roman Catholic priest have hugged each other in the streets of Chicago in broad daylight!

We did a wonderful ceremony in the park, we did a full moon, blue moon ritual. We planted pumpkin seeds in the park and watered them with the idea of seeding the world with health and with love, communication, consideration, and awareness. Then we went into a spiral dance, and everybody had a good time.

I walked home with a tall black gentleman from North Carolina, and we were talking about the Parliament. He too was a member of the assembly. I was saying that perhaps the "Global Ethic" would go around the world like a pumpkin seed. I said, "You know how when you plant pumpkin seeds they will come up where you plant them, but they will also come up on the other side of the garden and over by the garage and then on the neighbor's lawn? They just go out anyway they want to go." I was using the garden analogy because he was from North Carolina, and I figured he would understand. We got to the hotel and shook hands goodnight, and I read his name tag, because we all wore name tags the whole time; they gave your name and your tradition. He was a bishop of the African Methodist Episcopal church. Again, here was the matter of the Witch and the bishop talking about the spreading of the pumpkin seeds, the nature analogy.

Sitting here in western Massachusetts, I don't remember the local papers carrying anything about the Parliament. I hear that the Boston Globe *ran something, but I don't generally read that. It doesn't seem to have been an event that fired the popular imagination.*

Well, no. Religion isn't sexy, and that's why. How excited can you get about the media? The media were interested in the fact that the Greek Orthodox contingent walked out. They got excited about some of the Jews who were upset with Louis Farakhan. They got excited about the Witches having a problem getting a permit to put on the ritual in the park.

But it did hit the media in religious circles. And that's really what it was intended to do. They got together an assembly of the religious leaders so that the leaders would disseminate these concepts to their congregations, to the people that they came in contact with. It wasn't designed as a media event in the first place.

Can you summarize what the Global Ethic was trying to say?

The last paragraph reads, "Earth cannot be changed for the better unless the consciousness of individuals is changed first. We pledge to increase our awareness by disciplining our minds, by meditation, by prayer, by positive thinking. Without risk and a readiness to sacrifice there can be no fundamental change in our situation. Therefore, we commit ourselves to this global ethic, to understanding one another, and to socially beneficial peace-fostering and nature-friendly ways of life." The initial declaration ends with that, and the concluding paragraph of the whole thing says, "In conclusion, we appeal to all the inhabitants of this planet. Earth cannot be changed for the better unless the consciousness of individuals is changed."

And that is one of the things that I have been saying about the Parliament. That when we saw each other one to one, when people saw the Witches and heard what we had to say, when people saw the Native Americans and the Rastafarians or any of the less than totally Christian mainstream, they saw that we were just people who were as spiritual and as conscientious as anybody else.

"We pledge to work for such transformation in individual and collective consciousness . . . . Together we can move mountains. Without a willingness to take risks and a readiness to sacrifice there can be no fundamental change in our situation. Therefore, we commit ourselves to a common global ethic, to better mutual understanding, as well as to socially beneficial peace-fostering and earth-friendly ways of life." That is the way the Global Ethic ends. There will be no new global order without a global ethic. The global ethic is to be responsible adults, and I'm not talking grownups. Certainly, in this culture "adult" is a tough word. "Responsible" means cleaning up your own shit, and if there is other people's shit, cleaning that up too.

Another point that they make is "a fundamental demand that every human being must be treated humanely. There must be a commitment to a culture of nonviolence and a respect for life. A commitment to a culture of solidarity and a just economic order. A commitment to a culture of tolerance and a life of truthfulness. A commitment to a culture of equal rights and of partnership between men and women." Those are the large issues covered by the document.

How did the different groups react to the theme of equal partnership between men and women?

There is no way to answer that question, because we only met for three days. Each table discussed different things. This is a beginning document. The point of this was for people to take it all over the world and then to discuss it, to consider these matters. It says, "You shall not commit sexual immorality." Or in more positive terms, "Respect and love one another." Also, "We condemn sexual exploitation and sexual discrimination . . . . Young people must learn at home that sexuality is not a negative, destructive, or exploitative force, but creative and affirmative."

I don't even know how the Witches did with this, because we weren't going back to the hotel and gathering everybody together and discussing it. Everybody there was speaking on their own. There was no press, no reporters. It was very much a private enclave. There was no taping; none of that was allowed, so everything that was said in the assembly was private. The press didn't like it either.

Some things are more sacred than the press!

Exactly. There were very extraordinary people in that room, the great religious leaders, the Dalai Lama, and other people as important as he is, Hindus and Muslims and Sufis and so on.

Will there be anything like this in the future, or do we have to wait another century?

They are working on that. As a member of the assembly I do get the information and the newsletters and letters. Ideally, it will be in different countries, but I don't know. It's too early to tell. This is a thing that has to be digested. It's also very expensive and very complicated to put on.

Religious assemblies do go on around the world all the time; one just isn't aware of them. This was the first time that Pagans and indigenous peoples were there. We were not going to be hushed up or pushed to the back of the room, either.

The Native Americans were not going to have this happen. The Witches were polite, and they were there and people came to our lectures. I didn't do a presentation, but the ones that were given were packed. People stopped you in the halls when they saw your name tag. People would see the word "Wicca," and they would ask, "What's that?" and then you would describe your religion in three well-chosen sentences, which is an interesting exercise.

What do you think are the implications of this for the Pagan movement as a whole?

That's hard to answer. How can you make any statement about "the Pagan movement"? It's like trying to trap amoebas. I have had requests for copies of the Global Ethic from all over the world. I took it as a directive to send it out. That was part of my gift to the ethic, my gift to the people who put in all of the work. I think that people *are* thinking about it.

All I know about is Witches. I think the Craft is increasing greatly, and as people mature, as people have children, as people deal with how to raise their children in "our faith," as people battle for religious freedom, as people go after women's rights, black rights, gay rights, there is much more political awareness than there was. There is certainly much more environmental awareness than there was ten years ago. I think that the Witches are doing a great deal to teach environmental awareness, whether they are doing it deliberately or not. All of our public celebrations are related to the earth and to the care of the earth.

MAGNUS (JEFF) MCBRIDE is an extraordinary stage magician, shaman, and drummer. The Magic Castle Award currently caps McBride's long list of honors, which includes the Mandrake d'Or (Paris), International Magic Award, the Grands Prix Magique de Monte Carlo, Magician of the Year by the American Society of Magicians, and the rarely bestowed Star of Magic in the International Brotherhood of Magicians. His many television credits include PBS's *The Ring of Truth*, CNBC's *Dick Cavett Show*, CNN's *Show Business This Week*, HBO's *Entertainment Weekly*, and dozens of shows throughout Europe and Asia. He recently appeared in an episode of *Star Trek: Deep Space 9*, playing, appropriately, a hallucination!

To encourage his fellow magicians to explore the ancient roots of their art,

McBride has founded the Mystery School, and he is cosponsor of the WorldMagics Festival, which celebrates multicultural traditions and "enviro-magic." He was interviewed by phone on May 1, 1994.

When did you first discover that you were a Pagan?

I think it was very early on in my life. I used to find myself making shrines in the woods. I grew up in the forest in Rock Hill, New York, in the Catskill Mountains. I would build my little special places in the woods out of stones. I'd find special stone formations and build on to them, or I'd bring old hides and animal bones that I found in the woods and dress them up. That was really my first theater, in the forest, playing magic in the woods.

What religion were you raised in?

Roman Catholic. I was an altar boy. Now I'm an "altered boy."

What was it about Roman Catholicism that led you away from it?

I don't think it led away from me . . . it just fell off. I think it was one of the influencing factors behind me wanting to be a magician, watching the Catholic mass and the eucharist. It was very magical with the incense and the singing. When I was going to church, the mass was still done in Latin, and that was all very strange and mysterious. That's where the words "hocus pocus" come from. In medieval times the street conjurers would do a parody of the Catholic mass. The high magic of the Catholic mass is when the priest holds up the eucharist and says, "Hoc est corpus diem"—"This is the body of Christ." When the magician would hold up his prop and it would disappear or change, he would say, "Hocus Pocus." So magic and religion were linked in many ways.

Can you talk about the connection between magic and Paganism?

I think that if we trace the roots of theater, we find ritual. When we trace the roots of ritual back, we find shamanism. The origin of all performance theater, of all show business, is shamanism. My path has been to reconnect the shaman and the showman—"Showmanism," as it were.

How did you get your training as a magician, and how did you get your training as a Pagan?

I think that magic is a "way." The way I got to the way of magic was through music, because I wanted to be a drummer. When I was in third or fourth grade, I took out a music book in the library, and right next to the music books were the magic books. The first thing it said in the magic book was "never reveal your secrets," so I had to make the book disappear. I kept it in my private collection.

I started as a self-taught magician. In my excursions to New York City I would run into other professional magicians at the magic shops. That's where I started on my path to being a "showman" magician. But my original love was the drum. That is what brought me back to the origins of magic after I trained at the American Mime Theater and studied Japanese dance and Kabuki and martial arts in Asia.

I came back to the U.S. and attended a Rainbow Gathering in Central Park around May Day. Someone handed me a drum during one of the drum circles there. It was Garrick Beck, the son of Julian Beck, who was one of the founders of the Living Theater. Garrick Beck is one of the elders of the Rainbow Family. He handed me his drum, and that turned me back on to drumming again. During the course of the day I was back in a drum circle and wanting to know more about the drum as a transformational tool. I got the name and address for the Earthspirit Community and attended my first Rites of Spring that year.

Is that where you officially began your training as a Pagan?

No. A couple of years before that I had been studying the connection between stage magic and ritual magic. In the underground magic scene there was a journal called *The New Invocation*, which explored the connections between performance magic and ceremonial magic. There has been an underground movement for the last twenty years exploring the connections between the two magics, which a lot of people feel were one and the same in their intention and their design.

The shamanic healer creates a mood of possibility of magical transformation and takes people into nonordinary reality to access different states of consciousness where healing is possible. I think that in today's world that is still what the magician does. The magician reawakens people's sense of wonder in the natural world and reminds them that reality is subject to change without notice. They give people a place where they can journey to when life gets difficult.

You have been working that more and more into your performances haven't you?

Yes, much more. We've also been exploring it in larger groups. Every year in May, at Ananda Ashram in upstate New York, we run "Mystery School." Eugene Burger, America's foremost philosopher on performance magic, and Robert Neale are two of the other teachers who teach there. The school is set up as an experiential magical retreat, a place for magical entertainers who are interested in exploring other aspects of magical arts, as well as people who are involved in ritual theater who want to know more about the practical performance side of theatrical magic.

We do initiations and group rituals that are designed by those who attend the school, as well as workshops, master classes, and classes on theory and technique of performance magic and the history and origin of magic. We use drumming, dance, movement, and mask work. We have sessions to go over works in progress, where we explore new and alternative ways and contexts in which we can present magic for modern audiences. We use techniques from all different traditions of magic, not just Western magic or just stage magic. We expand it out to a global magic community.

Are the people who come to this primarily stage magicians, or are they Pagans?

Many are stage magicians, and there are many who are exploring spiritual paths which have led them to explore performance magic as a way to awaken people, as a way to open people up to the wondrous and the miraculous. Magic is something that alters your state of consciousness. What we are doing is exploring new ways and some very old ways of working magic for modern audiences using all of what we know.

As a result of all this, have people had mystical or spiritual growth experiences?

I think that on an individual basis people have experienced certain break-throughs. For one they have discovered that there are many more people pursuing magic as a spiritual path than they once thought. There is a growing community of magical folk who are walking this path and who think that it accelerates inner growth.

Are stage magicians working actively to bring this back to stage performance?

Yes. We get to do that at the World Magics gathering at Brushwood Folklore Center every summer. We take what we do at Mystery School, and we work it for the public during the first week of August. The World Magics Festival is a cross between a magical gathering and a performance magic convention. It's a very alternative gathering, people stay at nearby bed and breakfasts or they camp on the land. For three days we have very intense workshops exploring the different aspects of magical performance, and we create group performances and installations in the forest. It's all open to the public, and it's an annual event.

You have received some pretty impressive awards in your career. Could you give a sketch of the highlights of your performance work?

I tour Asia, mostly Japan and Taiwan, every few years. That is where a lot of my inspiration in mask and movement has come from. I think my first big break came when I was working in Atlantic City, and Diana Ross saw me. I toured with her as her opening act after that. I was combining many alternative theater disciplines that were not being utilized by the magicians. I worked with mime, mask, movement, percussion, and a lot of shaman's tools in my performance. That was very unusual at the time. That's why Diana Ross picked me up.

I got to work at Radio City Music Hall and opened my own show in New York off Broadway called "Mask, Myth, and Magic." That was in the late eighties. In 1986 I won the Grands Prix Magique in Monte Carlo. I was presented with the silver wand by Prince Rainier of Monaco. That's an invitational where the best magicians from all over the world are invited to compete. There is a jury that judges the competition.

In 1992 the American Society of Magicians' parent assembly gave me the

Magician of the Year award. That is the magic society founded by Harry Houdini.

In 1994 I received the Magician of the Year award from the Academy of the Magical Arts at the Magic Castle in California, which is the magician's "Oscar."

When you received all of these awards, did people ask you about the Pagan or mystical underpinnings of what you were doing, or do you discuss that with people?

Most of my performances are wordless performances where I use a lot of symbolism that speaks to the subconscious. Although I never overtly discuss my personal spiritual beliefs, I am sure that a lot of it is impacting the audience on many different levels. I am more about showing than telling. I'm not trying to use my performance platform as a pulpit from which to convert. I work symbolically and metaphorically and use the tools of a magician.

Most of my work centers around masks, around peeling away different levels and different layers. I think that's a metaphor that works in today's society. Many people feel trapped at different times in masks of their own creation. My character on stage creates all these marvelous masks that give him all these marvelous powers and ends up trapped within them. I think that's a statement that reflects today's society. People create these social and political personas and then get trapped in them and are unable to be liberated from them.

As a magician on stage I realize that the magician just mirrors the personal magician within everyone. If they can see me create, get trapped, and then liberate myself from these masks, perhaps they are living my experience vicariously through my performance. It's like all shamanic performances, where the shaman goes through different ordeals for the good of the patient and the tribe. There is a healing that takes place by witnessing this in theater. It has different levels that it works on. People like to be taken into another world, of nonordinary reality. People are always looking for safe ways to alter their state of consciousness, and magic is a very safe and clean way to do this in today's world. It also gives me the opportunity to work my personal magic inside of my public magic and to integrate the two worlds and heal the split between the two magics.

How do you see your path in relation to the earth?

Working with groups of magicians and forming intentional communities of magicians and deciding to have our gatherings on the land rather than in hotel rooms has put us more in contact with and in balance with the magic of nature. One of the things that we are working on is called "enviromagic," which is a double-edged word. We create these ritual dramas in beautiful sacred spaces in nature and bring the audience into them. Some of the messages and underlying themes are about how inseparable the magic of nature is from the magic of the individual and how the different elements work around and within everybody in their daily lives. And how an earth out of balance is a dangerous place to live. When we live in a global society that is rushing toward the brink of catastrophe, it is very important to balance the elements of nature around us and within us. A lot of our magical performances have environmental themes, and they take place in natural environments, allowing people to experience wonderful times out in nature. I think it's very necessary for artists to reflect that in their work.

You have won all of these awards now; you are at the top of your profession. What are your personal goals at this point? Where do you see yourself headed, and what are your challenges?

Many magicians are coming up with new ways to saw a lady in half or new ways to float a woman. I'm trying, with the help of the alternative magic community, to create a new context for people to experience magic in. And to create ritual spaces where magicians can go to have magical experiences. One of the things that I believe as an entertainer and as a person is that in order to give an audience a magical experience, you must first *have* a magical experience to give. You can't give a gift that you don't have to someone.

That is why I am working toward creating a new context for people to be able to enter into new places to experience magic in new ways instead of just creating new illusions and new effects to blow audiences away in a theater. My goal is to take people out into new environments to explore any type of magic that reflects a new type of thought and a new type of idea.

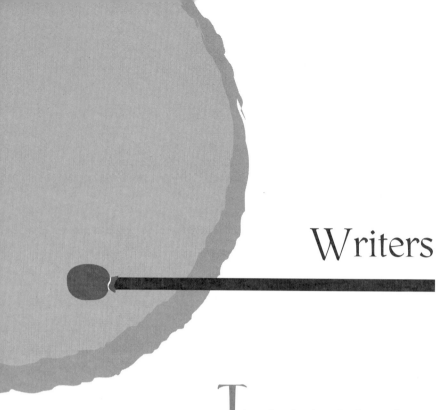

Writers

The role of writers in the modern world functions much in the same way as that of the bards and traveling storytellers of the past. Instead of knowledge, news, and folklore being transmitted orally around the campfire, they are transmitted via the books and publications that fill the libraries of our spirit. These modern shamans of the printed page have many times changed the courses of our lives with a single book. Consider the profound impact that Margot Adler's *Drawing Down the Moon* and Starhawk's *The Spiral Dance* had on the existing Pagan community and how these two books help to create the larger movement of today. So it is only fitting that we conclude by talking with some of the people who have been able to express so well the idealogies and cosmologies of the modern Pagan community.

STARHAWK is best known as the author of *The Spiral Dance*, one of the most widely-read books in the Pagan community. She is also the author of *Truth or Dare*, *Dreaming the Dark*, and a fantasy novel, *The Fifth Sacred Thing*. She has contributed articles to many publications and was included in the "100 Visionaries Who Could Change Your Life" article in the January-February 1995 issue of *Utne Reader*.

She is a very active lecturer and workshop facilitator as well as a founding member of the Reclaiming Collective, which regularly holds Witch camps to explore Goddess-centered spirituality and political action.
Starhawk was interviewed by phone on March 9, 1994.

When did you first discover that you were a Pagan? How did that happen?

When I was in college in the late sixties I was doing an anthropology project on Witchcraft, about which at the time I knew nothing. In the course of that I met some people who were Celtic Witches, and they began telling me about their tradition. Immediately it felt to me like, "Aha! this is what I have always believed." I just never knew there was actually a framework for it and other people that believed the same thing.

What religion were you raised in?

Jewish.

What was missing in Judaism for you?

At the time I was raised in it, there wasn't any sense that there was any role for women to be leaders and to be responsible, active agents in Judaism. That has changed since then, but at the time there were no women rabbis. There was nobody even thinking about it or talking about it.

Secondly, for me it was the importance of the connection of nature with spirituality. That was where I had always had my deepest spiritual experiences. While nature is certainly a part of Judaism, it wasn't central the way it is in Paganism.

What was the first kind of Witchcraft that you were introduced to?

I believe that the people who were practicing it were Celtic Witches. When I moved to San Francisco in 1975, I met Victor Anderson at a Covenant of the Goddess meeting. I had read a couple of his articles in a Pagan magazine, and it just struck me that here was somebody that I could learn from, he was someone to study with. So I asked him if I could come and see him, and he was very gracious and said yes. I began to study with him, and I was later initiated into the Faery tradition.

Most people don't know much about the Faery tradition, it seems to be a rather elusive kind of thing. Most people are familiar with Gardnerian Wicca; that seems to be almost a universal form. How does the Faery tradition differ from Gardnerian Wicca?

Well, the liturgies are different. The Faery tradition has a different system of degrees from the Gardnerian. It is also much more gay positive. There is within it a sense that there's a need for all kinds of different types of sexualities, not just one. And that this is something that's good. It's not a problem to be solved;

it is something to be celebrated, and it's an important part of the community to have lesbians and to have gay men and to have different kinds of circles of different kinds of people.

Victor talks about the Faery tradition as coming out of Africa?

When you talk to Victor, it sort of changes depending on who he is talking to. What he originally told me was that it came from Scotland, from the "little people." It's quite possible that there are links to Africa. There are so many links between the Craft and African spirituality that I think there are some links way, way back.

Does the Faery tradition use the four directions and the four elements and the Lord and the Lady?

Yes, it does. I don't use those terms myself anymore, so sometimes it takes me a moment to try to think back. What I practice now is not the Faery tradition per se. It has changed a lot since I was taught by Victor, although one of the things I was taught by Victor is that the Craft is supposed to change. You are supposed to be creative with it. It's not a fixed, dogmatic system.

What I do now is the tradition that has evolved with the people that I have worked with during the last fifteen or twenty years. That is what we call the Reclaiming Collective. Reclaiming got started back in 1981 out of some of the women who were in my coven at the time who wanted to teach. We felt that in our coven we had gone through a lot of power struggles together and had come to a good place where the power flowed smoothly and where there was no one leader in the group. We had evolved beyond the point where I was running the group.

We wondered if we could somehow create a way for other people to have that without having to go through quite as much struggle as we had. So we decided to co-teach together rather than as individuals, and we started a class. The class was so successful that it turned into another class and another class. There was also a very large ritual we did the year that *The Spiral Dance* came out. In 1981 a number of us who were planning the ritual ended up going down to the Diablo Canyon nuclear power plant and blockading, so other people took over the ritual planning. We were protesting the building of a nuclear power plant on an earthquake fault. That just seemed to us like asking for it.

When we came back, we discovered that we had a collective. The Reclaiming Collective in the larger community are people who see a connection between the Craft and Paganism and feminist politics and environmental and antimilitarist and social justice politics.

You recently got into some trouble at Clayoquot Sound, didn't you?

Yes. I was up there in British Columbia with my partner. We had been staying with one of his daughters. He has four daughters, and we were having a family vacation with all of us together on Cortez Island, which is on the other side of Vancouver Island from Clayoquot.

We had heard about the blockade because a number of people who were taking part in the blockade were also part of the Reclaiming Collective summer intensives up in Vancouver. They were people we had taught and trained, and they were personal friends of ours. We went up there to do a ritual for the camp and to offer some moral support, firmly intending that would be it. I really *don't* like to get arrested in foreign countries. I don't particularly like to get arrested at home! If I have to get arrested somewhere, I prefer to do it closer to home.

Just driving to the site of the blockade we drove through these magnificent, beautiful areas, and then we would hit these clear-cuts that were just devastating. The camp was in a clear-cut that had been cut fourteen years ago and still hadn't grown back. They don't grow back very well when all of the trees are cut down.

We felt a very powerful call to do more than just lend moral support and we decided to actively participate in the blockade. Myself and David and his daughters took part. His fourth daughter didn't because she has two very young children.

Now we are facing trial in May. As it turns out, they have been giving very heavy sentences to some people, and other people they have been giving suspended sentences to, so we are not sure what is going to be the outcome of our action as yet.

What do you think is the role of environmentalism in the Pagan movement?

For me the Pagan movement is about the sacred being embodied in the earth and in the human community. Environmentalism is simply what we have to do in order to keep some of the environment alive in order to have something to practice our religion around.

I actually would be perfectly happy never to blockade again, never to go to another political meeting in my life. I much prefer doing ritual or working in the garden or hanging out and watching TV to going to meetings and dealing with courts and dealing with all of that stuff. It has always seemed to me that when what's sacred to you and what's most important to you is threatened, you have to take a stand around it. You can't just be complacent and sit back and let somebody else take care of it.

For me the Goddess is not an abstraction. She is something that's real. She's alive, in the earth, and in the systems that we create in the human community, in all of us. We don't encounter Her through what goes on in the mind alone. We grow and develop spiritually through what happens when we take some real action about what is sacred to us, when we engage with the Goddess in the world.

You have just released a new book called The Fifth Sacred Thing, which seems to be about what you were just addressing.

Yes, very much so. It's set in the mid-twenty-first century, and it's about the urgency of changing our way of living and being on the earth before we destroy the earth. I'd say that the central question in the book is: "How can a nonviolent society deal with violence and with conflict without becoming what it is fighting against?"

I talked recently with someone in the FBI and he said that there has never been a single case of satanic ritual murder that has ever been confirmed by the FBI. I talked to Margot Adler yesterday, and her sources say that they have found exactly one satanic family in ten years. Yet at the same time we are seeing thousands and thousands of people coming forward and claiming to be satanically and ritually abused by Witches and so on. Do you have any thoughts on what's going on there?

Well, Margot and I have actually talked about writing something about this. It is something that I would like to do a lot more research on because it raises all kinds of difficult and fascinating questions. It is something that has been very hard for the feminist community to talk about because if you raise any skepticism at all, you are in this position of disbelieving women when they talk about their pain, which is what has always happened to women. We have talked about what has happened to us, and no one has believed it. Yet there is also a very unhealthy kind of sense of not being able to raise any of these questions without being immediately called an abuser or accused of being in denial about your own abuse.

When I have heard people talk about these things, I've been very interested in trying to find out what is happening. I often hear people say things that don't really make any sense. Someone will say she had a friend who went back to look for the site of her abuse with the police, and they couldn't find it. That showed her that the police were still involved in the whole satanic abuse conspiracy. So you say, "Wait a minute. Couldn't that also show that perhaps the site didn't exist?" There is no opening for that kind of question. I think it's a question that needs to be looked at in real depth.

On the one hand, I'm perfectly willing to believe that anything could and has happened to women. I think that abuse is, in a sense, part of our whole culture. There certainly are families that are as nutty and as sick as one could possibly imagine. But in terms of a widespread satanic conspiracy, that just does not seem to be happening in the reality that you and I generally live in. In a sense it has nothing whatsoever to do with Pagans.

The unfortunate thing is that now there is a backlash happening around, not just satanic abuse, but around all kinds of abuse. We run the risk of going back to the days where women aren't believed about what are, I think, the much more common, garden variety, in-your-family, someone-you-know, day-to-day kinds of abuses that continue to happen.

I think the feminist movement has made a kind of mistake in taking an all-or-nothing position. Either you always have to believe every woman about anything she might possibly say or claim, or it means you don't believe anything.

I think every case has to be looked at on a case-to-case basis, and it has to be looked at carefully, and we can't throw out rational evidence. A lot of the stuff about recovered memories, for example. Yes, it's perfectly possible for a memory to be buried and not surface for many years and to be repressed, but everything that surfaces is not necessarily a real memory. When memories do surface, they often surface attached to other images. They don't necessarily surface with the kind of accuracy you need to convict somebody in a court of law.

A friend of mine tells a story about her son, who swears that at one time he fell out of a stroller and was bitten by a dog. What actually happened was that there was one incident when he was a child where he fell out of a stroller and another incident where he was bitten by a dog. But his memory has combined the two, and that was about something where there was no attempt to hide it or disguise it. There was no shame attached to it. It was just two traumatic incidents.

As someone who does trance and who leads trance, I'm very skeptical about memories that are recovered through hypnotic induction. It's just too possible, too easy to implant ideas. Not even by saying anything but just by having the expectation that this is what somebody is going to find.

As somebody who is trained as a psychologist and who is the adult child of a psychotherapist, who comes from a family where just about everybody was some sort of social worker or psychotherapist and has been since the forties, I have a lot of wariness about therapists. About what they can do and about what they are up to.

As someone who writes fiction, I know that the fiction I have written has as much force for me as a memory of something that has actually happened to me. Some of it has even more force. Some of the incidents that I have written about were done by taking something from my own life and changing it. I have to really stop and think, and sometimes I have a hard time remembering, which way it actually happened. The fictional way actually carries more emotional power.

I think we need to look at the question of why this particular story, why this particular set of images is surfacing now. Why have so many people who are not fundamentalists latched on to them? I think we have to look at whether women are being healed by recovering these memories. And what is healing? That's one of the things that the therapeutic community has never really answered. What constitutes health? How do you know when your client is better? How do you yourself know when you are better? There aren't any objective standards for measuring that.

And what does it mean if people are being healed by remembering things which may or may not be true? Does it mean that they are true if you are being healed? Is that the proof? Or does it mean that something else is going on? Is it possible that binding one's pain into a powerful story of almost any sort could be healing? Or could it at least encapsulate it enough to make for better functioning?

That's very interesting because that's almost what the ancients would have done. They would have made something into a myth.

Yes. And so if that's what's happening, why this myth? Is this the myth that we really want to work with? The one that we really want to choose? And where has this myth come from? You are getting my raw thoughts on an issue that is very touchy and will probably get me into a lot of heat, flack, and noise, but those are some of the things that I'm thinking about. I would stress that it's something that I'm looking at doing some more in-depth research on. I would say that at this point I have more questions than I have hard and fast conclusions.

But the one thing I do feel is vitally important for the health of the feminist community and the Pagan community is that we have room to express skepticism and that we have room to express doubt. It doesn't mean that we don't support women in their healing, but otherwise we fall into the grasp of "the censor." As I wrote about in *Truth or Dare*, we can fall into the grasp of the worst sort of inner embodiment of patriarchy, where we are censoring ourselves and we are not allowed to speak.

What I have noticed as I travel around is that many women say to me privately that they have doubts about this, but they can't say it publicly because they are afraid. That is not a healthy climate for a movement that wants to bring about political change and that wants to bring about positive changes in women's lives.

Your book **The Spiral Dance** *is probably the most significant book for modern neo-Paganism. I think that* **Drawing Down the Moon** *is probably a close second. I just wonder if you could talk about what the Craft was like before you wrote that book and the kinds of influences that came into play to get you to write it, and what happened afterwards. How do you think that book helped to shape the community? Or did it?*

When I was writing *The Spiral Dance* in the mid-seventies, the Craft was in its third postwar incarnation. First, you had the Gardnerian roots and the stuff in the fifties that began to surface after Witchcraft was no longer a capital crime in England. Then in the sixties you had people who got into it through the counterculture. In the early seventies you began to get a small number of women who were getting involved through the feminist movement and feminist Spirituality.

I actually got into it in the sixties through the counterculture before I was even aware that there was such a thing as a feminist movement. Throughout most of the seventies there wasn't much in writing that you could turn to, either for history or for any idea of how to do it. You had to luck out and find someone to train you in order to get involved in it. The people who could train you were very few and far between, and a lot of them were not necessarily the people you would most want to hang out with. Particularly if you were a feminist.

What I did with *The Spiral Dance* was to try to write the book that I wish I had had when I was beginning—something to lay out the principles and the structure of how to go about it. I think in a sense that's why it has continued to sell and be read by people. There's nothing like writing what you need yourself. Margot Adler's book *Drawing Down the Moon*, which came out the same year, was the first independent survey of the movement that was happening. It has since been updated in another edition. The two of them together provided material for people to grab hold of. Since then many people have taken *The Spiral Dance* and started their groups and done their rituals and used it as a resource, which is very gratifying for me. That was what I hoped would happen.

Of course, there has been an enormous explosion of writing and research, resulting in all the material that is available now. Now the problem isn't that there's nothing available. As you go into a bookstore you are overwhelmed. What to read first? That is very healthy for the Craft, and it's very healthy for everybody. Now there is more diversity and more of a variety to choose from.

Do you have any comments about the standard of scholarship in a lot of the books that are coming out now? Does it bother you at all?

I'd say that the standard of scholarship ranges from very bad to somebody like Marija Gimbutas, who was an incredible scholar. I think that people have to pick and choose just like they would with anything else. If you picked up books on any other religion, there would be a wide range of standards of scholarship. It's partly up to the reader to look for the stuff that does come from a more sound academic base. It also depends on your criteria. There are a lot of things you can read that might not have good scholarship but that might be interesting or that might spark an idea for you about what you want to do and how you want to practice.

You travel all over the world and all over the U.S. You are in a position to meet many people and keep the pulse of the "big picture" of what's going on in Paganism. Do you see any particular problems that are coming up right now that need to be addressed? And where would you like to see Paganism move in the future?

What I see is not a problem, it's more of a challenge. We now have people who have been involved in the Pagan movement for many years who are growing up, who are a little older. They have kids, they are middle-aged, and the numbers are growing. There is starting to be more of a pull toward some kind of institutionalization. People are starting to ask why their kids don't have a summer camp to go to or why isn't there a place for their group to meet instead of always having to meet in someone's living room. They want the kinds of things that other religions have, and I think that's positive and that's healthy. That's a way in which the Pagan movement as a whole is coming out of the closet and seeing itself less as this strange outlaw religion and more as a religion with rights like any other religion.

It's a religion that has been persecuted and that has a lot of educating to do, but that's no reason we should skulk around in broom closets. That's also a challenge because much of what's best about the Craft has been based on its anti-institutionalist quality—that we don't have a hierarchy, that we don't get a lot of money involved in what we do. We don't have someone driving around in a Mercedes. It is something where you and your three friends can get together in your living room and do it. You don't need a lot of paraphernalia. It's great to have some training, but even without training you can find some way to express in ritual your own connection with the Goddess.

So that is a kind of tension that I see happening. I think it's a healthy tension, and it has to come as we grow and as we mature.

If you could dream in the future, where would you like to see it go?

I would like to see us have some institutions but also maintain some recognition that the religion is something that anyone can do. People often have debates about paid clergy, but I think what we need is not so much to pay priestesses to do our rituals for us but to pay organizers. We need to have the church secretary on salary rather than the priest. It's the people who are willing to take on the task of organizing the rituals and keeping the books and doing all of those sorts of things which are less fun than creating rituals who need to be paid.

Personally, I'd love to see us in the Bay Area have our own ritual space that we could use on Halloween so that before I die we can do a big Halloween ritual and not have to run around as soon as we get out of trance and start tearing down the altars and breaking down the lights and loading up the trucks like the circus leaving town in order to get out of there before the rented space we've got sends the janitor to kick us out. Having your own place is wonderful. Having a temple would be wonderful, but then it brings with it other questions, like what do you have to do to finance it and keep it going? How do you run it, and how do you do the accounting?

Reclaiming has been moving toward getting its books in order. We've applied for federal tax-exempt status. We incorporated a few years back after many years of running as a nonofficial entity, with no official existence. We found that as we began to do more things and take on larger projects we had to have things like a tax ID number. We had to have a bookkeeper. It's kind of like growing up in life. I've always been one of those people who has resisted the idea that you had to do all of those dull and boring things like taxes every year when what you really want to do is turn on.

Do you support yourself full-time with your writing and your workshops?

Yes, with my workshops and my writing and with some local teaching.

Before that did you have a mundane career of some kind?

I practiced as a therapist for a couple of years, and before that I had jobs, none of which I would dignify by calling them a career.

Can you talk on a personal level about what it has meant for you to be a Pagan? How it has affected your life?

It's always hard to give an answer to that question because being a Pagan has *been* my life. Pretty much all of my adult life has centered around being a Pagan. It has affected *everything*.

MARGOT ADLER is a well-known reporter for National Public Radio. She is also the granddaughter of pioneer psychiatrist Alfred Adler. She is a Witch and author of *Drawing Down the Moon*, which is considered by many to be one of the quintessential books on Paganism. Ms. Adler was interviewed by phone on March 8, 1994.

What religion did you grow up in, and how did you discover that you were a Pagan?

I was brought up in a completely agnostic, atheist household. I was told when I was five that we believed in the brotherhood of man and that was our religion. Then later on my mother said, "You're Jewish," and my father said, "No, you're not." Our family actually celebrated Christmas, even though we were Jewish by heritage. We celebrated an Austrian secular Christmas because my father is Viennese.

My mother was born in New York City, and she came from a shtetl Jewish background. Her parents came over in steerage in the 1890s. She grew up in the Lower East Side in Brooklyn, and her mother never learned to read and write. Her father taught himself to read and write. It was a very working-class background. My father grew up in a fairly affluent, intellectual, "intelligentsia" kind of family. He was the son of Alfred Adler, so he was in a very different situation.

My parents were both left wing, and while they were never members of any particular organization like the Communist party, I was basically a red-diaper baby. My earliest memories are of the McCarthy period and of being very afraid and having friends of the family who were blacklisted. My mother was involved with a lot of theater people, and many of them were blacklisted, Zero Mostel and so forth. My earliest memories are of being on the "outside" of America. Of not being someone who was part of the American way because I was sort of a Communist and I was from a nonreligious background.

When my mother died and I looked through all her books, she had works by Alan Watts and Allen Ginsburg and books about the Beat poets, so she was actually a very spiritual person. I have old letters of hers from the sixties talking about Zen. There was that alternative spiritual sense going on in my family.

I found the brotherhood of man trip that was presented to me to be very sterile. One of my best friends was Catholic, and at eight she had her first communion with the white dress and all that, and I thought she had a better deal going than me. At that time, of course, the Catholic mass was in Latin, and you could go into a church and immerse yourself in the beauty and the pageantry without knowing what it meant. I was very taken with the incense and ritual.

I had two experiences, one when I was ten and one when I was twelve, that probably led me to Paganism more than anything else. I went to a very wonderful progressive school called City and Country. When I was ten, our parents brought us to school at four in the morning on May 1. We were taken in a car to the home of a sister of one of the teachers. We had learned all of these medieval May Day carols, and we picked flowers as the sun rose. We came back to the school at about nine-thirty to strew flowers from classroom to classroom singing these medieval carols and then dance around the Maypole. I was just overwhelmed by the joy of it. I think that on some level I realized at a very young age that I loved ritual. Two years later, when I was twelve, my class spent the whole year studying ancient Greece. We spent an entire year immersed in the myths of the Gods and Goddesses.

Growing up in the fifties there weren't a lot of wonderful images of women to think about, and so Artemis and Athena became powerful images for me. I'd pour libations of water to them and things like that, even though way down deep I didn't want to worship them, I wanted to *be* them. They were these incredible images of what I wanted to be, of my higher self. They had such *energy* and pizzazz.

Then as I got older, I did what I think we all do. I said to myself that you don't worship the Greek Gods or pretend that you are them without ending up in a mental hospital. By the age of fourteen I had stuffed all of this away, and I began to be political. By 1960 I was very involved in politics. When I went to college, I was in Berkeley and in the Free Speech movement and I was in Mississippi as a civil rights worker and I was in Cuba with the Venceremos brigade. I put all of the psychic and spiritual stuff in a psychic drawer.

It wasn't until about 1970 and the first Earth Day when I became involved in the Environmental Movement and I started reading all these nature writers like Thoreau and Loren Eisley and Rachel Carson, that I had this startling revelation. I understood intuitively that I was reading a religious literature, not as it was described, solely a political literature. I understood that this was a religious movement and that this was about the connection of everything with everything else. That there was a deeply spiritual understanding of our connection to nature and the vitality and aliveness of everything.

As I was reading this stuff I came across an essay by Arnold Toynbee about the religious roots of our environmental crisis. I was reading a lot of other things that were very revelatory as well, but this was particularly amazing. Arnold Toynbee said that there is a problem in Genesis. That there is a problem in the Judeo-Christian notion of "Subdue the earth and multiply and have dominion over it." That the older, Pagan, animistic traditions understood that everything was alive and vital and that human beings were not *above* the earth. That they were a part of everything and that this Pagan animistic notion gives less license to exploit the earth and that the Judeo-Christian notion *gives* license to exploit the earth.

I was awed by this idea. I realized then that I was looking for an ecological religion. I didn't know what it was, but I knew there was *something* out there. I was looking for a holistic religion of the earth. I went to England to visit a friend, and I looked for "Druids" under "D" in the phone book. I got books on the Druids, and I continued with my research. That summer, 1971, I came across all kinds of Pagan organizations in England, the Pagan movement in Ireland and Wales, the Order of Bards, Ovates, and Druids, and I started subscribing to a magazine called *The Waxing Moon*, which I didn't understand a word of. It was talking about the "Lughnasad celebration" and how to make your own athame. I had no idea what they were talking about.

Suddenly out of the blue I got a letter from a coven in Essex, England. They said, "Dear Margot: We see you are a member of the Pagan movement . . ." and I thought, "Wait a minute, I'm not a member of anything." They said they were high priest and high priestess of a coven of Witches in Essex, and they were trying to sell their tape. They had a tape of their rituals, and they had sent me a sample. So for about a month it was a joke. I was corresponding with Witches. I had this tape, and I didn't even have a tape recorder that played the right speed. One day I put this tape on the tape recorder, and on it was the Drawing Down of the Moon ritual, the Charge of the Goddess.

It was done beautifully with these English accents and Brahms in the background. There was a man saying, "Hear ye the words of the Great Mother who is also called Artemis . . ." and all the names that I had used when I was twelve. Then this woman started speaking as the Goddess: "I am the beauty of the green earth . . ." and so on. I found myself convulsively crying. I realized that this woman was an adult and she wasn't in a mental hospital, and she was essentially doing what I had been doing when I was twelve, and it was all right.

So this woman gave me permission to open the drawer. Then I started looking for a group. I found the New York coven of Welsh traditionalist Witches and then the Pagan Way. This was in the fall of 1971. I ended up in a training coven and then left that group and spent time with the Gardnerians, where I was initiated as a Witch in the Gardnerian tradition. Then I had my own coven and the Manhattan Pagan Way.

I had started out very skeptically because I came from this very antireligious background. My father really was an atheist and a Marxist. People would say to me, "We believe in the threefold law, everything you do comes back three times," and I would say, "Wait a minute, why not two and a half?" Every time I was presented with a dogma I'd say, "I'm not sure I believe that."

But I suddenly understood this greater truth, that the Pagan religions of old and the contemporary Pagan religions of today are not based on belief. They are based on what you *do*. They are not based on creed, they are based on process, they are based on ceremony. It's like in Judaism where you don't have to believe in God to be a Jew; you are part of a tribe. It's a similar thing with Paganism. If you are involved in the ritual and involved in the ceremony and involved in the beauty of the religion, there are very few creeds that you have to believe in. Those few are "An ye harm none do what thou will" and the beauty and vitality of our relationship to nature and very few other things. It wasn't a dogmatic religion, so I started feeling incredibly comfortable in it. It was something I had always believed my whole life. I had never known that it had a name, but I had always known that it was what I was.

Then through completely crazy circumstances, the book happened. It was one of the few bizarrely psychic experiences I have ever had. I am not a particularly psychic person. I walked into a restaurant bar with a man who introduced me to his agent, and this woman looked at me and said, "What kind of things do you do?" I had never thought about doing a book, it never occurred to me in my wildest dreams, and as I turned to her a voice in my head said, "You are standing on a nexus point in the universe. Whatever happens now is going to really influence your life." So I told her I was involved in Witchcraft and Wicca, and her eyes got bigger and bigger. She said she had just left an agency, and she was starting out on her own, and she asked if I had ever thought of writing a book. And I said, "Quite frankly, no." The written word seemed much too eternal to me. I said I had been in radio for ten years and I was not sure about writing. She said to call her in a couple of weeks and she would show me how to write a proposal. I didn't call her because I was completely frightened by the idea. Two weeks later she called me. She said we should get together and talk. She showed me how to write a proposal, and I took six weeks to do it, rewriting it over and over again. Six months later I had a book contract.

I got a total advance of about $7,500, of which they gave me half, but it was the seventies and you could live cheap in a way that you can't do now. I spent six months running around the country interviewing people, and it changed me totally. I had been involved in the Craft, in the Gardnerian tradition, in a coven that was run essentially by very well-meaning, very lovely, Brooklyn street people. They were more authoritarian than I was. Our values weren't the same, although they taught me some very good things. I was already subscribing to *Green Egg*, so I went through it and figured out every interesting person that existed in the Pagan movement at the time, and I planned a trip that would take me to a lot of them.

I'd land in Los Angeles, and I'd go to one group that I knew and they'd introduce me to another group, who would introduce me to another group. Suddenly I was experiencing rituals from ten, twelve, fifteen different traditions, and I was suddenly understanding the breadth and depth and the philosophical principles which were not being expressed in the traditions of Wicca I had been brought up with. They were much more being expressed by the people I would call Pagan. By people like the Zells [G'Zells] and Aidan Kelly and a lot of people who were not in the tradition I had been brought into.

The understanding that I have come to is that we are talking about a religion that is tribal, not creed based. It's not based on prophets or the written word. It's based on process and what you do, not what you believe. It's based on the immanence of Divinity, not transcendence. It's based on what some people call an open metaphysics, that there is always more, that it's always flexible, and that it's always more interesting, etc. The implication was that this religion was very tied to diversity and freedom and that it really had things to say about the salvation of the planet. It had things to say about who we are and about men and women and feminism, all of which I hadn't completely gotten from the traditions I had started out with.

Since I was also a feminist, and since I was also involved in a consciousness-raising group, the Goddess stuff suddenly hit me in a big way. It was very powerful to become aware of all the different traditions, but I also got disillusioned to some degree. I had an image of the Craft as very egalitarian with men and women, as being pro-ecology, and suddenly I was meeting these groups that were pro–nuclear power. When I asked them about ecology, they would say, "Oh yeah, ecology. We try to put our trash out, but frankly we are really interested in the magic and we're not really interested in the ecology stuff." I was meeting people who were incredibly sexist. There was one coven where the people literally walked out on me because I told some guy to fuck off. So I suddenly had the realization that the movement was much more diverse than I had realized it was. It was much more complicated, and there wasn't a political line.

That's good in a way, I like it, but it became apparent that people did not necessarily hold values in common. I became very depressed about it for a while. I have this joke with Starhawk that we both wrote these books that came out in 1979. *The Spiral Dance* and *Drawing Down the Moon* came out on the same day, and we both had the image of this movement as a much more political, feminist one.

The movement that exists now, while it's just as diverse and just as crazy, is actually much more like the movement we envisioned in 1979. So our joke is that we helped create the movement we wanted but which was not there when we started.

Good for you! You are the foremothers.

Yes, maybe we have done some service.

What is it like to be Jewish and a Pagan?

My father was brought up in a Lutheran household even though he was Jewish, and my mother was brought up in a Jewish household but basically had been very oppressed by it. She ran away from home when she was eighteen and married a violinist and became sort of a beatnik. She came from a house where if you were a man you got the fifty-cent Hebrew teacher and you learned the words. If you were a woman you got the twenty-five cent one and you only learned how to mouth the words with no idea what they meant. So Judaism was a very complex subject in our household. I was brought up with a cultural Jewish identity by my mother after I was five or six and she went to Germany and had a freakout and decided she wanted to have a rapprochement with her Jewish heritage. But the fact was that she had let it all go, and my father had never known any of it.

Now I think that there are wonderful things about Judaism, but I think that there really are problems with monotheism. I think that the notion that so-called primitive people with multiple Gods have a lower kind of religion is a form of racism. I now think, along with James Breasted, an Egyptologist who died about seventy-five years ago, that monotheism is a form of imperialism. That "monotheism is imperialism in religion."

I tend to have a very polytheistic perspective. If I think that there is any problem in the Goddess spirituality movement, it is that there is a tendency to Goddess monotheism. That the Great Mother Goddess is the image of salvation just like Jesus or the Father God, instead of understanding that there are thousands of Gods and Goddesses. It is certainly more interesting to have a world with all of these multiple images.

Can you talk about the way that the media has been treating Pagans and Witchcraft? Has it changed or is it going backward? What do you see happening?

I think it's complicated. There are several different things happening at the same time. It is still true that most people's images of Witches are coming from Hollywood films. Even though very often we get positive write-ups, the fact remains that it's generally only on Halloween that we get interviewed, and that creates distortions.

But more people do understand who we are, and this mainstreaming is being aided by the fact that some of the churches are starting to get involved. The fact that a course of study like "Cakes for the Queen of Heaven" has run rampant through the Unitarian Universalist church and that it has led to the establishment of the Covenant of Unitarian Universalist Pagans, which now has chapters in Unitarian churches all over the country is one example. Within Judaism there are now Moon circles and New Moon circles and an effort at reclaiming Jewish nature rituals. There are Tu B'Shvat seders [ancient tree-planting ceremonies] being done by Jewish ecological groups all over the country. They are basically doing rituals for ecology. The United Church of Christ has a new book of common prayer in which the prayers say, "Oh God, from the womb of your Being." They are starting to use inclusive language that is both male and female.

So there is this enormous mainstreaming of some of the ideas that are involved in Wicca and Paganism. But at the same time there is still a lot of negative media play. The thing that I am constantly confronted with is the idea that Witchcraft and Satanism are the same. What I am also confronted with, and which is much harder to deal with, is the kind of people who are antsy about any form of spirituality and who have no idea that any of this stuff is happening.

Most people in National Public Radio are antsy about anything to do with spirituality. They have no idea that there are millions of people going to growth centers and taking workshops on shamanism or affirmations or whatever. They just don't even know that this whole world exists and that it's growing by leaps and bounds.

Some people say that you are a Unitarian. Are you?

Yes. I have recently affiliated with a Unitarian church, mainly because it had a lot of resources for my child. I am on the board of CUUPS, and I have served as a delegate at two of the UUA's general assemblies. I also speak before many Unitarian groups.

Can you talk about Pagan parenting, what that's like?

The last time I got asked this question, I said, "I look at my kid and I realize that I may be a Pagan, but he is being brought up as a secular humanist." It's terrible to say that.

He's not being brought up that much differently from how I was brought up, I must admit. He may go to Rites of Spring this year, and he'll probably love it and have a very good time. He gets to go to a couple of rituals a year. But I don't think he's being brought up that much differently from what I would call old-style progressive parenting. That is where you basically emphasize the whole person. You emphasize creativity and love of life and love of joy and love of nature. Things like that. That's probably what I was brought up with in my school, and I don't think it was particularly Pagan.

My husband's religion is basically quantum physics. He is very much a scientist, so I don't think our son is getting a particularly Pagan upbringing. He's certainly not being schooled in Wicca at this point; he's only three years old.

I'm actually not even sure what it would be to bring him up as a Pagan. He will certainly be shown the beauty of Paganism. He will be taken to rituals, and hopefully he will gravitate to it, but I just assume that he will be whoever he is. He will make his spiritual decisions based on what he sees. So I'm really not sure if he's being brought up that differently from the kids in his building. He probably has less money than the kids growing up in his building!

You are one of the foremothers of the modern Pagan movement, and you've had a unique position in that you have had the "eagle view" of many different groups for twenty years now. I'm wondering what kinds of problems or concerns do you have, are there any issues that you think should be addressed? Where do you think it's all going? And where would you like it to go?

I think the movement that I originally entered was a movement that was based on the coven and the grove. It was a much more private movement. You struggled to find a group, and you found whatever you could find and you stayed in that group until you got trained. Because there were very few groups that were public, you took whatever group was in your neck of the woods. A lot of people couldn't get into groups because the movement was hard to find, and when they found it they didn't always agree with the group they found. It was a very private kind of movement, and certain abuses came out of that. There was a lot more possibility at that time of people being authoritarian. There were groups that had the same problems as many of the religious movements have, such as gurus.

On the other hand, the advantage was that it was a living-room–based movement. Someone brought the wine, someone brought the cheese, no money changed hands, any five people were a coven, any twenty people were a group. You could start your own group after a certain amount of training no matter what the tradition was. You weren't beholden to anyone. There were many advantages to that kind of gentle anarchism. Communication was by newsletter; everyone subscribed to *Green Egg* or *Nemeton*. You found out what was going on in the movement by subscribing to journals, reading letters, etc.

In the late seventies the big Pagan festivals began. The movement changed drastically as a result. A national Pagan culture began, with people in all parts of the country knowing the same chants, knowing the same songs, and beginning to see each other's traditions through watching these traditions at festivals. Lore was passing from coast to coast, and the coven lost its power to some extent. People no longer needed to find a group to get into. They could find a Pagan festival, spend five or six days, and come away with a mass of contacts, having been introduced to five or six different traditions. They could start their own group or join another person's.

There was much more flexibility as a result, which was good. There was less authoritarianism, which was good, but, on the other hand, it became a much more public movement. The stars, instead of the private coven leaders, were people like myself, authors of books. I think the advantages were that it took away some of the problems that come with "How are you going to keep them down on the farm when they have seen gay Paris?" There were many people who had been forced into groups that they didn't really like, in traditions that they didn't really feel good about, and suddenly there was much more ability to have that "eagle view" you were talking about.

With that growth came all the questions that any religion has to deal with about institutionalization. What kind of a movement do we want to be? Do we want to be a movement as the Craft is in which everyone is a priest and priestess? Or is there going to be a laity? Do we want a movement with a laity?

If you have a larger movement, you start to get more followers and leaders. There are some of us who don't think that's so great. That's why we left the churches and the synagogues we left. We wanted the religion without the middle person. We wanted a group of equal participants. But on the other hand, if we are a larger movement maybe there are people who really don't want to be priests and priestesses and who want a larger movement with the values that we share. So maybe we *should* institutionalize more. These are large questions. What happens when people make their living from this movement? Does that lead to corruption? Should we have a paid clergy as some people like Z. Budapest and Isaac Bonewits would like us to have? These are large questions that every single religion as it gets bigger has to answer for itself.

We now are beginning to deal with children. We are beginning to have a support network to deal with questions that we never dealt with before, like alcoholism. Aidan Kelly left Paganism and went back to the Catholic church for a while because his alcoholism was not being helped. There was nowhere for him to go within the Pagan community. Now there are Pagan AA groups and so forth.

There is a real change in the movement becoming bigger and dealing with this kind of stuff, most of which is good, I think. But there are still questions that I have. I tend to come from the anarchistic, radical, participatory, anti-authoritarian stream, so I have some questions about institutionalization and becoming *big*. I'm not sure that I want Paganism to be the state religion ever, ever, ever. There is something good about being a minority religion in this culture. You get to critique the culture.

I once went to the Michigan Women's Music Festival, which was a wonderful experience. But you go there, and you are with six thousand women, and Wicca is the state religion. And it's a *very odd* feeling. On the one hand, it's incredibly moving—you are in tears because you have never been in a place where your religion was the accepted religion. Then there's a part of you that says, "Do I really want the world to be like this? I'm not so sure . . . it's a little scary. I'm not sure that if Wicca was the state religion they wouldn't be making the same mistakes that all the other religions are making."

There is just as much dogmatism within us, potentially, as anyone else. I think we have to be very, very careful about that. I think there is less of a tendency toward guruism and dogma because the basic tenets of the Pagan religion say that there is no need for prophets, you can do it yourself. The Gods are there for you to contact, you can be your own channeler, just a few years of training and you can start your own group.

But that doesn't mean that human beings, being what they are, don't revert to all kinds of shit and end up being just as authoritarian and dogmatic as everyone else. I've seen some *bizarre* stuff go on. And the hardest question that I have to say about the whole Pagan movement is that I've been involved in it for twenty-four years, and it is where my heart is. I'm into it not only because I believe in it philosophically, but also because it is *beautiful*. I really think it serves my need for imagination, for having roots, for being rooted to an earth-based culture. But having said that and knowing that it's my religion for my life, I have to say that my best friends aren't necessarily Pagan or Craft. The people who I have the most interesting intellectual discussions with in my life are not necessarily Pagan or Craft. I'm not sure what that means, but I find that interesting.

You sound a little sad when you say that.

Yes, I do. I *am* sad when I say that. It's always been true. My husband isn't a Pagan; he's sympathetic, but he's not a Pagan. The people who I hang out with at work aren't all Pagan. Actually, my office is very Pagan. It's amazing. In the NPR office in New York there are at least three people out of seven who would consider themselves Pagan. It's not true in NPR's main office in Washington, but we have a very, very Pagan bureau.

I have very mixed feelings about being at my job. There's a whole complicated thing about being a journalist right now, and every once in a while I say to myself that I could do lectures and workshops for my living. Then I say to myself, "I don't want to do that for a living." I want to be partly rooted in the "real" world. I want to have part of my job being with people who are not Pagans.

I think some of the problems that I see in the Pagan movement, some of the fights, some of the "wars," are being done by people who don't have anything else in their life. This is their *whole* life, and so they need to be big fish in these little small ponds. It's sobering, but it's also helpful for me to realize that the majority of the people I work with know nothing about Paganism. They don't care about Paganism, and yet some of them live a very moral life and some of them are very pro-nature and pro-ecology. I'm not really sure what I'm trying to say about this, but I think it's really important for there to be a sense of balance in people about what they are doing here.

We are still a small religion even though we are growing. That may be good. I'm not sure that I want us to be a huge religion. I'd like us to be bigger and better understood by everybody, but I am not sure that we should be the path for everyone.

The biggest idea in Paganism, as far as I am concerned, is that there is no one path to the ultimate. The whole idea of polytheism is that there are multiple pathways to the Divine, and that is good. The whole point of life is to be able to live in comfortableness with multiplicity and diversity and with people who are different from you. The world is a richer, more vibrant place when there are more traditions, more pathways. If we try to make ourselves into one belief system, we are really screwed, as culture, as a nation, as the earth. So I spend a lot of my time trying to argue for this kind of multiplicity. What I call the polytheistic perspective in life. I argue this within Paganism, too, because I hear a lot of people saying, "*This* is the right way" or "The traditional Craft is the only *real* Craft." And I don't think it's true.

I think it's really important to talk about how we are part of this larger picture. I think one thing you *can* say is that the earth-based traditions (and I include indigenous Paganism and neo-Pagans and Goddess religion and sha-manism and all that stuff) are making a very important statement about the earth. And about the way to live in freedom and diversity. That statement will hopefully be respected and even loved by a lot of different people. I think it's a helpful statement for surviving in our times. I think we have to really guard ourselves against seeing ourselves as *the* answer for everybody's spiritual quest.

This is something that I have just started thinking about recently, and I don't know exactly how to ask you, but I seem to be getting a lot of comments from people about certain Pagan publishers. People seem to be annoyed with the level of integrity and editing, or lack of it, that goes on. At the same time there is a recognition that these books are selling and that more and more people want to find out about Paganism and earth religions in general. There are efforts being made now to reach out to the New Age community, people are advertising in New Age journals, they are giving workshops, and then people want to buy the books. For these publishers, obviously the bottom line is profit. But they are not paying any attention to quality or scholarship or integrity. Where do you see that going? Is that a problem, or is it just the nature of commercial publishing?

I actually think that the quality of books is better than it was. I'm not saying that there isn't crap out there.

I think there is a problem in some of the scholarship in the Goddess spirituality movement. There is a lot of stuff that is what you could call wish-fulfillment thinking. Many people say that because there was equality of men and women in ancient art here and there, that means that there was equality in the culture, like in Crete, for example. That is still not clear. On the other hand, there is really interesting stuff like Marija Gimbutas's writings.

I must say that I get completely flipped out every time I hear somebody say "the nine million Witches that were burned." There's no evidence that nine million Witches were burned anywhere. There may have been a million. The nine million figure was dreamed out of thin air. Half of these people weren't Witches anyway, they were Protestants in Catholic countries and Catholics in Protestant countries or women who were good Christians, like in Salem, who basically had some property and someone wanted to do them in.

I get annoyed when I see shoddy scholarship. I see it all the time. But if you think about the books that people had fifteen or twenty years ago when they wanted to read about the Craft . . . they had *nothing*. They had Gardner, they had Margaret Murray. They had one book by Doreen Valiente and one book by Justine Glass and one book by Sybil Leek. There was one Stewart Farrar book. That was it! Then there was Hans Holzer. It was pretty pathetic. Now look at what HarperCollins is publishing on women's spirituality and what Oxford University Press is publishing. It's amazing what there is out there.

So, yes, there are some shoddy and rather silly books around, but actually they aren't nearly as bad as the books that were being published twenty years ago.

People are not complaining about those kinds of books. I think what people object to is the lack of editing, the lack of scholarship, and especially the sexism. In particular, there are two recent books on Druidism that have come out, and both are incredibly sexist.

When I started in the Craft I went to the first big Pagan gathering, which was Pan Pagan '80. It was in the Midwest, and it was unbelievable. Z. Budapest came there and did a women's ritual, which was one of the first in a mixed Pagan gathering. It was the first time a lot of lesbian feminists were there. There was a man who came in with a staff and tried to get his wife out of that ritual. He started doing violence in the middle of the ceremony. As a result of what happened during that ritual, the organization that was putting on the festival split into three groups. It was clear that there were many people who had been brought into the traditional Craft, the Gardnerian, British, Alexandrian-type traditions who were very, very antifeminist. And homophobic.

Take a look at the chapter on feminism and the Craft in my book. I have a section in there on how sexist the Craft was in the middle seventies. What happened was, they learned. They were challenged. The Gay Faery movement challenged the Craft and the Pagan movement on homophobia. It happened over a number of years, and there really has been change. Now you might get a weird book here and there, but most people are no longer in that situation. There really has been progress.

Is there anything else you want to talk about?

I am worried about the reporting of ritual abuse that is going on right now and the fact that there just doesn't seem to be much concrete evidence for it. I don't understand why the Zeitgeist is serving this up. Every age has its own psychological problems. There was schizophrenia, and then in the eighties it was borderline personality. The two forms that you are getting right now are people who say they have been abducted by aliens and people who are talking about ritual abuse. Plus there is the truth about abuse, of which there is a lot, and that should be dealt with.

But there are thousands of people coming up with these ritual abuse stories and alien abduction stories, and they are very similar. In both cases they say that they have been taken or that their babies have been taken from them. In one case, the babies are used for experiments; in the other case, they are sacrificed. In both cases women claim to have been "breeders."

When you talk to police, especially about the ritual abuse stuff, they find very little evidence for any of it. I talked to a guy who investigates ritual abuse for all of Washington and Maryland. He said he had come across exactly one intergenerational satanic family in the last ten years of investigations.

This stuff is coming out particularly in the feminist community and in the multiple personality therapy community. I remember reading a lesbian magazine and looking through the letters column; I saw ten letters from people who said that they were ritual abuse survivors. In one case the woman said she had ten babies taken from her. There was not a single letter questioning this. *Ms.* magazine had an article called "Ritual Abuse, Believe It." It was written by someone under a pseudonym. There was no way that anyone could question it. In some cases this ritual abuse is remembered only after hypnosis with a therapist, which brings up other questions.

I had a neighbor who is a multiple personality; she's been in therapy, and she's been hospitalized. She came to me one day and handed me a document that her therapist had given her. She had never on her own said that she was a ritual abuse survivor as far as I know, but the therapist had given her a list of the supposed satanic holidays. Most of them I had never heard of in my life. The therapist had said to this woman, "These are dates around which you may have more problems." First of all, that is *incredibly* suggestive. But let's forget that for a moment.

I have a friend who does a lot of research into this stuff. It turns out that this document comes from the fundamentalist Christian community, and that there are therapists who are not Christians who are handing this out completely unawares in New York City and telling their clients that the satanic holidays are the ones that they will be having more problems around.

What really scares me about it, the thing that I am wrestling with, is that—as someone who has been a feminist my whole life—I have always believed that one of the most important lessons the feminist movement gave us was that the personal is political. That from someone's own personal experiences one can get the real meaning of life. That one should trust one's intuition, etc. In therapy you are supposed to believe what the patient says, right? So you suddenly have all kinds of people coming up with these stories. I don't think they are lying. I think that *something* traumatic has happened. But the form that these stories are taking are not necessarily exactly correct. Maybe they are coming from the dream reality that happens within us, but they are not literally correct.

One of my close friends is Whitley Strieber, the guy who wrote *Communion* and *Transformation*, which are two books about having been personally abducted by aliens. Do I believe he was abducted by aliens? No. Do I believe he is lying? No. I believe in Whitley's case that the walls between the world of dream and the otherworld are thinner than for most, and that he travels between those two worlds, sometimes unknowingly. And that sometimes he can't figure out what is coming from which world. He has clearly had a traumatic experience, and he has named that experience as having been abducted by aliens, but I don't know that is in fact what happened. In the case of many of these women I'm not sure what happened either. I don't think that they are lying, but I also don't think that they have been having these ritual abuse experiences.

I also worry about the confusion of Wicca with ritual abuse, the possibility of a witch-hunt.

There is something I'd like to finish with. There are all kinds of stupid squabbles going on in the Pagan community about who is right and who is wrong, but on the good side what is happening is that every day there are new groups of people who are coming into Paganism who are freshly energized. Some of these people are incredibly talented. Their creativity will define Paganism for the future.

ZSUZSANNA BUDAPEST is a feminist Witch and the author of *The Holy Book of Women's Mysteries, Anna Perenna: The Grandmother of Time, Goddess in the Office,* and *Grandmother Moon.* She is the director of the Women's Spirituality Forum, a nonprofit organization that hosts an annual Goddess Festival. Her two sons are both fully grown. The interview was conducted on January 19, 1994.

How long have you been a Pagan?

I am a genetic Witch, originally from Hungary. My family tree goes back to 1270 and I am a miracle. We survived the Witch burnings, we survived the Communists, we survived *every-thing.* I am here to tell the tale and resurrect the whole thing again.

What was it like to be raised in the tradition?

When you are raised in the tradition, you don't realize that you are. You think that everybody is into Goddesses. My mother was a sculptress, and she would make Goddesses all the time, one Goddess statue after the other. She made a Queen of Swords, a Queen of the Winter, they were all female Goddesses of some sort.

Our friends were all people who were steeped in classical mythology. The first piece I ever wrote was about Zeus and Hera and their marital problems. It was only when I went to school that I realized there were people who were Christians who didn't have the Goddess. They had this dead man on a dead cross, which was always sort of nightmarish to look at. The symbol of the cross just turned me off to Christianity; I would get nauseous.

They talked a good line, and they practiced something else. I was put in a nunnery because it was postwar Europe, and the Christians had the only food. Nobody had anything to eat except the Christians. My mother was afraid that I would end up brain damaged if I didn't get enough to eat.

What kinds of things did your mother teach you?

She taught me that if you don't have any enemies, you haven't done anything. That you can tell the quality of your work by the quality of your enemies. She said, "I want you to be so strong that if I drop you on an iceberg and I come back two weeks later you are thriving." In other words, she stressed resourcefulness, escaping from situations. You had to have moxy in my family, or you didn't count.

My mother taught me that life is female and the source of life is female and that the God is female.

How does the kind of Paganism that you grew up with compare to the neo-Paganism that you see in America and in Europe today?

It is a pampered and spoiled Paganism that I see here. Lots of living-room Paganism, reading of paper in a ceremony, a lot of boring Paganism. The kind that I teach is fundamentally different. First of all, I teach women the female Goddesses and not the male Gods. We just don't pray to male Gods, period. No more bowing down to male Gods. First we acknowledge that the male principle of the Universe is not a patriarch, he's a good boy. I was raised like that, we never prayed to male Gods.

Is that traditional European Paganism?

No, that is the tradition of women's mysteries. It was just a family tradition that Mother practiced mostly with her friends. It helps a great deal to anchor the identity of women if they don't see men in the sky anymore.

You get unused to the idea of a male God, and you get used to all of it as the Mother and Her children. If you pray to the Mother, She reaches Her children; whatever you need the mother takes care of it. This is what makes us different from all the other Pagan traditions—we don't evoke male Gods or pray to them.

My mother taught me to never be boring, to be spontaneous, that creativity has to be without sweat. As an artist she would make something really beautiful, and she would look at it and say, "Oh, it's a little sweaty, don't you think?" Like somebody tried too hard. It was hard to measure up in our family. Very difficult.

My mother taught me that the ancestors are living on the winds and that you can talk to them. She did a lot of wind and weather magic. That is really the Central European shamanism—wind work. The winds have different personalities, and they are different Goddesses and Gods. She believed that is what you have to use to reach the ancestors. She would pray, and the wind would wake, and she would say, "Oh, they are here!"

What about Americans who are of European heritage—their ancestors are in Europe and they are living over here—does that make a difference?

The ancestors are everywhere. If they are dead, they are everywhere. They are not in this country or that country, they are not bound by continents. They are simultaneously everywhere. It gives me great comfort to walk into a cemetery and to see Mother's grave. But I walk into a cemetery in Hungary, and I know she's not there. Her grave is there, but I know she is not living there. If I pray to her there, she is apt to find me there, but she also has to come there. The soul is not in the earth where her ashes are. The soul is part of the great All. I can pray to her anywhere, and she will find me there. We believe that once you are dead and once you are on the other side, all the limitations that are placed on organic life forms no longer apply.

So you find that it's easier to work with someone once they have passed over?

In fact, yes. They get smarter on the other side. My father got smarter. He was not much of a father, but since he went there he doesn't bother me anymore, he doesn't say nasty things to me anymore. He is emanating support, and he seems to have changed for the better. I've noticed that that happens.

What do you think the impact of Paganism would be for women in the world?

When women rediscover the earth, they also rediscover the moon. Women breed by the moon and not by the sun. Animals are classified by how they breed. Everybody else breeds by the sun. We are the only primates that are lunar. Everybody else has estrus. Menstruation and ovulation are the separation of two polarities. They follow each other by two weeks. We are under the tutelage of the gentle moon; we don't rush out and present ourselves like cats and dogs. Every month we have a choice and we make it based on feeling rather than on the shortening or lengthening of sunlight, which is what most primates do.

So women find the earth and then the moon, and then they find themselves. For women the Goddess is everything. The Goddess is strength, consciousness, integrity, divine experiences, no longer being a victim of slave mentality. The Goddess is a lot for women in general and for me personally.

You were involved in a trial in 1975?

In 1975 I had a shop called Feminist Wicca on Venice Boulevard in Venice, California. I was getting very successful and very visible, and a lot of people came to me to have their Tarot cards read. I was reading for stockbrokers and hobos, you name it. The police set me up with a policewoman who requested a reading and after her reading the plainclothes policemen came and arrested me for reading. I was put in jail. Then we had a trial, and I lost, but we kept on appealing. The charge was "foretelling the future."

Now we have these psychic networks on television!

That's right. If they only knew what it took. I was convicted as a guilty Witch who predicted the future. If I had done it for entertainment, or if I had said I was pretending, I would have been okay. But everything I said *did* occur by the time I came to trial. The policewoman had to testify to that—that everything I said was for real and had happened. There was no doubt in the jury's mind that I was a Witch. They just said, "Yes, she's a Witch, she predicted the future, she's guilty."

They actually used the word "Witch"?

Yes. I was convicted of breaking the law 4330, which was a municipal code.

That law forbids finding water, uniting friends, finding lost lovers. It forbids astrology, any kind of magic, numerology, you name it; it just forbids it.

That law has now been repealed?

[The California Supreme Court] took one look at this law and struck it down. But it still stands in other states. I am pretty sure it still exists in Texas and probably in some other places.

You mentioned before that Pagans today practice "living-room Paganism" and that they are "pampered and spoiled." Can you comment on that a bit more?

I think it's probably because I was raised to be artistic, but for me it's just too boring. They just seem to stand around—like Christians. They don't worship Christ, but they have lots of degrees and a hierarchy. Some traditions are really just bad literature.

Well, here you are, you are the Wise Woman. If you could speak to the Pagans of America and of Europe, what would you like to say to them?

That they should *always* do ritual from the heart. That they should always speak from the heart. They should put down only a minimum of structure, and they should use improvisation. Improvisation is the very lifeblood of Witchcraft. In my experience if things just sort of fall out of your mouth, they come true much faster than if you have sweated over it for two weeks and you read it off aloud and everybody says "Blessed Be."

The things that I do just fall out of my mouth. Spontaneity and creativity have to be fostered, and there should be as *little* hierarchy as possible. I've thrown out all the degree stuff. We only have initiation when you embark on the path, ordination if you are already a proven high priestess who is writing, leading ritual, and teaching in the community. That's it. You are either an initiate or you are ordained, and there is nothing else.

Many people turn their entire self-worth into thinking they are "first degree" or "second degree," and there is all this hush hush. It really turns me off. But that is because I had this thriving upbringing as an artist. I was brought up to not be "normal" or to ever be settled.

I don't know if this is good advice for the world or even if it can be followed. The truth is that most people just aren't as talented. They just aren't into theater as, for example, I am. So improvisation may be a very tall order. Yet they also worship the Goddess, they are good people, and they are true Pagans, and here I am telling them what to do. I believe my upbringing was so extreme that to project it on the general population would be unfair.

Theater actually grew out of ritual, that is where theater was born. Ritual is the Mother of the Theater. We came back to the theater, and we do a lot of performance-quality ritual. I also put performance into ritual instead of doing it in a concert hall. If I do a concert in a concert hall, I put a concert within the concert.

I was trained in improvisation, which is a very daring kind of theatrical format where you allow the unconscious to seize you and you give it a voice. We do have a structure, we do have four people call in the four corners of the universe, we do have to have a purpose for the circle, which is decided communally. Everybody has to hold that.

We thank the spirit people, and we do have a high point where we direct the energy, but other than that everything is up to the people who are there. The middle is improvised by the people who are present. We dance and we do whatever bubbles up from their psyche. We all play instruments too. Music is very important with us.

You mentioned "wind magic." Can you give a little primer on what that is?

First of all, in Central Europe as a shaman you have to know your local winds. You have to know if it's the northwest wind that brings the rain, you have to find the rain-bringing wind if you want to have a job. Your number one job is to make rain. Each wind has a different function. It's good to be born when the north wind blows. It is said that when the North wind blows great souls come to be incarnated, great teachers.

I was born during a huge Siberian snowstorm on January 30, 1940. My father bought a newspaper that day, and it said that Budapest was standing still under the weight of all that snow. The east wind is a good one to begin new things. When the south wind blows, it's good to make love then because healthy, happy children will be born.

When the West wind blows, that is a good time to die. The west wind gathers the souls and takes them to the Mother. The north wind is called Nemere. That's a very important wind, it's *the* most important wind. It's the one you call on when you don't want to fall or get blown off a cliff, for example.

Where would you like to see Paganism move in the future?

This is sort of a challenging question because I like Paganism the way it is now. It is decentralized. There is not one of us who can be taken out and the whole thing collapses. That keeps us safe. When the mainstream accepts the Goddess, then they are also going to water it down. I already see some signs of that. There are t-shirts and mugs you can buy with the Goddess on them—pop Goddess worship.

But I want to see it permeating everybody's life and consciousness and actions. The Earth is our Mother, She is the mother of our species, and beyond nature there is *more* nature and there is no end to nature. We should all live our lives as if we are going to die tomorrow. This would be good.

CERRIDWEN FALLINGSTAR is a priestess of Wicca and author of *The Heart of the Fire.* She teaches metaphysical classes and leads tours to sacred sites in Greece, Malta, and Scotland.

When did you first discover that you were a Pagan?

I became a Witch formally at the age of twenty-two, about twenty years ago. I grew up in a family where my father used to refer to us as being Pagan, but we were not really practicing Pagans. What he meant was that we were nature lovers who didn't go to church. I think he actually resonated with Paganism quite a bit, but he didn't realize that it was an actual alternative. He was certainly not displeased when I got involved with Witchcraft.

My father had been brought up Presbyterian—"God's frozen people" was how he would refer to them. I was raised agnostic with Pagan leanings. My mother was also brought up agnostic. I'm the black sheep of the family because I am the only one who is seriously interested in spiritual matters. The rest of my family is more materialistically oriented.

When did you become interested in neo-Paganism?

I wasn't aware of it until I was twenty-two. As soon as I found people who were practicing I got involved. I had been fascinated with Witchcraft since I was a little girl. My grandmother kept a little journal of my first cute sentences and words, and when she died my mother found it and showed it to me. Everything was about Witches. Witches this, Witches that, on and on.

I had very strong past-life memories from when I was very small. I remember talking to my family about things I remembered and being very confused as to why they didn't remember the things I was trying to tell them about. I remember saying to my parents, "Oh. I'm so glad we are rich now." And they said we were *not* rich, and I said, "Oh, yes we are! We have a rug on the floor now instead of dirt and we eat meat every day." And they would laugh. I'd go to the bathroom and turn on the hot water and say, "Look! Hot water whenever we want it! We're rich."

I could clearly remember living in a hut with a dirt floor and having to go to a well to get water. I couldn't remember how we got from point A to point B. I certainly didn't have the concept that this was a different life. When my mother said she was going to have a baby, I said, "Oh, when are we going to the lake to pick the plants?" And she said, "Pick the plants? I'm going to a hospital." I was confused again because I thought you had to have certain kinds of plants at an occasion like that.

Once I found out more about Witchcraft and Witch burnings I came to the conclusion as a kid that it was all over and there wasn't anybody else out there anymore. It wasn't until I was twenty-two that I found out differently. At that time I was working for a feminist newspaper, and they came in one day and said there was a woman on trial for fortune telling and she was a Witch. I said, "Wow! I'll take that story!" That was Z. Budapest's fortune telling trial in 1975. So I was there as a reporter. She was eventually found guilty of fortune telling, and I ended up joining her coven.

What are some of the most important things that you learned in your training?

I'm mostly self-trained. I've studied with a lot of teachers, but I haven't had one particular, formal course of Witchcraft training. I teach an apprenticeship program which is pretty thorough. I hadn't encountered anyone teaching with that much depth when I was a novice, and so I had to do an awful lot of learning from the School of Hard Knocks.

Z. Budapest did teach me to read Tarot cards, and she also taught the power of spontaneity, of going with the flow with magical energy, of using intuition and letting that be more important than a particular formality. I taught myself hypnosis and trance work. I did most of my psychic development on my own. Twenty years ago there weren't a lot of good books, Starhawk's *The Spiral Dance* was really the first one that was a good, solid, beginner's book.

Can you describe what you mean by magic?

A magical spell is sort of like an active prayer. In some religions people will pray for something. A spell just takes it into a little more active participation with the Universe instead of just passively asking God to give you X. It's a matter of using your consciousness to change yourself in such a way that you would be more likely to attract what it is that you want. I like Dionne Fortune's definition of magic: that it's the art of changing consciousness at will. With a spell you are interested in shifting your own consciousness so that you develop psychic Velcro that will attract to you what you want.

Do you need to have special in-born abilities to do this, or is this something that anyone can do?

Magic is very metaphorical, you put together a certain number of symbols that characterize the thing that you want. You might put those together in a charm, and then burn a candle so you can focus your intention. All of this is a way of talking to your mind so that it responds.

People talk about the "supernatural," but that is not a very good term. What we are doing here is completely natural. It's just that we are dealing with some natural laws that are not yet commonly understood or defined. We are working as pioneers in an area that has been neglected and feared even by this culture.

Anyone who wants to develop that side of their brain can certainly do so.

Some people will have more of an aptitude for it, just as some people have more of an aptitude for languages or mathematics. But it won't be out of their reach as long as they are not brain damaged.

How has Paganism affected your life? I know you are a mother, do you have a mundane job?

All my work is related to my priestessing, classes in magic and ritual, and counseling. As far as being a mother, I don't know that it's all that different from what anybody does. I would say one big difference is I have been teaching him to be sensitive to his own intuitive energy since he was very young. I teach him how to practice that and to trust his own instincts.

Can you talk about what it means to be a priestess?

Well, it's a comparable word to minister. I have a license through Covenant of the Goddess, which is an organization that was founded in response to the trial I mentioned earlier. I can do weddings and baptisms and funerals and ministerial counseling and visit prisons and those sorts of things. I perform several weddings a year, and I do psychic counseling and hypnosis work. I do what I call shamanic counseling because I am coming from a shamanic back-ground rather than psychotherapy. They do tend to overlap; modern therapists are like our modern shamans in many ways. They just don't have the spiritual underpinnings, which I think are actually pretty important.

As a priestess, I have an apprenticeship program which meets one day a month for thirteen sessions. It's a small group of about fifteen people.

Do you get paid for your teaching?

People who take the class pay me for it. People also pay me for counseling sessions.

Do you represent any particular Goddess or pantheon?

I would say that my special Deity is Aphrodite. I have a special connection with her. I channel all sorts of different archetypal energies, but that one in particular feels very natural to me. It has to do with how comfortable I feel with my sexuality and my sensuality. I can teach people how to be more "in" their bodies. I do a lot of healing in that area. That does not mean that I make love to clients, because I don't. But I am able to channel that energy in a very healing way. I role model.

I do what is popularly called belly dancing, Middle Eastern dance. When I am performing, I am channeling that sacred energy. That is something that needs a lot of healing in this culture. Sex has been separated from the sacred. It's impor-tant for us to reconnect those things and that seems to be a gift that I can give.

You have authored a book?

Yes, it's called *The Heart of the Fire*. It's a historical novel about Witchcraft in sixteenth-century Scotland.

That is a book that came to you through past-life memories?

Yes, it was from some of those early childhood memories I was talking about. I believe that chronologically it was the last lifetime I had before this one. I think I took a fairly long break in between incarnations.

I had always had memories, bits and pieces here and there. I was working as a journalist, and I was having trouble writing anything personal. Something was trying to come through which was actually this book, but I didn't know it. Whenever I sat down to try to work in a more personal way, I would have this panicky thought that if I told the truth, everyone that I loved was going to die. This didn't make a whole lot of sense to me. I went to my therapist; we tried to track it down, but we really couldn't get a handle on why this was happening.

I had recently taught myself self-hypnosis, and I thought I might be dealing with past-life stuff, so I started working with one of my coven sisters named Isis. She did a reading for me, and as she laid out the cards I spontaneously regressed to Fiona McNair, the character in the book. She regressed into a woman named Mina, a friend of mine in that lifetime and one of my teachers. We both had the complete story open up to us; it was extremely dramatic.

Has being a Pagan affected your life in any other way?

It's really joyful to find your spiritual path if you are a spiritual person. It's like finding your true love, like being in the perfect-mate relationship. You find a way of relating to God-Goddess, to Source, and it just opens your heart. It brings peace and ecstasy and contentment. I think people are suffering because they don't know what their path is.

As an artist, a writer, I seem to have a muse, a Goddess energy. I think that creativity comes from the feminine side of the brain, the intuitive, the acausal and arational part of consciousness. I would say that the more you are in touch with that aspect, the more your creativity can flow. The rational part of the brain is very useful—we couldn't even be having this conversation without it. But if you get too tied up there, it can block the creativity, which is more free-form. There needs to be a balance there.

There is very little creativity in this culture. It's amazing how imitative people are and how shallow what passes for art in this culture is. I am not speaking of the Pagan culture but rather the dominant, mainstream culture. Pagans do tend to be more creative than the average people. Most seem to do some kind of craft or art or writing, even if it's just a hobby. I was working with Starhawk at the Reclaiming collective and at least half of the people would be working on embroidery during meetings.

As a priestess is there anything particularly unique about how you celebrate rituals, or is your path unique in any way?

I think I'm on the cutting edge of uniting the Goddess-God energy in an equal and balanced way between the masculine and the feminine. I don't want that to be unique. I envision myself as being a forerunner in this way of working.

In the Craft there is still a lot of emphasis on the Goddess as being dominant and as having a more primary position, and I am more interested in a genuine partnership approach. In my apprenticeship program there are equal numbers of men and women.

I've integrated a lot of things into what I teach at this point. I've studied with different kinds of teachers, not just Wiccans or Pagans. I've studied with Native American teachers, I studied Kundalini Yoga for six years. I've studied Taoism. I've studied with New Age teachers. My way of doing things is unique because it is what is filtered through me, it's all the different things I have explored and synthesized and brought to my students. The way I do things is always changing and evolving.

Are there any problems in the Pagan community that you are aware of?

No! [laughter]. Certainly not! We are all perfect. . . . Every community has its problems. I would say that mostly we have the same problems as the dominant culture.

An issue that I see is when Pagans identify with the image of the oppressed Witch. I tend to see myself as a leader of the culture, someone who is leading the culture into a healthier place. I don't see myself as a victim or an outsider.

I think it's important to visualize ourselves as the people of power to make a good and healthy influence in the larger culture. People are just alienated.

I think it's getting better, but for a long time there has been a fair amount of adolescent rebellion among Pagans who unfortunately are well past the age of adolescence. They adopt this "us against the world" mentality. It's a victim stance. It's always interesting for me to see people who say they are on a path of power who obviously relate to themselves as victims.

There is much we are doing *right*. The Pagan movement is obviously exploding. It's growing quickly. It's the kind of spirituality that people really want—it's comfortable with the body and grounded in immanent Divinity. It's right here, right now, in the earth, in the trees.

We need an ecological spirituality. We are on the brink of ecological disaster, and that consciousness has to change or people as a race are not going to make it. We as Pagans are providing something invaluable for the culture, which is a turn away from the destructive patterns to more life-affirming patterns.

Our spirituality says that everything is a web, the web of life. That all creation is interdependent. Our spirituality is not that of dominance or submission. It is not that of hierarchy. It is a spirituality that honors all beings. Pagans are at least making attempts to recycle and to not be overly wasteful in their personal consumption.

Do you see a connection between neo-Paganism and Native American spirituality? Most Pagans like to say that neo-Paganism is basically a European phenomenon, the celebration of ancient European culture. Most people don't talk about the Native American influence.

I don't think that is true where I live. Here on the West Coast there are a lot of Native American activities and groups that we all belong to. The difference with Native Americans is that they are not neo-Pagan, they have a more continuous tradition, which in many cases has been passed down unbroken. Our traditions are mostly revived traditions, reconstructed traditions. They are not old Pagan.

The two traditions are extremely similar. I have also worked with Louisa Teish, who follows the West African tradition, and we are very similar to that as well. We are doing the same kinds of things.

You live in the country. Is there anything you do that is special being a Pagan living on the land?

I like to make love in my garden before we plant the seeds! I don't know how many other people do that. I don't know how many of my neighbors copulate in the garden in spring, but I'm certainly going to! Actually, I do it year-round. I do it ritually to help things germinate.

Where I live there are a lot of people practicing Native American and Buddhist paths. I'm in a zone where there are many people of similar consciousness. I don't feel at all isolated or strange. I'm known as a Witch, and I'm accepted as a Witch.

How does what you are doing relate to mainstream American culture?

I really do believe that we are coming into another level of consciousness in a planetary sense. I think that people like myself are on the cutting edge. We are some of the early ones to be using different parts of our minds. I think we will all be telepathic in another generation. I think that's coming right up.

Someone like me can still be called a psychic, and people still act as if it's something extraordinary, but soon the kinds of things that I do will seem very ordinary. I just see myself as being somewhat ahead of my time. Somebody has to do it.

Can you give me some anecdotes about magical things that have happened to you as a result of being a Pagan?

The first time that I ever cast a circle by myself a bear walked out of the bushes and walked all the way around the edge of the circle and then walked off. I thought that was pretty amazing. My father happened to be watching me, and when I talked with him later, he said, "That was a pretty good trick with the bear!"

Another circle that we cast was at the beach, and we were coming to the end of the ritual. It was one of the first times we had worked at that beach, and we had not bothered to check tide tables. The tide was coming in very rapidly. It came up to the edge of the circle and the water parted and started to go around the outside. We were still pretty novice Witches, so we were pretty startled by this. The next wave did it again; it went around the periphery of the circle and then receded. When the next wave came, it went all the way around the circle and touched in the back. We totally freaked. We then quickly dismissed the circle, which was a mistake because when the next wave came it took all of our magical tools that we had not yet picked up. Novices! If we had been older, we would have been cooler about it. Of course the ocean was parting for us.

Is there anything left that you have not said?

One thing is that I recently led a group on a tour of the metaphysical sites of Scotland. I felt that to be a really extraordinary experience. I had not anticipated just how powerful those stone circles would be and what an incredible gateway to the past they are.

The energy of the neolithic time period is still very much there, and it's a beautiful energy. We went into a chambered tomb in the Orkneys at night and did ritual. It was so sweet. You could feel how those people were not afraid of death. It was a part of life to them, part of the in-breath and the out-breath. You could just feel that. I was deeply moved, and it made me realize how important it is to deeply connect with the past and to feel which parts of it would still work now. Not to blindly follow tradition. I think that's one of the weaknesses in the Native American practice. You ask them why they did something, and they say it's because Grandfather did it that way.

In the past there was a comfortableness with the flow of life, that trust that death isn't the end, there is always rebirth, and love never passes. You can always reconnect with those you love. That feeling of spirit being present in everything is so needed. You can see where the alienation has gotten to. We live in a culture where people do horrible things to each other—rape and child abuse. It takes such an incredible level of unconsciousness for people to do things like that.

I'm not saying that the past was perfect, but there were some very peaceful cultures in the neolithic, the Pictish people in Scotland, for example. There were some very long-term peaceful cultures. People have not always lived in a state of stress and warfare. It's important to check into that. There are overall reasons for why we have had to explore this rather difficult way of being on the planet, but there *are* other options. I'm not saying technology is bad; let's have *more* of it, but let's have it be technology that really helps us instead of just how to build a bigger bomb.

The paleolithic and even into the neolithic was very much a right-brained culture. When Sappho says that she had a conversation with Aphrodite, she means it! She saw her; it's not a metaphor to her. She hallucinated her. People had visions all the time. The shift from that is described in the Bible where it says, "And they ate from the tree of the knowledge of good and evil. And then they knew suffering." The knowledge of good and evil is the left brain that asks if something is "good" or "bad," "right" or "wrong." It divides things into a dichotometric either-or. It also asks how a house was built and why did the baby die? How did you do it? How much? How can we fix it? It analyzes and figures things out. We needed that part of the brain, but then we started using it exclusively and we got into domination, hierarchy, good and evil, black and white, male and female, and the world was split and divided. We are now at a similar leaping-off place where we will start using both sides. That is why we have to look back and feel into what worked.

REVEREND PAUL BEYERL is the author of *The Holy Books of the Devas, The Master Book of Herbalism, A Wiccan Bardo,* and *Painless Astrology.* Works in progress include *The Little Unicorn and the Goddess* and *The Holy Book of the Devas, II.* Paul is founder of *The Unicorn Newsletter,* the Rowan Tree Church, and the tradition of Lothlorien. He was interviewed by phone on March 19, 1994.

What does "Pagan" mean to you and what does "Wiccan" mean to you?

"Pagan" is a lifestyle word. It includes anybody who wants to call themselves Pagan. Depending on who is using it, it can include Buddhists and Native Americans. Other uses of the word include people who like to get very drunk, and so I don't always use the word for myself. Wicca is a very specific religion rather than a lifestyle. I tend to call myself a Wiccan.

When did you first discover that you were Wiccan?

In 1975. I had left the Catholic church during my teens, and for years, throughout college and beyond, I was involved in Eastern studies. That was the early seventies. I was studying Tibetan Buddhism, Taoism, Eastern philosophy and religion in general. That led me to Wiccan teachers. Through what I would now call Buddhist magic I was able to get a job that I wanted by using visualization. I met a new coworker, and we talked about our respective interests, and she said I should meet her teachers. So I met them and studied from them.

It was very direct. It was a neo-Alexandrian tradition, and they still work in private. They are in the Minneapolis–St. Paul area. I went through formal training and three degrees of initiation with them. I was a third-degree initiate by 1979.

And you have been a Wiccan ever since. What is it about Wicca that is the most important for you? Why did you stay interested? Why didn't you go on to Vedanta or something like that?

For me personally it's the fact that I'm able to work in the type of Wicca I work with just as intently as the people who work within the mystery schools and traditions of Buddhism in Tibet to transcend more than one incarnation. It's very different from what Wicca is for most people.

Does this have anything to do with the second book that you wrote, A Wiccan Bardo?

Yes. The word *Bardo* is a Tibetan word that is like the aboriginal word "dreaming." It deals with the space between lives. In *The Tibetan Book of the Dead*, the *Bardo Thodol*, this is described. I founded a Wiccan tradition based on the way that I practice, and *A Wiccan Bardo* deals with that. One of the primary focuses is based on what is done in some traditions in Tibet in which it is possible through ritual work and certain acquired skills to come back and continue working within the same tradition in your next life. We have verification that this is done in Tibet. I find that Wicca, if approached in certain ways, can use that tradition in a comparable manner. The tradition that I founded is called *Lothlorien*.

That's from Tolkien, isn't it? What is the Tolkien connection, or is there one?

In Tolkien's work the Lothlorien is a magical tree. Almost all religions have a Tree of Knowledge or a Tree of Wisdom. The tree in Tolkien is one in which the hobbits and their friends had to be blindfolded and lifted up by rope, which was a very initiatory metaphor. The tree was presided over by a Lord and Lady who represented the polarities. It existed in the Elven kingdom, so it's a very ideal metaphor.

In what other ways is your tradition unique? How does it differ from what most people think of as Wicca, which is the standard Gardnerian approach?

We work with a more universal approach to the symbols, such as unicorns rather than archangels or watchtowers. Unicorns are less defined in terms of gender. People who are studying for initiation have to be able to work either polarity.

Probably the largest difference is the way our legal structure is. We have members scattered throughout North America. We are incorporated as a church, but we don't have a focused geographical location.

So how do you handle the teaching and the counseling aspect when people are scattered?

Telephones, computers, cassette tapes.

What is the Rowan Tree Church ?

That is the legal, tax-exempt, incorporated church. There is no building; we are just scattered in many places.

What do you do in your mundane life, for a job?

I teach. Right now I am teaching a twelve-week course in astrological prognosis, which is the use of astrology in modern healing. It's a college-level course, but it's not taught in a college. I teach twelve-week courses in Tarot, twelve-week courses in astrology, and ten-week courses in herbal healing. That's what I do. I teach out of my home, wherever I live.

You are probably best known for another book that you wrote called **The Master Book of Herbalism.** *It is probably one of the classics of magical herbalism. Can you talk a little bit about the role that green beings, plants, can have in a person's spiritual path?*

There are about three dozen courses that I teach, and my bookshelves are just full of material. Here is a clipping from a friend of mine who is an Ojibwa elder who may be moving to Seattle to help us establish a center there: "The greatest part of life lies in the fact that human food consists entirely of souls. All the creatures that we have to kill and eat, all those that we have to strike down and destroy to make clothes for ourselves have souls that do not perish with the body." The quote is from an Igluluk elder.

So does that sum it up for you?

In a sense, yes, it really does, because everything has a soul, and so working with that energy by ingesting it or by surrounding yourself with it, whether in a tea or a bath, is all a form of altering your energy. It can be used for healing, it can be used for magic, it can be used to open the mysteries to you. That's my work. But I would make the same statement in terms of the planets, gems, and minerals. I have just finished my research for a book on gems and minerals.

Most herbalists seem to have a favorite plant. Do you have a favorite plant that you work with?

No. I don't have a favorite color, either. In terms of a favorite herb I could probably narrow it down to about seventy or eighty. As far as colors, there are a couple of shades that I don't like; otherwise, they are all my favorites. The United States is one of the strangest countries. It's one of the few countries in the world where people run around having a "favorite."

Is there an herb that you take every day?

No. They are all my favorites. I am serious about that.

Is there one that you are working with now?

At the moment, coffee.

If people wanted to join the Rowan Tree Church, what could they expect to get from joining it?

The primary things that the church offers are communities in a number of cities. That is a growing process. Any geographical area where there are three or more people can form a community. That allows them to work in group situations for rituals. There is a calendar so that people observe the same holidays, frequently at the same time. They work simultaneously and with the same things, so that we are actually creating a web of energy as opposed to being solitary. There is a central library in Minnesota that has about three thousand volumes. There is a central cassette tape library. There is a monthly newsletter. There are healing rituals. There are things that people have access to through members who belong to other traditions. Some people study in the Mystery School. That's a course of study towards initiation and ordination.

One of the questions I have been asking folks is whether there are any issues or problems that are facing Paganism or Pagans that you think need to be addressed.

The ongoing process of "Witch wars" which are based upon ego needs to be addressed. It is something that has been going on for at least the twenty years that I have been involved, and it's still going on today. It ruins our credibility and is probably the biggest impediment to our growth and progress.

What would be your suggestion for how to deal with that?

That's difficult. The people who get involved in them would have to change, and that's not anything that anybody's advice is going to make happen. But it's the biggest problem that I am aware of. I've done workshops coast to coast, north to south, and there is no place that's exempt from them. It sort of goes with the territory, I guess. People attracted to magic tend to have big egos and believe that theirs is the only way. It's slowly changing, but it still goes on.

How do you see that Paganism relates to the earth, or does it?

Because the tradition that I founded is both Eastern and Western in a number of respects, one of the differences is that we take an active rather than passive role. The other difference is that in Eastern cultures where the climate and poverty make life extremely difficult, one of their primary religious goals is to escape the wheel of incarnation.

One of my primary goals is to come back. The earth is very fertile. I feel that despite all the changes that alarm humans so dearly, the earth is much stronger than people recognize.

How do you think that your path or Paganism in general could influence American culture and world culture?

I would say that Pagan and Wiccan views in general have contributed to the increased awareness of the feminine aspect of the Divine. And there is a very astounding revolution which is taking place around that. Most major religions, with a couple of exceptions, and those exceptions are the minority, are now acknowledging the feminine aspect of the Divine. That doesn't mean that everyone has accepted it, but Judaism, the Roman Catholic church, and the Episcopal church are showing a growing awareness of people who now look at the word God and accept the fact that that could be masculine and/or feminine.

This is one of the biggest things which I believe is connected to modern Paganism. But we also need to be aware, and frequently Pagans forget this, that Buddhism defines Deity as both masculine and feminine. There are about five million Buddhists in the United States. There are probably about a hundred and fifty thousand Pagans.

Do you think that Buddhism will ultimately have a more dominant role than Paganism?

It does now. Just in terms of sheer numbers it's a far bigger influence in the world. Paganism is very splintered, it's very fractionalized. There is no cohesiveness amongst its people.

Yet it's kind of ironic that when we get together in groups we recognize each other as a tribe.

Yes, I know. But you have to be aware of all the wars in COG or surrounding COG or any group that exists. That's what I was referring to earlier. Nothing really gets done in terms of social change; there is so much energy being spent on all the conflict. Every other religion is out there making social change, feeding the poor, doing all this beyond their isolated community. Paganism is not doing this, and that's a generalization, but it's by and large true.

So what is your vision for the future of Paganism? Where would you like to see it go from here?

I am going to answer that, but I need to separate Wicca and Paganism. What I consider to be Wicca is not designed to be a large public religion. Religions that deal with the deeper mysteries are never mainstream or widespread religions. By nature of the mysteries themselves, that's just the way it is.

Paganism, on the other hand, which by my definition includes Native American religions, has made a lot of changes in the last twenty years. Native Americans are making greater efforts to preserve their religions, Buddhism is spreading—and Buddhism is often considered a Pagan religion because it is Pantheistic. The things which we call "Paganism" are becoming more widely associated.

This is not necessarily what I want, but I have studied the evolution of religions over thousands of years, and I think that it is possible that the need for Paganism and Wicca will decrease in the next century or two. Much of what attracts us to it is that we came from a patriarchal background and we didn't want that. But how strong will the attraction be to Paganism when you grow up as a Christian knowing that God is a Mother?

If Paganism and Wicca are to be a viable option in the long-term future, the communities will need to try to shift the emphasis of their work considerably. There needs to be more long-term planning. A lot of people talk about wanting Pagan schools, for example. What they are really saying is that they want to perpetuate their specific tradition. There isn't a tradition out there that's large enough to support a school.

Somehow getting people to come together to work to create a school where they could all teach is a more likely answer, but that's when you run into all of the difficulties. If they were trying to come up with a common space to do ritual, who gets to use it and on which hours and on which days if they all want to do a full moon or a Sabbat? So I'm not sure that Wicca will become a common religion.

What about the idea of Pagans being the carriers of the European Earth observances? Keeping them going?

In part they do. I think that Wicca is more something that helps preserve the mysteries, not just the European mysteries. That's a preferred view anyway, which may not be accurate. The European folk cultures—those ways of looking at things—there is far more than Wicca or Paganism that is keeping those alive. When I lived in Minneapolis, every time a Christian holiday came along, there were major articles in the newspaper describing the origins of all that stuff. And it was very accepted. There is a lot of work done in the mainstream community that keeps that information alive. It's one of the things that we do, but it's not enough.

They may keep the information alive, but are they really practicing it?

Oh, yes, they are. There are things done with candles, there is a lot still going on. For one thing what we are doing is a reconstruction, and there is no recorded history for what we say we are keeping alive. We are not really doing it the same way it used to be done, but we like to tell people that we are. How many books of the Druids exist? None. That's my whole point. We are keeping a lot of things alive, but we are keeping them alive in new ways. So it's not necessarily that much better than some of the customs that are being kept alive in the Christian culture.

Can you give a few anecdotes about things that have happened when you were working magic?

After twenty years? How would I even think of one? It's been nonstop. For me that's the same kind of question as a favorite color. My whole life is magical, and it is a constant process of having my dreams manifest. At the same time I live healthwise with something that's supposed to be terminal. And yet on a month-by-month basis more and more happens.

In three months we are moving to a place with land and a stone circle. Between us we have everything that we want. That's magic. It's been moving in that direction since before I came into the Craft, since I started with my Tibetan work. So there is no one thing I can focus on. It's all been constantly interconnected. I do ritual, but I don't do spell stuff. I don't do magic to make things happen because if you do ritual, things do.

I focus instead on keeping my ethics together and on just embracing change. Sometimes it goes to hell, but that's the way it always is in the mysteries.

Mythology describes what it does; sometimes you have to go through hell to open things up. That's just as wonderful as getting money in the mail, which is where most Pagans are at in terms of magic. They talk about doing all this magic and you get what you want. If that's true, then they shouldn't be poor.

You mentioned the word ethics. You are a priest. Can you talk a little bit about what Pagan ethics are?

I can only talk for myself. If you live your life very ethically as a Wiccan and you are not afraid to look at all aspects of incarnate reality and to maintain your ethics, you will probably be vilified by other people, including most Pagans. What I am talking about is that if you really look at what most Pagans and Wiccans would think of as the charges of the Goddess—"All acts of love and pleasure are my rituals"—or if you say you can do anything you want as long as it's not harmful, those are real intense dictums by which to live your life. It means you can do lots of things which are not socially acceptable and lots of things which Pagans, many of whom like to be politically correct, would consider politically incorrect.

I have taught workshops dealing with sexuality throughout the United States. One of the examples of what a couple could use to explore the Great Rite would be the man humbling himself before his priestess/partner and worshipping her. That is a little bit too strange for some, although a lot of women think it's a great idea. There are also tremendous stories in mythology in which the Gods or Goddesses place each other in bondage. There are all sorts of things that could take place that have absolutely no moral judgment of right or wrong, but which people will automatically judge as wrong. People, including Pagans, tend to be very inhibited, even though some of them are very promiscuous. Promiscuity is sometimes a symptom of inhibition.

That's interesting. How is promiscuity a symptom of inhibition?

Rather than dealing with the deepest levels of intense magical sex that a person could have, the energy gets channeled into many shallow experiences. I can give you a metaphor. It's very common for people rather than being quiet about the magic that they are doing to talk about it to everybody until they have no power left. It's the same process with some people who, rather than having to confront some of their deepest feelings, their own dark side, seek reassurance in an endless stream of partners.

Another issue, and this is another reason why Pagan religions should not be mainstream, is that they are designed to deal much more openly with intense sexuality even though in practice many of them do not.

When I first went to Pagan gatherings in the seventies, it was fairly shocking. I had gone with expectations that the people I would be encountering would be very spiritual and it would be extremely intense. Parts of it were, but much of what was going on was alcohol, drugs, and people out there fucking by the bonfire all night long. And it's still that way. I'm not against it, because to me that's part of the Pagan lifestyle, but it's not the mysteries that I deal with.

In about A.D. 50 I would probably have been an underground mystical Christian rather than a Pagan. Because the Pagans at that time were busy slaughtering Christians, and Paganism at that point was very comparable to Christianity today. It was the end of the age of Aries getting ready for a new age. So I don't always define myself as Pagan, that's only part of who I am.

HARVEY WASSERMAN is a noted historian and author of *Killing Our Own: The Disaster of America's Experience with Atomic Radiation, Harvey Wasserman's History of the United States, America Born and Reborn,* and *Energy War.* He is a senior advisor to Greenpeace, as well as a longtime activist in the antinuclear movement. He was interviewed at the Montague Farm in Montague, Massachusetts, in August of 1993.

Are you a Pagan?

Well, I tend to resist labels, so let's trace the cosmology. I was born Jewish in New England but grew up in Ohio. In terms of my intellectual cosmology I am very fond of Buddhism. I'm an environmentalist, an ecologist, and I believe very strongly that we are inseparable from the planet both spiritually and physically. If the latter precept is Pagan, well then, why not?

I first met you at Starwood, one of the largest Pagan gatherings. When did you first become interested in Paganism?

I guess my contact came at Starwood about five years ago. I don't have much detailed knowledge of Paganism, but I find it fascinating. Clearly, because it's planet centered and nature centered and ritual centered and attached to ancient animistic beliefs, it is very aesthetically appealing and exciting, and I'm intrigued by it. As manifested at Starwood and in the writings of my friend Margot Adler, it has a nice feel to it.

What is it about Paganism that keeps you coming back?

At Starwood it's fascinating and fun. I really like the drumming and the dancing and the exotic worship and connection with natural things: the stars, the planets, the earth, the rivers, the trees, the forests, the animals. It feels very strong. Very natural. I like the way people dress, the astrology and the Tarot, all the artifacts and the cultural trappings, the sense of an ancient connection . . .

Is there anything you have picked up from being around Pagans that has been useful to you in your life?

Perhaps an awareness of the natural cycles and different ways of being. It's good to see people being unrestrained and free with each other and with themselves. Free to connect with the planet and the natural energies.

Do you still practice Judaism?

Judaism for me is a set of ancient traditions. It's a communal and a family way of being. We light candles on Friday night. I like the singing of Shlomo Carlbach. He's very fluid and animated and passionate. He is Hasidic.

I like the passion of Paganism. It's also very compassionate. It's very non-hierarchical.

Judaism is an old, big, expansive tradition, and I take from it a warm feeling of communing with people who are also Jews. Hitler made it very clear that if you are born into it, you are Jewish whether you choose to be or not. So you might as well embrace it. Hitler didn't care if you had never practiced Judaism. If you happened to have one great-grandparent who was Jewish, you were on your way to the chambers. Both my parents are Jewish, and I feel comfortable with the vibration of it. I like the Jewish emphasis on family and community and the liberal traditions, and I like hearing Hebrew. Beyond that I know I'm Jewish whether I like it or not, and I choose to like it.

Intellectually I am very taken with Buddhism. I believe empirically in the enlightenment experience. I think it's there and it's worth pursuing. I love the discipline of meditation, the cosmic view that if you clear your mind and attain a certain inner order and connection you can advance to another level of consciousness. It has a beautiful aesthetic simplicity, and it is also profoundly nonviolent and nonhierarchical.

In 1967 you participated in a march on the Pentagon which was an exorcism ritual. That strikes me as a very Pagan thing to do.

It was also a lot of fun. Somebody decided that in addition to our standard political protest march we would surround the Pentagon, hold hands, and chant "Out Demons Out," and the Pentagon would lift off the ground. The police would not let us surround the Pentagon. In fact, I understand that it's illegal to walk around the Pentagon. But I recently did that, and I did chant "Out Demons Out" at each side. Back then the Pentagon looked really fierce and oppressive and violent and mean. When I recently circled it, it looked kind of shabby, like everything else in post-Reagan America. It had seen stronger days. Like either the demons had left, or they had lost their power. They were nowhere near as threatening or as oppressive as they were then. It was more like just a place to work. You know, all the people lining up for the bus after a day's work. It didn't seem to have the same malignant, omnipotent aura as during the Vietnam War when it was devouring so much life.

Was that your first radical action?

No. My first political action was a demonstration in 1962. I was sixteen years old and picketing a local roller rink that was not allowing blacks in. We chanted, "Don't skate, integrate!"

What was it that first caused you to become radicalized?

My parents were Kennedy liberals from Boston and Jewish. They were supporters of F.D.R. They are exactly the age of John Kennedy. My father was born three months before him and my mother five months after him, in the same area of Boston, and they were following the Jewish liberal intellectual tradition.

I went to Mississippi for a march during the civil rights movement, but I really became radicalized by the war in Vietnam. It was such a heinous, vile event that it demanded opposition. I was 1A draft status for a while, and that really did it, I guess. I was in the class of '67 at the University of Michigan, working on the student newspaper. I just felt it *had* to be opposed. I demonstrated at the draft board in Chicago and at several places in Ann Arbor and California. I was at the Chicago Convention in '68. The war was a cosmic affront, so full of hypocrisy and violence and greed. It was a great thing to work against the war.

Around that time you also joined a commune, which was what hippies did in those days.

We had a radical news service, the Liberation News Service, and the commune grew out of that. I felt very comfortable coming back to Massachusetts in 1969. The farm was a place where we became gardeners. The first decision made here was to not use chemicals on the garden. That has held for twenty-five years.

This farm was very influential in getting the antinuclear movement fueled up in America, wasn't it? It was also the birthplace for the Clamshell Alliance . . .

In 1973 Northeast Utilities wanted to build a nuclear plant four miles from our house. Here we were, all these refugees from the antiwar movement, with all these skills and beliefs. We just decided we weren't going to let them build it. We organized and stopped them. The farm served as a center for the antiwar movement and the antinuclear movement for twenty years. It still is in a lot of ways. Certainly spiritually. We were among the first to really organize against the technology and to successfully stop a plant. There were filmmakers and activists and organizers and writers and speakers. It was an amazing confluence of events.

By that time we were pretty deep into organic farming. For many of us who had grown up in the suburbs, it was our first introduction to nature and to living on the land. And to doing things in harmony with the planet as opposed to being at war with it. So that is really where it all started for us.

We are still farming organically, and we still have the political commitments, so it has been a great blessing. There has always been a great interest in astrology and Tarot and those sorts of disciplines. We certainly weren't going to mass every Sunday. We were spiritual as well as political pioneers, but there was no formal discipline to it. We were activists, healers, craftspeople, writers, poets, musicians, and farmers.

It seems like everything you were doing was ultimately for the benefit of the earth.

I think we understood implicitly that what you do for the earth you do for yourself. And what you do *to* the earth you do to yourself.

That's a pretty mainstream Pagan value.

Well, I suppose in my own searchings it came from Native America. That strikes me as a clear thread through Native American spirituality, the oneness with the earth. The Calvinist tradition in the West is totally the opposite. These were the people who founded Puritan Massachusetts. They believed that we are separate from nature, and that nature is the playground of the Devil. That we are here to subdue nature, to consume it, and to be at war with it. They hated the Indians. They hated feminists, they hated anything that challenged the view of a male-dominated authoritarian universe.

They had a linear monocultural view of history as opposed to a diverse cyclical view. They feared sexuality. You could have sex to reproduce but anything that deviated from the missionary position could lead to capital punishment. You couldn't wear bright-colored clothing. Everybody was encouraged to spy on everybody else. It was almost the exact opposite of Paganism as we see it at Starwood and elsewhere.

Is Paganism the religion of the left?

The core of Paganism seems to be the idea of oneness with nature, with all beings. I would hope most Pagan people are progressive in their politics.

Do you see Paganism having an effect on American culture?

Sure. It's like the effect of rock and roll or that the hippie subculture had. It oozes into the mainstream and really redefines a lot of assumptions that are taken for granted. Obviously astrology has a certain hold on people. That's clearly one of the artifacts of Paganism. The drumming which permeates so much of popular music comes from it. If you trace rock and roll it comes from the New Orleans blacks who came from Africa. There was a place where they drummed called Congo Square. That drumming has certainly permeated American music to a healthy and positive extent.

Do you think that Paganism is an effective ideology to help the earth?

I think it's a worldview that's of use. Just the acknowledgment that we are inseparable from the earth, that all beings are connected, and that if you administer pain to another being you are basically doing it to yourself. It's the Golden Rule made into sacrament. That's really where it's at as far as making evolutionary progress with our species, as far as I am concerned.

That is the *most* important insight for the environmental movement. If we can just make people understand that if you pollute, you are destroying your own body, and that there is no such thing as a corner of the earth that you can destroy without harming yourself. That it's a physical reality as well as a spiritual one.

Paganism has all these ritual communications with the Goddess and with the animistic essences and so on. But that is the fundamental insight: Do unto your planet—all beings—as you would do unto yourself. Once we get that understood I think we can jump through to the next stage of evolution. Paganism the way I see it is all the attractive and funny and interesting and challenging and intellectual and ancient artifacts that surround that basic core belief.

Is the Native American religion a Pagan religion? It is non-Christian.

I don't know if I'd say that to a group of Native Americans! I'm not sure they would really want that term used on them. I've never used the term "Pagan" in connection with Native Americans. One of the things I wrote about in *America Born and Reborn* was that the Native American influence on the United States has been at least as strong as the European influence.

This is never dealt with by historians. Conservative historians say that the Indians got wiped out, and that's too bad. The liberal historians wring their hands over it a little more, but no one gives proper credit to the influence of Native America on mainstream American culture. The reality is that the Constitution and the Bill of Rights and the environmental movement and the feminist movement and the sexual liberation movement can all trace their roots to Native America.

The European influence that came here was male-dominated and authoritarian and anti-natural. At least as it was exhibited by the Puritans, which was the *most* reactionary of the Christian cultures.

The Native American culture was immensely influential, and one cannot overestimate the impact that it had. The historians and the politicians don't want to deal with it. Although in the last couple of years Congress actually formally acknowledged Native American influence on the writing of the American Constitution. It's the first time they ever did that. It was an actual resolution of Congress.

Can you give some anecdotes about Paganism as you have experienced it?

Dancing around the fire [as big as a house] year after year at Starwood has been tremendously liberating. It stays with me all year. You have six hundred people cavorting around the bonfire and the drummers set up and two hundred people dance around and a couple dozen of them go all night.

The most memorable one was at the last Starwood on a Friday night. There was drumming and people were dancing and Magnus the magician was there.

There was this wonderful convivial feeling, very, very spiritual. Very liberating. Very beautiful. It was better than any organized service I have ever gone to. It was just a purely spiritual, ethereal way of Being for several hours, and I really didn't want the dawn to come. If only life could be like that all the time!

And then the dawn came and people started asking, "Where are you from?" and all that. In the night we were Gods. When the day dawned, we were people again. But the love still vibrates.

One time we went to a New Age gathering that was on the Solstice and on a full moon. That happens very rarely. It was also on a Saturday, which only happens once a century. We went to southern Ohio very near to where Tecumseh was born, one of the great Native American leaders. That night we conceived our twins. There were a hundred people dancing around the fire under a full Shahbos moon, Summer Solstice night, on a Saturday. And there was a sweat lodge ceremony that night. Now here we are with perfect, beautiful twin daughters. What greater proof of the power of pure spirituality?

Sources and Resources

![black bar]

Welcome to the sources and resources section! Here you will find an extensive bibliography of books, articles, and audiotapes by interviewees as well as many others of interest to those in the Pagan movement; a listing of magazines and other publications; information on contacting Pagan organizations, groups, and individuals; electronic resources for on-line newsgroups; and a directory of merchants offering a wide variety of Pagan-oriented supplies and services. Many of those listed operate at a deficit. Please be sure to include a business-size self-addressed and stamped envelope with your information requests.

If you would like to contact any of the interviewees, please check the list of organizations, groups, and individuals. Many of these people can be contacted in care of author Ellen Evert Hopman, P.O Box 219, Amherst, MA 01004. Enclose the letter you would like her to forward inside a blank, stamped envelope. (The authors and publisher regret that we cannot be responsible for those who choose not to reply.)

Books and Articles

Abelar, Taisha, *The Sorcerer's Crossing* (New York: Penguin Arkana, 1993).

Adler, Margot, *Drawing Down the Moon* (Boston: Beacon Press, 1986).

Agrippa, Cornelius Henry, *The Philosophy of Natural Magic* (Kila, MT: Kessinger Publishing, 1992).

———, *Three Books of Occult Philosophy* (Hastings, England: Chthonios Books, 1986).

Anderson, Cora, *Fifty Years in the Feri Tradition* (self-published), 1529 153rd Ave., San Leandro, CA 94578, $7.50 plus $3.00 s/h.

Anderson, Victor, *Thorns of the Blood Rose*, 1529 153rd Ave., San Leandro, CA 94578, $6.50 plus $1.00 postage.

Arguelles, Jose, *Surfers of the Zuvuya* (Santa Fe, NM: Bear and Company, 1989).

Arthen, Deirdre Pulgram, *Walking with Mother Earth* (1994), D& J Publications, PO Box 129, West Boxford, MA 01885–0129.

Ashcroft-Nowicki, Dolores, *The Shining Paths* (Northamptonshire, England: Aquarian Press, 1983).

Aswynn, Freya, *Leaves of Yggdrasil* (St. Paul, MN: Llewellyn Publications, 1992).

Bates, Brian, *The Way of Wyrd* (San Francisco: HarperSanFrancisco, 1992).

Beyerl, Paul, *The Holy Book of the Devas* (Palm Springs, CA: International Guild of Occult Sciences, 1980).

———, *The Master Book of Herbalism* (Custer, WA: Phoenix Publishers, 1984).

———, *Painless Astrology* (Palm Springs, CA: International Guild of Occult Sciences, 1993).

———, *A Wiccan Bardo* (Dorset, England: Prism Press, 1989)

Blavatsky, H. P., *Isis Unveiled*, Vol. I, II (Pasadena, CA: Theosophical University Press, 1976).

Bolen, Jean Shinoda, M.D., *Goddesses in Every Woman* (San Francisco: Harper and Row, 1984).

Bonewits, Isaac, *Real Magic* (York Beach, ME: Samuel Weiser, 1989).

Bord, Janet and Colin, *Earth Rites: Fertility Practices in Pre-Industrial Britain* (London: Granada Publishing, 1982).

Brunaux, Jean Louis, *The Celtic Gauls: Gods, Rites, and Sanctuaries* (London: B.A. Seaby, 1988).

Budapest, Zsuzsanna, *Anna Perenna: The Grandmother of Time* (San Francisco: Harper and Row, 1989).

———, *Grandmother Moon* (San Francisco: Harper and Row, 1990).

———, *Goddess in the Office* (San Francisco: Harper and Row, 1993).

———, *The Holy Book of Women's Mysteries* (Berkeley, CA: Wingbow Press, 1989).

Budge, E. A. Wallis, *The Egyptian Book of the Dead* (New York: Dover Publications, 1967).

Buenfil, Alberto Ruz, *Rainbow Without Borders* (Santa Fe, NM: Bear and Company, 1991).

Butler, E. M., *Ritual Magic* (Cambridge, England: Cambridge University Press, 1979).

Caesar, Julius, *The Battle for Gaul*, Anne and Peter Weisman, trans. (London: Chatto and Windus, 1980).

Caldecott, Moyra, *Women in Celtic Myth* (Rochester, VT: Destiny Books, 1992).

Cameron, Anne, *Tales of the Cairds* (British Columbia: Harbour Publishing, 1989).

Campanelli, Dan and Pauline, *Ancient Ways* (St. Paul, MN: Llewellyn Publications, 1992).

———, *Circles, Groves, and Sanctuaries* (St. Paul, MN: Llewellyn Publications, 1992).

Carmichael, Alexander, *Carmina Gadelica, Hymns and Incantations, With Illustrative Notes of Words, Rites and Customs Dying and Obsolete*, vol. I, II (Edinburgh, Scotland: Oliver and Boyd, 1900).

Carson, Anne, *Feminist Spirituality and the Feminine Divine* (New York: Crossing Press, 1986).

Chadwick, Nora, *The Celts* (New York: Penguin Books, 1970).

Colum, Padraic, *The Children of Odin—A Book of Norse Myths* (New York: MacMillan, 1948).

Condren, Mary, *The Serpent and the Goddess* (San Francisco: Harper and Row, 1989).

Corrigan, Ian, *Druidheachd: Symbols and Rites of Druidry*, ADF, PO Box 516, East Syracuse, NY 13057–0516.

Cottrell, Leonard, *Lady of the Two Lands, Five Queens of Ancient Egypt* (Indianapolis, IN: Bobbs-Merrill, 1967).

Crawford, O. G. S., *The Eye Goddess* (Oak Park, IL: Delphi Press, 1991).

Crossley-Holland, Kevin, *The Norse Myths* (New York: Pantheon, 1980).

Crowley, Aliester, *Magick in Theory and Practice* (Secaucus, NJ: Castle Books, 1991).

Cuhulain, Kerr, *Law Enforcement Guide to Wicca*, Horned Owl Publishing / Wiccan Information Network, 3906 Caboro Bay Rd., Victoria, BC V8N 4G6, Canada.

Cunningham, Scott, *Encyclopedia of Magical Herbs* (St. Paul, MN: Llewellyn Publications, 1993).

———, *Living Wicca* (St. Paul, MN: Llewellyn Publications, 1993).

Darkstar, Erynn, *Na gCloch Machnamh* (The Stones of Meditation) (1993), Preppie Biker Press & Inis Glas Productions, 7912 39th Ave. SW, Seattle, WA.

———, *Ogham, Tree-Lore and the Celtic Tree Oracle* (1993), Preppie Biker Press & Inis Glas Productions, 7912 39th Ave. SW, Seattle, WA.

Darkstar, Erynn, and Taine Bwca, *The Cauldron Of Poesy* (1993), Preppie Biker Press & Inis Glas Productions, 7912 39th Ave. SW, Seattle, WA.

Davidson, H. R. Ellis, *Gods and Myths of the Viking Age* (New York: Bell Publishing, 1981).

———, *Lost Beliefs of Northern Europe* (New York: Routledge, 1993).

———, *Myths and Symbols of Pagan Europe: Early Scandinavian and Celtic Religion* (New York: Routledge, 1989).

Department of the Army, *Religious Requirements and Practices of Certain Selected Groups: A Handbook for Chaplains* (Washington, D.C.: Department of the Army, 1978), Pamphlet 165–13.

Dexter, Miriam Robbins, *Whence the Goddesses* (New York: Pergamon Press, 1990).

Douglas, Alfred, *The Tarot* (New York: Penguin Books, 1981).

Dubie, Francesca, *Her Winged Silence: A Shaman's Notebook* (self-published chapbook), 2261 Market St., San Francisco, CA 94114.

D'vora, "Reflections from the Orgynizor," *Mezlim*, Sacred Prostitute Issue, vol. 3 no. 3, Lammas, 1992.

Eisler, Riane, *The Chalice and the Blade* (San Francisco: Harper and Row, 1988).

Eliade, Mircea, *A History of Religious Ideas*, vol. I, II, III (Chicago: University of Chicago Press, 1978, 1982).

———, *Symbolism, the Sacred, and the Arts* (New York: Crossroad Publishing, 1985).

Elie, *Ahavat Aretz* (Love of the Land) (Rananna, Israel: Hotsaot Pratiot Am Ha Aretz, 1971).

———, *Derech Ivrim, Derech Falcha* (Ways of the Hebrews, Ways of the Land) (Rananna, Israel: Hotsaot Pratiot Am Ha Aretz, 1989).

———, "The Hebrew Earth Festivals," *Mezlim*, Spring/Beltane 1993, Autumn/Samhain 1992, Winter/Candlemas 1993.

————, "On Hebrew Paganism," *Mezlim*, Imbolc 1992.

————, "Shir Bereshit" (Song of the Beginning) *Mezlim*, Samhain 1991.

Ellis, Peter Berresford, *The Druids* (London: Constable, 1995).

Evans-Wentz, W. Y., *The Fairy Faith in Celtic Countries,* Library of the Mystic Arts (New York: Citadel Press, 1990).

————, *The Tibetan Book of the Dead* (New York: Oxford University Press, 1960).

Fallingstar, Cerridwen, *The Heart of the Fire* (1990), Cauldron Publications, PO Box 282, San Geronimo, CA 94963.

Farrar, Janet and Stewart, *A Witch's Bible Compleat* (New York: Magickal Childe, 1984).

————, *The Witch's Goddess* (Custer, WA: Phoenix Publishing, 1987).

————, *The Witch's Way* (Custer, WA: Phoenix Publishing, 1984).

Farrar, Stewart, *What Witches Do* (Custer, WA: Phoenix Publications, 1983).

Faulkner, R. O., *The Ancient Egyptian Pyramid Texts* (Oxford, England: Clarendon Press, 1969).

————, trans. *The Ancient Egyptian Book of the Dead* (Austin, TX: University of Texas Press, 1990).

Fortune, Dion, *The Mystical Qabalah* (York Beach, ME: Samuel Weiser, 1984).

Frost, Gavin and Yvonne, *The Witch's Bible*, Church and School of Wicca, PO Box 1502, New Bern, NC 28560.

Freidrich, Paul, *Proto-Indo-European Trees* (Chicago: University of Chicago Press, 1970).

Frey, Otto Hermann, V. Kruta, B. Raftery, and M. Szabo, *The Celts* (New York: Rizzoli International Publications, 1991). This book is *very* expensive, and worth it.

Gantz, Jeffrey, *Early Irish Myths and Sagas* (New York: Penguin Books, 1984).

————, *The Mabinogion* (New York: Penguin Books, 1984).

Gardner, Gerald, *High Magic's Aid* (London: Michael Houghton, 1949).

————, *The Meaning of Witchcraft* (London: Aquarian Press, 1959).

————, *Witchcraft Today*, Magickal Childe, 35 W. 19th St., New York, NY 10011.

Gardner, Kay, *Sounding the Inner Landscape* (Trenton, NJ: Caduceus Publications, 1990).

Gimbutas, Marija, *Bronze Age Cultures in Central and Eastern Europe* (New York: Mouton de Gruyter, 1965).

————, *The Civilization of the Goddess: The World of Old Europe* (San Francisco: Harper, 1991).

————, *Goddesses and Gods of Old Europe* (Berkeley, CA: University of California Press, 1982).

————, *The Language of the Goddess* (San Fransisco: Harper and Row, 1989).

Gomm, Phillip Carr, *The Druid Way* (Dorset, England: Element Books, 1993).

————, *The Elements of the Druid Tradition* (Dorset, England: Element Books, 1991).

Goodrich, Norma L., *Priestesses* (New York: Franklin Watts, 1989).

Graves, Robert, *The White Goddess* (New York: Farrar Straus and Giroux, 1966).

Green, Miranda, *Dictionary of Celtic Myth and Legend* (New York: Thames and Hudson, 1992).

————, *The Gods of the Celts* (Totawa, NJ: Barnes and Noble, 1986).

————, *The Gods of Roman Britain* (Aylesbury, Bucks, England: Shire Publications, 1983).

————, *The Sun-Gods of Ancient Europe* (London: B. T. Batsford, 1991).

————, *Symbol and Image in Celtic Religious Art* (London: Routledge, 1989).

Gregory, Lady, *Visions and Beliefs in the West of Ireland* (Gerrards Cross, England: Colin Smythe, 1979).

Guiley, Rosemary Ellen, *The Encyclopedia of Witches and Witchcraft* (New York: Facts on File, 1989).

Gunardson, Kveldulf, *Teutonic Magic* (St. Paul, MN: Llewellyn Worldwide, 1990).

————, *Teutonic Religion* (St. Paul, MN: Llewellyn Publications, 1993).

Hart, Mickey, *Drumming at the Edge of Magic* (San Fransisco: Harper, 1990).

Hawkins, Gerald, *Stonehenge Decoded* (New York: Doubleday, 1965).

Heath, Robin, *A Key to Stonehenge* (Dyfed, Wales: Bluestone Press, 1988).

Herm, Gerhard, *The Celts* (New York: St. Martin's Press, 1976).

Hollander, Lee M., trans. *The Poetic Edda* (Austin, TX: University of Texas Press, 1962).

Hopman, Ellen Evert, *A Druid's Herbal for the Sacred Earth Year* (Rochester, VT: Destiny Books, 1995).

————, *Tree Medicine, Tree Magic* (Custer, WA: Phoenix Publishers, 1991).

Hornung, Erik, *Conceptions of God in Ancient Egypt, The One and the Many* (Ithaca, NY: Cornell University Press, 1990).

Hutton, Ronald, *The Pagan Religions of the Ancient British Isles* (Oxford, England: Blackwell Publishers, 1993).

James, Geoffrey, *The Enochian Evocation of Doctor John Dee* (Berkeley Heights, NJ: Heptangle Books, 1984).

Johnson, Buffie, *Lady of the Beasts* (San Francisco: Harper, 1988).

Joyce, P. W., *A Social History Of Ancient Ireland* (London: Longman's Green, 1903).

Judith, Anodea, *The Sevenfold Journey: Reclaiming Mind, Body and Spirit Through the Chakras* (Marshall, MN: Crossing Press, 1993).

————, *Wheels of Life: A User's Guide to the Chakra System* (St. Paul, MN: Llewellyn Publications, 1987).

Kelly, Aiden, *Crafting the Art of Magic, Book I: A History of Modern Witchcraft, 1939–1964* (St. Paul, MN: Llewellyn Publications, 1991).

Knight, Gareth, *A Practical Guide to Qabalistic Symbolism* (York Beach, ME: Samuel Weiser, 1978).

Kraig, Bruce, and Leon E. Stover, *Stonehenge, The Indo-European Heritage* (Chicago: Nelson Hall, 1978).

Lamb, F. Bruce, *Wizard of the Upper Amazon* (Boston: Houghton Mifflin, 1974).

LaPuma, Karen, *Awakening Female Power* (Fairfax, CA: SoulSource Publishing, 1991).

Leek, Sybil, *Diary of a Witch* (New York: Signet Books, 1969).

Leland, C. G., *Aradia, Gospel of the Witches* (Freemont, CA: Technology Group,1986).

Lewis, Bernard, *History—Remembered, Recovered, Invented* (Princeton, NJ: Princeton University Press, 1975).

Lichtheim, Miriam, *Ancient Egyptian Literature,* vols. I, II, III (Berkeley, CA: University of California Press, 1980).

Lines, Marianna, *Sacred Stones, Sacred Places* (Edinburgh, Scotland: St. Andrews Press, 1992).

Littleton, C. Scott, *The New Comparative Mythology, An Anthropological Assessment of the Theories of Georges Dumezil* (Berkeley, CA: University of California Press,

1980).

Llewelyn, Morgan, *Bard: The Odyssey of the Irish* (New York: Tor Books, 1987).

————, *Druids* (New York: William Morrow, 1991)

Lonegren, Sig, *Labyrinths, Ancient Myths and Modern Uses* (Glastonbury, Somerset, England: Gothic Image Publications, 1991).

————, *Spiritual Dowsing* (Glastonbury, Somerset, England: Gothic Image Publications, 1986).

Lorde, Audre, *Use of the Erotic As Power* (New York: Out and Out Books / Crossing Press, 1982).

Luhrman, T. M., *Persuasions of the Witch's Craft* (Cambridge, MA: Harvard University Press, 1989).

MacCana, Proinsias, *Celtic Mythology* (New York: Peter Bedrick Books, 1968).

Malaclypse, The Younger, *Principia Discordia* (Lilburn, GA: Illuminet Press, 1991).

Markale, Jean, *The Celts* (Rochester, VT: Inner Traditions, 1993).

Mathers, S. Liddell Macgregor, *The Key of Solomon the King (Clavicula Salomonis)* (New York: Samuel Weiser, 1972).

Mathews, Caitlin, *The Elements of the Celtic Tradition* (Dorset, England: Element Books, 1989).

Mathews, Caitlin, and Prudence Jones, *Voices from the Circle* (London: Aquarian Press, 1990).

Maxwell, Ed, *Occult Awareness: A Handbook for Law Enforcement Officers,* HC 62, Box 3304, Long Pond, PA 18334.

Merrifield, Ralph, *The Archaeology of Ritual and Magic* (New York: New Amsterdam Books, 1987).

Merry, Eleanor C., *The Flaming Door, The Mission of the Celtic Folk Soul* (Edinburgh, Scotland: Floris Books, 1983).

Miller, Hamish, and Paul Broadhurst, *The Sun and the Serpent: An Investigation into Earth Energies* (Launceston, England: Pendragon Press, 1994).

Miller, Richard Alan, *The Magical and Ritual Uses of Herbs* (New York: Destiny Books, 1983).

Mills, Theodore, "Quest for a Witche's Jewel," *The Witche's Almanac* (Aries 1992–Pisces 1993) PO Box 318, Milton, MA 02186.

Miners, Scott, *A Spiritual Approach to Male/Female Relations* (Wheaton, Ill: Theosophical Publishing House, 1984).

Mohen, Jean-Pierre, *The World of the Megaliths* (New York: Facts on File, 1990).

Murray, Liz and Colin, *The Celtic Tree Oracle* (New York: St. Martin's Press, 1988).

Murray, Margaret A., *The God of the Witches* (London: Oxford University Press, 1952).

Murray, Margaret, *The Witch-Cult in Western Europe* (London: Oxford University Press, 1921).

Naddair, Kaledon, *Keltic Folk and Faerie Tales* (London: Century Hutchinson, 1987).

Nichols, Ross, *The Book of Druidry* (Northamptonshire, England: Aquarian Press, 1990).

O'Boyle, Sean, *Ogam the Poet's Secret* (Dublin: Gilbert Dalton, 1980).

O'Flaherty, Wendy Doniger, *Women, Androgynes and Other Mythical Beasts* (Chicago: University of Chicago Press, 1982).

O'Gaea, Ashleen, *The Family Wicca Book* (St. Paul, MN: Llewellyn Publications, 1993).

Olson, Carl, *The Book of the Goddess Past and Present* (New York: Crossroad Publishing, 1989).

Ouspensky, P. D., *The Symbolism of the Tarot* (New York: Dover Publications, 1976).

Pepper, Elizabeth, *The Moon Diary and Love Charms* (Cambridge, MA: Pentacle Press, 1989).

Pepper, Elizabeth, and John Wilcock, *Magical and Mystical Sites: Europe and the British Isles* (Grand Rapids, MI: Phanes Press, 1983).

———, *Witches All* (New York: Grosset and Dunlap, 1977).

Piggott, Stuart, *The Druids* (New York: Thames and Hudson, 1986).

Qualls-Corbett, Nancy, *The Sacred Prostitute* (Toronto: Inner City Books, 1988).

Rebsamen, Fredrick, trans., *Beowulf* (New York: HarperCollins, 1991).

Rees, Alwyn and Brinley, *Celtic Heritage* (New York: Thames and Hudson, 1961).

Regardie, Israel, *The Complete Golden Dawn System of Magic* (Scottsdale, AZ: New Falcon Publications, 1990).

———, *Foundations of Practical Magic* (London: Aquarian Press, 1982).

Ross, Anne, *Everyday Life of the Pagan Celts* (London: Carousel Books, 1972).

———, *Pagan Celtic Britain* (London: Constable, 1993).

———, *The Pagan Celts* (Totowa, NJ: Barnes and Noble, 1970).

Ross, Anne, and Don Robins, *The Life and Death of a Druid Prince* (New York: Summit Books, 1989).

Roth, Gabrielle, *Maps to Ecstasy* (San Rafael, CA: New World Library, 1989).

Rutherford, Ward, *Celtic Mythology: Nature and Influence of Celtic Myth—Druidism to Arthurian Legend* (Wellingborough, England: Aquarian Press, 1987).

Smith, Brian K., *Reflections on Resemblance, Ritual and Religion* (Oxford, England: Oxford University Press, 1989).

Simpson, Jaqueline, *Scandinavian Folk Tales* (London: Penguin Books, 1988).

Squire, Charles, *Celtic Myth and Legend* (North Hollywood, CA: Newcastle Publishing, 1975).

Starhawk, *Dreaming the Dark* (Boston: Beacon Press, 1988).

———, *The Fifth Sacred Thing* (New York: Bantam, 1993).

———, *The Spiral Dance* (San Francisco: Harper and Row, 1979).

———, *Truth or Dare* (San Francisco: Harper and Row, 1987).

Starke, Shirley, *Celtica, Songs for the Harp* (Woodside, NY: Celtic Heritage Press, 1990).

Stein, Diane, *Casting the Circle* (Freedom, CA: Crossing Press, 1990).

Stewart, Robert J., *Celtic Gods and Goddesses* (London: Blandford, 1990).

Stone, Merlin, *Ancient Mirrors of Womanhood* (Boston: Beacon Press, 1984).

Storms, G., *Anglo-Saxon Magic* (The Hague: Martinus Nijhoff, 1948).

Strozzi Heckler, Richard, *In Search of the Warrior Spirit* (Berkeley, CA: North Atlantic Books, 1990, revised 1992).

Taylor, Tony and Sable, *Book of Ritual* (self-published), Henge of Keltria, PO Box 48369, Minneapolis, MN 55448 ($12 plus $3 s&h).

Taylor, Rogan, *The Death and Resurrection Show* (London: Blond, 1985).

Thompson, C. J. S., *The Mysteries and Secrets of Magic* (New York: Olympia Press, 1972).

Valiente, Doreen, *An ABC of Witchcraft* (Custer, WA: Phoenix Publishers, 1975).

———, *Witchcraft for Tomorrow* (Custer, WA: Phoenix Publishers, 1978).

Vendryes, Joseph, *Choix d'Etudes Linguistiques et Celtiques* (Paris: C. Klincksieck, 1952).

———, *Lexique Etymologique de L'Irlandais Ancien*, vol. 25 (Dublin: Dublin Institute for Advanced Studies, 1959).

Waite, Arthur Edward, *The Pictorial Key to the Tarot* (New York: U.S. Games Systems, 1986).

Walker, Barbara G., *The Women's Dictionary of Symbols and Sacred Objects* (San Francisco: Harper and Row, 1988).

———, *The Women's Encyclopedia of Myths and Secrets* (San Francisco: Harper and Row, 1983).

Wasserman, Harvey, *America Born and Reborn* (New York: Macmillan, 1984).

———, *Energy War* (Westport, CT: Lawrence Hill, 1979).

———, *Harvey Wasserman's History of the United States* (New York: Four Walls, Eight Windows, 1989).

Wasserman, Harvey, Norman Solomon, Robert Alvarez, and Eleanor Walters, *Killing Our Own: The Disaster of America's Experience with Atomic Radiation* (New York: Dell/Delta, 1982).

Weed, Susun, *Healing Wise*, Ash Tree Publishing, PO Box 64, Woodstock, NY 12498.

———, *WiseWoman Herbal for the Childbearing Year*, Ash Tree Publishing, PO Box 64, Woodstock, NY 12498.

———, *The WiseWoman Way for the Menopausal Years*, Ash Tree Publishing, PO Box 64, Woodstock, NY 12498.

Williamson, Robin, *The Wise and Foolish Tongue* (San Fransisco: Chronicle Books, 1991).

Wolfe, Allyn, "Good News, Bad News: West Country Wicca," *Red Garters International*, vol. 19, no. 3, 1990.

Zabkar, Louis V., *Hymns to Isis in Her Temple at Philae* (Hanover, NH: University Press of New England, 1988).

Audiotapes

Arthen, Andras Corban and Deidre Pulgram
We Believe
Serpent's Egg Publishing
PO Box 513
Medford, MA 02155

Bonewits, Isaac
Avalon is Rising, and
  Be Pagan Once Again
ADF Regalia Department
PO Box 2536
N. Babylon, NJ 11703

Corrigan, Ian
Once Around the Wheel, Songs of the Wheel, Ian Corrigan Live at Starwood!
Association for Consciousness Exploration
1643 Lee Rd.
Cleveland Heights, OH 44118

Elie and Friends
Earth Is My Temple
Sabra Enterprises
PO Box 15636
Lockland, OH 45215
(Inquire about accompanying booklet)

Grosvenor, Vertamae
Goddess Spirituality
NPR Horizons audio cassette tape no.
  HO 881220C001
NPR Customer Service
975 Observatory Dr.
Madison, WI 53706

Haines, Julia
Odyssey, an Afro-Celtic harp cassette
A. Howl Records
53 West Willow Grove Ave.
Philadelphia, PA 19118

Heymann, Ann
The Harper's Land, Queen of Harps
Clairseach Productions
PO Box 637
Winthrop, MN 55396
(Inquire about her books and instruc-
tional materials for the Celtic
wirestrung harp)

Hopman, Ellen Evert
*The Herbal and Magical Powers of
Trees, Celtic Gods and Goddesses,*
and *The Druid Path: Herbs & Festivals*
Creative Seminars
PO Box 203
West Hurley, NY 12491
(914) 679–6885

MotherTongue
*All Beings of the Earth, Firedance!,
Wheel of the Year: Mothertongue
Live!,This Winter's Night (A Celebra-
tion of the Winter Solstice)*
Earthspirit Community
PO Box 365
Medford, MA 02155

Scott, Molly, and Sarah Benson
We All Come from the Goddess
Medicine Song Productions
Molly Scott c/o Sumitra
PO Box U
Charlemont, MA 01339

Weed, Susun
Menopause
Ash Tree Publishing
PO Box 64
Woodstock, NY 12498

Williamson, Robin F.
*Five Bardic Mysteries, Five Celtic Tales of
Enchantment, Five Legendary Histories
of Britain, Five Celtic Tales of Prodigies
and Marvels, Rory Mor and the
Gruagach Gaire*
Robin Williamson Productions
PO Box 27522
Los Angeles, CA 90027

Videotapes

Borroughs, William (narrator)
Witchcraft through the Ages (1920)
(spoof with film footage from the
1920s and bizarre jazz accompaniment)
MPI Home Video
15825 Rob Roy Dr.
Oak Forest, IL 60452

Gaup, Nils
Pathfinder (1987) (Lapp with English
subtitles)
Fox-Lorber Home Video
419 Park Ave. South
New York, NY 10016

Gimbutas, Marija
World of the Goddess
distributed by New Leaf Distributing Co.
5425 Tulane Dr. SW
Atlanta, GA 30336

Hopman, Ellen Evert
Gifts from the Healing Earth, vol. I
(1993) (herbal video)
EFP Services
21 Kettle Hill Rd., RFD #3
Amherst, MA 01002
(413) 548–8058

Hopman, Ellen Evert
Pagans (1995)
EFP Services
21 Kettle Hill Rd., RFD #3
Amherst, MA 01002
(413) 548–8058

Reed, Donna
Goddess Remembered and *The Burning
Times*
Direct Cinema
PO Box 10003
Santa Monica, CA 90410

Schiffman, Suzanne
Sorceress
Mystic Fire Video
Box 9323
S. Burlington, VT 05407

Weed, Susun
Weeds to the Wise
Ash Tree Publishing
PO Box 64
Woodstock, NY 12498

Magazines and Other Publications

Accord
PO Box 33274
Austin, TX 78764

Aerious
93640 Deadwood Creek
Deadwood, OR 97430

Aisling
PO Box 196
London WC1A 2DY England

All Acts of Love and Pleasure
(Pagan erotica)
2049 S. Federal Blvd., #286
Denver, CO 80219

All My Relations
PO Box 352
Hazleton, BC VOJ 1YO Canada

Ambrosia
PO Box 212
Springfield, MO 65801–0212

Artemisia's Magick
PO Box 144
Payette, ID 83661

The Azrael Project Newsletter
(dedicated to a macroscopic understanding of the Angel of Death)
Westgate Press
5219 Magazine St.
New Orleans, LA 70115

Bard's Circle
PO Box 760
Campellford, ON KOL 1LO Canada

The Beltane Papers
(women's mysteries)
PO Box 8
Clear Lake, WA 98235

Calendar of Events
(Lists most festivals and events nationwide)
Larry Cornett
9355 Sibelius Drive
Vienna, VA 22182–1632

The Cauldron
Mike Howard
Caemorgan Cottage
Caemorgan Rd.
Cardigan, Dyfed
Wales SA43 1QU 11 UK

The Cauldron of Cerridwen
Kindred Spirit
PO Box 141
Willow Grove, PA 19090–0141

Celtic Connections
c/o David James, Tamarisk Farm
West Bexington, Worchester
Dorset DT2 9DF England

Circle Network News
PO Box 219
Mt. Horeb, WI 53572

Compost Newsletter
729 Fifth Ave.
San Francisco, CA 94118

Connections
1705 14th St., #181
Boulder, CO 80302

Creation Spirituality Magazine
160 E. Virginia St. #290
San Jose, CA 95112–5848

Crone Chronicles
(conscious aging)
PO Box 81
Kelly, WY 83011

Cultwatch Response Inc.
Attn. V. Copeland
PO Box 1842
Colorado Springs, CO 80901

Dalriada Magazine
2 Brathwic Place
Brodick, Isle of Arran
KA27 8BN, Scotland
(Ask about Celtic Heritage Society and correspondence course.)

Daughters of Nyx
PO Box 1187
White Salmon, WA 98672

Demeter's Emerald
(Pagan parenting)
PO Box 612603
South Lake Tahoe, CA 96152

Diipetes Quarterly
PO Box 20037
GR 11810 Athens, Greece

Directory to Canadian Pagan Resources
PO Box 2205
Clearbrook, BC V2T 3X8 Canada

Di Schmatteh
(Judeo-Pagan newsletter)
PO Box 7616
Minneapolis, MN 55407

Dragon's Song
PO Box 408, Woden
ACT 2606, Australia

The Dreamweaver
PO Box 150692
Fort Worth, TX 76108

A Druid Directory
(a guide to modern Druid orders)
Phillip Shallcross, editor, B.D.O.
PO Box 29
St. Leonard's-on-Sea
East Sussex TN37 7YP England

Druidisme
BP 13
93301 Auberviliers
Cedex, France

Druid's Progress
PO Box 3495
Jersey City, NJ 07303

The Druid's Voice
COBDO
PO Box 29
St. Leonard's-on-Sea
E. Sussex TN37 7YP England

Earth Circle News
PO Box 1938
Sebastopol, CA 95473

Egyptian Religion Newsletter
Neter
PO Box 290011
Tampa, FL 33687–0011

Eidolon
PO Box 4117
Ann Arbor, MI 48106

Emania
(excellent non-Pagan Celtic scholarship
  from Ireland)
Ford and Bailie
PO Box 138
Belmont, MA 02178

Emerging Self
c/o Mary Paruszkiewicz
129C Lucille Ct., 225
Bartlett, IL 60103

Enchante
30 Charlton St.
Box 6F
New York, NY 10014

The Enchanting News
PO Box 145
Marion, CT 06444

The Entheogen Review
PO Box 778
El Rito, NM 87530

Factsheet Five
PO Box 170099
San Francisco, CA 94117–0099

The Flatland Witch's
Pen Pal Listing (send a #10 SASE)
Wolverine
PO Box 117
Cascade, MT 59421

From The Hearth
(Pagan parenting)
c/o K. Hinds
728 Derrydown Way
Decatur, GA 30030

Good Heavens
PO Box 674
Defiance, OH 43512

Green Egg
PO Box 1542
Ukiah, CA 95482
5878037@mcimail.com

The Green Man
(for Pagan men)
PO Box 641
Pt. Arena, CA 95468

H.A.M. (How About Magic?)
(for Pagan youth)
Nemeton
PO Box 488
Laytonville, CA 95454

The Hazel Nut
PO Box 186
Auburn, AL 36831–0186

The Heart Beat
New Dawn Publishing Company
20526 County Route 59
Dexter, NY 13634–9743

Hecate's Loom
PO Box 5206
Station B
Victoria, BC V8R 6N4 Canada

Hexen Zeit Schrift
Palraune Verlag
Schmezer Strasse 18
Ladenburg W–6802, Germany

Hidden Path
(for Gardnerian Wiccans only)
Three Sister's Ltd.
PO Box 934
Kenosha, WI 53141

Ho
(lists Rainbow Gatherings)
1614 Camp Springs Rd.
Riedsville, NC 27320

Hole in the Stone
2049 S. Federal, #286
Denver, CO 80219

Horns and Crescent
c/o J. Powell
PO Box 382053
Cambridge, MA 02238

Idunna
PO Box 25637
Tempe, AZ 85285–5637

Indigenous Woman
PO Box 174
Lake Elmo, MN 55042

Inner Circle News
c/o Mystical Powers Curio
3421 E. Tropicana, #G
Las Vegas, NV 89121

Keltoi
(non-Pagan Celtic)
PO Box 20153
Dag Hammarskjold Postal Center
New York, NY 10017

Keltria, A Journal of Druidism and Celtic Magic
PO Box 48369
Minneapolis, MN 55448
Keltria@aol.com
(Ask about their Book of Ritual and correspondence course)

Kindred Spirits Quarterly
PO Box 101
Bega, NSW 2550, Australia

The Little Folk
(for parents and children)
PO Box 10715
Glendale, AZ 85318–0715

Llyr: The Magazine of Celtic Arts
3313 North Mont Rd.
Baltimore, MD 21244

Magic Wand
PO Box 27164
Detroit, MI 48227

Magical Blend
PO Box 11303
San Francisco, CA 94101–7303

Magical Unicorn Messenger
817½ Park
Findlay, OH 45840

Mezlim
PO Box 19566
Cincinnati, OH 45219

Military Pagan Newsletter
PO Box 2610
McKinleyville, CA 95521–2610

Millenial Chronicles
RR1, Box 478
Williams, IN 47470

The Minstrel: A New Tune
PO Box 3068
Winnipeg, MB R3C 4E5 Canada

Moira: Revue de Paganisme, de Magie et de Sciences Traditionelles
Moira/CDD, BP 68
33034 Bordeaux
Cedex, France

Moondog Journal
c/o David Koons
RD1, Box 338
Landisburg, PA 17040

Mystagogue Magazine
PO Box 15955
Sacramento, CA 95852–0955

Native Nations
245 Fifth Ave.
New York, NY 10016

The New Invocation
PO Box 17163
Phoenix, AZ 85011

New Moon Rising
8818-G Troy Street
Spring Valley, CA 91977

Ocean Gypsy
(for mermaid lovers)
PO Box 828
Nyack, NY 10960

Ocular: Illustrated Paganism & Occult
Rosewood Cottage
Langtoft, Driffield
E. Yorkshire YO25 OTQ England

Odinic Rite
Briefing B.M.
Runic, London WC 1N 3XX England

Odinism Today
B.M.
Edda, London WC 1N 3XX England

Of a Like Mind
PO Box 6021
Madison, WI 53716
(Ask about network membership, Pentacle Pals, and hotline)

Out of the Broom Closet
Pentamerous Publishing
PO Box 2298
Athens, OH 45701–2298

Pagan Life
Irish Pagan Movement
The Bridge House
Clonegal, Enniscorthy
Wexford, Ireland

Pagan Muse and World Report
PO Box 850
Freemont, CA 94537

Pagana
(Pagan/occult/Witchcraft Sig of Mensa)
c/o Valerie Voight
PO Box 9336
San Jose, CA 95157

Pagans for Peace
PO Box 2205
Clearbrook, BC V2T 3X8 Canada

Pagans in Recovery
c/o Church of Earth Healing
22 Palmer St.
Athens, OH 45701

Pallas Society News
PO Box 18211
Encino, CA 91316

Pan American Indian Association News
PO Box 244
Nocatee, FL 33864–0244

Panegyria
Aquarian Tabernacle Church
PO Box 57
Index, WA 98256

The Pathfinder
PO Box 11
Valley Head, AL 35989

Pax Deorum
(Roman Paganism)
PO Box 12104
Tucson, AZ 85732

The Quill and Sword
WLPA
PO Box 8736
Salem, MA 01971–8736

Quintessence
PO Box 10634
Winston-Salem, NC 27108

Rainbow Tribe / Stoneman
122925 Fifth Ave. So.
Burnsville, MN 55337

The Raven's Call
(Strega, Italian traditional Witchcraft)
Moon Dragon Publications
PO Box 301831
Escondido, CA 92030

Red Garters International
NWC
PO Box 162046
Sacramento, CA 95816

Rosegate Journal
PO Box 5967
Providence, RI 02903

Sacred Circle
(Baltic Paganism)
Vilija Witte
Romuva/Canada
PO Box 232 Stn. D
Etobicoke, Ontario M9A 4X2 Canada

Sacred Hart
PO Box 72
Kenmore, NY 14217

Sacred Serpent
(journal of Baltic Paganism)
Iron Wolf
PO Box 232, Stn. D
Etobicoke, Ontario M9A 4X2 Canada

Sagewoman
PO Box 641
Point Arena, CA 95468

The Serpent's Tail
PO Box 07437
Milwaukee, WI 53207

Silver Chalice
PO Box 196
Thorofare, NJ 08086

Snake Power
5856 College Ave., #138
Oakland, CA 94618

Survival
PO Box 1502
New Bern, NC 28563

The Sword of Dyrnwyn
PO Box 674884
Marietta, GA 30067

Symphony, A Newsletter of Magick and Harmony
PO Box 27465
San Antonio, TX 78227–0465

Talking Leaves
1430 Willamette, #367
Eugene, OR 97401

Tarot Network News
TAROCO
Box 104
Sausalito, CA 94966

Tranet
(alternative technologies and living)
PO Box 567
Rangeley, ME 04970–0567

Trans
PO Box 121851
Nashville, TN 37212

The Unicorn, and The Littlest Unicorn
(for children)
Rowan Tree Church
PO Box 8814
Minneapolis, MN 55408

The Web
(spiritual women's publication)
401 Cumberland Dr.
No. Augusta, SC 29841

The Wiccan
BM Box 7097
London WC1N 3XX England

The Wiccan Rede
Silver Circle
PO Box 473
NL–3700 Alzeist The Netherlands

Wild Woods Forum
PO Box 61413
Virginia Beach, VA 23462

The Witches' Almanac
PO Box 318
Milton, MA 02186

Woman of Power
PO Box 827
Cambridge, MA 02238–9990

Wood and Water
77 Parliament Hill Rd.
London NW3 2TH England

WPPA Update
(trade paper of the Wiccan/Pagan Press
 Alliance)
WPPA
PO Box 1392
Mechanicsburg, PA 17055

Yggdrasil
Freya's Folk
537 Jones Street #165
San Francisco, CA 94102–2007

Organizations, Groups, and Individuals

Aerious
Mark McNutt
93640 Deadwood Creek Rd.
Deadwood, OR 97630

Amer
(for people experiencing religious
 discrimination and those wanting
 information on the occult)
PO Box 16551
Clayton, MO 63105

**American Druidic Church, Jay and
 Patricia Tibbles**
PO Box 2642
Fontana CA 92334

Ancient Order of Druids
Ted Williams
125 Magyar Crescent
Nuneaton CV11 4SJ England

Ancient Ways
4075 Telegraph Ave.
Berkeley, CA 94609

Aos Dana
Fiona Davidson
Invergowrie House
Ninewells, Dundee DD2 1UA Scotland

The Aquarian Tabernacle Church
PO Box 57
Index, WA 98256

Ar nDraíocht Féin (ADF)
Box 516
E. Syracuse, NY 13057–0516

The Artemisian Tradition
c/o Orieythyia
PO Box 7184
Capitol Station
Albany, NY 12224

**Association for Consciousness
 Exploration (ACE)**
(sponsors the Starwood Festival)
1643 Lee Rd.
Cleveland Heights, OH 44118

Avalon East Pagan Gathering
PO Box 36135
Halifax, NS B3J 3S9 Canada

Bardic Order Group
Alex Gunningham
Flat 2
20 The Common
Ealing, London W5 3JB England

Bay Area Pagan Assemblies (BAPA)
PO Box 850
Freemont, CA 94537

B.C. Witchcamp
PO Box 21510
1850 Commercial Dr.
Vancouver, BC V5N 4AO Canada

The Bear Tribe
PO Box 9167
Spokane, WA 99209

Bethel Festival (Spirit of the 60s)
Rich Suraci
67 Maple St.
Newburgh, NY 12550

Rev. Paul Beyerl
9724 132 Ave. NE
Kirkland, WA 98033

Brighid's Fire Festival
(Imbolc Gathering)
Pagan CC of Ohio
PO Box 02089
Columbus, OH 43202

British Druid Order
Box 29
St. Leonard's-on-Sea
East Sussex TN37 7YP England

Callista
HC PO Box 282
Somerset, VA 22946

The Celtic League, American Branch
PO Box 20153
Dag Hammarskjold Center
New York, NY 10017

The Celtic Research and Folklore Society
Spion Kop
Lamash, Isle of Arran
Scotland KA27 8NL

Charleston Pagan Net
PO Box 62563
N. Charleston, SC 29419

Chattanooga Intertribal Association
(Cherokee, Creek, Choctaw, Iroquois, Tlingit, Pueblo, Lakota)
PO Box 71585
Chattanooga, TN 37407

Church and School of Wicca
PO Box 1502
New Bern, NC 28560

Church of All Worlds (CAW)
PO Box 1452
Ukiah CA 95482
listserv@netcom.com

Church of All Worlds Australia
Anthorr & Fiona Nomchong
Box 408
Woden ACT 2606 Australia

Church of All Worlds Canada
Kathryn Millar
Site 16, c26
Gabriola Is., BC VOR 1XO Canada

Church of All Worlds Germany
Ulrich Glaser, Ostergasse 9
Markgroningen 714 Germany

Church of All Worlds Switzerland
Dio Weir
Postfach 8109 Zurich
CH 8036 Switzerland

Church of The Eternal Source
(Egyptian Pagans)
PO Box 371353–1353
San Diego, CA 92137–1353

Church of the Goddess
PO Box 583
Capitola, CA 95010

Church of the Iron Oak
PO Box 060679
Palm Bay, FL 32906–0679

The Church of the Sacred Earth
PO Box 321
Bethel, VT 05032

Circle des Amis du Druidisme / Ollotouta Druidique des Gauls
BP13, 93301 Aubervilier
Cedex, France

Circle Cithaeron
PO Box 15461
Washington, DC 20003

Circle of Pink Triangle
Gay Neo-Pagan Faerie Gathering
9808 Cypress St.
Tampa, FL 33635

Circle Sanctuary
PO Box 219
Mt. Horeb, WI 53572

Circles of Exchange
9594 First Ave NE
Seattle, WA 98115

Congregationalist Witchcraft Association
PO Box 2205
Clearbrook, BC V2T 3X8 Canada

Cougar
PO Box 201
Frenchtown, NJ 08825

The Council of British Druid Orders
PO Box 29
St. Leonard's-on-Sea
E. Sussex TN37 7YP England

Council of British Druid Orders
Elizabeth Murray [secretary]
76 Antrobus Road
London W4 5NQ England

Council of the Magical Arts
PO Box 33274
Austin, TX 78764–3274

Covenant of Gaia Church
PO Box 1742
Station M
Calgary, Alberta T2P 2L7 Canada

Covenant of the Goddess (COG)
PO Box 1226
Berkeley, CA 94704
pio@cog.org

Covenant of Unitarian Universalist
    Pagans (CUUPS)
PO Box 640
Cambridge, MA 02140

Craft Wise
PO Box 457
Botsford, CT 06404

CraftWorks /UFO III Fest
PO Box 1328
Bloomington, IN 47402

The Crow Call
PO Box 187
Bogota, NJ 07603

Crow Coven: A Pagan/Alternative
    Network Alliance
PO Box 8456
Burlington, VT 05402

Crystal Fox
433 Main St.
Laurel, MD 20707

Culturewatch
(dedicated to keeping track of the right
    wing's assault on civil rights)
464 19th St.
Oakland, CA 94612

Danica Paulic
Mosnje 20
Rdovljica, Slovenia 64240

Diana's Grove
(sponsors numerous festivals)
PO Box 159
Salem, MO 65560

Dragonfest
PO Box 6927
Denver, CO 80206

Dream Catchers
340 E. Maple
Birmingham, MI 48009–6313

Druid Clan of Dana
Lady Olivia Robertson
Clonegal Castle
Enniscorthy S. Ireland

Druuidica Comardiia Eriutalamas
582 Boul. Des Praries
Laval QE H7V 1B5 Canada

D'vora
PO Box 1048
Buffalo, NY 14213–9998

The Earth Conclave
(sponsors Power of Words and Culture
    Conference)
PO Box 14377
Madison, WI 53714

Earth Drum Council
PO Box 1284
Concord, MA 01742

Earth First!
PO Box 5176
Missoula, MT 59806

Earth Medicine Journeys
PO Box 1239
Lebanon, TN 37088

Earth Rhythm
2488 Nadine Circle
Hinckley, OH 44233

Earthkeeper Medicine Society
PO Box 304-G
Montezuma, NM 87731

Earthskills Workshops
Darry Wood
Unicoi State Park
Helen, GA 30545

The Earthspirit Community
PO Box 365
Medford, MA 02155

Ecole Drudique Des Gaules
Bernard Jacquelin
Villa Montmorency
75016 Paris, 45 27 74 79 France

Ecumenicon Festival
5400 Eisenhower Ave.
Alexandria, VA 22304

Edge of Perception
PO Box 159
Salem, MO 65560

Elderflower Womenspirit Fest
PO Box 7153
Redwood City, CA 94063

Elf Lore Family
(Wild Magic Gathering and Elf Fest)
PO Box 1082
Bloomington, IN 47403

Elie
c/o Sabra Enterprises
PO Box 15636
Lockland, OH 45215–9998

Enchantments Ltd.
PO Box 2867
Toledo, OH 43606

Etheracon Festival
c/o Tom Sheeley
40 Mobile Manor
Middle Road
Hudson, NY 12534

**Ethnobotany and Psychoactive
   Plants, Botanical Preserve Center**
PO Box 1368
Sebastopol, CA 95473

Evolution
PO Box 833
London NW6 England

**Rowan Fairgrove and Russell
   Williams**
PO Box 90304
San Jose, CA 95109

The Fellowship of Isis (FOI)
Clonegal Castle
Enniscorthy, S. Ireland

Feral
(Fellowship of Earth Religions, Awakenings,
   and Lore)
PO Box 733
N. Hollywood, CA 91603

Finnish Pagans, Kati-ra and Tapio
Mandragora Dimensions
PO Box 452
00101 Helsinki Finland

Forever Forests
(tax-deductible tree plantings)
PO Box 212
Redwood Valley, CA 95470

Four Oaks Center
PO Box 930
Blue Hill, ME 04612

Foxwood Temple
PO Box 5128
Laurel, MD 20726

**Free Spirit Festival/ Free Spirit
   Alliance**
PO Box 5358
Laurel, MD 20726

French Druid Groups
  Muller Alain
  10/1 Cite Cadres
  67510 Lembach France

  Pierre Collier
  8 rue Pierre Curie
  59195 Herin France

  Pierre Duchesne
  B.P. 5
  35540 Plerguer France

  Regis Blanchet
  Le Prieure
  27120 Rouvray France

Freya's Folk
537 Jones St., #165
San Francisco, CA 94102

Fungofile Inc.
(Telluride Wild Mushroom Fest)
PO Box 48503
Denver, CO 80248–0503

Gay and Lesbian Pagan Coalition
PO Box 26442
Oklahoma City, OK 73126–0442

GFRNETwor
(dedicated to healing of the Earth Mother)
PO Box 243GE
Madisonville, TN 37354

Glastonbury Order of Druids
R. Maughfling and J. Paterson
Dove House
Barton-St. David
Somerset TA11 6DF England

Gorsedd De Bretagne
c/o Bertran Borne
An Neiz
Kerhenri, Saint-Thurien 29380 France

Greenleaf Church of Wicca
PO Box 924
Springfield, MO 65801

The Guardians of the Fourth Face
c/o Tuitéan
PO Box 24213
Edina, MN 55424

Gulf Coast Women's Fest
(Memorial Day Weekend)
Hensen Productions
1806 Curcor Dr.
Gulfport, MS 39507

Harvest of Light
2401 Bernadette, #123
Columbia, MO 65203

The Haven
3064 East Main Rd
Portsmouth, RI 02871

Haven [Elspeth and Nybor]
PO Box 0948
Cumberland, MD 21501

**Hawkwind Earth Renewal
   Cooperative**
PO Box 11
Valley Head, AL 35989

Hawthorn Grove Inc.
PO Box 706
Monticello, NY 12701–0706

Heartland Spiritual Alliance
(sponsors Heartland Spirit Festival)
PO Box 3407
Kansas City, KS 66103

The Henge of Keltria
PO Box 48369
Minneapolis, MN 55448
Keltria@aol.com

Ellen Evert Hopman
PO Box 219
Amherst, MA 01004

Illuminati of Indiana
PO Box 5793
Bloomington, IN 47407

Imago
553 Enright Ave.
Cincinnati, OH 45205

Institute for Deep Ecology
PO Box 2290
Boulder, CO 80306

Ishpiming Retreat Center
PO Box 340
Manitowish Waters, WI 54545

Japanese Pagan Network
Ikari Segawa
7–22–4 Minamisyowa-Cho
Tokushima City 770 Japan

Journeys of Wisdom
4889 Sinclair Rd., #108
Columbus, OH 43229

Keltria Publications
"Kaer Eidyn"
PO Box 307
Edinburgh EH9 1XA, Alban Scotland

Lady Liberty League
c/o Circle
PO Box 219
Mt. Horeb, WI 53572

Lake Circle
(sponsors Beltane gathering)
PO Box 83, Hell Gate Station
New York, NY 10029

Lifespring Gathering
PO Box 30327
Jacksonville, FL 32230–0327

Lifeworks
PO Box 5362
Atlanta, GA 31107

Deborah Ann Light
PO Box 2669
Sag Harbor, NY 11963

London Druid Group
Gordon Gentry
74 Riversmeet
Hertford SG14 1LE England

Lumens Gate Festival
N'Chi
PO Box 19566
Cincinnati, OH 45219

Lunatic Fringe
PO Box 126
Saxapahaw, NC 27340

The Lyceum of Venus of Healing
PO Box 698
Ayer, MA 01432–0698

Macaw
PO Box 24124
Milwaukee, WI 53224–0124

Magic Circle Drummers (hands-on workshops)
Jeff McBride and Abbi Spinner
305 W. 52nd St.
New York, NY 10019

Magical Education Center of Ann Arbor
PO Box 7727
Ann Arbor, MI 48107

Magnus (Jeff) McBride
c/o Tobias Beckwith & Associates
305 West 52 St., Suite 1L
New York, NY 10019

Majkia Temple
PO Box 901
Ardmore, PA 19003

Merriam Hill Education Centre
148 Merriam Hill Rd.
Greenville, NH 03048–9729

Midwest Pagan Council
PO Box 160
Western Springs, IL 60558–0160

Military Pagan Network
PO Box 2610
McKinleyville, CA 95521

MIT Pagan Students Association
c/o Association of Student Activities
MIT
77 Mass. Ave.
Cambridge, MA 02139

Moonweb
PO Box 15461
Washington, DC 20003

Morningstar
2801 Buford Hwy., # 435
Atlanta, GA 30329

Mythcon
c/o Irv
5465 N. Morgan St., #106
Alexandria, VA 22312

National Women's Music and Spirit Conference
(June event)
Women in the Arts
PO Box 1427
Indianapolis, IN 46206

Nepthys Lodge
PO Box 1075
Edmonton, Alberta T5J 2M1 Canada

New England Covens of Traditionalist Witches
PO Box 29182
Providence, RI 02909–1116

The New Invocation
PO Box 17163
Phoenix AZ 85011

New Moon / New York
PO Box 1471
Madison Square Station
New York, NY 10159–1471

New Reformed Druids of North America
Stephen Abbott
PO Box 6775
San Jose, CA 95150

New Reformed Orthodox Order of the Golden Dawn (NROOGD)
2140 Shattuck Ave., #2236
Berkeley, CA 94704

The New Wiccan Church
PO Box 162046
Sacramento, CA 95816

North Shore (Massachusetts) Covenant of Unitarian Universalist Pagans
First Universalist Society
211 Bridge Street
Salem, MA 01970

Oak Dragon Project
PO Box 5
Castle Cary
Somerset BA7 7YQ England

Olwydd
(Pagan discussion group)
PO Box 574
Hudson, NH 03051

Order of Bards, Ovates, and Druids
Philip Carr-Gomm
PO Box 1333
Lewes, E. Sussex BN7 32G England

Our Lady of the Shining Star
(sponsors Feast of the Gods Festival)
PO Box 520
Church Rock, NM 87311

Our Lord and Lady of the Trinacrian Rose
(Italian traditional craft)
33 Everlyn Ave.
Medford, MA 02155

Pagan CC of Ohio
PO Box 02089
Columbus, OH 43202.

Pagan Education Network
(monitors anti-Pagan activity and press in the U.S. and Canada)
PO Box 1364
Bloomington, IN 47408–1364

The Pagan Federation
BM Box 7097
London WCIN 3XX England

Pagan Leadership Conference
Goddess Studies
c/o Lauri Debayner
1402 Hill St.
Ann Arbor, MI 48104

Pagan Summer Gathering
c/o Draconis Nest
PO Box 408
Woden, ACT 2606 Australia

Pagans for Peace
PO Box 2205
Clearbrook, V2T 3X8 Canada

Pagans for Peace
c/o Barbara Honish and Ulrich Glaser
Ostergasse 9
D–7145 Markgroningen Germany

Pagans in Recovery
c/o The Church of Earth Healing
22 Palmer St.
Athens, OH 45701

Pagans in Recovery Project
c/o Circle
PO Box 219
Mt. Horeb, WI 53572

Panathenaia
PO Box 488
Laytonville, CA 95454

Pan Pacific Alliance
G.P.O. G498
Perth 6001 Western Australia

Pan Pagan Festival, M.P.C. Inc.
PO Box 160
Western Springs, IL 60588

Pantheos
(gay men's network)
PO Box 9543
Santa Fe, NM 87504

Partnership Way
1770 N. Camino Sabidell
Tucson, AZ 85715

Peace and Justice Center
1016 18th Ave.
So. Nashville, TN 37212

**Qadash Kanankhu (Canaanite/
Phoenician Paganism)**
PO Box 7092
Berkeley, CA 94707

Rabenclan
c/o Foreign Contacts Coordinator
Postfach 1214, D-48348
Everswinkel Germany

Rainbow Retreats
PO Box 856
Warrenville, IL 60555

**Ravenwood Church and Seminary of
the Old Religion Inc.**
PO Box 5586
Atlanta, GA 30307

Reclaiming Collective
PO Box 14404
San Francisco, CA 94114

Reformed Druids of North America
c/o The Archdruid
Carleton College
Northfield, MN 55057
(Inquire about Druid Archives project)

The Ring of Troth (Asatru)
PO Box 25637
Tempe AZ 85285

The Rowan Tree Church
PO Box 8814
Minneapolis, MN 555408

Rites of Spring Festival, Earthspirit
PO Box 502
Medford, MA 02155

Sanctuary Phoenicia
(Middle Eastern Paganism)
PO Box 22112
Sacramento, CA 95831

School of Wicca
PO Box 1502
New Bern, NC 28563

The Society of the Evening Star
PO Box 29182
Providence, RI 02909–1116

Solfinna
PO Box 123
Haddam, CT 06438–0123

Solitary, By Choice or by Chance
(federally recognized church for those who
practice their Pagan spirituality alone)
DE-Anna Alba
PO Box 6091
Madison, WI 53716

The Southern Delta Church of Wicca
(a branch of the Aquarian Tabernacle
Church)
PO Box 91
Lake City, AR 72437

Annie Sprinkle
c/o Barbara Carrellas
420 West 46th St.
New York, NY 10036
(212) 265-3796

Stones Scenes
Silver Ravenwolf
PO Box 1392
Mechanicsburg, PA 17055–1392

Tapestry Coven
PO Box 10
Stevenson, MD 21153

Tecumseh Lodge Powwow
(midwinter dances, ceremonies)
Mel Hoefling
1831 Timbercrest
Nashville, IN 47448

Temple of Wicca
PO Box 2281
Lancaster, OH 43130

The 3rd Road
(School of the Faery tradition, Francesca
Dubie)
2261 Market St., #423
San Francisco, CA 94114

Thoth
PO Box 317
BU Station
Boston, MA 02215

Transformational Adventures Tours
25521-E Indian Hills Lane
Laguna Hills, CA 92653

The Turning Wheel
8039-A Ritchie Hwy.
Pasadena, MD 21122

The United Council of Pagans Network
PO Box 91
Lake City, AR 72437

Universal Life Freedom Quest Society
PO Box 2754
Jonesboro, AR 72402

University of Maryland Pagan
Students Association
U.C. Center, PO Box 5
5401 Wilens Ave.
Baltimore, MD 21228

University of Massachusetts Pagan
Students Association
PO Box 117
Student Union Bldg.
U. of Mass.
Amherst, MA 01003

UPPITY
PO Box 672
Dahlonega, GA 30533–0672

Vasudeva Korbiatiev
Basseomaua St. 56–106
St. Petersburg 16135 Russia

Vision Weavers
PO Box 3653
Fairfax, VA 22038

Voices of Women
7407 Aspen Ave.
Takoma Park, MD 20912

The Whole Earth
142 Washington St.
Binghamton, NY 13901

Whole Earth Travel
660 Venice Blvd, #181
Venice, CA 90291

The Wiccan Church of Canada
109 Vaughn Rd.
Toronto, Ontario Canada

Wic-can Fest
PO Box 125
3090 Danforth Ave.
Scarborough, Ontario M1L 1B1 Canada

The Wiccan Information Network
(monitors anti-Wiccan activities, groups,
   and individuals in the U.S. and
   Canada)
PO Box 2422
Main Post Office
Vancouver, BC V6B 3W7 Canada

Wiccan/Pagan Press Alliance
PO Box 1392
Mechanicsburg, PA 17055

Winterfire Festival
Pagan CC of Ohio
PO Box 02089
Columbus, OH 43202

Winterstar Festival, A.C.E.
1643 Lee Rd., #9
Cleveland Hts., OH 44118

The Wisewoman School of Herbal
   Healing
PO Box 64
Woodstock, NY 12498

Witches' League for Public
   Awareness
PO Box 8736
Salem, MA 01971–8736

Witches Today
(information network)
PO Box 221
Levittown, PA 19059

Wolf Spring Song
(Seneca history)
Rte 1, Box 357
Wingina, VA 24599

The Women's Spirituality Forum
PO Box 11363
Oakland, CA 94611

World Magics Festival
c/o Frank Barney
Brushwood Folklore Center
Route 1, Box 154
Sherman, NY 14781

Wyrd Sisters Productions / Spiral
   Festival
PO Box 26414
Albuquerque, NM 87125

Electronic Resources

Mailing Lists

Aphrodite
(mailing list for female Witches)
to send mail: aphrodite@lysator.liu.se
to send mail to the administrator:
aphrodite-request@lysator.liu.se
to apply for membership: aphrodite-request@lysator.liu.se

Church of All Worlds
5878037@mcimail.com

Dalriada Celtic Heritage Society
BBS Isle of Arran, Scotland
+44 0770 302532
(8 bit, N1 ANSI, all speeds up to 14400)

Druid information
Keltria@aol.com

Pagan (the religion)
pagan-request@drycas.club.cc.cmu.edu

Pagan Federation online (Europe)
netco@paganfed.demon.co.uk (general info requests);
antidef@paganfed.demon.co.uk (news requiring a faster response);
secretary@paganfed.demon.co.uk (nonmember inquiries and general business);
pagdawn@paganfed.demon.co.uk (articles, letters to the editor of *Pagan Dawn* magazine); and
parents@paganfed.demon.co.uk (Pagan parenting).

WMSPRT-L
(open discussion group for women and men interested in Goddess spirituality and feminism)
listserv@ubvm.cc.buffalo.edu
Or on bitnet to: listserv@ubvm
To subscribe leave the subject line blank and in the body of the message type: subscribe wmsprt-1 First name Last name. List owner is Gail Wood
To post messages: wmsprt-1@ubvm (bitnet) or wmsprt

E-Mail Info

Nigris, Frater I.
A Mage's Guide to the Internet
(tyagi@houseofkaos.abyss.com)
has information on Magick, mysticism, occultism on the Net
Mailing addresses, FTP sites, and gopher info
Available by FTP at: netcom.com/pub/alamut/mageguide, or quartz.rutgers.edu/pub/occult/magesguide, or from gopher at Clearinghouse of Subject Oriented Internet Resource Guides (UMich)

Newsgroups

alt.discordia
alt.fan.kali.astarte.innana
alt.magick
alt.pagan (nature religion/polytheism discussion group)
to join send a message to:
paganrequest@drycas.club.cc.cmu.edu

Merchants and Services

Abramelin Ritual Artisans
124 Baptist Hill Rd.
Palmer, MA 01069
(413) 283-6502
Rare books, custom jewelry and ritual supplies.

Abyss
RR1 Box 213
Chester, MA 01011
(413) 623-2155
FAX (413) 623-2156
Wholesale/retail books, jewelry, ritual items, Tarot cards.

Arena Press
PO Box 5
Point Arena, CA 95468
Pagan-owned printers.

Feather Anderson
PO Box 1039
Sebastopol, CA 95473
Dowser and Feng Shui master.

The Broom Squire
233 Shingowack Tr.
Medford Lakes, NJ 08055
(609) 654-6128
Unbelievably beautiful natural broom corn with handles made from crooked tree branches. Perfect for handfastings, ritual use, and, of course, flying. Inquire about broom making supplies, instructions, seeds, books.

Celtic Folkworks
RD4 Box 210
Willow Grove Rd.
Newfield, NJ 08344
(609) 691-5968
Beautiful and hard to find Celtic jewelry, clothing, books and other items.

Ecstatic Intuitive Tattooing
c/o Tom Dunn
PO Box 102
Craftsbury Common, VT 05827

Ross Jennings
Hearthstone
RD 1, Box 179
Wilton, NH 03086
Earthwright, geomancer.

JBL Devotional Statues
PO Box 163-G
Crozet, VA 22932–0163
(800) 290-6203
Indian, Middle Eastern and European Deities.

Sig Lonegren
PO Box 218
Greesboro, VT 05841
Dowser, sacred numbers and architecture.

Dr. Patrick MacManaway
Westbank Centre
Strathmiglo, Fife KY14 7QP Scotland
Dowser, intuitive healer, geomancer.

Magus Books
1316 South East St.
Minneapolis, MN 55414
(612) 379-7669
Rare and used books, ritual supplies.

McNamara's Green
PO Box 51188
Seattle, WA 98115
(206) 523 0306
Celtic books, jewelry, decals, bumperstickers, cards.

David Morgan
11812 North Creek Parkway N., Suite 103
Bothell, WA 98011
(800) 324-4934
Welsh jewelry, books, clothing.

Ragnarok
7954 W.3rd St.
Los Angeles, CA 90048
Norse books, jewelry, runes, etc. Send $3.00 for mail order catalog.

Rainbow Serpent
11722 Crownover
Williamsport, OH 43164
Images of the Goddess.

White Light Pentacles
PO Box 8163
Salem, MA 01971–8163
(800) 627-8379
Wholesale to stores only.

Wildwood Studio
717 Spruce
Boulder, CO 80302
Incense, oils, spell kits, books, supplies for Wicca, Celtic, Ceremonial, Native American Traditions.

Witchery
PO Box 16122
Worcester, MA 01601–6122
Celtic-style bodhrans, many varieties of shamanic frame drums, bagpipes, chanters, harps, lyres, hammered dulcimers, lutes, and more.

Herbal Suppliers

Penn Herb Company
603 North Second St.
Philadelphia, PA 19123
(800) 523-9971
Western medicinal herbs, mail order, and retail.

St. John's Herb Garden Inc.
7711 Hillmeade Rd.
Bowie, MD 20720
(301) 262-5302
FAX (301) 262-2489
Culinary and medicinal herbs.

Herb Closet/Osaanyin Herb Cooperative
PO Box 964
Montpelier, VT 05602
(802) 223-0888
Oils, extracts, incense, elixirs, rare and exotic botanicals.

Herb Technology
1305 NE 45th, Suite 205
Seattle, WA 98105
(800) 659-2077
FAX (206) 547-4240
Chinese and Ayurvedic herbs.

Herbalist and Alchemist
PO Box 553
Broadway, NJ 08803
908) 689-9020
Chinese and Western medicinal herbs.

Mountain Rose Herbs
PO Box 2000
Redway, CA 95560
(800) 879-3337
FAX (707) 923 7867
Organic and wildcrafted herbs, oils, cosmetics, supplies, books.

Frontier Cooperative Herbs
3021 78th St.
Norway, IA 52318
(800) 669-3275

Seeds Of Change
PO Box 15700
Santa Fe, NM 87506–5700
(505) 438-8080
FAX (505) 438-7052
Rare, organic medicinal and edible plant seeds.

Two Dragons Trading Co.
4638 SW Beaverton
Hillsdale Hwy
Portland, OR 97221
(800) TWO-DRAG
Rare and difficult to obtain oils and perfumes.

North East Herb Association
PO Box 146
Marshfield, VT 05658–0146
Classes, meetings, newsletter; catalog of practitioners, teachers, suppliers.

American Herbalists Guild
PO Box 1683
Soquel, CA 95073.
Conferences, classes, newsletter,